J2EE Design Patterns Applied

Craig A. Berry
John Carnell
Matjaz B. Juric
Meeraj Moidoo Kunnumpurath
Nadia Nashi
Sasha Romanosky

Wrox Press Ltd. ®

J2EE Design Patterns Applied

Published by Wrox Press Ltd,
Arden House, 1102 Warwick Road, Acocks Green,
Birmingham, B27 6BH, UK
Printed in the USA
ISBN 1-861005-28-8

Trademark Acknowledgments

Credits

Authors
Craig A. Berry
John Carnell
Matjaz B. Juric
Meeraj Moidoo Kunnumperath
Nadia Nashi
Sasha Romanosky

Additional Material
Mike Swainston-Rainford

Commissioning Editor
Craig A. Berry

Technical Editors
Dipali Chittar
Kalpana Garde
Niranjan Jahagirdar
Matthew Moodie
Nilesh Parmar

Managing Editor
Adam MacLean
Vijay Tase

Project Manager
Christianne Bailey

Author Agent
Nicola Phillips

Technical Reviewers
Jeelani Basha
Ersin Eser
Phil Powers De George
Dave Hudson
Steve Parker
Don Reamey
Matt Staples
Paul Wilt

Production Coordinator
Neil Lote

Proof Reader
Chris Smith

Cover
Natalie O'Donnell

Index
John Collin

Illustrations
Santosh Haware
Manjiri Karande

About the Authors

Craig A. Berry

Craig Berry is a Commissioning Editor, Technical Editor, Technical Architect, writer, or whatever the title of the week is at Wrox Press, where he has worked for the past four years on 25 odd programming titles, including *Professional Java Server Programming* J2EE and J2EE 1.3 Editions, *Professional EJB, Professional JMS Programming, Professional Java Servlets 2.3*, and *Professional J2EE EAI*. Craig came to Java and publishing by the rather round about route of zoology and film journalism, so when not masterminding the latest Wrox Java publication, he can usually be found in the bowels of a cinema somewhere. Craig can be reached at craigb@wrox.com.

Craig contributed Chapter 4 to this book.

John Carnell

John Carnell has had an obsession with computers since he was 12 years old working on his Commodore 64. John is an avid writer and professional speaker on the topics of system architecture and design. John currently works as a System Architect for the Centare Group, a leading provider of e-software solutions. John lives in Waukesha, Wisconsin with his wife Janet, his son Christopher, and his two pups Lady Bug and Ginger.

John can be reached at john_carnell@yahoo.com

To my wife Janet: You are the foundation in which my house is built on. Everyday you fill my life with laughter.

To my son, Christopher: You are the culmination of your father's hopes and dreams. Looking into your eyes, I can, for a brief time, put aside my own short-comings and doubts, and realize just how wonderful and special life can be. I love you both.

John contributed Chapter 3 to this book.

Matjaz B. Juric

Matjaz B. Juric holds a Ph.D. in computer and information science and is an Assistant Professor at the University of Maribor. He has been involved in several large-scale object technology projects. In cooperation with the IBM Java Technology Centre, he worked on performance analysis and optimization in RMI-IIOP development, an integral part of the Java 2 Platform. Matjaz has co-authored *Professional J2EE EAI* and *Professional EJB*, both from Wrox Press, and has published a chapter in More Java Gems, from Cambridge University Press. He has published in journals and magazines, such as *Java Developer's Journal, Java Report, Java World, Web Services Journal, EAI Journal*, and ACM journals, and presented at conferences such as OOPSLA, SIGS Java Development, Wrox Conferences, XML Europe, SCI, and others. He is also a reviewer, program committee member, and conference co-organizer.

My efforts in this book are dedicated to my family. Special thanks go to all my friends at Wrox, at the University of Maribor, and everyone else who supported me.

Matjaz contributed Chapters 1 and 6 to this book.

Meeraj Moidoo Kunnumpurath

Meeraj works with EDS as a Senior Information Specialist. He support Chelsea FC, runs twenty-five miles a week, and eats tuna and broccoli in the evening.

Meeraj contributed to Chapter 5 of this book.

Nadia Nashi

Nadia trained originally as an architect, completing a first class postgraduate diploma in architecture at the University of Greenwich in 1993. She moved from designing real-world objects to designing virtual objects, completing an MSC in Software Engineering at Westminster University in 1994. Nadia works full time as an independent object-oriented analyst/designer, Java consultant, and software developer.

To my husband Adrian and my daughter Mariam.

Nadia contributed Chapters 2 and 7 to this book.

Sasha Romanosky

Sasha holds a Bachelor of Science in Electrical and Computer Engineering from the University of Calgary, Canada and has been working with computer and Internet technologies for over seven years. His research interests include cryptography, PKI, security patterns and role based access control. His passion is Internet security.

Sasha contributed to Chapter 5 of this book.

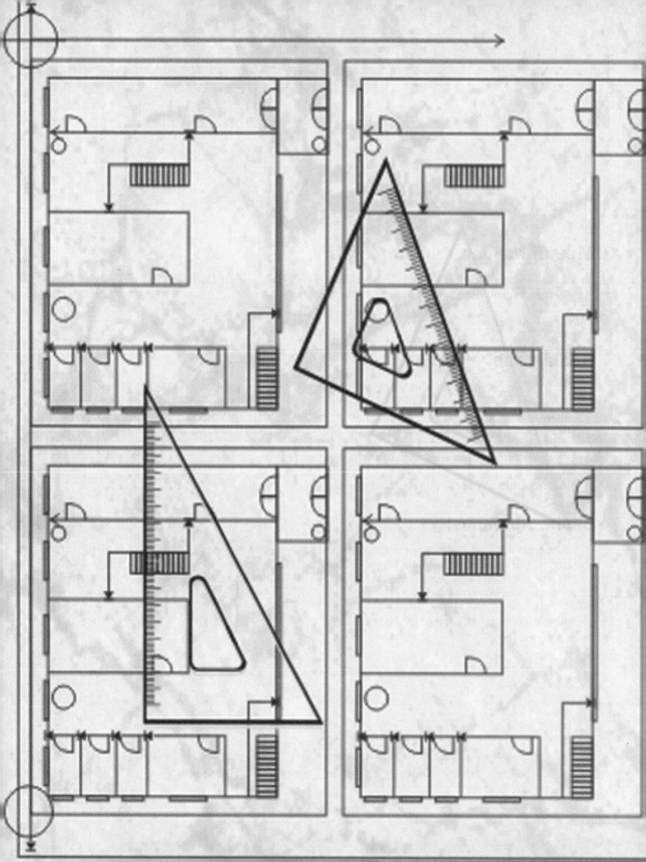

Table of Contents

Table of Contents

Table of Contents

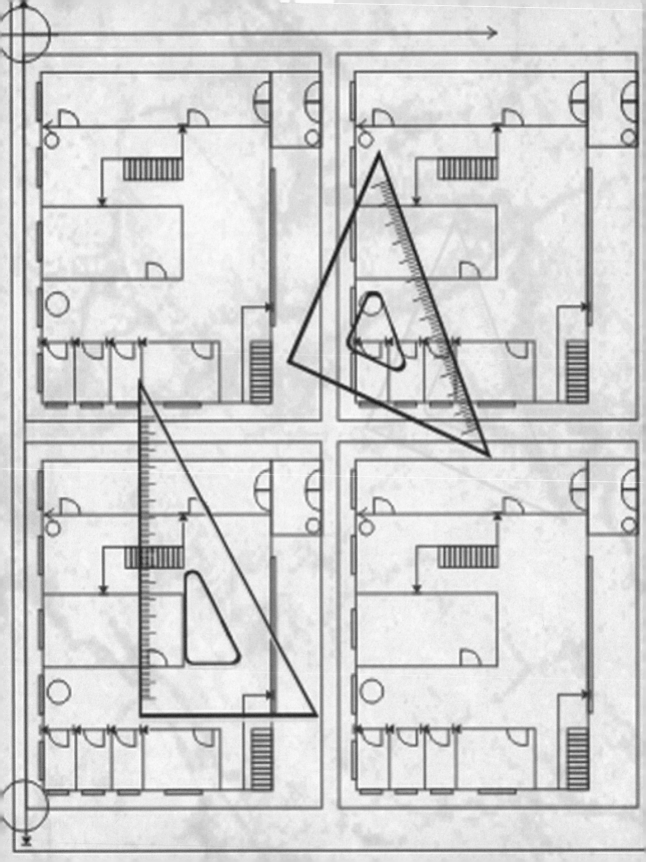

Introduction

Welcome to *J2EE Design Patterns Applied*. As the title suggests, this book will use the J2EE design patterns and apply them to build quality applications. Over the years, patterns have proved to be an effective way to gather, formalize, and disseminate experience about recurring solutions to common problems in some contexts. The J2EE platform design patterns add to the existing wealth of software design patterns. However, these patterns do not exist in isolation, and inevitably they need to be assembled to form larger and more complex frameworks.

Selecting patterns and turning them into real-world solutions is never an easy task. Furthermore, applying patterns in general, or J2EE patterns in particular, to address business and technical requirements poses enormous challenges. This book is a guide to creating scalable and secure J2EE applications using J2EE patterns, including good object-oriented design principles and real-world practices.

In this book we'll not only describe the common problems that we face in enterprise development with J2EE and provide sound solutions for them, but also show how to apply these solutions to real world-projects.

Who is this Book For?

This book is for developers who are reasonably familiar with the Java 2 Platform, Enterprise Edition, and want to learn how to leverage this technology into better practice. They can be:

- ❑ Proficient J2EE Developers who are interested in moving with the technology and pushing their J2EE knowledge to its limits

- ❑ J2EE Architects who are tasked with setting system specifications, orchestrating Java 2 Enterprise solutions, and integrating them with backend systems like databases and legacy systems

What's Covered in this Book?

This book will cover the various patterns that are used while designing enterprise applications. We'll cover these patterns in individual chapters and apply them to various areas of design and development. We'll discuss each of these patterns with the help of a case study and apply them. The chapters in this book are organized as follows:

❑ **Chapter 1: Design Patterns Applied to J2EE**
This chapter provides an overview of patterns and focuses more specifically on design patterns and J2EE. Some guidelines as to how to use patterns in an effective way are also discussed.

❑ **Chapter 2: Patterns Applied to the Web Tier**
This chapter describes issues that surround designing and managing the top layer of a web application. We discuss the technical requirements expected of the client layer and how the J2EE presentation design patterns can address these.

❑ **Chapter 3: Patterns Applied to a Persistence Framework**
This chapter focuses exclusively on developing the data tier using a combination of common data persistence design patterns and J2EE technologies. Specifically, this chapter covers the topics such as what persistent frameworks are and discusses extensively the core patterns that should be considered while building a persistence framework.

❑ **Chapter 4: Patterns Applied to Improve Performance and Scalability**
In this chapter we look at a number of patterns that lead to a better performing and more scalable design.

❑ **Chapter 5: Patterns Applied to Manage Security**
In this chapter, we introduce security patterns and their benefits. Security patterns provide techniques for addressing security issues as J2EE and other object-oriented patterns provide proven techniques for solving known programming problems.

❑ **Chapter 6: Patterns Applied to Enable Enterprise Integration**
In this chapter, we discuss the most important integration patterns and show how to apply them in the J2EE standards.

❑ **Chapter 7: Patterns Applied to Enable Reusability, Maintainability, and Extensibility**
This chapter discusses the application of design patterns for the specific purpose of reusing software and developing more maintainable and extensible software. We shall then focus on a group of patterns that demonstrate these aspects in a generic framework, which is composed of a series of components in the context of a J2EE framework.

What You Need to Use this Book

The code in this book was tested with the Java 2 Platform, Enterprise Edition SDK 1.3 Reference Implementation, which is available for download from http://java.sun.com/j2ee/download.html. Several chapters also require access to a database. For these chapters, we used MySQL, an open source database server, which is available free from http://www.mysql.com/downloads/index.html.

Conventions

To help you get the most from the text and keep track of what's happening, we've used a number of conventions throughout the book.

For instance:

> **These boxes hold important, not-to-be-forgotten information, which is directly relevant to the surrounding text.**

While the background style is used for asides to the current discussion.

As for styles in the text:

- ❑ When we introduce them, we **highlight** important words
- ❑ We show keyboard strokes like this: *Ctrl-K*
- ❑ We show filenames and code within the text like so: `persistance.properties`
- ❑ Text on user interfaces and URLs are shown as: Menu

We present code in two different ways:

```
In our code examples, the code foreground style shows new, important, pertinent
code.
While code background shows code that's less important in the present context, or
has been seen before.
```

Customer Support

We always value hearing from our readers, and we want to know what you think about this book: what you liked, what you didn't like, and what you think we can do better next time. You can send us your comments, either by returning the reply card in the back of the book, or by e-mail to feedback@wrox.com. Please be sure to mention the book title in your message.

How to Download the Sample Code for the Book

When you visit the Wrox site, http://www.wrox.com/ simply locate the title through our Search facility or by using one of the title lists. Click on Download in the Code column, or on Download Code on the book's detail page.

The files that are available for download from our site have been archived using WinZip. When you have saved the attachments to a folder on your hard-drive, you need to extract the files using a de-compression program such as WinZip or PKUnzip. When you extract the files, the code is usually extracted into chapter folders. When you start the extraction process, ensure your software (WinZip or PKUnzip) is set to use folder names.

Errata

We've made every effort to make sure that there are no errors in the text or in the code. However, no one is perfect and mistakes do occur. If you find an error in one of our books, like a spelling mistake or faulty piece of code, we would be very grateful for your feedback. By sending in errata you may save another reader hours of frustration, and of course, you will be helping us provide even higher quality information. Simply e-mail the information to support@wrox.com; your information will be checked and if correct, posted to the errata page for that title, or used in subsequent editions of the book.

To find errata on the web site, go to http://www.wrox.com/, and simply locate the title through our Advanced Search or title list. Click on the Book Errata link, which is below the cover graphic on the book's detail page.

E-Mail Support

If you wish to directly query a problem in the book with an expert who knows the book in detail then e-mail support@wrox.com, with the title of the book and the last four numbers of the ISBN(5288) in the subject field of the e-mail. A typical e-mail should include the following things:

- ❑ The **title of the book**, **last four digits of the ISBN**, and **page number** of the problem in the Subject field

- ❑ Your **name**, **contact information**, and the **problem** in the body of the message

We *won't* send you junk mail. We need the details to save your time and ours. When you send an e-mail message, it will go through the following chain of support:

- ❑ Customer Support – Your message is delivered to our customer support staff who are the first people to read it. They have files on most frequently asked questions and will answer anything general about the book or the web site immediately.

- ❑ Editorial – Deeper queries are forwarded to the technical editor responsible for that book. They have experience with the programming language or particular product, and are able to answer detailed technical questions on the subject.

- ❑ The Authors – Finally, in the unlikely event that the editor cannot answer your problem, they will forward the request to the author. We do try to protect the authors from any distractions to their writing; however, we are quite happy to forward specific requests to them. All Wrox authors help with the support on their books. They will e-mail the customer and the editor with their response, and again all readers should benefit.

The Wrox Support process can only offer support to issues directly pertinent to the content of our published title. Support for questions that fall outside the scope of normal book support is provided via the community lists of our http://p2p.wrox.com/ forum.

p2p.wrox.com

For author and peer discussion join the P2P mailing lists. Our unique system provides **programmer to programmer**™ contact on mailing lists, forums, and newsgroups, all in addition to our one-to-one e-mail support system. If you post a query to P2P, you can be confident that it is being examined by the many Wrox authors and other industry experts who are present on our mailing lists. At p2p.wrox.com you will find a number of different lists to help you, not only while you read this book, but also as you develop your applications.

To subscribe to a mailing list just follow these steps:

1. Go to http://p2p.wrox.com/

2. Choose the appropriate category from the left menu bar

3. Click on the mailing list you wish to join

4. Follow the instructions to subscribe and fill in your e-mail address and password

5. Reply to the confirmation e-mail you receive

6. Use the subscription manager to join more lists and set your e-mail preferences

Why this System Offers the Best Support

You can choose to join the mailing lists or you can receive them as a weekly digest. If you don't have the time, or facility, to receive the mailing list, then you can search our archives. Junk and spam mails are deleted, and your own e-mail address is protected by the unique Lyris system. Queries about joining or leaving lists, and any other general queries about lists, should be sent to listsupport@wrox.com.

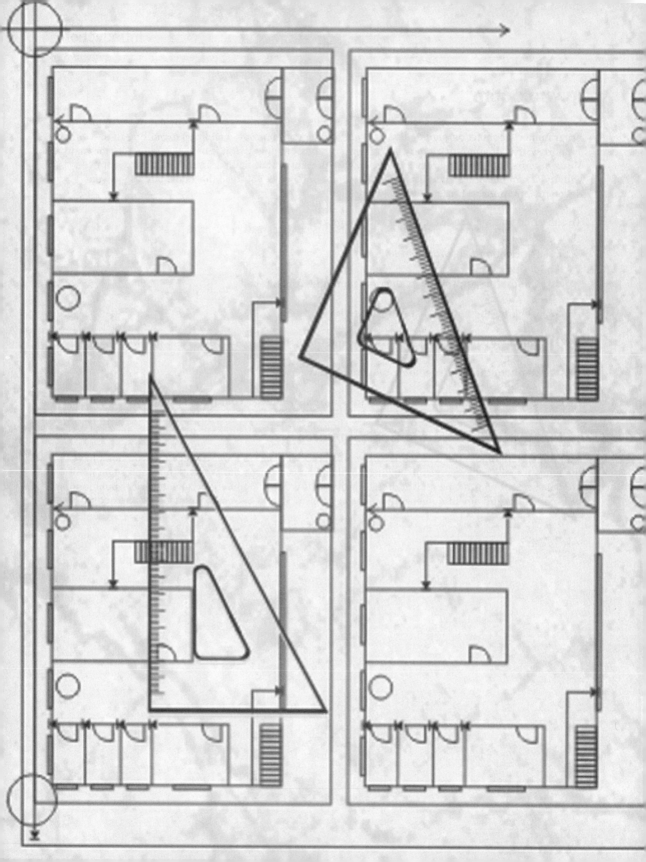

Design Patterns Applied to J2EE

Developing enterprise applications is a difficult task even if we use the most advanced software platform – the Java 2 Platform, Enterprise Edition (J2EE). Through APIs, J2EE provides a high level of abstraction of technologies and services, which makes enterprise development easier. However, knowing the J2EE APIs is not enough. To design sound architectures that will result in quality applications, we also have to know when and how to use these APIs in the right way. This book will teach us how to use the J2EE APIs, technologies, and services in the best way.

The fact is that, through lack of experience in a new technology, we are often on our own to figure out how to use it in the most appropriate way. It is likely that we will not find out the best possible solution in our first attempt. It is more likely that we will need several iterations until we figure out the best practices. Good solutions are evidently based on experience. They are not invented; they are *discovered* and *refined*.

Learning by experience and reusing solutions that have proved to be successful in the past is very important in engineering disciplines – so is it for enterprise applications. Experience helps us to build good solutions faster and with less effort, thus saving cost and improving quality. The only problem is that we have to gain the experience somehow. Instead of learning from our own experience, we can learn from the experience of others. This book will save us the effort of gaining our own experience. It will show the sound design practices based on the experience of many developers.

But, how are the experiences of others described? Over the years, **patterns** have proved to be an effective way to gather, formalize, and disseminate experience about recurring solutions to common problems in some contexts. In this book, we will focus on J2EE design patterns. We will not only describe the common problems that we face in enterprise development with J2EE and provide sound solutions for them, but also show how to apply these solutions to real-world projects.

In this chapter, we will provide an overview of patterns, focus more specifically on design patterns and J2EE, and give some guidelines as to how to use patterns in an effective way. We will cover:

❑   The evolution of patterns

❑   What design patterns are

❑   Identifying patterns

❑   How design patterns solve design problems

❑   Selecting a design pattern

❑   Using a design pattern

❑   Antipatterns

❑   J2EE and design patterns

❑   J2EE-specific patterns vs. patterns in a J2EE context

❑   Problem domains for J2EE patterns

The Evolution of Patterns

It all started in civil engineering and architecture. In the seventies, architecture was considered as a discipline that required a lot of experience. The three books by Christopher Alexander et al. surprised the community. Their objective was to make architecture useful for people without highly specialized knowledge and experience. They identified the similarities between architectures that proved to be good, and identified the common principles and wrote them as solutions to common design problems. They named these solutions "patterns" in architecture.

However, even years after publishing the 253 patterns, Alexander et al. did not succeed in making architecture a mechanical process. Why, then, have these architectural patterns been so important? Making architecture a mechanical process has never been the goal of patterns. The patterns have been important because they did succeed in making the solutions to common architecture problems accessible to a wider population and made less experienced architects more productive and more effective. This has been the major objective of architectural patterns.

Patterns in architecture have had a large influence on other engineering disciplines. It has become obvious that each mature engineering discipline should have documented solutions to common problems; so should software engineering, where patterns have proved to be successful in describing solutions to common software problems. Patterns do not only give sound solutions, but they also help in communicating between people and help them reason what they do and why.

Patterns in Software Engineering

So, what are patterns in software engineering? Unfortunately, there is no single definition that would cover all relevant aspects.

> **Simply defined, "a pattern is a proven solution to a problem in a context".**

However, this simple definition can lead to wrong understanding of what patterns actually are. Alexander has written:

> *"Each pattern describes a problem which occurs over and over again in our environment, and then describes the core of the solution to that problem in such a way that you can use this solution a million times over, without doing it the same way twice."*

The most influential publication on patterns in software engineering in the recent years has been the book *Design Patterns: Elements of Reusable Object-Oriented Software* by Erich Gamma, Richard Helm, Ralph Johnson, and John Vlissides, alias the Gang of Four (GoF); Addison-Wesley (ISBN: 0-201-63361-2). According to their definition:

> *"A pattern is a three-part rule, which expresses a relation between a certain context, a problem, and a solution."*

According to this definition, patterns are solutions to problems, usable in more than one scenario.

An interesting definition is the one provided by Richard Gabriel:

> *"Each pattern is a three-part rule, which expresses a relation between a certain context, a certain system of forces which occurs repeatedly in that context, and a certain software configuration which allows these forces to resolve themselves."*

Patterns are gathered through experience and are based on proven solutions. A pattern becomes a pattern only after it has been verified several times in real-world systems. Hence patterns on one side promote reuse and on the other side prevent us from reinventing the wheel, which eventually makes us work faster and more efficiently.

Patterns also give us a vocabulary, which improves communication between architects and designers and let us think about common architectural solutions in ways that we haven't considered them before. Patterns encourage us to combine them to solve larger problems.

Having said that, we could say that there is actually nothing new about patterns. Experienced designers read the patterns and figure out that they have done this before, often many times. We've known for ages that experts don't think about problems in terms of low-level constructs, rather they build high-level abstractions. Patterns, however, motivate people to identify and document these high-level abstractions. The motivation for these people to identify patterns includes:

❑ Finding patterns is a matter of experience, not novelty. Novelty introduces risks, because new approaches and techniques have to be verified and tested before they can claim to be useful. In real life, success is often more important than novelty. Therefore, new patterns have to be tried before we can assess their value. Good patterns arise from practical experience.

❑ Patterns accelerate the communication between developers, allowing them to learn faster, and thus developing better software every day. To achieve efficient communication, we have to represent patterns somehow, preferably using a standard format. We will come back later to formats in which we can represent patterns.

❑ Patterns allow qualitative and quantitative validation of knowledge. Thus, we can assess the efficiency of patterns. This allows presenting and understanding the advantages and disadvantages of patterns and the architectures we build out of them.

Patterns have been applied almost everywhere. Over the years, many different kinds of software patterns have been identified, including:

❑ Design patterns, which cover software design and are probably the most important patterns. Often they are object-oriented and cover architectures (system design), design (component interactions), and programming idioms (language-specific techniques). In this book, we will focus on design patterns.

❑ Analysis patterns, which describe reusable analysis models and are very helpful in domain analysis. They cover a wide range of domains including trading, measurement, accounting, and organizational relationships. To find out more on analysis patterns, please refer to *Analysis Patterns: Reusable Object Models* from Addison-Wesley (ISBN 0-201-89542-0).

❑ Process patterns, which describe the software process design. More exactly, they describe proven and successful approaches and activities for developing software. For more information, please refer to *Process Patterns: Building Large-Scale Systems Using Object Technology* (ISBN 0-521-64568-9) and *More Process Patterns: Delivering Large-Scale Systems Using Object Technology* from Cambridge University Press (ISBN 0-521-65262-6).

❑ Organizational patterns, which describe structure and practices of organizations and projects. For more information on these, please refer to http://i44pc48.info.uni-karlsruhe.de/cgi-bin/OrgPatterns.

❑ Implementation patterns, which describe implementation concepts. For more information, please refer to *Essential Java Style: Patterns for Implementation* from Prentice Hall (ISBN 0-13-085086-1).

❑ Other domain specific patterns.

Patterns can also be categorized based on what problem aspect they cover, including:

❑ Creational patterns

❑ Structural patterns

❑ Behavioral patterns

We can see that patterns exist in several abstraction levels and can be classified in different schemes. In this book, we will focus on J2EE design patterns. Before that, let's have a look at what design patterns are.

What are Design Patterns?

Design patterns are recurring solutions to standard design problems in contexts. Design problems are something that we cannot solve without further investigation. Problems typically occur in a certain environment or a situation – which we call **context**. Solutions are answers to these problems that help us to resolve the problem in a given context.

For example, we have a small living room, and the question is where to put the door to make the room convenient. After trying different positions, we might figure out that we should put the door in the southeast corner of the room. We have found a solution to a specific problem. In the same way, we could find a specific solution for a software design problem.

The obvious question is whether all solutions to design problems are design patterns. The answer is that it is not necessarily true. Design patterns are only those solutions that are useful in different contexts, that is, solutions that can be applied repeatedly, solving the same problem occurring in different contexts.

Returning to the position of the doors, our solution is not yet a pattern, because its use is limited to our specific scenario. If we would, however, find out a general solution for all smaller rooms, then we could call our solution a pattern. That's exactly what Alexander did. He figured out that the room doors should not be placed anywhere on the wall. Moreover, the success of a room depends to a great extent on the position of the doors. Therefore, he recommended that, except in very large rooms, the doors should be put as near the corners of the room as possible. He called this *pattern* the "Corner Doors".

We can see that although a simple concept, design patterns are difficult to define. Therefore, we don't wonder anymore why we have so many different definitions. To get a practical understanding of what design patterns are, let's elaborate more on this.

Design patterns focus on software design. They systematically name, explain, and evaluate important software design. Design patterns enable easier reuse of successful and proven design and architectures and make them more accessible to developers of new systems, particularly those with less experience. Design patterns help us to select alternative designs. As we will focus on design patterns in this book, henceforth we will use the word "pattern" for design patterns.

Let's say that we have to develop a `Customer` entity bean and expose the customer data to the clients. The naïve solution would be to define a remote interface with fine-grained methods (such as `get/setName()`, `get/setAddres()`, and so on) and allow remote clients to access the entity beans directly. To figure out (without help from patterns) that this solution is not scalable and therefore inappropriate for any real application would require implementing the component and the client, deploying, and testing it. Quite a lot of effort, isn't it? Remember that in real-world applications we would most likely face several such components, not just `Customer`.

The knowledge of design patterns, such as Value Object and Session Façade, would make it clear that the remote interfaces of EJBs should be coarse-grained. The Value Object pattern would show us a sound solution of how to make interface coarse-grained and still transfer all the necessary data in an elegant way, saving several remote method invocations. The Session Façade pattern would show us that we should not access entity beans directly. Rather we should develop a session bean, which will act as a façade. It would also teach us that we could further improve the performance if we add a local interface for the entity bean and deploy both EJBs in the same container.

If you are not familiar with Value Object and Session Façade patterns, you might not have understood the last paragraph. Don't worry, because all these patterns will be discussed in detail in the subsequent chapters of this book. You might have noticed however, that both these patterns have a context in which they can be applied. This is true for all patterns. They also have to balance a set of forces that are often opposing. When describing patterns, we have to clearly define all these things. According to Design Patterns by the Gang of Four, a pattern has four essential elements:

❑ The *pattern name*, which should identify a pattern and thus increase our vocabulary.

❑ The *problem*, which describes when to apply this pattern. It should explain the problem and the context.

❑ The *solution*, which should not describe a particular concrete design or implementation, but rather should describe a pattern as a template, which can be used in many different contexts (situations).

❑ The *consequences*, which are the results and tradeoffs of applying a certain pattern. Consequences are critical for evaluating alternatives and for making decisions.

> **Design patterns are the descriptions of how to solve general design problems in particular contexts.**

Design patterns name, abstract, and identify the key aspects of common design structure. They identify who is participating in the solution, what roles and responsibilities they have, and how they collaborate. In most cases, these will be objects and components. Each design pattern focuses on a particular problem. An important point is also that each pattern describes its tradeoffs and consequences.

Related patterns, woven together, form *pattern languages*. Pattern languages are not formal languages; they are a collection of related patterns. Both patterns and pattern languages are important for learning, communicating, and solving problems in a better, faster, and more efficient way. In this book, we will focus on pattern languages for J2EE. However, before we focus more explicitly on J2EE design patterns and their applications, let's first discuss how we can identify patterns.

Identifying Patterns

We identify patterns from experience. Every experienced architect or designer has figured out that in all or the majority of projects, similar problems occur and, most interestingly, solutions to these problems are also similar. This does not mean that the actual solution will be exactly the same. However, it does mean that all solutions share basic concepts. When looked at from a point of abstraction, we could say that all these solutions and problems represent a common abstract problem with a common abstract solution.

Having that in mind is a good start for identifying patterns. We should look at our past projects and identify the problems we have dealt with. For each problem, we should try to identify its characteristics. We should also document the solutions for these problems. Then we should gather similar problems and solutions and figure out the similarities.

It is very likely that similar solutions will represent a single pattern. Remember Alexander's Corner Doors pattern, discussed in the earlier section? Alexander identified this pattern investigating a large number of rooms with well positioned doors. All rooms with doors near the corners of the room represented this pattern. The same holds true for the Value Object and Session Façade patterns, which we've mentioned before. They too have been identified through analysis of several good performing applications.

However, a set of solutions becomes a pattern only after it has been verified. So, as Alexander had to verify that the corner position of the doors is really useful, similarly we have to verify patterns that we identify. Verifying complex patterns in software engineering might be a little more difficult than verifying simpler architectural patterns, such as the Corner Doors pattern.

We therefore say that we do not identify patterns directly; we identify pattern candidates. Pattern candidates should be standalone solutions with as few connections to the outer world as possible. Don't forget – patterns are about reuse. We have to validate the pattern candidates. The community often uses the Rule of Three. This rule states that each candidate pattern should be proved in at least three different systems before it can become a real pattern. This rule is not very exact; therefore the authors of this book suggest that a pattern candidate should be verified as extensively as possible. Only this will give the pattern practical value.

Patterns that haven't been verified enough can do a lot of harm. Why? The fact is that the majority of architects, designers, and developers will not identify patterns. They either don't have time or motivation to do this, or they lack experience. The majority of them will, however, learn patterns and use them to improve their solutions. A pattern that cannot fulfill the goals can do damage to a large number of applications, and can bring patterns a bad reputation.

Another important question to answer is at what level of abstraction the patterns should be and how much implementation details they should include. A commonly accepted concept in the J2EE patterns community is that patterns should be at a high abstraction level. However, each pattern can (and should) include details about the solution. These solution details are often at a lower abstraction level than the pattern itself and are called strategies. Obviously, there is no precise and hard distinction between patterns and strategies.

Since this book is about applying patterns, we will give a lot of attention to these strategies to show exactly how patterns can be used in different contexts.

The authors of the book *Core J2EE Patterns* from Prentice Hall PTR (ISBN 0-13-064884-1) define the following difference between patterns and strategies:

❑ Patterns should be at a higher abstraction level than strategies. Therefore, patterns should recommend the best strategies for their implementation.

❑ Developers can, through strategies, extend the use of patterns and find new ways to implement certain patterns.

❑ Patterns and strategy names improve communication.

After identifying patterns, we have to represent them. This brings us to the representation of patterns, which we will cover in the next section.

Representing Design Patterns

Figuring out how to represent patterns is as difficult as defining patterns. Simple graphical representation, for example Unified Modeling Language (UML), will not be sufficient. To make patterns really promote reuse, we have to represent the intent, motivation, decisions, consequences, and so on. To apply patterns successfully, we should also provide concrete examples.

Over the years, many patterns have been identified. The authors who have identified those patterns have published them in pattern catalogs. Probably, the most important pattern catalog is the 23 patterns from Design Patterns by the GoF. For J2EE developers, a pattern catalog is taking shape as a community process under the Java Developer Connection at http://java.sun.com/. Another important pattern catalog for J2EE developers can be found at http://www.TheServerSide.com/.

Patterns can be represented in a formal or a non-formal way. Most pattern catalogs today use a non-formal representation for the patterns. The problem, however, is that they do not use the same format, they differ in some way. Probably, the major source of differences between pattern representations is that design problems addressed by different types of patterns are not very similar. For example, GoF patterns address OO design problems whereas core J2EE patterns address problems encountered in building J2EE applications.

The majority of non-formal pattern representations use several sections. Some of them are found in the majority of representations, the others differ. The majority of these non-formal representations are based on the representation used in the GoF book. The GoF representation uses the following template:

❑ **Pattern name and classification**
   Each pattern should have a unique name, which is important for a pattern to become a part of our vocabulary.

❑ **Intent**
   Briefly answers what a pattern does, its rationale and intent, and what design problem it addresses.

❑ **Also Known As**
   Provides a list of other well-known names for the pattern.

❑ **Motivation**
   Describes a scenario that makes it obvious what the problem is and how the pattern solves the problem.

❑ **Applicability**
   Describes where the design pattern can be applied, examples of poor design, and how we can recognize them.

❑ **Structure**
   Provides a graphical representation. A good idea is to use the UML notation.

❑ **Participants**
   Shows what classes, objects, and components participate in the design pattern, and what are their responsibilities.

❑ **Collaborations**
   Answers questions as to how participants collaborate.

❑ **Consequences**
Provides a list of how the pattern supports its objectives, what are the results and tradeoffs of using the pattern.

❑ **Implementation**
Hints, techniques, and strategies for implementing the pattern. We should also mention language-specific issues and possible pitfalls.

❑ **Sample code**
Gives code fragments that illustrate how we should implement the pattern.

❑ **Known uses**
Where can this pattern be found in real-world systems?

❑ **Related patterns**
Lists the closely related patterns and mentions the most important differences.

Before we look at the patterns that will be discussed in this book, let's take a quick look at the benefits of design patterns and how they can help solving our problems.

How Do Design Patterns Solve Design Problems?

Now that we are familiar with patterns, let's try to explain how design patterns solve design problems.

> **Design patterns can help us to make sound software design, or to design software better than we would without the knowledge of the patterns.**

In general, design patterns help us solve the most common problems encountered during the application design phase. These include:

❑ Identifying components, internal structures of components, and relationships between components

❑ Determining component granularity and appropriate interactions

❑ Defining component interfaces

The design patterns targeted to the J2EE platform address common design problems using J2EE services and technologies. These include:

❑ View management

❑ Request processing

❑ Service location and activation

❑ Remote communication and communication between tiers

❑ Component selection

❑ Persistent state, transaction, and security management

❑ EIS integration

Design patterns also help us to make our design:

- ❑ More appropriate for reuse
- ❑ More robust for changes in the future

J2EE applications are built of components, which can be found on the client tier, web-component tier and business-logic (EJB) tier. Components, if developed in the Java language, follow the object-oriented approach. When designing such applications, architects are faced with a difficult problem: how to identify the components, how to select their types, and how to identify the internal structure of components (for example, the objects as building blocks of components)? It is difficult to determine the right abstraction level, granularity, and flexibility, and so on without enough experience.

Here, software development methods are not always helpful. Although they provide different ways to identify and analyze model objects, they are often not too explicit on design model components and objects. Real-world development also shows that applications are often made of components that do not model real-world objects directly – although in analysis models, we often define objects based on their real-world counterparts.

We can therefore have problems with the selection of appropriate component types, offered by J2EE, particularly when the choice is not obvious, or we have to fulfill additional requirements on performance or security for example. This holds true for web components, where we might have difficulties choosing between JSP (Java Server Pages) and servlets, as well as for business-logic tier components, where we first have to choose between different kind of EJBs (stateless session, stateful session, entity, and message-driven beans), and also between CORBA and RMI-IIOP distributed objects and JMS. The decision will have long-lasting consequences.

When applying design patterns, we will get guidance in making these decisions. The following are some other benefits:

- ❑ They help us make the appropriate abstractions
- ❑ They help us make the appropriate generalizations
- ❑ They help us determine the appropriate granularity to enable reuse
- ❑ They help us make the design flexible and more adaptable to future changes

Particularly, granularity plays an important role here. Selecting the appropriate granularity of components regulates the amount of communication required, which is particularly important in distributed applications (J2EE applications are distributed). The decision about granularity can make the difference between a well performing and an inadequately performing application.

The selection of granularity is reflected in the component interfaces. J2EE, as a distributed platform strictly follows the concept of separating the interface and the implementation. It reduces dependencies between clients and components, thus increasing flexibility. Clients depend on interfaces only, and are therefore unaware of changes in the component implementations. This enables us to change the implementation without influencing the clients. This concept is very useful for distribution and integration.

However, these benefits can be realized only as long as the interfaces stay unchanged. This requires that we place a lot of effort in defining interfaces that will not require modification too soon or too often. Design patterns can be helpful in defining the interfaces with appropriate granularity and signatures.

Design patterns also help us with the architecture of view management and help us to design the presentation-tier components flexible enough to accommodate future modifications and centralize certain tasks, such as user authentication, authorization, and personalization. They can also help in separating the request processing from generating the view, which further increases the flexibility.

Design patterns are also helpful for promoting reuse. Reuse in software development has a long history and has come through a long way from simple reuse of source code (or implementation artifacts) through the reuse of artifacts that represent the abstraction of a problem, all the way to the reuse of artifacts that represent the ideas of problem solutions. Patterns are nothing but the reuse of ideas and have proved to be a successful way and a catalyst for reuse of ideas. Design patterns also help us make our design more appropriate for a lower level of reuse – for reuse of components and objects. In this sense, patterns are probably one of the most successful forms of reuse.

Last, but not the least is achieving designs that are robust for changes in the future. Requirements in software development are changing rapidly. Good software designs are those that can anticipate these changes. However, it requires that we base our designs on the aspects of the domain that are least likely to change; and that we foresee the possible future changes from the very beginning. This will save use of extensive redesigns in the future.

Design patterns in general as well as those focused on J2EE provide help in avoiding these situations. If we use design patterns, our architecture will be more flexible. This is because each pattern defines a general solution that allows us to change certain aspects independent of the others.

To realize these advantages of design patterns, we, however, need to select the appropriate patterns. Therefore, in the next section we will look at how to select appropriate design patterns.

Selecting a Design Pattern

The number of patterns has been growing fast in recent years. This makes selecting the right pattern a non-trivial process, particularly if we are not familiar with the patterns listed in the catalog. Choosing the right pattern is important, because if we apply a pattern that has not been intended to solve our design problem, we will not benefit from it. Therefore, before using pattern catalogs we have to study all the patterns carefully and understand them.

Still, after a careful study of patterns, we might conclude that there are several patterns that might come into our selection for a specific design problem. For example, to hide the complexity of the business-logic tier and to decouple the communication between the EJB and clients, the J2EE pattern catalogs list at least three similar patterns: Session Façade, Message Façade, and EJB Command. We can then follow different approaches, which will help us to find and select the appropriate pattern. The following are some of the useful approaches:

❑　Pattern catalogs usually group patterns based on their purpose. It should not be difficult to identify the appropriate group. We should then study the patterns in this group and select the most appropriate one.

❑　For each pattern we should find out the design problem that a pattern solves. This will narrow the set of potentially useful patterns for our problem.

- We should read the problem and solution parts of each pattern description. The problem section will help us to identify the patterns that might be appropriate. We will then do the final selection based on the solution part.

- We should figure out the interrelations between the patterns. The relations can help us to select the group of potentially useful patterns.

- A useful approach is to consider what parameters should be variable in our design. We should identify what we would like to change without redesigning the system. This is called "encapsulation of the concept that varies" (GoF) and is defined with many patterns. Once we know this, we can select the appropriate pattern based on this criterion.

- The opposite approach is to identify causes for the redesign. We should identify the causes (or forces) that require a redesign. Then we should identify those patterns that will help us to avoid these causes.

The following activity diagram shows the described steps graphically:

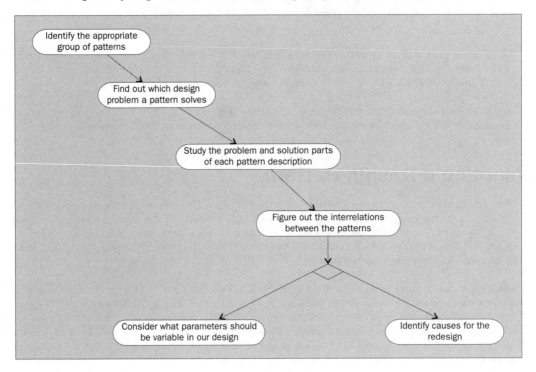

Although these steps might look difficult at first, we will provide enough guidelines throughout the book to help you in the pattern selection process. The more we become familiar with patterns the easier it will be to select them.

For now, let's look how we should use a design pattern after we have selected it.

Using a Design Pattern

To gain benefits from patterns, it is very important to select them appropriately. Even more important is to use and apply the selected pattern the right way. Otherwise, we will not see the benefits of it.

To use the patterns effectively, we should follow these guidelines:

- ❏ Before using a pattern, we should understand it completely. This requires that we study the Solution section, where we should understand all components, classes, and objects that take part in the pattern and their relationships. We should also be familiar with Strategies section and understand the guidelines for applying the pattern in different scenarios.

- ❏ We should check once again that we have selected the appropriate pattern. We should study the pattern description carefully, particularly the Consequences and Related Patterns sections.

- ❏ We should look at the Applying Pattern section and study carefully the examples. If we are already familiar with the pattern, a quick look at the sample code in the Strategies section might be sufficient. The goal is to learn how to implement the pattern.

- ❏ We should choose names for the pattern participants that are meaningful for our application. The names in the pattern catalog are usually too abstract to use them directly. Choosing appropriate names will simplify further development and will make our design (and code) more understandable.

- ❏ The next step is to define the interfaces, components, classes, and relationships. Particularly, relationships with other classes in our design are important. From the relationships, we will see which other classes the pattern affects. Often, we will have to slightly modify these classes and ideally avoid any type of coupling between classes.

- ❏ We should also choose appropriate names for operations in the pattern. Here the name used in the patterns catalog is also abstract. We should also watch out that we follow the naming conventions.

- ❏ Finally, we should implement the pattern. Here, the Applying Pattern section will be very helpful, because it will give concrete examples on how to implement each pattern appropriately.

The following figure shows the described steps:

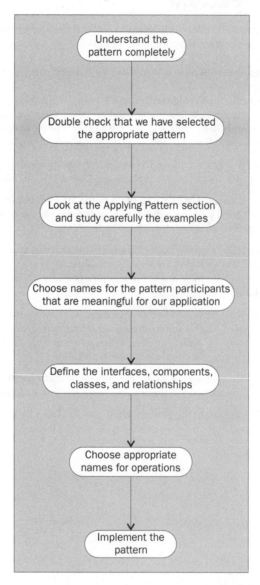

We should be aware that patterns introduce certain flexibility into the design. They achieve this by adding extra abstraction layers, which might complicate our design and affect the performance. Therefore, we should be aware why we use a pattern and be able to justify why we actually need it. We should always ask whether we really need the flexibility offered by the pattern. We should never use patterns just because they seem to be useful; we should also study (and understand) the consequences of each pattern.

In the next section, we discuss more on inappropriate use of patterns and how refactoring comes into play.

Refactoring

We have seen that design patterns present useful solutions for common design problems. However, learning many design patterns is not sufficient for becoming a good designer. We have to understand the patterns and assess when to use them and what benefits a certain pattern will bring if we apply it.

We also have to be aware that using too many patterns and using them in the incorrect way can lead to over-engineering. Over-engineering is a situation where we make our architecture more sophisticated than it needs to be. A major reason for over-engineering is the wish that we produce flexible architecture to accommodate all possible future changes. The key, however, is to not over-engineer the code; otherwise we would waste time and money.

On the other hand, we also have to be aware of under-engineering. With under-engineering, we are focused on adding functionality to the system as quickly as possible. A consequence is that we do not improve the design, which is a time bomb. Using this approach, we might be able to develop the first version quicker, but we will definitely have troubles with later releases.

In both scenarios, we can use refactoring.

> **Refactoring is a "behavior-preserving transformation". According to Martin Fowler, it is "a change made to the internal structure of software to make it easier to understand and cheaper to modify without changing its observable behavior".**

If we apply refactoring continuously, it will improve the design of our application on one hand, and on the other hand it will prevent under- and over-engineering. Often, when refactoring, we will find out that patterns can provide help. Practical experience shows that we often identify patterns during refactoring. This is called refactoring to patterns and it corresponds to Martin Fowler's words: "Patterns are where you want to be; refactorings are ways to get there from somewhere else". More information on refactoring can be found in the book *Refactoring: Improving the Design of Existing Code* from Addison-Wesley (ISBN 0-201-48567-2).

So far, we have figured out that patterns document proven good design approaches. However, there are also several bad design approaches. Documenting them can help us prevent using them; this is exactly what antipatterns are about. We'll look at antipatterns in the next section.

Antipatterns

Design patterns document praxis-proven solutions and are based on successfully working applications where patterns have fulfilled their objectives. We all know, however, that there are also several applications that did not fulfill their goals. Not much (often nothing at all) is said about the design and architecture of such applications. What did the architects of these applications do wrong? Documenting these wrong decisions, which have often emerged spontaneously, can help us prevent making the same mistakes in our applications.

For example, a typical wrong design decision, made in the first J2EE applications was to model entity beans with fine-grained interfaces and accessing them directly. This added a considerable remote method invocation and transaction management overhead, which resulted in poorly performing and un-scalable applications.

This and similar mistakes are documented as antipatterns. Antipatterns describe negative solutions, which cause more problems than they address. Antipatterns describe design solutions that do not work in practice due to unintended and unforeseen negative consequences. Elaborating why we made a bad solution and what consequences this bad solution had will help us to avoid such cases in the future. Antipatterns will help us to avoid using bad solutions and to recover and correct these mistakes, because antipatterns offer refactored solutions for successful development.

Antipatterns can therefore be seen as the exact opposite of patterns. Patterns help us to identify solutions that work. Antipatterns help us to identify solutions that will not work and/or good solutions applied in the wrong context or situation. Identifying mistakes as early as possible is the key to risk minimization. Therefore antipatterns are very important for each designer, architect, and developer.

Antipatterns can be identified in all phases of software development; therefore we can classify them similarly as patterns. Like patterns, we have to identify them appropriately and then use the refactorings to improve the design. In this book, we will not focus on antipatterns although in the following chapters, we will provide some examples of wrong design decisions and categorize them as antipatterns. For more information on antipatterns, read the following books:

- *AntiPatterns: Refactoring Software, Architectures, and Projects in Crisis* from John Wiley & Sons (ISBN: 0-471-19713-0)

- *AntiPatterns In Project Management* from John Wiley & Sons (ISBN: 0-471-36366-9)

- *Java AntiPatterns* from John Wiley & Sons (ISBN 0-471-14615-3)

Now that we are familiar with design patterns in general, with refactoring and antipatterns, let's look at design patterns in the context of Java 2 Platform, Enterprise Edition (J2EE).

J2EE and Design Patterns

J2EE provides a rich set of technologies that are useful for developing enterprise applications. In version 1.3 J2EE supports the following technologies:

- **Enterprise JavaBeans (EJB) version 2.0** provides services for developing, deploying, and managing business-logic tier components on the EJB tier.

- **JavaServer Pages (JSP) version 1.2** allows development of dynamic web-based user interfaces.

- **Java Servlets version 2.3** provides a mechanism for extending the functionality of the web server to access the business systems.

- **JDBC API version 3.0** provides services for connectivity with relational databases.

- **Java Message Service (JMS) version 1.0.2** is a standardized API for accessing Message-Oriented Middleware (MOM), and supports the Point-to-Point and Publish/Subscribe models.

❑ **Java Remote Method Invocation, RMI-IIOP**, part of the Java 2 SDK version 1.3, Standard Edition, provides the ORB services and enables transparent remote method invocation between distributed objects and components. The ORB is protocol-independent and currently supports the RMI native protocol (JRMP) and the CORBA-compliant IIOP protocol.

❑ **Java Interface Definition Language (IDL)**, part of the Java 2 SDK version 1.3, Standard Edition, is a CORBA-compliant ORB that enables interoperability with external CORBA distributed objects using the IIOP protocol.

❑ **Java Transaction API (JTA) version 1.0.1** and **Java Transaction Service (JTS) version 1.1** provide support for transactions and provides interfaces for application-level transaction demarcation.

❑ **Java Authentication and Authorization Service (JAAS) version 1.0** provides security services, particularly authentication and authorization. It provides the Pluggable Authentication Module (PAM) framework implementation for authenticating users.

❑ **Java Naming and Directory Interface (JNDI) version 1.2**, part of the Java 2 SDK version 1.3, Standard Edition, is a standardized API for accessing naming and directory services.

❑ **Java API for XML Parsing (JAXP) version 1.1** provides support for handling XML-formatted data. It provides DOM (Document Object Model) and SAX (Simple API for XML) parsers and an XSLT (XML Style Sheet Language for Transformations) transformation engine.

❑ **J2EE Connector Architecture version 1.0** is a service provider interface that enables the development of resource adapters through which the access to enterprise information systems is enabled. It defines a standard set of system-level contracts between a J2EE-compliant server and a resource adapter.

❑ **JavaMail version 1.2** provides an API for managing e-mails and requires the JavaBeans Activation Framework (JAF).

In addition to these technologies, which are a standard part of every J2EE 1.3-compliant application server there are additional JAX (Java API for XML) interfaces:

❑ **JAXM – Java API for XML Messaging**
Provides an API for packaging and transporting business transactions using the wire protocols defined by ebXML.org, Oasis, W3C, and IETF.

❑ **JAX/RPC – Java API for XML-based Remote Procedure Calls**
Supports XML-based RPC standards.

❑ **JAXR – Java API for XML Registries**
Provides an API for a set of distributed registry services that enables business-to-business integration between business enterprises, using the protocols defined by ebXML.org.

❑ **JAXB – Java API for XML Binding**
Allows us to compile an XML Schema into one or more Java classes that can parse, generate, and validate documents that follow the Schema.

❑ **JWSDL – Java Web Service Definition Language**
Provides a standard set of APIs for representing and manipulating services described by WSDL (Web Services Description Language) documents. These APIs define a way to construct and manipulate models of service description.

There is also a new version of JAXP – version 1.2 – under development. To ease the installation and use of these APIs, Sun has gathered under the name Java XML Pack (JAX Pack) the following technologies: JAXM, JAXP 1.2, JAXR, and JAX-RPC. Sun has also published the Java Web Services Developer Pack (WSDP), which gathers the Java XML Pack, JSP Standard Tag Library (JSTL), Ant Build Tool, Java WSDP Registry Server, Web Application Deployment Tool, and Apache Tomcat dev container. Familiarity with these APIs is a prerequisite for developing Web Services and for applying the patterns related to them.

In addition to these, we might also be interested in APIs that have been optional additions, but are now a standard part of J2SE version 1.4, and will therefore become a part of the J2EE 1.4. These include:

❑ Java Secure Socket Extension (JSSE) for enabling secure communications using SSL and TLS protocols. JSSE includes functionality for encryption, authentication, and validating message integrity.

❑ Java Cryptography Extension (JCE), which provides a framework and implementation for encryption, key generation, key agreement, and MAC (Message Authentication Code) algorithms.

❑ Java Generic Security Services (JGSS), an API for generic authentication and secure messaging interface that supports pluggable security mechanisms.

❑ Java Management Extensions (JMX), an API for management and monitoring.

To use J2EE, we therefore have to learn at least all standard J2EE technologies and preferably the aforementioned additional options too. This is not a trivial task. But, is learning these technologies enough for designing good applications on J2EE? Unfortunately, the answer is "no" because learning the technologies only answers the question *how* to use them, not *when* and *why*. Learning the technologies is also not the same as learning to design applications with J2EE. When designing applications we have to make decisions about the architecture and the technologies.

> **Learning J2EE technologies is the foundation for learning how to design applications with J2EE.**

If we would like to be successful designers, we will have to know more than just the facts about technologies. We need to know:

❑ Which technology to use for which problem

❑ How to use it the best way – in other words, what are the best practices for each technology

❑ What are the common pitfalls and how we should not use a technology

❑ Which are the best solutions for common problems

❑ How to improve bad solutions

Each J2EE designer, architect, and developer has been faced with these questions while using J2EE technologies. Servlets, JSPs, EJBs, JMS, JNDI, JCA, and other J2EE technologies do a fair job of abstracting technical details from the developer. However, we still have to know how to use them. Figuring this out ourselves would require a lot of studying of the underlying concepts – exactly what J2EE tries to abstract and hide from us – the underlying complexity.

In the past, there have been numerous applications that have used J2EE technologies in a wrong way. This led to applications that did not perform as expected and did not meet the requirements and objectives. To be honest, these problems are not limited to J2EE. With each technology, we can develop useless applications if we don't use the technology in the right way.

Although J2EE abstracts the underlying technologies in a high-level manner, we still have to model and design our solutions to use these technologies. Designers, architects, and developers are seeking the answer to the aforementioned questions, which in practice are more concrete, such as:

- ❑ Which kind of enterprise beans is most suitable for a specific task
- ❑ How to design EJBs for adequate performance and scalability
- ❑ How to take most advantage of container-managed transactions, persistence, and security
- ❑ Should we look up components each time or should we store the references
- ❑ Where to store session data
- ❑ Should we use JSPs or servlets
- ❑ Should we treat content and presentation separately
- ❑ Who should be responsible for data validation
- ❑ How should we define effective relationships between entity beans
- ❑ How to minimize remote method invocations
- ❑ How much data should we send between the tiers
- ❑ How should we integrate existing applications

These and several other questions are the ones that we have to answer on a daily basis. Design patterns for J2EE have started to emerge to answer these questions. Today, there are two large catalogues of J2EE patterns. One is TheServerSide.com pattern repository, which can be accessed online at http://www.theserverside.com/patterns/index.jsp. The most important patterns from this catalog have been published in the book, *EJB Design Patterns: Advanced Patterns, Processes, and Idioms* from John Wiley & Sons (ISBN 0-471-20831-0).

The other important source of J2EE patterns is the Sun Java Center, which has defined a set of 15 J2EE patterns. These can be accessed online too at http://developer.java.sun.com/developer/technicalArticles/J2EE/patterns. These patterns have been published in the book *Core J2EE Patterns* from Prentice Hall (ISBN 0-13-064884-1).

Why Use Patterns in J2EE?

Using J2EE patterns has all the advantages of using general-purpose patterns, plus the advantage that these patterns have been focused on J2EE development precisely. Therefore, they are more focused on J2EE and less abstract than general-purpose patterns; this simplifies their identification, use, and adaptation to our specific application or system.

J2EE patterns, if used in the correct way, will improve the design of our applications. As we have mentioned before, we have to understand the patterns before we start to use them. Although patterns might look simple at first sight, they are generally not simple to apply. Therefore in this book we will place a lot of effort to demonstrate how we should apply the patterns in the best way.

J2EE patterns document the best-proven approaches for solutions to common problems faced when designing and developing J2EE applications. They have been used over and over again and have proved that they can successfully solve similar problems in different projects.

J2EE patterns define a common vocabulary for J2EE developers. This enables better communication between developers. Every developer who starts using patterns quickly starts using pattern names in their communication with other developers.

This fact highlights the importance of naming the patterns appropriately. Although a consensus on naming J2EE patterns has not been reached yet, the situation is quite good, having only a few almost identical patterns under different names. Different names for the same pattern add confusion. The fact is also that the situation is resolving quickly.

Using patterns has another important benefit; it constrains the solution space. Patterns define boundaries within which the solution can be applied. Patterns therefore suggest the boundaries to the developer.

J2EE-Specific Patterns vs. Patterns in a J2EE Context

We have started to use the phrase J2EE design patterns. Now, how do J2EE design patterns relate to general-purpose design patterns? Most general-purpose patterns are applicable to J2EE platform, and we will call these patterns in J2EE context. Some patterns are specific to J2EE, because they solve J2EE-specific problems. We will call these J2EE-specific patterns.

When trying to classify patterns, we figure out that design patterns range from more general to more specific. Based on their generality, patterns can be classified into the following three categories:

- ❏ Fundamental design patterns, which are not bound to a specific domain, platform, or programming language. For example, Façade (as defined by GoF) is a fundamental design pattern.

- ❏ Design patterns, related to a specific programming language or platform, because they are partly or completely realized with constructs of this platform or language (Java, J2EE, for example). Examples include Session and Message Façade, EJB Command, Generic Attribute Access, etc. We will make an overview of J2EE patterns a little later.

- ❏ Design patterns, related to a specific domain. They represent solutions for problems in a limited context. For example, patterns related to transactions, persistence, EIS integration, etc. Domain patterns can be derived from fundamental design patterns directly, or they can be defined as specializations of platform-specific patterns.

Determining whether a pattern is specific to a programming language or platform requires knowledge about that language or platform. Please recall that patterns are identified as successful solutions that have been implemented in a certain language or platform (such as J2EE). Patterns are then generalized. The important question is whether the generalization could present the pattern in a way that it does not use any language- or platform specific-constructs.

The other criterion is whether the pattern is application-domain specific or not. The less domain specific the pattern, the more broad usage domain the pattern has.

Another criterion can be whether the pattern is *atomic and elementary*, or is it built of several other patterns. Although these analyses are interesting, they are not very important for the application of patterns. However, they help us understand patterns better.

To go back to J2EE patterns, we can see that in J2EE pattern catalogs we will find patterns that are specific to J2EE and Java, but we will also find general-purpose patterns that have been adapted to the J2EE platform. Some J2EE patterns might also be domain specific, while the others might be used in different domains. As we will see later, this book classifies the J2EE patterns based on their technology domains. This simplifies the selection and application.

The hierarchy of the patterns is shown on the following figure:

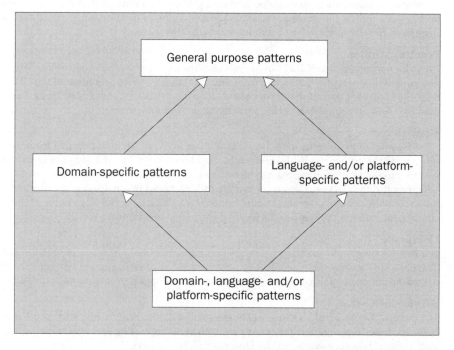

J2EE patterns represent the expertise and experience of the Java designers, architects, and developers. In the next section, we'll make a short overview of the most important J2EE patterns.

The Most Important J2EE Patterns

As we have already mentioned, with J2EE there are two important J2EE pattern catalogs. One is supervised by the Sun Java Center, which has defined 15 patterns, which are also published in the *Core J2EE Patterns* book. The other is TheServerSide.com. Its catalog publishes a larger number of patterns; the most important of them have been gathered in the book *EJB Design Patterns: Advanced Patterns, Processes, and Idioms*. We'll look at the most important patterns from both catalogs.

Sun Java Center J2EE Patterns Catalog

The Sun Java Center has organized the patterns into tiers, similar to J2EE, in a multi-tiered platform. As we saw earlier, each tier has its own responsibilities and is separated from other tiers. The Core J2EE patterns are focused mainly on the web component and business logic (EJB) tier. They are organized as follows:

❑ Presentation-tier patterns for web-component tier

❑ Business-tier patterns for business-logic (EJB) tier

❑ Integration tier for connection with systems on the EIS tier

The catalog defines the following presentation-tier patterns:

❑ **Intercepting Filter**
Provides a solution for preprocessing and post processing a request. It defines a flexible architecture, which allows us to declaratively apply filters for intercepting requests and responses. Servlet filters are an implementation of this pattern.

❑ **Front Controller**
Provides management and handling of requests through a centralized controller. The controller takes over the common processing that occurs on the presentation tier. Thus it takes over the controller part of the Model View Controller (MVC) pattern. The front controller manages content retrieval, security, view management, and navigation.

❑ **View Helper**
Provides a solution for separating the programming logic, which is responsible for presentation (formatting the output – view) from the other (business) logic. The presentation formatting is placed into the view components, which can be composed of multiple subcomponents to compose a complex view. The business-logic code is placed into helper components. Typical functions of helper components are content retrieval, validation, and adaptation. Helper components can use the Business Delegate pattern to access business services.

❑ **Composite View**
Is a flexible solution for creating aggregate presentations (views) from atomic subcomponents. The presented architecture enables easy piecing together of elementary view components, which makes the presentation flexible and allows among other things personalization and customization.

❑ **Service-to-Worker**
Is a pattern composed of a Dispatcher component with the Front Controller and View Helper patterns. It performs request processing prior to view processing and is suitable for larger applications. It is very similar to the Dispatcher View pattern.

❑ **Dispatcher View**
Is similar to Service to Worker. This pattern also combines a Dispatcher component with the Front Controller and View Helper patterns. In contrast to Service-to-Worker, this pattern performs request processing during the view processing. Therefore it is more suitable for smaller systems.

The business-tier patterns from the catalog are:

❑ **Business Delegate**
Provides a solution for reducing the coupling between tiers, particularly between the presentation and the business-logic tier. It provides a proxy to the façade, which can serve as a universal entry point for services on the business-logic and EIS tier. The proxy can also cache the remote method invocations for improved performance. The Business Delegate pattern can be combined with the Service Locator pattern.

❑ **Value Object**
Solves the problem of exchanging the data between tiers and the related remote overhead. Value Object gathers all required data within a serializable object, which is transferred between the tiers with a single remote method invocation. This pattern is commonly accepted as the best technique for communication between and exchanging data between the tiers. It successfully minimizes the number of remote method invocations, which are costly in distributed systems.

❑ **Session Façade**
Hides the complexity of the business components and centralizes the workflow. It provides coarse-grained interfaces to the clients, which reduces the remote method overhead. It also fits well with declarative transaction and security management. Session Façade pattern is usually combined with other patterns, such as: Service Locator, Value Object, Value Object Assembler, Value List Handler, Service Activator, and Data Access Object. It is one of the most important J2EE patterns.

❑ **Composite Entity**
Addresses the remote interface overhead with the EJB 1.1 entity beans and provides a solution for designing coarse-grained entity beans by grouping parent dependent objects into a single entity bean. It is focused on the EJB 1.1 persistence model and outdated with the EJB 2.0 persistence model, local interfaces, and managed relations.

❑ **Value Object Assembler**
Provides a flexible solution for composing a Value Object from different sources, which can be EJBs, Data Access Objects, or Java objects. The pattern is useful for creating data that has to be passed to the client. The Value Object Assembler pattern is related to the Value Object pattern.

❑ **Value List Handler**
Provides a sound solution for query execution, and results processing. It may also cache results for further performance improvement. This pattern is based on the Iterator pattern from the GoF catalog.

❑ **Service Locator**
Provides a solution for looking up, creating, and locating service factories, and encapsulating their complexity. Multiple clients can use the Service Locator object, which reduces complexity, provides a single point of control, and can improve performance through caching.

There are also two integration-tier patterns defined:

❑ **Data Access Object**
Provides a flexible and transparent access to the data, abstracts the data sources, and hides the complexity of the EIS persistence tier. The advantage is the resulting loose coupling between the business and the EIS tier. This pattern is also useful for entity beans with bean-managed persistence.

❑ **Service Activator**
Provides a solution for enabling asynchronous processing with synchronous EJB components, particularly session beans. This pattern provides similar functionality to the message-driven beans in the EJB 2.0 specification. The advantage of this pattern is that it can be applied to EJB 1.1 as well.

Some of the Sun Java Center J2EE Patterns, particularly business-tier patterns, are a little outdated because they have been defined with respect to EJB specification version 1.1. As we know, EJB version 2.0 has brought several important modifications, among others, message-driven beans, local interfaces, and a new persistence model.

These new features invalidate the Composite Entity pattern, because local interfaces in EJB 2.0 now allow making finer-grained entity beans, and defining relationships among them without performance penalty. Actually, the EJB 2.0 specification favors the latter approach. The message-driven beans also call for another pattern, the Message Façade. Also, Service Activator has been outdated due to the same functionality provided by message-driven beans. Some of these new patterns have been defined in the second pattern catalog on TheServerSide.com.

TheServerSide.com Patterns Catalog

This pattern catalog organizes the patterns a little differently. It uses the following categories:

❑ EJB Layer Architectural Patterns

❑ Inter-Tier Data-Transfer Patterns

❑ Transaction and Persistence Patterns

❑ Client-Side EJB Interaction Patterns

The important EJB Layer Architectural Patterns include:

❑ **Session Façade**
Provides the same solution as the indentically named pattern from the Sun Java Center J2EE Patterns catalog.

❑ **Message Façade**
Is similar to Session Façade pattern. However, it uses message-driven beans instead of session beans. This enables asynchronous, fault-tolerant access.

❑ **EJB Command**
Is a competitor to the Session Façade pattern. It wraps business logic in command beans, decouples the client and the business-logic tier, and reduces the number of remote method invocations.

❑ **Data Transfer Object Factory**
Provides a factory for data transfer objects.

❑ **Generic Attribute Access**
Provides a generic solution to set and retrieve attributes for entity beans in a dynamic way though `HashMaps`.

❑ **Business Interface**
Provides a solution for achieving compile-time consistency checking of EJB interfaces. For this purpose, it defines a business interface, which is implemented by both the local/remote interface and the enterprise beans class.

The important Inter-Tier Data-Transfer Patterns include:

❑ **Data-Transfer Object**
Provides a solution for transferring data using serializable objects. This pattern is related to the Data Transfer Object Factory pattern and similar to the Value Object pattern.

❑ **Domain Data-Transfer Object**
Is a specialization of Data Transfer Object for a specific domain.

❑ **Custom Data-Transfer Objects**
Shows how to define custom Data-Transfer Objects.

❑ **Data-Transfer HashMap**
Provides a solution to marshal arbitrary sets of data between client and EJB tier using HashMaps.

❑ **Data-Transfer RowSet**
Shows how to use RowSets for marshaling raw relational data directly from a ResultSet in the EJB tier to the client tier.

The important Transaction and Persistence Patterns include:

❑ **Version Number**
Provides a solution for maintaining consistency and protecting against concurrency problems for use cases that span transactions.

❑ **JDBC for Reading**
Shows how to perform listing operations on relational databases using JDBC.

❑ **Data-Access Command Beans**
uses Command beans for data access. Similar to the EJB Command pattern.

❑ **Dual Persistent Entity Bean**
Shows how to write entity beans that support both BMP and CMP through inheritance. The final selection is done through the deployment descriptor.

The important Client-Side EJB Interaction Patterns include:

❑ **EJB Home Factory**
Provides a solution to improve the performance when looking up EJB Home interfaces. The solution is to use the EJB Home Factory, which can implement caching and thus improve performance.

❑ **Business Delegate**
Is similar to the indentically named pattern in the Sun Java Center catalog.

Relations Between J2EE Patterns

The fifteen patterns from the Sun Java Center catalog and the seventeen patterns from TheServerSide catalog are related. Some of the patterns are also similar and provide similar solutions for same problems. We have identified the following similarities:

❑ Service to Worker and Dispatcher View

❑ Session Façade, Message Façade, and EJB Command

❑ Service Locator and EJB Home Factory

❑ Value Object and Data-Transfer Object with all variations: Domain Data-Transfer Object, Custom Data-Transfer Object, Data-Transfer `HashMap`, and Data-Transfer `RowSet`

❑ Value Object Assembler and Data-Transfer Object Factory

❑ Data-Access Object and Data-Access Command Bean

To get a better overview of both pattern catalogs, we will show their relationships and dependencies in the next figure. Gray shadowed boxes represent patterns from TheServerSide catalog, while white boxes represent Sun Java Center patterns:

The relationships, groupings, and dependencies are shown below:

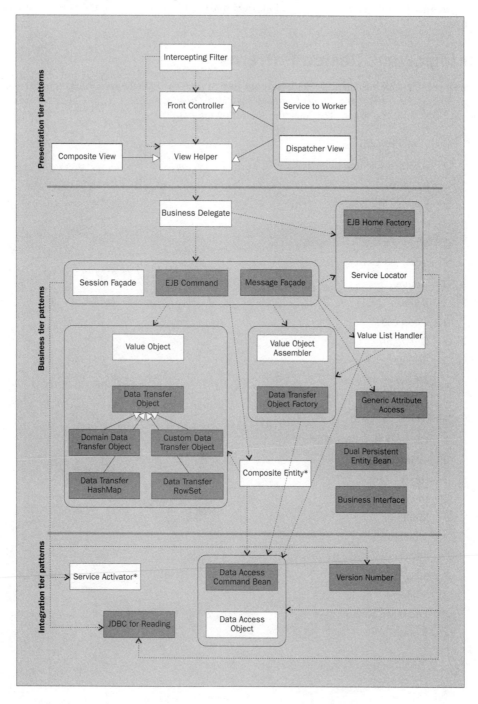

Several J2EE patterns from both catalogs correspond to Java-related patterns and general-purpose design patterns. Therefore, in the next section, we'll make a short overview of the other most important design patterns.

Other Important Design Patterns

The most popular and influential general-purpose design patterns have been published in the GoF pattern catalog, *Design Patterns: Elements of Reusable Object-Oriented Software by the GoF,* from Addison-Wesley (ISBN: 0-201-63361-2). This includes the following patterns:

- ❏ Creational patterns:
    - ❏ Abstract Factory
    - ❏ Builder
    - ❏ Factory Method
    - ❏ Prototype
    - ❏ Singleton
- ❏ Structural patterns:
    - ❏ Adapter
    - ❏ Bridge
    - ❏ Composite
    - ❏ Decorator
    - ❏ Façade
    - ❏ Flyweight
    - ❏ Proxy
- ❏ Behavioral patterns:
    - ❏ Chain of Responsibility
    - ❏ Command
    - ❏ Interpreter
    - ❏ Iterator
    - ❏ Mediator
    - ❏ Memento
    - ❏ Observer
    - ❏ State
    - ❏ Strategy
    - ❏ Template Method
    - ❏ Visitor

In addition to the GoF catalog, there are some important Java related catalogs. Probably the most influential is the book, *Patterns in Java, Volume 1* from John Wiley & Sons (ISBN 0-471-25839-3). It defines the following important patterns:

- ❑ Delegation
- ❑ Interface
- ❑ Immutable
- ❑ Marker Interface
- ❑ Object Pool
- ❑ Layered Initialization
- ❑ Dynamic Linkage
- ❑ Cache Management
- ❑ Little Language
- ❑ Snapshot
- ❑ Single Threaded Execution
- ❑ Two-Phase Termination

By now you might have got the feeling that there are currently quite a few important patterns. Selecting and using them requires that we know and understand them. In this book, we will show how to apply the most important patterns in J2EE.

In the next section, we will look at the problem domains for J2EE patterns and discuss the organization of the rest of the book.

Problem Domains for J2EE Patterns

We have seen that different pattern catalogs structure patterns in different ways. This book is not a pattern catalog, and neither is it a formal discussion about J2EE patterns. Rather we concentrate on how to apply existing design patterns in J2EE applications.

To simplify the selection of patterns, we have organized the patterns based on the domain they might be used for. This corresponds well with our practical focus to show how to *apply* design patterns.

The patterns and their application in this book are organized into following sections:

- ❑ Patterns Applied to the Web Tier
- ❑ Patterns Applied to a Persistence Framework
- ❑ Patterns Applied to Improve Performance and Scalability
- ❑ Patterns Applied to Manage Security
- ❑ Patterns Applied to Enable Enterprise Integration
- ❑ Patterns Applied to Enable Reusability, Maintainability, and Extendibility

The section on *Patterns Applied the Web Tier* covers the following patterns:

- ❑ Intercepting Filter (from the J2EE catalog)
- ❑ Front Controller (from the J2EE catalog)
- ❑ View Helper (from the J2EE catalog)
- ❑ Composite View (from the J2EE catalog)
- ❑ Service-to-Worker (from the J2EE catalog)
- ❑ Dispatcher View (from the J2EE catalog)

The section on *Patterns Applied to a Persistence Framework* covers the following patterns:

- ❑ Data Access Object (from the J2EE catalog)
- ❑ Value Object (from the J2EE catalog)
- ❑ Service Locator (from the J2EE catalog)

The section on *Patterns Applied to Improve Performance and Scalability* covers the following patterns:

- ❑ Value Object (from the J2EE catalog)
- ❑ Value Object Assembler (from the J2EE catalog)
- ❑ Business Delegate (from the J2EE catalog)
- ❑ Session Façade (from the J2EE catalog)
- ❑ Message Façade (from TheServiceSide.com catalog)
- ❑ Service Locator (from the J2EE catalog)

The section on *Patterns Applied to Manage Security* covers the following patterns:

- ❑ Risk Assessment and Management
- ❑ Single Access Point
- ❑ Check Point
- ❑ Role

The section on *Patterns Applied to Enable Enterprise Integration* covers the following patterns:

- ❑ Integration Broker
- ❑ Wrapper
- ❑ Integration Mediator
- ❑ Virtual Component (Integration Façade)
- ❑ Data Access Object (from the J2EE catalog)

- ❑ Data Mapping

- ❑ Process Automator

The section on *Patterns Applied to Enable Reusability, Maintainability, and Extendibility* covers the following patterns:

- ❑ Façade (from the GoF catalog)

- ❑ Abstract Factory (from the GoF catalog)

- ❑ Decorator (from the GoF catalog)

- ❑ Template Method (from the GoF catalog)

- ❑ Builder (from the GoF catalog)

Relationships Between Patterns

We can see that in the next chapters we will cover patterns from four sources. In addition to J2EE, TheServerSide.com, and GoF patterns we will also cover integration patterns. To understand the most important relations among them we will show them graphically. We will use the following shading for different groups of patterns:

The following figure shows the relationships between patterns covered in this book:

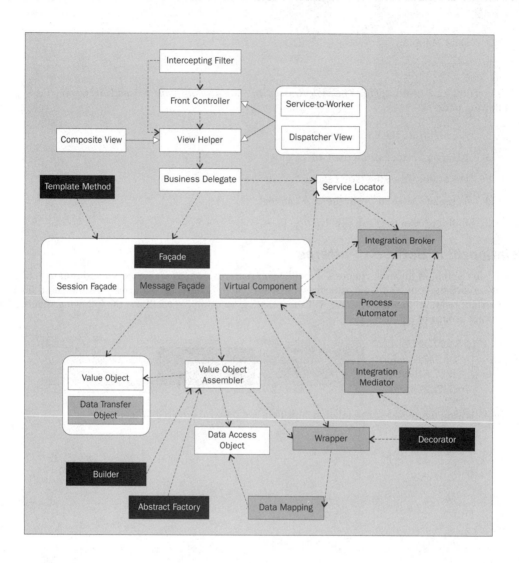

Summary

In this chapter, we have seen that patterns are important for achieving higher-level reuse – the reuse of ideas. Patterns are best solutions for common problems in a context. Although their roots lie in architecture and civil engineering, they have become very important in software development. Patterns are a way towards catalogs of best solutions to common problems.

Patterns can be applied to almost all phases of software development. Probably the most important are the design patterns, which focus on design problems. Patterns are not invented; they are identified. To identify patterns, we need a lot of experience and a bunch of successful projects. Identifying patterns is a difficult and responsible task because they should present the best possible solutions for design problems. Therefore, patterns should be verified as extensively as possible.

Fortunately, the majority of us will not identify patterns; we rather use the patterns. To successfully use a pattern, we should be able to select the most appropriate one. Although many recommendations exist on how to best select a pattern, we will not be able to make a good selection without understanding what problem a pattern solves and what the solution is. Knowing the relationships between patterns is also very helpful.

Using patterns is a good way to design software. Still, we have to use patterns intelligently. This means that we should not use too many of them, but should always assess their advantages and disadvantages, otherwise we will over-engineer our applications. On the other side, if we don't use patterns at all, we could under-engineer our application. In both cases, we can use refactoring to improve our design.

When talking about patterns, we cannot avoid antipatterns. They are just the opposite of patterns and show the bad practices and bad solutions in software engineering. Knowing antipatterns helps to avoid these common pitfalls.

Design patterns can be general purpose and independent of a specific programming language, platform, or domain. They can also be specific. Our focus will be primarily on J2EE design patterns. These patterns show how to solve common design problems with applications based on J2EE. In this chapter, we have made a short overview of most important J2EE patterns and pattern catalogs.

In the following chapters, we will go into the details of how to apply J2EE patterns in specific domains. We will show concrete examples and best practices for applying the most important J2EE patterns.

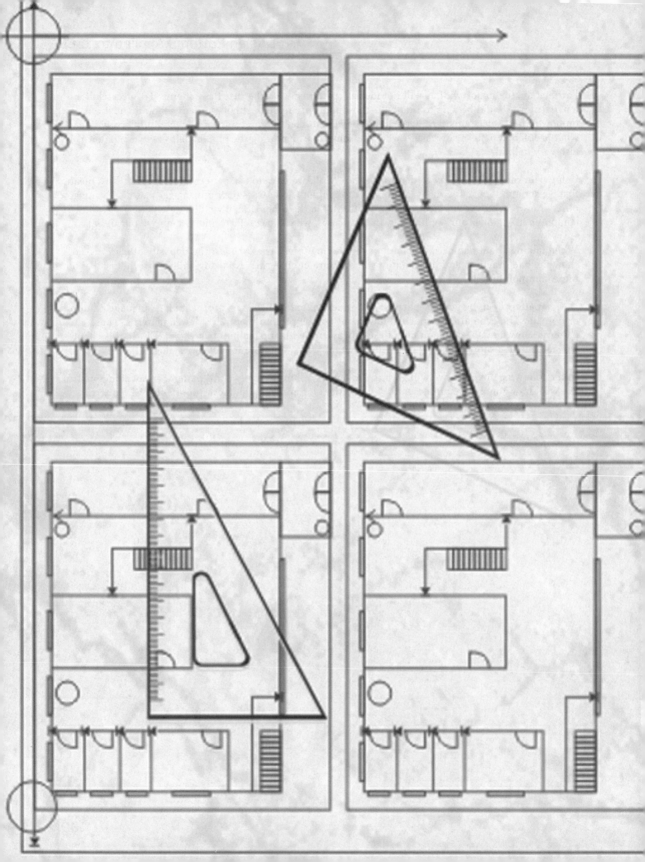

Patterns Applied to the Web Tier

2

One of the challenging problems in designing web applications is creating a well-structured, thin, and clean client layer. The challenge is to combine the right look and the correct behavior, while encapsulating the presentation logic without any business logic creeping into this layer, and at the same time create easy-to-read and easy-to-maintain code. In addition, the presentation layer often caters for extra requirements such as user authentication, data encryption, session management, user personalization, and request processing.

In this chapter, we shall describe issues that surround designing and managing the top layer of a web application. We shall discuss the technical requirements expected of the client layer and how the J2EE presentation design patterns can address these.

We shall discuss these patterns by developing an application for a hotel booking management system. This application focuses on the J2EE presentation patterns but can be considered as a complete deployable enterprise application in its own right.

Presentation Patterns

The **Model View Controller (MVC)** was one of the first design patterns that introduced the notion of the separation of the presentation layer and the business-logic layer. The MVC introduced the concept of a view (presentation layer), the model (data), and the controller that coordinates the two. Prior to MVC, the user interface designs tended to merge these layers together, but now MVC decouples them to increase flexibility and reuse.

MVC defines a 'subscribe' or 'notify' protocol to decouple the view from the model. The view must ensure that it reflects the state of the model. Whenever the model data changes, all views get notified and each view can then update itself. This approach allows attaching different presentations to a model. New views can be created without major changes to the controller or model. This is no longer automatically expected of a web application. The *View Management* section later in this chapter discusses this extensively.

With the introduction of the J2EE design patterns from the Sun Java Center, the designer of an enterprise application has a wider choice of solutions that can address multiple problems and can be applied to achieve elegant solutions.

The following are the J2EE presentation-tier patterns that we shall cover:

❑ Intercepting Filter

❑ Front Controller

❑ View Helper

❑ Composite View

❑ Service-to-Worker

❑ Dispatcher View

The following are the support patterns:

❑ Model View Controller

❑ Observer

❑ Command

❑ Abstract Factory

Case Study: A Hotel Bookings Management System

The focus of this application is on the client-management aspect and a demonstration of utilizing the core J2EE presentation patterns. We will use this example to describe the patterns adopted as they are introduced in the example solution.

Before we start, let's examine the application requirements and its use case model.

The application provides management of the hotel details, a search facility for hotels based on certain criteria, and a booking system. It also includes adding hotel information such as name, location, type, room booking, change of hotel details, and so on. It enables a group or chain of hotels to use a single remote system to manage its various booking requirements. The web application could be extended to provide a universal hotel booking system to enable users to find a particular hotel that matches their requirements, check availability and cost, and then make a reservation.

The hotel system must be flexible in providing a variety of functions, which will also depend on the role of the user. The following is a list of user roles that are expected to interact with the hotel system:

❑ Customers will search for hotels to match specified criteria, view details on a selected hotel, check availability of and cost of the room, and place a booking request.

❑ Hotel employees would act on behalf of the customer to place a booking request having received the customer's instructions either by fax, e-mail, or phone.

❑ Administrators can act as web customers or hotel employees. In addition, they perform tasks such as creating entries for new hotels, removing hotels, and managing information.

The scope of this application is quite large. However, for the purpose of this case study, we have limited it to the design domain and implementation domains of the specific areas relating to the administrator's use cases.

The Use Case Model

The following diagram shows the use case model for the hotel application, and has the following use case divisions:

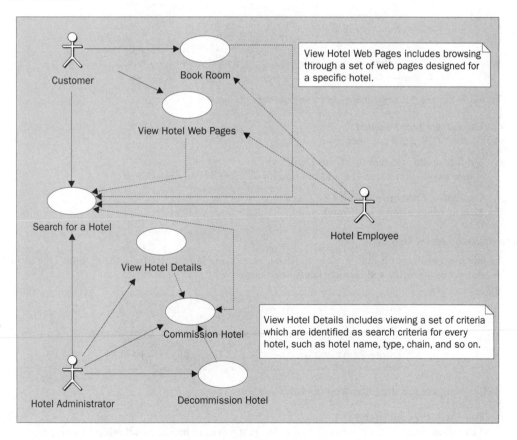

The Hotel Administrator Use Cases

In this section we shall discuss a set of three use cases that the administrator actor interacts with. These are:

❑   Commission Hotel

❑   Decommission Hotel

❑   View Hotel Details

Since these use cases are very similar in their format, it has been possible to devise a common solution for all three of them. After a brief description of each use case, we will discuss their pattern identification and their realization.

Commission Hotel Use Case

The administrator is able to create a new hotel entry into the system including its selection criteria. In addition, a set of web pages that describes the new hotel need to be deployed on the system as well:

The following are the steps involved in evaluating a use case:

❑   **Use Case Preconditions**
Access privileges have been granted

❑   **On Successful Outcome of the Use Case**
A new hotel entry is created and the hotel web pages are commissioned

❑   **On Failed Outcome of the Use Case**
Fails to commission a new hotel

Decommission Hotel Use Case

The administrator actor is able to decommission an existing hotel entry from the system. This includes the removal of the entry and its associated web pages.

The following are the steps involved in evaluating a use case:

❑   **Use Case Preconditions**
The chosen hotel entry to be removed exists in the system including all relevant web pages

❑   **On Successful Outcome of the Use Case**
The hotel entry and all its related information is successfully removed from the system

❑ **On Failed Outcome of the Use Case**
The specified hotel entry and its related information does not get deleted from the system

View Hotel Details Use Case

The view hotel details include viewing a set of criteria, such as hotel name, type, chain, and so on, which are identified as search criteria for every hotel:

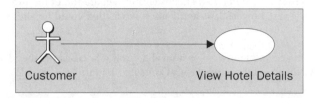

❑ **Use Case Preconditions**
The hotel entry chosen exists in the system including all relevant web pages

❑ **On Successful Outcome of the Use Case**
The hotel entry and all its related information is successfully displayed

❑ **On Failed Outcome of the Use Case**
The specified hotel entry and its related information does not get displayed

Identifying the Patterns

To identify the patterns required to fulfill the use cases described earlier, we need to address the main problem domain areas normally associated with a web application of this kind. We have identified five main problem domain areas, which we need to take into account. These are:

❑ Processing Requests

❑ Session Management

❑ View Management

❑ Validation

❑ Client Security

In the coming section we shall discuss the first four problem domain areas. The client security domain area is covered in Chapter 5. In the context of these problem domain areas, we will develop the Hotel Administrator part of the system.

Processing Requests

Most software applications require some kind of request-processing. This has always been a very interesting application design problem, particularly in web applications. In a simple scenario, request processing can be page oriented whereby each page manages its own request and response processing. In this case, it is easy to have a lot of duplication in code and inconsistency in the application behavior, making maintaining and extending the code difficult.

The best way to address the problem of processing requests is by introducing a controller.

The Front Controller Design Pattern

The Front Controller pattern centralizes control allowing common request-processing. It also delegates to the next view. Centralizing request-processing ensures that this logic is not mingled in different views and it is common between these views. Maintaining it and extending it will therefore be more straightforward. The Front Controller also encourages the separation of the presentation logic from the navigation logic. This is very powerful, as application navigation could be altered without affecting the presentation logic.

A Controller pattern can be implemented as a servlet, or as a JavaBean embedded in a JSP page. The diagram below shows the structure of the Front Controller pattern:

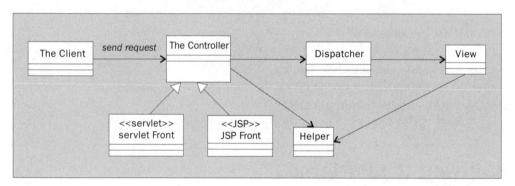

The participants of the Front Controller pattern are as follows:

- **Controller**
  The initial point for handling a request and delegating to the next view

- **Dispatcher**
  Responsible for view management and navigation

- **View**
  Represents and displays information to the client

- **Helper**
  Helps the view or the controller to complete its processing

In our hotel application we have implemented the Front Controller pattern as a servlet controller, using a command and controller strategy. We have chosen the servlet implementation of the controller over the JSP implementation for the following reasons:

- JSP pages are usually related to display formatting and not request processing. Making a controller a JSP will muddle these different purposes.

- In the servlet controller implementation, the request-processing code is easier to maintain because it is separated from the HTML.

This strategy allows separating the controller delegation tasks into separate command objects, decoupling the delegation processes even further. Command is a design pattern that represents a command or an action as an object, decoupling its behavior and allowing extra pluggable functionality like command logging and undoable operations.

The Front Controller Implementation

This pattern is realized in the `AdminHotelController` class. The `AdminHotelController` extends the `HttpServlet` class. It centralizes the processing of hotel requests. The following is the source code for this class:

```
package hotel.presentationtier;

import javax.servlet.http.HttpServlet;
import javax.servlet.http.HttpServletRequest;
import javax.servlet.http.HttpServletResponse;
import javax.servlet.ServletException;
import javax.servlet.ServletConfig;
import javax.servlet.RequestDispatcher;
import java.io.IOException;

import hotel.util.HotelDetails;
import hotel.ejb.HotelHome;
import hotel.ejb.Hotel;
import java.math.BigDecimal;
import java.util.Properties;
import hotel.util.Command;
import hotel.util.RequestHelper;

public class AdminHotelController extends HttpServlet {

    private void processRequest(HttpServletRequest request,
                                HttpServletResponse response)
            throws ServletException, IOException {

        String next = "";
        try {
          RequestHelper helper = new HotelRequestHelper( request, response );
          Command command = helper.getCommand();
          next = command.execute( helper );
        } catch( Exception e ) {
          e.printStackTrace();
        }
        dispatch( request, response, next );
    }
```

This method handles the HTTP GET request:

```
    protected void doGet(HttpServletRequest request,
                HttpServletResponse response )
            throws ServletException, IOException {
    processRequest( request, response );
    }
```

This method handles the HTTP POST request:

```
protected void doPost(HttpServletRequest request,
                HttpServletResponse response )
        throws ServletException, IOException {
  processRequest( request, response );
}

public String getServletInfo() {
  return getSignature();
}
```

Finally, this method dispatches the request to the next page:

```
private void dispatch(HttpServletRequest request,
                HttpServletResponse response,
                String page )
        throws ServletException, IOException {
  RequestDispatcher dispatcher=
    getServletContext().getRequestDispatcher( page );
  dispatcher.forward( request, response );
}
```

Please note the page is an absolute path, otherwise dispatcher will be null:

```
private String getSignature() {
  return "ServiceToWorker-Controller";
}
}
```

The Command Design Pattern

The Command Pattern represents a request as an object; it allows clients to parameterize requests. As each command is represented as an object, the behavior for a new command can easily be added as a new object without affecting any other commands. Also, new behavior for an existing command can be modified, or appended without affecting other commands. Command states can be persisted or logged if required.

The class diagram below shows the structure for the Command pattern:

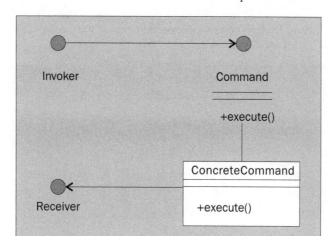

Participants in the Command design patterns are as follows:

❑ **Command**
Declares an interface for executing an operation

❑ **Concrete Command**
Defines a binding between a receiver object and an action

❑ **Invoker**
Asks the command to carry out the request

❑ **Receiver**
Knows how to perform the operations associated with carrying out a request

The sequence diagram below shows the sequence of calls for the Command pattern:

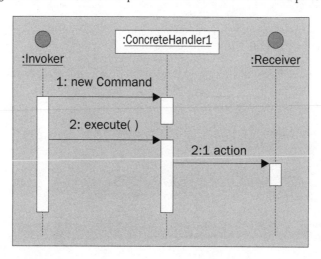

The Command Implementation

The command classes for the hotel administration views are encapsulated in the following diagrams. There are essentially three kinds of command objects; these are the `CreateCommand`, the `FindCommand`, and the `RemoveCommand`:

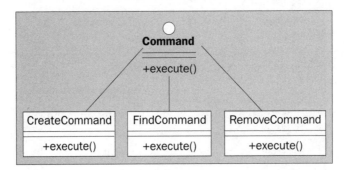

Each object has one method called `execute` to map the action for that command. The following is the source code for the `Command` interface:

```
package hotel.util;

import javax.servlet.ServletException;
import java.io.IOException;
```

This represents a `Command` object. Based on the Command design pattern, it encapsulates a request as an object to parameterize clients with different requests:

```
public interface Command {

    public String execute( RequestHelper helper )
                        throws ServletException, IOException;
}
```

For this interface we have provided three implementations; these are the `CreateHotelCommand`, the `RemoveHotelCommand`, and the `FindHotelCommand`.

The following class implements the `Command` interface for the `create` command:

```
package hotel.presentationtier;

import hotel.util.Command;
import hotel.util.HotelDetails;
import hotel.util.RequestHelper;

import hotel.businesstier.HotelBusinessDelegate;
import hotel.businesstier.HotelBusinessDelegateImpl;

import java.util.Properties;
import javax.servlet.ServletResponse;
```

```
import javax.servlet.ServletException;
import java.io.IOException;
import java.math.BigDecimal;

class CreateHotelCommand implements Command {
   private HotelDetails hoteldetails = null;
   private HotelBusinessDelegate delegate =
                          new HotelBusinessDelegateImpl();
   public CreateHotelCommand( ) {
   }

   private String getDisplayMessage( Properties properties ) {
     return properties.getProperty("id") + " is successfully created";
   }

   public synchronized String execute( RequestHelper helper )
     throws ServletException, IOException {
       try {
         Properties properties = helper.getProperties();
         hoteldetails = new HotelDetails(
                           properties.getProperty("name"),
                           properties.getProperty("purpose"),
                           properties.getProperty("regionOrTown"),
                           properties.getProperty("type"),
                           properties.getProperty("chain"),
          (BigDecimal)properties.get("swimmingPool"),
          (BigDecimal)properties.get("gym"),
          (BigDecimal)properties.get("conferenceRooms"));
         delegate.createHotel(properties.getProperty("id"), hoteldetails);
         helper.getRequest().setAttribute( "result",
                                this.getDisplayMessage( properties ) );
         helper.getRequest().setAttribute( "hotel", hoteldetails );
     } catch( Exception e ) {
         e.printStackTrace();
         helper.getRequest().setAttribute( "result",
                              "Error processing Create Hotel Command" +
                              e.toString() );
         return "/errorPage.jsp";
       }
       return "/adminHotelResult.jsp";
   }
}
```

The following class implements the Command interface for the remove command:

```
package hotel.presentationtier;

import hotel.util.Command;
import hotel.util.HotelDetails;
import hotel.util.RequestHelper;
import businesstier.HotelBusinessDelegate;
import businesstier.HotelBusinessDelegateImpl;
```

```
import java.util.Properties;
import java.io.IOException;
import javax.servlet.ServletException;

class RemoveHotelCommand implements Command {
    private HotelDetails hoteldetails;
    private HotelBusinessDelegate delegate =
                                new HotelBusinessDelegateImpl();

    public RemoveHotelCommand( ) {
    }

    private String getDisplayMessage( String id ) {
      return "Hotel Id " + id + " is successfully removed";
    }

    public synchronized String execute( RequestHelper helper )
        throws ServletException, IOException {
        try {
            String id = helper.getProperties().getProperty("id");
            hoteldetails = delegate.getHotel( id );
            delegate.removeHotel( id );
            helper.getRequest().setAttribute( "result",
                                        this.getDisplayMessage( id ) );
            helper.getRequest().setAttribute( "hotel", hoteldetails );
        } catch( Exception e ) {
            e.printStackTrace();
            helper.getRequest().setAttribute("result",
                            "Error processing Remove Hotel Command" +
                                e.toString() );
            return "/errorPage.jsp";
        }
        return "/adminHotelResult.jsp";
    }
}
```

The following class implements the Command interface for the find command:

```
package hotel.presentationtier;

import hotel.util.Command;
import hotel.util.HotelDetails;
import hotel.util.RequestHelper;
import hotel.businesstier.HotelBusinessDelegate;
import hotel.businesstier.HotelBusinessDelegateImpl;
import java.util.Properties;
import java.io.IOException;

import javax.servlet.ServletException;
    class FindHotelCommand implements Command {
        private HotelDetails hoteldetails;
        private HotelBusinessDelegate delegate =
                        new HotelBusinessDelegateImpl();
```

```
    public FindHotelCommand( ) {
    }

    private String getDisplayMessage( Properties properties ) {
      return properties.getProperty("id") + " is found";
    }

    public synchronized String execute( RequestHelper helper )
                              throws ServletException, IOException {
      try {
        Properties properties = helper.getProperties();
        HotelDetails hoteldetails =delegate.getHotel(
                              properties.getProperty("id") );
                              helper.getRequest().
          setAttribute("result", this.getDisplayMessage( properties ) );
          helper.getRequest().setAttribute( "hotel", hoteldetails );
      } catch( Exception e ) {
        e.printStackTrace();
        helper.getRequest().setAttribute(
                    "result",
                    "Error processing Find Hotel Command"  +
                    e.toString() );
        return "/errorPage.jsp";
      }
      return "/adminHotelResult.jsp";
    }
}
```

Please note that all the three command objects have package access, because the client of the Command objects need not know the specific concrete class of each object. All command types can be treated uniformly using the command interface.

In the following section, we shall describe how these command objects get created and defined by an abstract factory class called the CommandFactory.

The Abstract Factory Design Pattern

Since we have a number of command types, we need a clean way to build these commands to hand them to the controller so the controller can delegate to them. For this, we use the Abstract Factory design pattern. Abstract Factory allows the creation of families of related objects without exposing their concrete classes.

The following diagram shows the structure for the Abstract Factory design pattern:

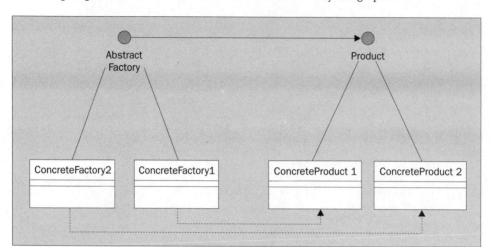

Participants in the Abstract Factory pattern are as follows:

- **Abstract Factory**
  Provides interface abstraction for creating a product

- **Product**
  Provides an interface for a product abstraction

- **Concrete Factory**
  An abstract factory implementation for creation of a concrete product

- **Concrete Product**
  The concrete product implementation

The Abstract Factory Implementation

This pattern is realized as a CommandFactory interface and a CommandFactoryImpl class, which implements this interface. The CommandFactory interface has a createCommand method to facilitate the creation of a command. The following is the source code for the CommandFactory interface:

```
package hotel.util;
```

This represents the abstract factory interface to create commands. Abstract Factory provides an interface for creating families of related or dependent objects without specifying their concrete classes:

```
public interface CommandFactory {

    public Command createCommand( String action );
}
```

This is the implementation for the Command Factory design pattern:

```
package hotel.presentationtier;

import hotel.util.Command;
import hotel.util.CommandFactory;

import java.util.HashMap;
import java.util.Enumeration;
import java.util.Properties;

class CommandFactoryImpl implements CommandFactory {

    private HashMap commands = new HashMap();
    private final static String
        ACTION_MAPPING_PROPERTIES = "actionMapping.properties";

    public CommandFactoryImpl() {
      try {
        Properties properties = new Properties();
        properties.load( getClass().getResourceAsStream(
        ACTION_MAPPING_PROPERTIES ));
        for( Enumeration e = properties.keys(); e.hasMoreElements(); ) {
            String action = ( String )e.nextElement();
            commands.put( action, ObjectCreator.createObject(
                        properties.getProperty( action ) ) );
        }
      } catch( Exception e ) {
        System.out.println( "Error: " + e.toString() );
        e.printStackTrace();
      }
    }

    public Command createCommand( String action ) {
      return ( Command )commands.get( action );
    }
}
```

This class loads action and class name mappings from a property file called
actionMapping.properties. The following is the mapping:

```
create= hotel.presentationtier.CreateHotelCommand
remove= hotel.presentationtier.RemoveHotelCommand
find= hotel.presentationtier.FindHotelCommand
```

The FactoryFacadeImpl uses the ObjectCreator class to dynamically instantiate the command
objects associated with each mapping. Discussing this class is out of the scope of our case study; please
refer to the source code downloadable from http://www.wrox.com for its implementation.

The Command design pattern and the Abstract Factory design pattern do not constitute enough to help
the controller complete its initial request-processing task. The final part required is the View Helper
design pattern.

The View Helper Design Pattern

The View Helper design pattern helps a view to complete tasks not associated directly with the presentation of the view. The main objective of using the view helper is to separate the interaction with the business tier from the presentation tier thereby decoupling the two layers as much as possible so any change to one layer will no have a big effect on the other.

The structure for the view is a very simple one. The following diagram shows the View Helper pattern:

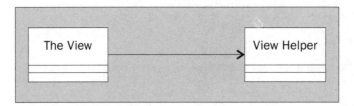

Participants in the Composite View pattern are as follows:

❑ **The View**
   This is presentation view in the context of a web application. It can be HTML, JSP, or a servlet.

❑ **The View Helper**
   This is the helper for the view, and holds information not directly associated with presentation formatting. A view helper can be implemented as one of the following:

   ❑ A Java bean implementation

   ❑ A Custom tag implementation

A value bean helper has a more specific use than a JavaBean helper. It is normally used within the JSP as a data holder. The following is the JSP tag for a value bean helper:

```
<jsp:useBean id="hotel" scope="request"
             class="hotel.util.HotelDetails" />
```

The following is a simple example of a custom tag helper:

```
<logic:iterate collection="<%=cdDB.getCds()%>"
               id="cd" type="database.CdDetails">
```

The View Helper Implementation

The helper classes for the hotel admin view are encapsulated in three interfaces and classes. These are the `RequestHelper` interface, the `AbstractRequestHelper` class, and the `HotelRequestHelper` class. The `RequestHelper` object gathers parameter-specific information.

The following diagram shows how these two classes relate to each other:

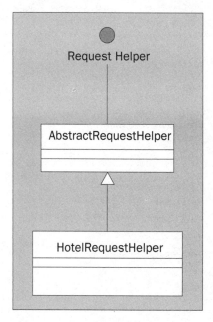

Here is the source for the RequestHelper interface:

```
package hotel.util;

import java.util.Properties;
import java.math.BigDecimal;
import java.util.Enumeration;
import javax.servlet.http.HttpServletRequest;
import javax.servlet.http.HttpServletResponse;

public interface RequestHelper {
    public HttpServletRequest getRequest();
    public HttpServletResponse getResponse();
    public Command getCommand();
    public Properties getProperties();
}
```

The following is the source code for the AbstractRequestHelper class:

```
package hotel.presentationtier;

import javax.servlet.http.HttpServletRequest;
import javax.servlet.http.HttpServletResponse;
import javax.servlet.ServletException;
import java.io.IOException;

import java.util.Properties;
```

```
import java.math.BigDecimal;
import java.util.Enumeration;
import javax.servlet.http.HttpServletRequest;
import javax.servlet.http.HttpServletResponse;
import hotel.util.RequestHelper;
import hotel.util.Command;

abstract class AbstractRequestHelper implements RequestHelper {

    private HttpServletRequest request = null;
    private HttpServletResponse response = null;
    private Properties properties = null;

    AbstractRequestHelper( HttpServletRequest request,
                           HttpServletResponse response){
      this.request = request;
      this.response = response;
      this.properties = getProperties( request );
    }

    public HttpServletRequest getRequest() {
      return request;
    }

    public HttpServletResponse getResponse() {
      return response;
    }

    public abstract Command getCommand();

    public Properties getProperties( ) {
      return properties;
    }
```

In addition to a direct translation, this method parses and filters user input text into actual Java objects and values. For example, string numbers such as "1" are parsed to a number:

```
private Properties getProperties(HttpServletRequest httpservletrequest) {
    Properties properties = new Properties();
    for( Enumeration enumeration =
                  httpservletrequest.getParameterNames();
                  enumeration.hasMoreElements();) {
      Object obj = enumeration.nextElement();
      String s = httpservletrequest.getParameterValues((String)obj)[0];

      System.out.println( "Parameter name ="+ obj.toString() + ", Parameter
                          value =" + s );
      if( ! isAny(s)) {
        try {
          properties.put(obj, new BigDecimal(s));
        } catch(NumberFormatException _ex) {
          properties.put(obj, s);
        }
```

```
        }
      }
    return properties;
  }

  private static boolean isAny(String s) {
      return s.equals("Any");
  }
}
```

And finally, the following is the specialization for the HotelRequestHelper class. This class is final and has package access only because it is not designed to be extended or be visible outside the domain of the presentation-tier package:

```
package hotel.presentationtier;

import javax.servlet.http.HttpServletRequest;
import javax.servlet.http.HttpServletResponse;
import hotel.util.CommandFactory;
import hotel.util.Command;
import hotel.util.RequestHelper;

import javax.servlet.ServletException;
import java.io.IOException;

final class HotelRequestHelper extends AbstractRequestHelper {

    private CommandFactory commandFactory = new CommandFactoryImpl();

    HotelRequestHelper( HttpServletRequest request,
                        HttpServletResponse response) {
      super( request, response );
    }

    public Command getCommand() {
      return commandFactory.createCommand(
        getProperties().getProperty("action") );
    }
}
```

Session Management

A client session can be defined as maintaining a conversation state between a number or group of a client's requests and a server. In most cases it is necessary to manage client sessions. Session management is split between the client layers and the server layers.

A client session can be persisted in the client code, by using hidden fields in the HTML, cookies, the URL, or in the server code. Some applications also use database persistence or serialization.

Sometimes it is also necessary to authenticate user sessions before dealing with the request. Typically, a server-side utility generates a unique session Id when a user logs in; the session Id gets passed in for each request forwarded for processing after a successful login for that user. The session expires if the user logs out or after some time.

This kind of design, without care can make the session client code fragmented and difficult to maintain. In adopting a clear structure or a design pattern these issues can be addressed. One method of doing this is to use the Front Controller design pattern described in the previous section to authenticate user sessions and help reduce fragmentation.

This version of the Front Controller design pattern shown in the sequence diagram below introduces a session helper, which creates a new session and authenticates existing sessions:

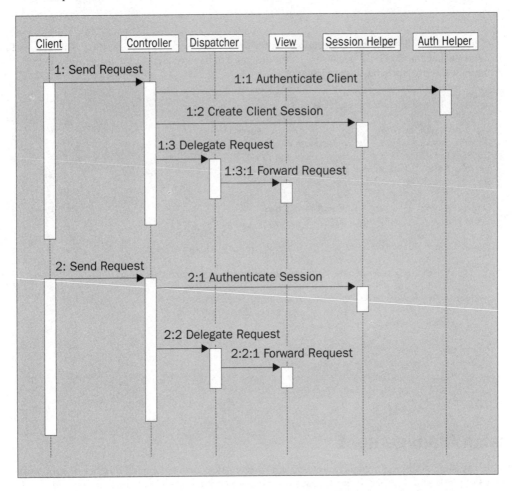

Another way to ensure session creation and authentication is to use the Intercepting Filter design pattern. This is the approach we have adopted in our hotel application. The reason for this is to put the session creation and authentication logic early on, before getting into the controller code. If a request session is not valid, the request is bounced back.

The Intercepting Filter Design Pattern

The Intercepting Filter design pattern allows intercepting a request and applying a set of filters to it and then rejecting the request or allowing it to pass through to its intended target.

The class diagram below shows the structure of the Intercepting Filter pattern:

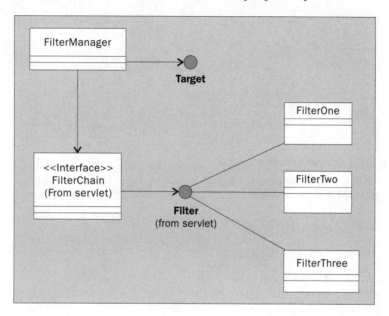

Participants in the Intercepting Filter pattern are as follows:

❑ **FilterManager**
The filter manager manages the filters, sequencing them and initiating their processing in a filter chain

❑ **FilterChain**
The filter chain is a structure comprising a sequence of individual filters

❑ **FilterOne, FilterTwo, FilterThree**
The independent filters that can be associated with specific destination or target

❑ **Target**
The target is the destination requested by the client

The following diagram shows different types of filters adopted for different purposes for the hotel application. In the coming section, we shall show the implementation for the SessionFilter and in the validation section of this chapter, we shall show the ValidationFilter implementation:

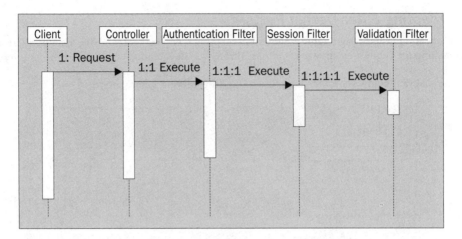

The Intercepting Filter Implementation

The Servlet 2.3 API provides out-of-the-box implementation for the Intercepting Filter design pattern. We have implemented the `javax.servlet.Filter` to create a `SessionFilter`:

```
package hotel.presentationtier;

import javax.servlet.ServletRequest;
import javax.servlet.ServletResponse;
import javax.servlet.FilterConfig;
import javax.servlet.FilterChain;
import javax.servlet.ServletException;
import javax.servlet.RequestDispatcher;
import javax.servlet.http.HttpServletRequest;
import javax.servlet.http.HttpServletResponse;
import javax.servlet.Filter;

import java.io.IOException;

public class SessionFilter implements Filter {

  private FilterConfig filterConfig = null;

  public void init( FilterConfig filterConfig ) throws ServletException {
    this.filterConfig = filterConfig;
  }

  public FilterConfig getFilterConfig() {
    return filterConfig;
  }

  public void setFilterConfig( FilterConfig filterConfig ) {
    this.filterConfig = filterConfig;
  }

  public void doFilter( ServletRequest request,
                        ServletResponse response,
```

```
                              FilterChain chain ) throws IOException,
                              ServletException {
    HttpServletRequest httpRequest = ( HttpServletRequest )request;
    HttpServletResponse httpResponse = ( HttpServletResponse )response;
    String session = ( String )httpRequest.getAttribute( "session" );
    if( session == null ) {
      httpRequest.setAttribute( "result",
                                "session is not valid" );
      RequestDispatcher dispatcher = filterConfig.getServletContext()
                            .getRequestDispatcher("/errorPage.jsp");
      dispatcher.forward( request, response );
    } else {
      chain.doFilter( request, response );
    }
  }

  public void destroy() {
  }
}
```

For the purposes of this book this filter does session authentication but not the creation of new sessions. The filter needs to be declared in the web.xml descriptor for the application. This is the XML for declaring a session filter:

```
<filter>
   <filter-name>SessionFilter</filter-name>
   <filter-class>hotel.presentationtier.SessionFilter
   </filter-class>
</filter>

<filter-mapping>
   <filter-name>SessionFilter</filter-name>
   <url-pattern>/AdminHotelServlet/*</url-pattern>
</filter-mapping>
```

View Management

In our hotel application there are two kinds of views: the view shared by the customer and the hotel employee, and the administrator view. Addition of views may be required at later stage of the product life cycle, and so flexibility can be built into the design. This suggests that we need to device a way to manage the views easily and neatly.

The best way to address this is to use the MVC design pattern, as shown in the diagram overleaf. The MVC separates the notion of a view from the model. An element can appear only once in a model, whereas it can appear multiple times in different views. The view can be tailored to suit a user's requirement, for instance the view can form a subset of the model:

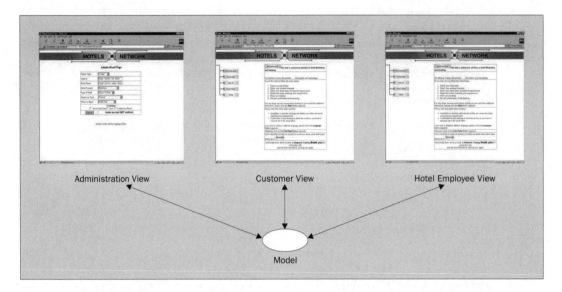

By adopting the Front Controller design pattern described earlier we have adopted a Model View Controller structure for the hotel application. The Front Controller design pattern introduced a view and controller elements; the model part lives outside the presentation tier.

To add to this, some users may have privileges to change the model. This will require an update mechanism; the most suited for this purpose is the Observer design pattern.

Observer defines a one-to-many dependency between objects so that when one object changes its state, all its dependants are notified and updated automatically. Updating a view in a web application is no straightforward task. It will require doing multiple refreshes, polling or keeping an HTTP connection open.

In our hotel example, it was seen that it is not necessary to have an update mechanism because this was not put forward as business requirement. Hotels can be commissioned/decommissioned with an acceptable delay period of 24 hours. It may be more frequent in the case for room booking, which was mentioned earlier, but is outside the scope of this example.

Our administrator views need some kind of structure because there is a need to have frame views and sub-views. For example, in our hotel user view we will need to show a banner at the top of the page, enter a set of criteria, and in another area show the result of the user action. For this we can use the Composite View pattern.

The Composite View Design Pattern

The Composite View pattern allows a parent view to aggregate sub-views. Hence, the overall view becomes a composite of smaller atomic parts. This reduces the amount of duplicate code for repeated parts among the different views and enforces a consistency between separate views making maintenance and manageability of the views more straightforward.

The following diagram shows the basic structure for the Composite View pattern. The Composite View pattern is based on the Composite pattern first introduced in the book *Design Patterns, Elements of reusable object-oriented software (ISBN 02-0163-361-2)*:

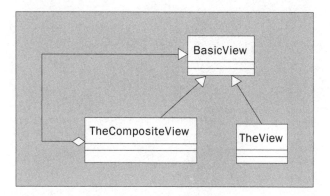

Participants of the Composite View Pattern are as follows:

❏ **BasicView**
   This is the basic abstraction for the view

❏ **TheCompositeView**
   A view that is composed of a number of sub-views

❏ **TheView**
   A simple view that has no sub-views

The Composite View Implementation

In our hotel example, there are four sub views that can be used within one composite view. These are the views of the administrator hotel:

❏ The admin hotel frame view

❏ The admin hotel view

❏ The admin hotel result view

❏ The error page view

❏ The banner view

The view composition is shown in the diagram below:

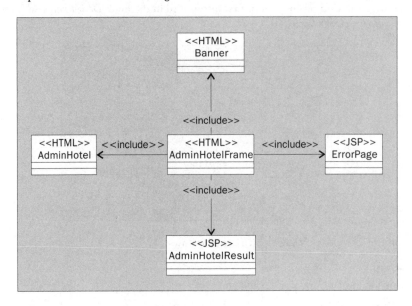

For the administrator view pages the composite view strategy we have used is a mixture of a simple HTML frameset strategy and a JavaBean view strategy. With the JavaBean view strategy, they are used with the context of the JSP page. JavaBeans are easy to create and integrate within the structure of the JSP page.

The following is the source for the `AdminHotel.html` page:

```
<html>
  <head>
    <title>Admin Hotel Page</title>
  </head>

<body>
  <h3><center>Admin Hotel Page</center></h3>
  <form action="AdminHotelServlet" method="GET" target="result">
   <p> </p>
    <div align="center"><center><table border="1" cellspacing="1"
        width="425" bgcolor="#FFFFFF" bordercolor="#FFFFFF"
        bordercolorlight="#FFFFFF" bordercolordark="#FFFFFF">
    <tr>
      <td width="125"><font size="2" face="Arial">Action Type</font></td>
      <td width="300"><select name="action" size="1">
      <option value="create">Create</option>
        <option value="find">Find</option>
        <option value="remove">Remove</option>
        </select></td>
    </tr>
    <tr>
      <td width="125"><font size="2" face="Arial">Hotel ID</font></td>
```

```
      <td width="300"><div align="left"><p>
        <input type="text" name="id" value="type hotel ID here" size="20">
      </td>
  </tr>

  <tr>
    <td width="125"><font size="2" face="Arial">Hotel Name</font></td>
    <td width="300"><div align="left"><p>
    <input type="text" name="name" value="type hotel name here" size="20">
    </td>
  </tr>

  <tr>
    <td width="125"><font size="2" face="Arial">Hotel Purpose</font></td>
    <td width="300"><select name="purpose" size="1">
      <option value="Business">Business</option>
      <option value="Cultural excursion">Cultural excursion</option>
      <option value="Skiing Holiday">Skiing Holiday</option>
      <option value="Beach Holiday">Beach Holiday</option>
      <option value="Business & Culture">Business & Culture</option>
      <option value="Beach & Culture">Beach & Culture</option>
      <option value="Business & Beach">Business & Beach</option>
     </select>
    </td>
  </tr>

  <tr>
    <td width="125"><font size="2" face="Arial">Type of Hotel</font></td>
    <td width="300"><div align="left"><p><select name="type" size="1">
      <option value="5 Star">Delux / 5 Star</option>
      <option value="4 Star">4 Star</option>
      <option value="3 Star">3 Star</option>
      </select>
    </td>
  </tr>

  <tr>
    <td width="125"><font size="2" face="Arial">Region or Town</font></td>
    <td width="300"><select name="regionOrTown" size="1">
      <option value="Ankara">Ankara</option>
      <option value="Istanbul">Istanbul</option>
      <option value="Cappadocia">Cappadocia</option>
      <option value="Bodrum">Bodrum</option>
      <option value="Erciyes">Erciyes (ski centre)</option>
      <option value="Side">Side</option>
      <option value="Palandoken">Palandoken (ski centre)</option>
      </select>
    </td>
  </tr>

  <tr>
    <td width="125"><font size="2" face="Arial">Chain or Agent</font></td>
    <td width="300"><select name="chain" size="1">
      <option value="Gold Trail">Gold Trail</option>
```

```
            <option value="Thomson">Thomson</option>
            <option value="LunnPoly">LunnPoly</option>
            <option value="First Choice">First Choice</option>
            <option value="Jmc">Jmc</option>
            <option value="Ottoman Hotels">Ottoman Hotels</option>
            </select>
        </td>
      </tr>

      <tr>
        <td width="425" align="center" colspan="2"><small><font
            face="Arial"><strong>Facilities:</strong><br>
          <input type="checkbox" name="swimmingPool" Value="1">
            Swimming Pool</font>,
          <input type="checkbox" name="gym" Value="1"><font
            face="Arial">Gym</font>,
          <input type="checkbox"
                name="conferenceRooms" Value="1"><font face="Arial">Conference
                Rooms.</font></small></td>
      </tr>

        <tr>
          <td width="125" align="center"><input type="submit"
              value="Submit"></td>
          <td width="300" align="center"<small><font
              face="Arial">
            <strong>Hotel servlet GET method:</strong></font></td>
        </tr>
      </table>
    </center></div>
    </form>

    </body>
  </html>
```

Please note that the action tag highlighted points to the `AdminHotelServlet`. This is the name mapped to the `hotel.presentationtier.AdminServletController` class in the `weblogic` `web.xml` descriptor for the `hotel.war` file.

Finally, we shall review the `AdminHotelResult` JSP page. This JSP page utilizes the value bean helper that is the second helper we have developed for the `Admin Hotel View`:

```
<html>
  <head>
    <title>Admin Hotel Result Page</title>
  </head>

  <body link="#FFFFFF" vlink="#FFFFFF" alink="#FFFFFF" bgcolor="#FFFFFF"
      text="#000000">
    <H3><center> "<%=request.getAttribute( "result" )%>"</center></H3>
    <p>

    <jsp:useBean id="hotel" scope="request"
```

```
                    class="hotel.util.HotelDetails" />
    <center>
    <h2>
       Hotel Details for
       <jsp:getProperty name="hotel" property="name"/>
    </h2>

    <table border=3>
       <tr>
         <td>
           Hotel Purpose :
         </td>

<td>
       <jsp:getProperty name="hotel" property="purpose" />
</td>
       </tr>

       <tr>
         <td>
           Hotel Region or Town :
         </td>
         <td>
           <jsp:getProperty name="hotel" property="regionOrTown" />
         </td>
       </tr>

       <tr>
         <td>
           Hotel Type :
         </td>
         <td>
           <jsp:getProperty name="hotel" property="type" />
         </td>
       </tr>

       <tr>
         <td>
           Hotel Chain :
         </td>
         <td>
           <jsp:getProperty name="hotel" property="chain" />
         </td>
       </tr>
    </table>
    </center>
  </body>
</html>
```

The View Helper Implementation

We have introduced the View Helper design pattern earlier in this chapter when we developed the RequestHelper classes. This is the second time we shall use this design pattern in our case study. We have developed a JavaBean helper called the HotelDetails as a second helper to store the hotel information once a hotel is retrieved to display its details to the user.

This is the code for the HotelDetails class:

```java
package hotel.util;

import java.io.Serializable;
import java.math.BigDecimal;

public class HotelDetails implements Serializable {

    private String name = "";
    private String purpose = "";
    private String regionOrTown = "";
    private String type = "";
    private String chain = "";
    private BigDecimal swimmingPool = new BigDecimal(0.0D);
    private BigDecimal gym = new BigDecimal(0.0D);
    private BigDecimal conferenceRooms = new BigDecimal(0.0D);

    public HotelDetails( String name,
                         String purpose,
                         String regionOrTown,
                         String type,
                         String chain,
                         BigDecimal swimmingPool,
                         BigDecimal gym, BigDecimal conferenceRooms ) {
      if( name != null ) {
        this.name = name;
      }
      if ( purpose != null ) {
        this.purpose = purpose;
      }
      if ( regionOrTown != null ) {
        this.regionOrTown = regionOrTown;
      }
      if ( type != null ) {
        this.type = type;
      }
      if ( chain != null ) {
        this.chain = chain;
      }
      if ( swimmingPool != null ) {
        this.swimmingPool = swimmingPool;
      }
      if ( gym != null ) {
        this.gym = gym;
      }
```

```
      if ( conferenceRooms != null ) {
        this.conferenceRooms = conferenceRooms;
      }
    }

    public String getName() {
      return name;
    }

    public String getPurpose() {
      return purpose;
    }

    public String getRegionOrTown() {
      return regionOrTown;
    }

    public String getType() {
      return type;
    }

    public String getChain() {
      return chain;
    }

    public BigDecimal getSwimmingPool() {
      return swimmingPool;
    }

    public BigDecimal getGym() {
      return gym;
    }

    public BigDecimal getConferenceRooms() {
      return conferenceRooms;
    }

    public String toString() {
      StringBuffer stringbuffer = new StringBuffer(getClass().getName() +
                                                             "::\n");
      stringbuffer.append("name=" + name + ", purpose=" + purpose + ",
                          region or town=" + regionOrTown + ", ");
      stringbuffer.append("type=" + type + ", chain=" + chain + ", ");
      stringbuffer.append("swimmingPool=" + swimmingPool + ", gym=" + gym +
                          ", ");
      stringbuffer.append("conferenceRooms=" + conferenceRooms);
      return stringbuffer.toString();
    }
  }
```

The diagram that follows shows the three patterns we have discussed in the *View Management* section assembled into one framework. These are the three patterns discussed earlier:

❏ **Model View Controller**
Separates the presentation logic and the business logic into separate tiers, by introducing a model (business data), a view (data presentation), and a controller, which coordinates the two

❏ **Composite View**
Allows a parent view to aggregate to sub-views. So the overall view becomes a composite of smaller atomic parts

❏ **View Helper**
Separates out logic not related to presentation formatting away from the view

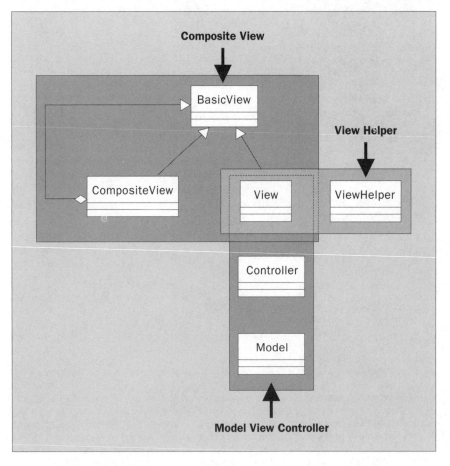

In the above diagram the boxes labeled "Composite View", "View Helper", and "Model View Controller" represent the individual design patterns, and the boxes labeled "BasicView", "CompositeView", "View", "ViewHelper", "Controller", and "Model" represent the participants of the patterns.

Validation

There are two types of validation possible in the presentation tier. These are client validation and server validation. Client validation lives in the front HTML layer and can be achieved using a scripting language such as JavaScript. It is important to filter out empty fields to do type validation, for example to differentiate between strings, numbers, and dates. Server validation happens in a bridging layer between the JSP page and servlet code, and can be achieved by using view helper classes and filters.

Both client and server validation are necessary to validate input effectively. Other strategies may involve using value beans or pushing validation down to the business logic layer.

The Intercepting Filter Implementation

Having previously introduced the Intercepting Filter design pattern, we can see that this pattern is also appropriate for the validation of user input. In this scenario we have a `ValidationFilter` implementing the `javax.servlet.Filter` interface and a separate `Validator` class and a factory to create `Validators`.

The following diagram shows the use of the validation filter as part of the Intercepting Filter design pattern to perform validation on the servlet request for the hotel administrator pages:

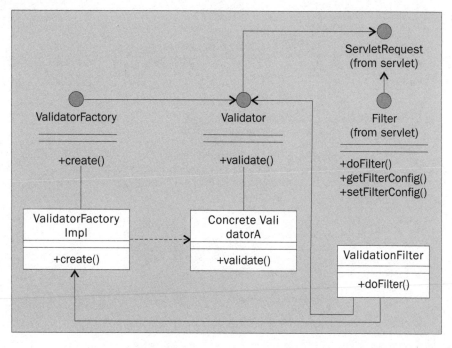

The `ValidatorFilter` class implements the `doFilter` method to perform the validation task:

```
package hotel.presentationtier;

import hotel.util.Validator;
import javax.servlet.ServletRequest;
```

```java
import javax.servlet.ServletResponse;
import javax.servlet.FilterConfig;
import javax.servlet.FilterChain;
import javax.servlet.ServletException;
import javax.servlet.RequestDispatcher;
import javax.servlet.http.HttpServletRequest;
import javax.servlet.http.HttpServletResponse;
import javax.servlet.Filter;

import java.io.IOException;
import javax.servlet.http.HttpServletRequest;
import javax.servlet.http.HttpServletResponse;

public class ValidationFilter implements Filter {

  private FilterConfig filterConfig = null;
  private Validator validator = new
                            ValidatorFactoryImpl().createValidator();
  public void init( FilterConfig filterConfig ) throws ServletException {
    this.filterConfig = filterConfig;
  }

  public FilterConfig getFilterConfig() {
    return filterConfig;
  }

  public void setFilterConfig( FilterConfig filterConfig ) {
    this.filterConfig = filterConfig;
  }

  public void doFilter( ServletRequest request,
                        ServletResponse response,
                        FilterChain chain )
          throws IOException, ServletException {
    HttpServletRequest httpRequest = ( HttpServletRequest )request;
    HttpServletResponse httpResponse = ( HttpServletResponse )response;
    if( ! validator.validate( request ) ) {
      httpRequest.setAttribute( "result",
            "Error data entered is not valid. Please check your input" );
            RequestDispatcher dispatcher =
            filterConfig.getServletContext()
            .getRequestDispatcher("/errorPage.jsp");
      dispatcher.forward( request, response );
    } else {
      chain.doFilter( request, response );
    }
  }

  public void destroy() {
  }
}
```

This is the interface for the `Validator` object. The `Validator` interface has one method called validate, which returns `true` or `false` and takes one parameter. The parameter is abstracted to type `Object` so it can be reused within any context:

```
package hotel.util;

public interface Validator {
    public boolean validate( Object object );
}
```

To build the validation objects we have adopted the abstract factory again so we can create `Validator` implementations without specifying their concrete classes. This is the `ValidatorFactory` interface source:

```
package hotel.util;

public interface ValidatorFactory {

  /** Creates a Validator instance
  */
    public Validator createValidator( );

}
```

The filter needs to be declared in the `web.xml` descriptor for the application. This is the XML for declaring a filter:

```
<filter>
<filter-name>ValidationFilter</filter-name>
<filter-class>hotel.presentationtier.ValidationFilter </filter-class>
  </filter>
  <filter-mapping>
    <filter-name>ValidationFilter</filter-name>
    <url-pattern>/AdminHotelServlet/*</url-pattern>
  </filter-mapping>
```

Please note that the complete source code including XML descriptors for this application is provided with the downloadable source code for this book.

Assembling the Patterns into a Framework

So far we have described and adopted the following patterns for the hotel Administrator use cases and we have shown how to implement each pattern:

❑ **Intercepting Filter**
  Intercepts requests and applies a filter so that the requests can be forwarded or bounced back

❑ **Front Controller**
  Centralizes control and request processing and manages delegation to the next view

❑ **View Helper**
Helps to separate out non-presentation-related logic away from the view into separate helper classes

❑ **Composite View**
Separates a view into small atomic sub-views; the layout of the page may be managed independently of its content

❑ **Command**
Encapsulates a command or action as an object

❑ **Abstract Factory**
Allows the creation of families of related objects without specifying their concrete classes

The final part is to compose and view the whole framework for the application. There are two J2EE presentation patterns that could be used as the basis for this framework. These are:

❑ Service-to-Worker

❑ Dispatcher View

Each of these two patterns resembles a macro pattern or a micro framework in its own right. We will describe and discuss each of these patterns in the coming two sections and compose a comparison table between the two to show the subtle differences between them.

The Service-to-Worker Design Pattern

The Service-to-Worker design pattern assembles two sub-patterns together into a micro framework. These are the Front Controller, and the View Helper. Its participants are a combination of a controller, dispatcher, views, and their helpers.

Assembling these patterns into a workable framework is important to utilize the benefits associated with each pattern.

As in the Front Controller design pattern, the Service-to-Worker pattern centralizes control, and improves modularity and reuse by providing a central place to handle system services and business logic across multiple requests. It also helps separate non-presentation logic from the view into helper classes, by decoupling model access from the view. The sequence diagram below shows the participants of the Service-to-Worker pattern:

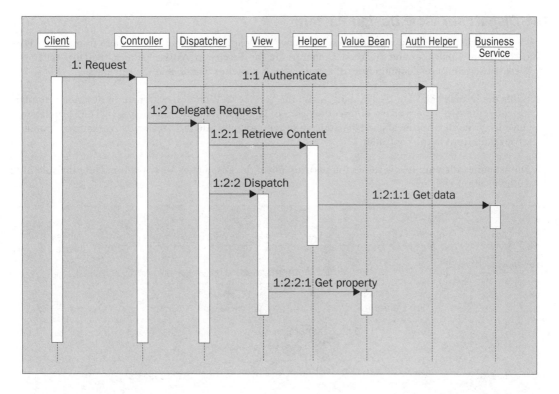

Participants in the Service-to-Worker design pattern are as follows:

❑ **Controller**
This is the initial point for handling a request and is a centralized request processing unit, which delegates to the next view using the dispatcher and uses helpers to separate out chunks of functionality into separate modules. It is responsible for authentication, authorization, and delegation.

❑ **Dispatcher**
This is responsible for view management and navigation. The dispatcher delegates to the next view. In the Service-to-Worker pattern the dispatcher uses a helper to push data into the view.

❑ **View**
This represents and displays information to the client.

❑ **Helper**
This helps the view or the controller to complete its processing. In the Service-to-Worker pattern it can be used to push data into the view.

❑ **Value Bean**
This is another name for a helper.

❑ **Business Service**
The service the client is seeking to access. This is the first point of access to the business tier. Typically it is represented as a business delegate.

The Dispatcher View Design Pattern

The Dispatcher View design pattern assembles two sub-patterns together into a micro framework. These are the Front Controller and the View Helper. As in the Service-to-Worker pattern, the Dispatcher View participants are a combination of a controller, dispatcher, views, and their helpers.

While the Dispatcher View design pattern and the Service-to-Worker design pattern describe a similar structure, the two patterns have different division of labour among their participants. The Dispatcher view delays content retrieval until dynamic view generation, while the Service-to-Worker does content retrieval up front in the controller.

The sequence diagram below shows the participants of the Dispatcher View pattern. Note the role of the Authentication Helper:

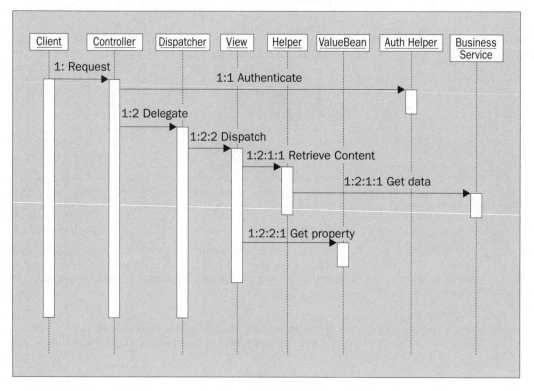

Participants in the Dispatcher View design pattern are as follows:

❑ **Controller**
This is the initial point for handling a request, centralizing request/response processing. It is also responsible for authentication and authorization, and delegation.

❑ **Dispatcher**
This is responsible for view management and navigation. The Dispatcher delegates to the next view.

- **View**
  Represents and displays information to the client. In the Dispatcher View, the view pulls the data from the data source using the view helper.

- **Helper**
  This helps the view or the controller to complete its processing.

- **Value Bean**
  This is another name for a helper.

- **Business Service**
  The service the client is seeking to access. This is the first point of access to the business tier. Typically it is represented as a business delegate.

Comparing the Service-to-Worker and Dispatcher View Patterns

Although the Service-to-Worker and the Dispatcher View patterns share the same structure and participants, they have subtle differences between them.

We have summarized the similarities and differences between the Service-to-Worker and the Dispatcher View patterns in the following table.

Service-to-Worker Pattern	Dispatcher View Pattern
Is a macro pattern or a micro framework of a couple of presentation tier patterns	Is a macro pattern or a micro framework of a couple of presentation tier patterns
Incorporates two sub-patterns: the Front Controller and the View Helper	Incorporates two sub-patterns: the Front Controller and the View Helper
Structure is composed of the controller, dispatcher, views, and view helper participants.	Structure is composed of the controller, dispatcher, views, and view helper participants.
Controller and dispatcher have a bigger role. In addition to centralizing request processing, view management, and navigation, the dispatcher also does content retrieval from the business tier.	Controller and dispatcher have a smaller role.
The view is responsible for presentation of data already retrieved by the dispatcher.	The view is responsible for content retrieval from the business tier at the point of its dynamic generation, and the display of this data.
Pushes more logic and behavior to the front, in the controller, dispatcher, and helpers, keeping the view quite simple.	Pushes more logic and behavior to the back to the view and its helpers, making the view more complex; scriplet code, or custom tags are typically needed to complete tasks not done in the controller.
Employs a push MVC.	Employs a pull MVC.

There is a real case here to have used the Dispatcher View pattern instead of the Service-to-Worker pattern. The Service-to-Worker has been used because it was seen as preferable to give the controller more responsibilities. This will make managing the views easier and understanding the view structures more straightforward giving a benefit for maintainability.

The Service-to-Worker Implementation

For our hotel example we have implemented the Service-to-Worker pattern using a controller servlet with command and controller strategy. As we have seen earlier in the chapter, it necessary to assemble the presentation patterns described into a workable framework. This is important to allow attainment of the benefits associated with each pattern. In addition, the Service-to-Worker pattern provides a good structure making the reuse and maintenance of these components more straightforward. A better structure also allows more flexibility for future changes.

For detailed implementation of the Service-to-Worker pattern please refer back to the following sections:

❑   The Front Controller design pattern implementation

❑   The Command design pattern implementation

❑   The View Helper design pattern implementation

❑   The Intercepting Filter design pattern implementation

❑   The Composite View design pattern implementation

Finally we are going to show all the patterns adopted and discussed earlier assembled into one framework:

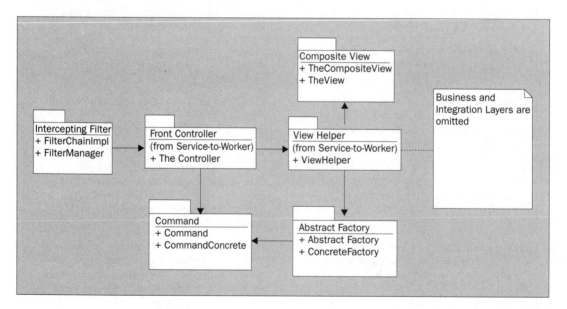

The following diagram shows the actual class relationships and how the patterns described above map to classes, interfaces, HTML, and JSP pages:

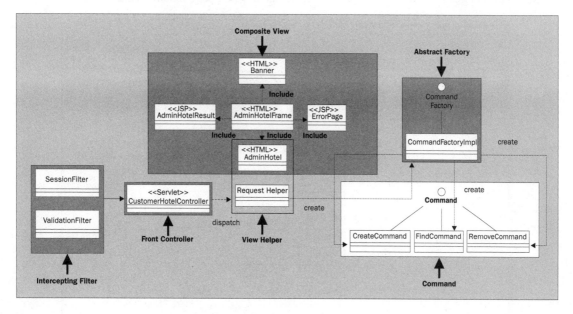

The Hotel Application Admin Site

When the application is deployed and running, the main admin page should look something like this:

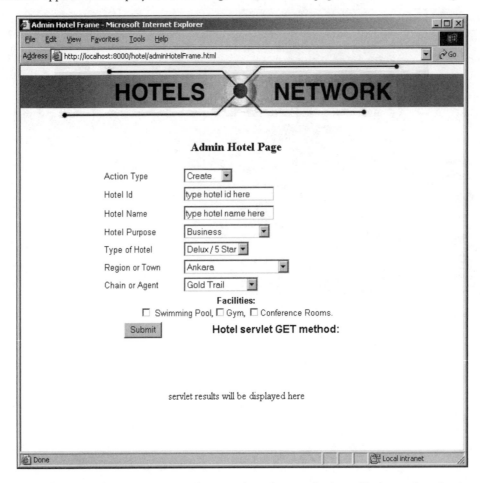

The screen has a simple composite view framework, with two sub views. These are the selection view and the result view. To create a new hotel entry, select the create option in the drop-down list, type the hotel ID and the hotel name, and then set the selection criteria. Click the Submit button.

The result is shown in the result view as in the following screen capture:

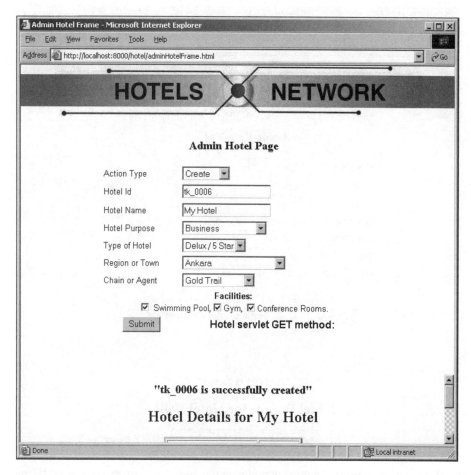

To find a hotel, select the find option in the drop-down list, type the hotel ID, and the hotel name. Click the submit button. The result is shown in the result view as in the following screen capture:

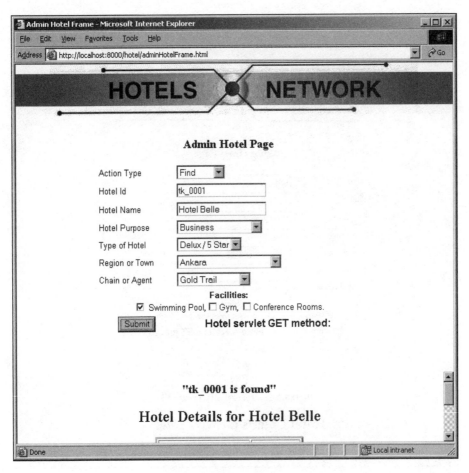

To remove a hotel entry, select the remove option in the drop-down list, type the hotel ID and the hotel name. Click the submit button.

The result is shown in the result view as in the following screen capture:

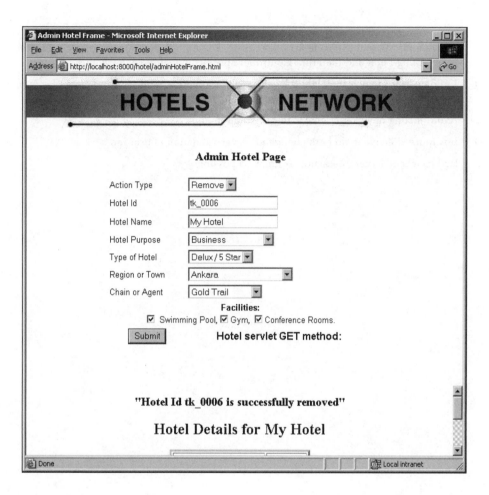

Summary

In this chapter we have discussed the design issues surrounding web-tier management and design of an enterprise application with emphasis on providing solutions within the J2EE presentation-tier patterns from the Sun Java Center. These are the Intercepting Filter pattern, the Front Controller pattern, the Composite View pattern, the View Helper pattern, the Service-to-Worker pattern, and the Dispatcher View pattern.

The patterns discussed also included the patterns of the original design patterns introduced in the book called *Elements of Reusable Object-Oriented Software*: Addison-Wesley (ISBN 0-201-63361-2). They are the Command pattern, and the Abstract Factory pattern.

The main points to take away are:

❑ Keep the design of the client layer thin with emphasis on the presentation logic only. The business logic should live in a different layer.

❑ Take into account the skill set available when structuring the client layer. For example, separate HTML and JSP code from Java code. Some J2EE presentation patterns like the Intercepting Filter and the Front Controller specifically help to achieve this.

❑ Validate user input at the highest level possible to reduce validation and error checking at the levels below this level.

❑ Avoid mixing navigation logic with presentation logic.

❑ It is more effective to do both client and server validation of user input.

❑ Reduce client-server interaction as much as possible.

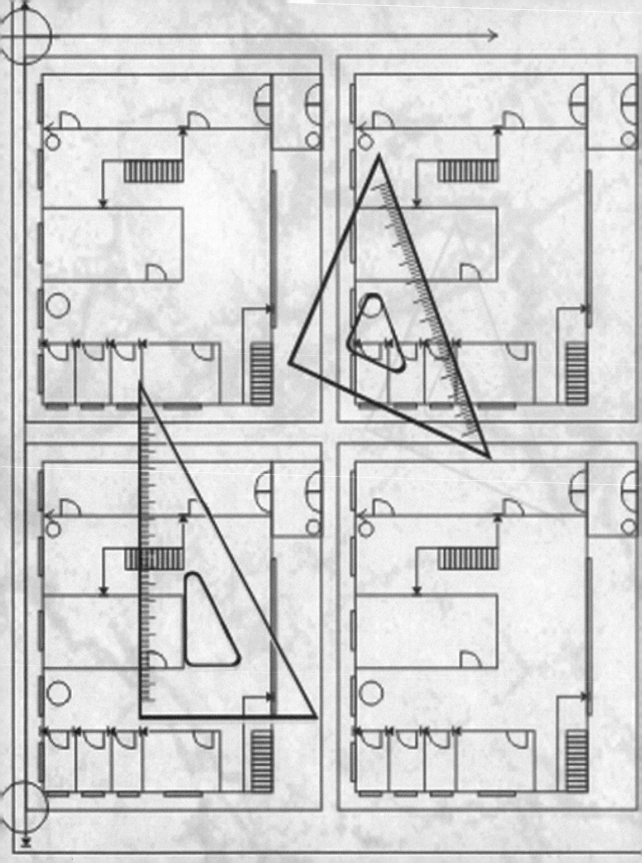

3

Patterns Applied to a Persistence Framework

Data is the lifeblood of the modern corporation. Over the last five to ten years, many corporations have become keenly aware that they can no longer function as viable entities without the data contained within their IT (Information Technology) systems. Data is no longer considered a byproduct of their day-to-day business operations, but rather a strategic asset. One might even go as far as saying:

> **An organization's data is in many cases the organization. Without a consistent and well-defined set of services for accessing the often heterogeneous data sources within an organization, building and integrating applications can become a nightmare.**

Unfortunately, even with the increased awareness of the importance of an organization's data, IT departments do not always have a well thought out strategy for how their applications access and manipulate data.

IT departments tend to look at data access as an application-level issue. They do not look at their data usage from a holistic, enterprise view. Thus, they miss opportunities to build a common framework for accessing and manipulating data locked within their corporate data sources.

Ask most software developers if their applications were written on a base development framework that can easily be modified and reused across applications and you are likely to meet one of the two types:

❑ The developers who have never been exposed to any kind of formal software architecture or design. Therefore, they do not know how to respond to your inquiry.

❑ The IT veterans who have tried to implement a framework, but found them too cumbersome to use and even more difficult to maintain. They believe frameworks would significantly reduce the complexity of their application development and maintenance efforts. However, they are rarely given the time or money to properly build a persistence framework and in the end design a solution that is not usable.

The sad reality is that most applications are not architected. They are "coded" on the fly with the tactical focus of delivering some piece of business functionality. They are not constructed with an eye towards the strategic goal of building a common set of software services that can be reused across multiple applications.

In the short term, the developer delivers what is required of them, but the organization that they work for loses out because of the long-term costs associated with supporting code that was never written with reusability or extensibility in mind.

Many IT departments are realizing that the only way they will be able to keep up with the ever-increasing demand for new applications, while trying to keep costs under control, is to build their applications around a framework that provides a common set of reusable services.

For an IT organization to properly design, deliver, and maintain any type of application framework requires:

❑ **Time and money**
Most organizations are not willing to appropriate time or spend any significant dollar amount to build a reusable framework. System architecture is one of the first sacrifices made by a development team when facing the (often relentless) time-to-market pressures placed on them by the different business units in their organization.

❑ **Incremental implementation**
Building system architecture requires identifying small deliverables that can deliver quantifiable results. Unfortunately, most companies try to implement a common system architecture using a "big bang" approach. However, they are often disappointed because they can rarely show any immediate business benefit for the several months they have to put forward in writing their initial framework.

❑ **Willing to change – Architectures are not designed; they evolve**
This means that there has to be willingness for an organization to refactor and redesign code, even if that code is serving its immediate purpose. Sometimes, entire pieces of architecture must be refactored to achieve the level of reuse and extensibility desired by the organization.

Many IT development teams have looked to the n-tier application model as a means of developing such a services-based framework. An n-tier application model splits an application into three logical tiers. Pieces of each tier might be physically located on different pieces of hardware throughout the enterprise. The three logical tiers in n-tier architecture are:

- ❏ A presentation tier – This is responsible for all logic that deals with presenting information to an end user.

- ❏ A business tier – This captures an organization's business rules as components that can be reused across multiple applications.

- ❏ A data tier – The data tier, also known as the integration tier, is responsible for abstracting away data sources so that the business rules can access and manipulate data regardless of where the data is located or how it is retrieved.

There has been a great deal of research done into the best practices of building a solid presentation and business tier. A walk into any bookstore will reveal that the topic of building presentation and business-tier logic has been going on over the last six to seven years.

In addition, there is a wide-range of open source presentation and business-tier frameworks available for ready use in application development projects. Two examples of these frameworks can be found on the Apache Software Foundation's Jakarta web site (http://jakarta.apache.org):

- ❏ Struts – Struts is a Model-View-Controller framework based on Sun's JSP Model-2 implementation. It offers a number of application plug-in points that cleanly separate an application's presentation, business, and data tiers into well-defined, maintainable pieces.

- ❏ JetSpeed – JetSpeed is an enterprise-portal development framework. JetSpeed provides a common presentation framework to quickly pull together web-based applications into a cohesive entry point for the enterprise's end users.

Frameworks like these are the result of a significant amount of focus being placed on how to cleanly separate the presentation and business-tier logic from one another.

However, until recently, few companies had thought of building their data tier using any kind of formalized, data-persistence framework. Most application developers focused exclusively on the business logic reuse in the middle tier. For many companies the data tier was a relational database or a corporate mainframe system that did not map cleanly to many of the object-oriented paradigms they were trying to implement.

The data access logic for an n-tier application is mixed with the business rules in the middle tier or vaguely defined in an amorphous set of stored procedures that attempts to hide the complexity of the data access from the developer.

However, more and more individuals are beginning to realize that failure to abstract away the physical and vendor-implemented details of their corporate data sources translates directly into a significant cost for maintaining an application long term. Some of these costs will be covered in the next section, *"What is a Persistence Framework?"*

This chapter is going to focus exclusively on developing the data tier using a combination of common data-persistence design patterns and J2EE technologies. Specifically, this chapter is going to cover the following topics:

- ❏ What is a persistence framework?

- ❏ Design patterns that can be used in the implementation of a persistence framework. The patterns covered will include:

- ❑ The Data Access Object pattern
- ❑ The Value Object pattern
- ❑ The Service Locator pattern
- ❑ Core strategies to consider when building a persistence framework:
  - ❑ Primary key generation
  - ❑ Concurrency management and locking
  - ❑ Transaction management
  - ❑ Performance issues

Remember, implementing a framework is often a matter of opinion. The design patterns presented in this chapter are just guidelines. In other words, they are example solutions to counter programming problems that occur repeatedly. The presentation shown in this chapter is not the only way of implementing these patterns. The key thing to remember with all data-persistence patterns is:

> **"Data-persistence patterns focus on building a logical façade that hides all of the ugly data access code associated with retrieving and manipulating data. They completely abstract away the physical details of the data sources that a development team uses to build its applications."**

Let's say you work in the IT department of the fictional magazine publishing company, IT World Now. Your team has built and deployed several Java, web-based applications that work at a functional level. However, the management of the IT department is growing increasingly frustrated with the cost of maintaining the existing applications. They are also frustrated with the lack of reuse of the existing code base when a new application is written. They want a common application development framework that will provide reuse at all the three tiers of the application.

You have been asked to look at different aspects of IT World Now's subscription database and also at how a persistence framework can be built on top of these databases to abstract away their underlying details. You have decided to take a few data entities from the subscription database and build a prototype on which the rest of the subscription persistence framework can be built.

The prototype would be built using three tables:

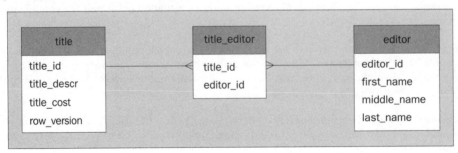

- ❏ `title` – This table is used to hold all of the titles currently in the subscription database.

- ❏ `editor` – This table is used to hold all the editors currently working for IT World Now.

- ❏ `title_editor` – There is a many-to-many relationship between titles and editors. Editors can work across multiple titles and a journal can have multiple editors. The `title_editor` table establishes links between the editors and the titles that they are working on.

The SQL DDL for the tables shown above is available for download at http://www.wrox.com/.

A Starting Model

The following JSP page highlights some of the more common mistakes made by developers when writing an application. This JSP page is going to query the subscription database for all of the titles in the database. It will then display the results of the query on the screen. Let's take a look at the code:

```
<%@page import="java.sql.*"%>
<%@page import="java.util.*"%>

<!--
    The following JSP page demonstrates a few of the more common mistakes
    made by application developers.
-->

<table border="1" align="center">
  <tr>
    <td align="center" nowrap>
      Id
    </td>
    <td align="center" wrap>
      Description
    </td>
    <td align="center" nowrap>
      Cost
    </td>
  </tr>
<%
    Connection conn = null;
    ResultSet  rs   = null;
    Statement statement = null;
    try{
      /* Problem # 1 */
      Class.forName("org.gjt.mm.mysql.Driver");

      /* Problem #2 */
      conn =  DriverManager.getConnection
        ("jdbc:mysql://192.168.1.98:3306/test/?username=gnu@192.168.1.98");

      /*Do something with the connection*/
      StringBuffer sql = new StringBuffer(64);
      sql.append("SELECT                   ");
```

```
sql.append("  title_id     ,          ");
sql.append("  title_descr  ,          ");
sql.append("  title_cost              ");
sql.append("FROM                      ");
sql.append("  title                   ");

statement = conn.createStatement();

rs   = statement.executeQuery(sql.toString());

while (rs.next()) {
  out.println("<tr>");
  out.println("<td>");
  out.println(  new Long( rs.getLong("title_id") ).toString() );
  out.println("</td>");

  out.println("<td>");
  out.println(   rs.getString("title_descr")   );
  out.println("</td>");

  out.println("<td>");
  out.println(   new Float (rs.getFloat("title_cost") ).toString() );
  out.println("</td>");
  out.println("</tr>");
}
} catch(SQLException e) {
  out.println("SQL Exception Error--> " + e.getMessage());
}
finally {
  if (statement!=null) try{ statement.close();} catch(SQLException e){}
  if (rs!=null) try{ rs.close(); } catch(SQLException e){}
  if (conn!=null) try{ conn.close();} catch(SQLException e){}
}
%>
</table>
```

This example was chosen because it demonstrates some of the typical mistakes made by database developers. These mistakes include:

❑ Not cleanly separating the presentation, business, and data logic into distinct tiers

❑ Exposing the application to what database platform the data is residing in

❑ Tying the application code directly to the physical structure of the database tables (in other words the `title` table)

❑ Forcing the application developer to learn and understand the complexity of the data access API used to retrieve and manipulate data

Separating Application Tiers

The first bullet point, not cleanly separating the presentation, business, and data logic into distinct tiers, is a still surprisingly common problem. Even with the score of n-tier architecture books and ready-to-use open source frameworks many developers fall into the trap of not separating their data logic from the other types of logic in their application:

```
while (rs.next()) {
      out.println("<tr>");
      out.println("<td>");
      out.println(  new Long( rs.getLong("title_id") ).toString() );
      out.println("</td>");

      out.println("<td>");
      out.println(   rs.getString("title_descr")  );
      out.println("</td>");

      out.println("<td>");
      out.println(   new Float (rs.getFloat("title_cost") ).toString() );
      out.println("</td>");
      out.println("</tr>");
   }
```

The JSP page example is lacking any business logic, but it does demonstrate a clear lack of separation between the presentation and data tiers. Failure to enforce a clean separation of data logic from presentation and business logic will result in database code being scattered throughout the application. For small application, this might not be an issue, but for large applications this can turn in a maintenance nightmare. Even small database changes can result in developers trudging through application code looking for business code.

Hiding the Database Platform

The JSP example demonstrates the second bullet in an extreme manner. In the JSP page above, the developer has directly embedded connection information inside of the JSP page:

```
/* Problem # 1 */
Class.forName("org.gjt.mm.mysql.Driver");

/* Problem #2 */
conn =  DriverManager.getConnection
        ("jdbc:mysql://192.168.1.98:3306/test/?username=gnu@192.168.1.98");
```

The JSP page has direct knowledge that it is talking to a MySQL database via the Java package and the class name of the MySQL JDBC driver is passed into the Class.forName() method call. In addition, the database connection information and user ID and password have been embedded inside of the code.

One might consider that the two problems highlighted above are minor, but they are common mistakes that often lead to a significant amount of overheads in maintaining code. Imagine a large application written in the style shown above. The application has 40 to 50 screens and any number of scenarios could force you to have to revisit each one of the screens and make changes to the database connection information. Revisiting these screens will require a significant amount of "grunt" programming work and extensive re-testing of the entire application to ensure that all database touch points were visited and changed. Some examples of the events that could trigger this include:

❑   Your database needs to be moved to a different server with a new IP address and machine name.

❑   You decide to change the database platforms that the application is working on. Your application might be using an open source database such as MySQL and you decide to move to the Oracle DBMS platform.

❑ The developer has compromised database security. Any one who can get access to the source code for the application now also has access to the database the application is accessing. This is especially true for JSP pages, because many developers do not pre-compile their code and leave the JSP source code directly on the service to be compiled by their application server.

❑ You have discovered that the pool manager you are using for your database connections has a serious flaw. You decide to switch to another vendor's pool manager.

Most developers have, finally, learned not to embed their database connection information directly inside their application code. They usually encapsulate the database connection process into some variant of a JDBC Connection factory class that instantiates the JDBC Connection for them. However, the code segment illustrates a common theme. Developers often tightly couple their application code with the database platform from which it is retrieving data. They create this tight coupling by not hiding the database connection information or using vendor-specific database features directly in their application code.

For example, the Oracle database gives the developer a database object to generate sequential numbers. This sequence and its use in the SQL syntax is Oracle specific. If the development team uses this object throughout their application, they could face a significant amount of downtime in porting the application to another database platform, as they have to search the entire application and change the code to use some other sequence generation mechanism.

Hiding the Physical Structure of your Data Entities

In the JSP example above, the developer is exposing the application to the physical structure of the data entities they are accessing. In our example, the JSP page is retrieving data from the title table by issuing a SQL statement directly inside of the JSP page.

```
sql.append("SELECT             ");
sql.append("  title_id     ,   ");
sql.append("  title_descr ,    ");
sql.append("  title_cost       ");
sql.append("FROM               ");
sql.append("  title            ");
```

By issuing the SQL code directly inside of the JSP page, the developers have effectively tied themselves to the physical structure of the title table. If any of the columns they use are changed or deleted from the title table, the developers will need to visit every application that touches the title table and ensure that they have not broken their code.

By exposing the physical format of your data entities to the application, there is also a risk that code will break if the data relationships between the title table and other tables in the subscription database change. The SQL statement above is retrieving data just from the title table. However, later in the chapter your will see that there is a many-to-many relationship between the title and editor tables. If the database were refactored to make this relationship a one-to-many relationship, again all of the applications that issued any SQL commands against the subscription database would have to be revisited.

Encapsulating Complexity

The last point to take away from this code example is that every time the developer wants to retrieve or manipulate any data from the subscription database, they must understand the complexities of a data access API, such as JDBC or JDO (Java Data Objects). The developer must understand how to connect to the database and the syntax of a query language, and properly understand such concepts as transaction management and isolation.

Most IT organizations want to divide their application developers into tiers. They want their novice and intermediate-level developers to focus on building business applications and leave the infrastructure and architectural code to more experienced and seasoned developers. The only way these organizations can accomplish this is by ensuring that complex and often repetitive tasks like accessing data from a corporate database are hidden from the business application developers. These developers should not have to know where or how they are getting their data. Business application developers should focus on writing business code and not infrastructure code.

What is a Persistence Framework?

A persistence framework is a set of software services that decouples an application from the data sources it uses and manipulates. A persistence framework sits on top of an organization's data sources and hides the data access APIs (such as JDBC, JDO, or entity EJBs) used to access these data sources. The services offered should completely abstract away the physical details of accessing and manipulating data from that data source. The diagram below illustrates the where in the system architecture the persistence framework sits:

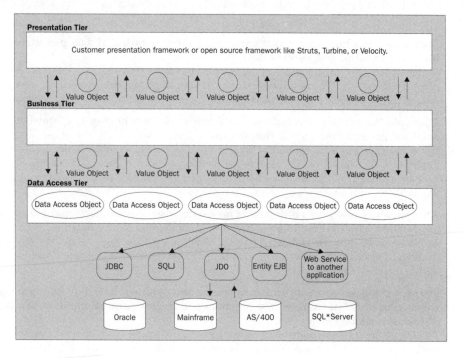

In the above diagram, the data persistence framework completely abstracts away how data is being accessed. It does this by strictly enforcing the separation of the presentation, business, and data tiers. To aid in this separation, two design patterns are used:

❑   The Data Access Object pattern

❑   The Value Object pattern

The Data Access Object pattern completely encapsulates the retrieving and manipulating of data. It also encapsulates the data access API used to interact with the database such as JDBC, JDO, SQLJ, and so on. The Data Access Object pattern communicates with the business tier by using value objects that encapsulate data being retrieved and sent to the database.

The Value Object pattern shown in the diagram encapsulates data sent to and from the database. The Value Object pattern hides the physical table structures from the business application developers and abstracts away what data relationships exist in the database, by providing a Java Collection mechanism for retrieving parent-child, one-to-many, and many-to-many relationships from the database. The value objects can also be passed up to the presentation tier and used in displaying information to the end users.

In large organizations, you might have dozens of systems that are using different mechanisms for data access. In addition, the organization can have data that is being accessed by application developers scattered throughout systems in the organization that are running on a plethora of database platforms. Why expose these differences to the developers trying to write business applications? A persistence framework hides these complexities from an application developer writing a business application.

The services offered in a persistence framework should do the following for the developers building applications on it:

❑   **Provide a clean mechanism that encourages the separation of data-persistence logic from presentation and business logic**
In the architectural diagram above, the business tier is the only tier allowed to access corporate databases. The business tier interacts with corporate databases by using the Data Access Object pattern. It never uses a data access API like JDBC to access a database.

❑   **Decouple the applications built on the framework from having any knowledge of the database platform the data is residing in**
By encapsulating all data connection logic inside the data access objects, the business application developer does not need to know what type of database platform they are connecting to, any of the security information (user ID and password) needed to connect to the database, or the network address of the database.

❑   **Abstract away the physical details of how data is stored within a database and also the relationships that might exist between data entities in the database**
Applications built on the architecture layout above never issue SQL queries directly against a database. They have no true idea of what the physical structure of the data is and use value objects to access the database.

❑   **Simplify the development process by hiding the details associated with opening a connection to a database, issuing commands to retrieve and manipulate data, and transaction management**
The Data Access Object and Value Object patterns completely decouple the business application developer from the data source they are using in their application. They do not need knowledge of a data access API and instead can use simple interfaces for retrieving and manipulating data.

Let's now dive into the first of the two patterns mentioned above, the Data Access Object pattern, and explore how it can be implemented.

The Data Access Object Pattern

The Data Access Object (DAO) and Value Object (VO) patterns were first documented at the Sun Java Center. The DAO pattern abstracts away how data is retrieved and manipulated from a data source. The DAO pattern serves two purposes:

❑   First, the DAO pattern completely abstracts away the data source in which the data the user is requesting resides. The user of the DAO pattern does not know whether the data they are retrieving is coming from an Oracle database, a Microsoft SQL Server, an LDAP server, or a web service. The data source is completely transparent.

❑   The second function the DAO pattern provides is that it abstracts away the CRUD (Create, Replace, Update, and Delete) logic normally associated with accessing a data source. As the user has no knowledge of how the data is being queried or retrieved, they will not be affected if the data access code (for example, a SQL statement issued inside the DAO) is changed or modified. A DAO pattern even allows an application architect to pull data from multiple data sources and present it to the user as one logical object (in other words a value object containing data from multiple data sources).

This flexibility provided by the DAO pattern comes from the fact that applications do not directly access a data source. Instead, they create a DAO object and use it to access a data source on their behalf. If they are retrieving data, they can use a value object to hold the retrieved data. The Value Object pattern abstracts away the physical structure of how the data is stored in the database. The Value Object pattern will be discussed in greater detail later in the chapter.

The diagram below illustrates conceptually how a piece of client code uses a DAO object to retrieve data on its behalf:

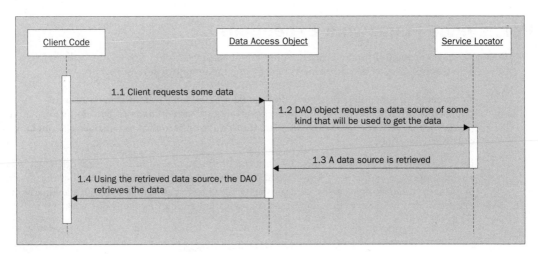

The DAO pattern is powerful because it:

❑ Abstracts away how data is actually being retrieved from a data source. A DAO pattern can use any number of Java data access APIs to carry out its work. Some of these APIs are:

❑ The JDBC API – The first standard database access API, JDBC is part of the J2SE with extensions in J2EE.

❑ SQLJ – SQLJ is relatively new API put forth by several leading database and Java application-server vendors. SQLJ allows the developer to embed SQL code directly into their Java code and then have it translated into Java code using a code preprocessor.

❑ Entity Enterprise Java Beans – The entity EJB specification is a data-persistence specification that allows the developer to abstract away database code behind a component-based architecture.

❑ Java Data Objects (JDO) – The JDO specification is newest addition to database access APIs. JDO allows you to retrieve and persist data from a database using standard Java objects. JDO objects are lighter weight than entity EJBs, while still providing much of the same functionality as an entity EJB.

❑ Provides a clean separation of business and data logic to minimize the temptation for application developers to mix their business and data logic. By centralizing all of the data access code within one logical construct, developers can use a logical interface for accessing and manipulating data.

❑ Provides a standard set of programming interfaces that will address the common database development issues of:

❑ Primary Key Generation

❑ Concurrency Management and Locking

❑ Transaction Management

❑ Performance Issues

Persistence Framework Exceptions

All exceptions both caught from and raised within the persistence framework will be rethrown as a `DataAccessException`. This rethrowing is being implemented for two reasons:

❑ By catching all exceptions thrown within the data persistence framework, there is an opportunity to process and catch all exceptions in a consistent manner. Developers using data-persistence framework classes like the `DataSourceFactory` need to worry about catching only one exception.

❑ By rethrowing any exceptions raised within the `DataSourceFactory`, or any other part of our data-persistence framework, we are able to abstract away the data sources that the persistence framework accesses. The persistence framework developer provides a consistent exception that can always be caught by the application code using the framework.

The code for the DataAccessException is shown below:

```
package dataaccess;

public class DataAccessException extends Exception {
  Throwable exceptionCause = null;

  public DataAccessException(String pExceptionMsg) {
    super(pExceptionMsg);
  }

  public DataAccessException(String pExceptionMsg, Throwable pException) {
    super(pExceptionMsg);
    this.exceptionCause = pException;
  }

  public void printStackTrace() {
    if (exceptionCause != null) {
      System.err.println("An exception has been caused by: ");
      exceptionCause.printStackTrace();
    }
  }
}
```

The DataAccessException class is a generalized exception. It is used to rethrow any non-persistence framework exceptions raised and any minor issues that might arise during processing within the persistence framework. Other more specialized exceptions within the framework reflect specific events that might want to be tracked and caught by the application using the DAO. These exceptions all extend the DataAccessException and include:

❑ NoDataFoundException

❑ OptimisticLockException

❑ ServiceLocatorException

These exceptions will be covered as they are encountered in our walkthrough of the persistence framework.

Implementing the Data Access Object Pattern

The DAO pattern abstracts away the tasks associated with retrieving and manipulating data by defining a Java interface that has five basic methods:

❑ findByPrimaryKey(Object pPrimaryKey)

❑ insert(ValueObject pValueObject)

❑ createValueObject()

❑ update(ValueObject pValueObject)

❑ delete(ValueObject pValueObject)

The `findByPrimaryKey()` method is used to retrieve a record from a data source. It takes a single input parameter, `pPrimaryKey`. This parameter is the unique ID of the record in the data source. In the examples for this chapter, this parameter represents a primary key field for a record in a relational database. The `findByPrimaryKey()` method returns an object of type `ValueObject`. A `ValueObject`, which is a wrapper, wraps the data retrieved from the data source the DAO represents as a Java class. Thus, the code using the DAO is never tied directly to the underlying data structure that the DAO encapsulates.

The `insert()`, `update()`, and `delete()` methods all carry out the actions that their names imply. They take a single parameter of type `ValueObject` that holds all the data that will be used in carrying out the `insert`, `update`, or `delete` actions.

You might wonder why on the `delete()` method you are passing in an entire `ValueObject` rather than just the primary key ID. The main reason is efficiency. If the data entity represented by the DAO has several conditions that must be met in order for the record to be deleted, it is easier to try to pass that data into the DAO as part of the `ValueObject` passed into the method. Otherwise, for each condition that must be checked before deleting the record, the DAO must perform a database lookup to confirm that condition has been met.

This condition often exists when you are building your DAO layer above a database written by a third-party vendor. As the persistence framework developer, you do not have control over how these vendors support referential integrity for their data entities when data is deleted. Many vendors embed their referential integrity code directly inside their application. This means you have to reverse engineer the database behavior and put this behavior in your DAO to ensure that the proper insert, updates, and deletes occur when a record is deleted from the database.

The `createValueObject()` method is used to create an empty `ValueObject` that can be populated with data and then passed to a DAO's `insert()` method for insertion into the data source represented by the DAO.

Since a DAO pattern abstracts the mechanism by which data is retrieved and manipulated, there are two different ways to implement it:

- ❏ As a standard Java class
- ❏ As a J2EE session EJB

All of the DAOs built in this chapter will be built as stateless session EJBs using JDBC. The DAO could also have been built using a simple Java class.

Simple Java classes are quicker to implement and take less time to debug because there is significantly less setup work to write a class. However, the J2EE stateless session EJB approach has been chosen for this chapter because the application server that the EJB runs in provides a number of core infrastructure services. These infrastructure services include:

- ❏ **Container-based transaction management**
  This relieves the database developer of the responsibility of having to code complex transaction management code within their application.

- ❏ **Declarative Access Control**
  Declarative access control allows the developer to control what users and application can use the session EJB to carry out their work.

❑ **Resource pooling**
Resource pooling improves application performance by keeping a pool of session EJBs available to process user requests.

In order to build a framework for EJB-based DAOs, we are going to extend the EJB remote interface (EJBObject) and the bean class (SessionBean) to include the five DAO method signatures defined earlier.

The DAO Remote Interface

The DAOObject interface will be used as the remote interface for our data access objects:

```
package dataaccess;

import javax.ejb.EJBObject;
import java.rmi.RemoteException;
import valueobject.ValueObject;

public interface DAOObject extends EJBObject {

  public ValueObject findByPrimaryKey(Object pPrimaryKey)
      throws DataAccessException, NoDataFoundException,
          ServiceLocatorException, RemoteException;

  public void insert(ValueObject pValueObject)
      throws DataAccessException, ServiceLocatorException,
          RemoteException;

  public void update(ValueObject pValueObject)
      throws DataAccessException, OptimisticLockException,
          ServiceLocatorException, RemoteException;

  public void delete(ValueObject pValueObject)
      throws DataAccessException, ServiceLocatorException,
          RemoteException;

  public ValueObject createValueObject()
      throws DataAccessException, ServiceLocatorException,
          RemoteException;
}
```

The DAOBean Class

The DAOBean class extends the SessionBean interface used in a standard session EJB implementation:

```
package dataaccess;

import javax.ejb.SessionBean;
import valueobject.ValueObject;

public interface DAOBean extends SessionBean {
```

```
    public ValueObject findByPrimaryKey(Object pPrimaryKey)
        throws DataAccessException, NoDataFoundException,
            ServiceLocatorException;

    public void insert(ValueObject pValueObject)
        throws DataAccessException, ServiceLocatorException;

    public void update(ValueObject pValueObject)
        throws DataAccessException, OptimisticLockException,
            ServiceLocatorException;

    public void delete(ValueObject pValueObject)
        throws DataAccessException, ServiceLocatorException;

    public ValueObject createValueObject()
        throws DataAccessException, ServiceLocatorException;

}
```

The TitleDAO Session Bean

We are going to build a DAO object to represent the `title` table in the subscription database. Since this DAO is implemented as a session EJB, it will consist of three Java files:

- ❏ TitleDAO
- ❏ TitleDAOHome
- ❏ TitleDAOBean

Firstly, the `TitleDAO` interface is the remote interface for the EJB. It extends the `DAOObject` interface as shown below:

```
package session.title;

import dataaccess.DAOObject;

public interface TitleDAO extends DAOObject {}
```

Next, the `TitleDAOHome` interface extends the `EJBHome` interface. This interface is responsible for returning the `TitleDAOBean` class:

```
package session.title;

import javax.ejb.EJBHome;
import java.rmi.RemoteException;
import javax.ejb.CreateException;

public interface TitleDAOHome extends EJBHome {

    public TitleDAO create() throws RemoteException, CreateException;

}
```

The TitleDAOBean Class

The TitleDAOBean class holds the actual implementation of the TitleDAO code. This class is a wrapper around all of the database code that is normally exposed and intermixed within presentation and business logic.

As you are looking through the TitleDAOBean implementation, it is important to keep these two key points in mind:

❑ The TitleDAO implementation shields the developer from how data is being retrieved and manipulated. It could easily be converted from JDBC to some other data access API.

❑ The physical structure of the title table can be easily restructured. The table can easily be normalized or denormalized.

Both of these tasks can be accomplished because the TitleDAO provides a public interface that completely hides the underlying database code. Radically change your data structures too much and event a DAO might not be able to keep the change from rippling through all of the applications in your organization. However, a DAO provides a buffer that will allow the application architecture to isolate applications from most changes made to a database. Without the abstraction layer that a DAO object provides, even small changes to the database can represent significant code rewrites and testing in multiple applications throughout the enterprise.

Shown below is the skeleton for the TitleDAOBean class (each method will be walked through in greater detail in its own section):

```
package session.title;

import dataaccess.*;
import valueobject.*;
import session.counter.*;
import session.editor.*;
import javax.ejb.*;
import java.sql.*;
import java.rmi.RemoteException;
import java.util.HashMap;
import java.util.Collection;
import java.util.Iterator;

public class TitleDAOBean implements DAOBean {
  private SessionContext ctx;
  /*
   * The findByPrimaryKey() method will retrieve a single title
   * record from the subscription database. It returns a TitleVO
   * that contains all of the title data.
   */
  public ValueObject findByPrimaryKey(Object pPrimaryKey)
      throws DataAccessException, ServiceLocatorException,
             NoDataFoundException {
  }
```

```
/*
 * The update() method will update a single record in the title
 * table with the valueobject passed in as a parameter.
 */
public void update(ValueObject pValueObject)
    throws DataAccessException, OptimisticLockException,
        ServiceLocatorException {
}


/*
 * The delete() record will delete a single record from the title
 * table in the subscription database. It does this based on the
 * id of the value object passed into the table.
 */
public void delete(ValueObject pValueObject)
    throws DataAccessException, ServiceLocatorException {
}


/*
 * The insert() method will insert a single record into the title
 * table. The data it inserts will be pulled from the value
 * object passed into the method.
 */
public void insert(ValueObject pValueObject)
    throws DataAccessException, ServiceLocatorException {
}


/*
 * The createValueObject() method will create an empty value
 * object prepopulated with any mandatory data.  n example of
 * this mandatory data might be a primary key that for a particular
 * record.
 */
public ValueObject createValueObject()
    throws DataAccessException, ServiceLocatorException {
}

public void ejbCreate() {}
public void ejbRemove() {}
public void ejbActivate() {}
public void ejbPassivate() {}
public void setSessionContext(SessionContext sessionCtx) {
  this.ctx = sessionCtx;
}

}
```

The findByPrimaryKey() Method

The findByPrimaryKey() method is used to retrieve a single record from the title table. It returns the data in the form of a ValueObject object. We'll see the implementation of this later in the chapter.

The code for the `TitleDAO.findByPrimaryKey()` method uses JDBC calls to retrieve the requested record from the `subscription` database and create a `ValueObject`, populate it with data, and return it to the application calling the `find()` method:

```
public ValueObject findByPrimaryKey(Object pPrimaryKey)
    throws DataAccessException, ServiceLocatorException,
           NoDataFoundException {

  String pkPrimaryKey = (String) pPrimaryKey
  ServiceLocator serviceLocator = ServiceLocator.getInstance();
  Connection conn =
    serviceLocator.getDBConn(ServiceLocator.SUBSCRIPTIONDB);
  ResultSet rs   = null;

  //Getting my SQL Code for retrieving all of the titles
  SQLCode sqlCode = SQLCode.getInstance();
  String sql =
    sqlCode.getSQLStatement("titledao.findbyprimarykey().select");

  TitleVO titleVO = new TitleVO();

  try {
    PreparedStatement preparedStatement = conn.prepareStatement(sql);
    preparedStatement.setLong(1, Long.parseLong(pkPrimaryKey));
    rs = preparedStatement.executeQuery();

    // Populate a the value object with the resultset data
    if (rs.next()){
      titleVO.setTitleId(rs.getLong("title_id"));
      titleVO.setTitleDescr(rs.getString("title_descr"));
      titleVO.setTitleCost(rs.getFloat("title_cost"));
      titleVO.setRowVersion(rs.getLong("row_version"));

      EditorDAOHome editorDAOHome =
        (EditorDAOHome)serviceLocator.getEJBHome(
                                    ServiceLocator.EDITORDAO);
      EditorDAO editorDAO = editorDAOHome.create();
      titleVO.setEditors(
          editorDAO.findEditorByTitle(String.valueOf(
                                    titleVO.getTitleId()))));
    } else {
      throw new NoDataFoundException(
              "Record id: " + pkPrimaryKey +
              "is not found in the title table.");
    }

    //Reset the flags so that we know the object is in pristine state.
    titleVO.resetFlags();
  } catch(SQLException e) {
    //Aborting the transaction
    ctx.setRollbackOnly();
    throw new DataAccessException(
```

```
                    "Error in TitleDAO.findByPrimaryKey()", e);
    } catch(RemoteException e) {
    //Aborting the transaction
    ctx.setRollbackOnly();
    throw new DataAccessException(
            "Error in TitleDAO.findByPrimaryKey()",e);
    } catch(CreateException e) {
    //Aborting the transaction
    ctx.setRollbackOnly();
    throw new DataAccessException(
            "Error in TitleDAO.findByPrimaryKey()",e);
    } finally {
    try {
      if (rs != null) rs.close();
      if (conn != null) conn.close();
    } catch(SQLException e) {
    System.out.println("I am unable to close a resultset, " +
                       "statement, or connection " +
                       "TitleDAO.findByPrimaryKey().");
    }
    return titleVO;
  }
}
```

The first several lines of code of the `findByPrimaryKey()` method may look unusual. The first thing the `findByPrimaryKey()` method does is cast the primary key argument to a `String`. This is because this is the data type we are going to be using in our application, but you could just as easily cast it to any object type.

Then the method uses is the `ServiceLocator` object to retrieve the JDBC `Connection` to the `subscription` database and `EJBHome` interfaces for all EJBs used within the persistence framework:

```
ServiceLocator serviceLocator = ServiceLocator.getInstance();

Connection conn =
  serviceLocator.getDBConn(ServiceLocator.SUBSCRIPTIONDB);
```

The `ServiceLocator.getDBConn()` method retrieves a JDBC database `Connection` to the `subscription` database. We will be covering the `ServiceLocator`'s code later in the chapter.

After the database connection is retrieved, we use an object called `SQLCode` to retrieve the `SELECT` statement used to retrieve data from the `title` table:

```
SQLCode sqlCode = SQLCode.getInstance();
String sql =
  sqlCode.getSQLStatement("titledao.findbyprimarykey().select");
```

The `SQLCode` class is used to hold all of the SQL statements used in the persistence framework in one location. A DAO needing a SQL statement can get an instance of the `SQLCode` class and then issue a call to the `SQLCode.getSQLStatement()` method. When this method is called, a key value is passed in that will map to the desired SQL statement. The SQL statement used in the `TitleDAO.findByPrimaryKey()` method looks like:

```
SELECT title_id, title_descr, title_cost, row_version FROM title WHERE
       title_id=?
```

The SQLCode class is based on the Singleton design pattern and has two purposes:

❑ Centralize all of the SQL statements used in the application within a single property file called sql.properties. Using the SQLCode class, all changes to the SQL code in the persistence framework take place in this one location.

❑ Eliminate the need to build the SQL statement directly inside of each of the find(), insert(), update(), and delete() methods in a DAO. The SQLCode class has only one static copy of a particular SQL statement. This way if a particular DAO method is a called a dozen times, there is only one String object representation of that SQL statement stored within in the virtual machine.

The SQLCode class is shown below. However, it is very straightforward Java code and will not be covered in greater detail in this chapter.

```java
package dataaccess;

import java.util.Properties;
import java.io.*;

/*
 *  The SQLCode class is a helper class that loads all of the SQL
 *  code used within the persistence framework into a private properties
 *  object stored within the SQLCode class.
 */
public class SQLCode {
  private static SQLCode sqlCode = null;
  private static Properties sqlCache = new Properties();

  /*Calling the SQLCode's constructor*/
  static {
    sqlCode = new SQLCode();
  }

  /*Retrieves the Singleton for the SQLCode class*/
  public static SQLCode getInstance() {
    return sqlCode;
  }

  /*
   * The SQLCode constructor loads all of the SQL code used in the
   * persistence framework from the sql.properties class into the sqlCache
   * properties object
   */
  private SQLCode() {
    try {
      String sqlFileName = "sql.properties";

      sqlCache.load(new FileInputStream(sqlFileName));
```

109

```
    } catch(IOException e) {
      System.out.println(e.toString());
    }
  }

  /*
   * The getSQLStatement() method will try to retrieve a SQL statement
   * from the SQLCache properties object based on the key passed into
   * the method.  If it can not find an the SQL statement, a DataAccess
   * Exception will be raised.
   */
  public String getSQLStatement(String pSQLKeyName)
      throws DataAccessException {

    //Checking to see if the requested SQL statement is in the sqlCache
    if (sqlCache.containsKey(pSQLKeyName)) {
      return (String) sqlCache.get(pSQLKeyName);
    } else{
      throw new DataAccessException("Unable to locate the SQL " +
          "statement requested in SQLCode.getSQLCode() " + pSQLKeyName);
    }
  }
}
```

After the abstractions offered by the ServiceLocator and SQLCode classes, the rest of the findByPrimaryKey() method executes the SQL statement and populates a TitleVO object with the data retrieved from the title table:

```
PreparedStatement preparedStatement = conn.prepareStatement(sql);
preparedStatement.setLong(1, Long.parseLong(pPrimaryKey));
rs = preparedStatement.executeQuery();

if (rs.next()){
   titleVO.setTitleId(rs.getLong("title_id"));
   ...
}
```

There are a few things to keep in mind about the findByPrimaryKey() method.

First, the base DAO interface defines a single findByPrimaryKey() method to retrieve a record by its primary key. However, there is nothing to stop a DAO developer from implementing multiple find() methods. Each implemented find() method on a DAO can retrieve data via different queries. If multiple records are retrieved from a query, the find() method should return a HashMap containing ValueObjects. Each ValueObject in the HashMap represents a single record retrieved from the query encapsulated within the find() method.

In the TitleDAO.findByPrimaryKey() method, the EditorDAO.findEditorByTitle() method is used to retrieve all of the editors assigned to that particular title.

> *For the sake of brevity, the EditorDAO code will not be shown in this chapter. However, as mentioned earlier, the code is available for download from the Wrox web site.*

This `findEditorByTitle()` method returns a `HashMap` containing all of the editors associated with that title. Why use a `HashMap` to hold the results of multiple records? Why not use an `ArrayList`? The `HashMap` object was chosen because it supports retrieving a record from within it by using a key value. In the `TitleDAO.findByPrimaryKey()` method, the `HashMap` being returned by the call to `EditorDAO.findByEditorTitle()` is keyed with the primary key of each editor.

If we know the editor's ID, we can retrieve the record directly from the `HashMap` without iterating through every item in the map. If we used a `Collection` object like an `ArrayList` or `Vector`, we would not have this flexibility in locating a record in the collection. The `HashMap` returned by the `EditorDAO.findByPrimaryKey()` method is then passed into the `setEditors()` method on the `titleVO` object:

```
EditorDAOHome editorDAOHome =
   (EditorDAOHome) new InitialContext().lookup("editor/EditorDAO");
EditorDAO editorDAO = editorDAOHome.create();

titleVO.setEditors(editorDAO.findEditorByTitle
                (new Long(titleVO.getTitleId()).toString()));
```

This `TitleDAO.findByPrimaryKey()` method demonstrates how our persistence framework can handle a one-to-many or many-to-many database relationship. A many-to-many relationship exists between the `title` table and the `editor` table. When a user tries to retrieve a `TitleVO`, the `TitleDAO.findByPrimaryKey()` method will also retrieve all of the editor records associated with that particular title and capture that relationship in the `TitleVO` object passed back to the end user.

If no data is found by the `findByPrimaryKey()` method, it will raise a `NoDataFoundException`. This exception inherits from the `DataAccessException` as described. This exception does not necessarily indicate that there is an error in the DAO, just that a record could not be retrieved.

There is one thing to be aware of with using the `EditorDAO.findEditorByTitle()` method to retrieve all of the editors associated with a title: this method call can become a performance bottleneck. For example, if you are retrieving 1000 title records, there will be 1000 calls to the `EditorDAO.findEditorByTitle()` method. This is a fundamental weakness inherent to a persistence framework.

Persistence frameworks are designed to handle small transactions that retrieve a few objects, make changes and update them. They are not meant for retrieving large data sets or performing bulk inserts, updates, or deletes. In the `findEditorByTitle()` case, if you believe that your are going to bring back a large dataset, you might want to evaluate whether or not you want to use the design patterns shown in this chapter for that data work.

The insert() Method

The code for the `insert()` method is shown below. Let's walk through the `insert()` method and discuss what is occurring within it. The first step in the `insert()` method is to retrieve the SQL code that is going to be used in the `TitleDAO.insert()` method:

```
public void insert(ValueObject pValueObject)
    throws DataAccessException, ServiceLocatorException {

  //Getting all of my SQL code for inserting a title
```

```
SQLCode sqlCode = SQLCode.getInstance();

String sqlTitle = sqlCode.getSQLStatement("titledao.insert().insert");
String sqlTitleEditor =
  sqlCode.getSQLStatement("titledao.insert().inserttitleeditor");
```

The `insert()` method is going to use two SQL statements while executing. The first SQL statement will insert the title data from the `TitleVO` passed into the `insert()` method into the `title` table. This SQL statement, represented by the key `titledao.insert().insert`, looks like:

```
INSERT INTO title (title_id, title_descr, title_cost, row_version )
VALUES ( ?,?,?,? )
```

Once the SQL code is retrieved, a database connection is obtained from a `ServiceLocator`. The retrieved database connection is then used to obtain a `PreparedStatement`:

```
//Building my SQL Code for inserting a record into the title table.
TitleVO titleVO = (TitleVO) pValueObject;
ServiceLocator serviceLocator = ServiceLocator.getInstance();
Connection conn =
    serviceLocator.getDBConn(ServiceLocator.SUBSCRIPTIONDB);

PreparedStatement preparedStatement = null;

try {
  //Populate the prepared statement with data from the value object
  preparedStatement = conn.prepareStatement(sqlTitle);
```

Note also in the above code, that the `ValueObject` passed into the `insert()` method is cast to type `TitleVO`. The `TitleVO` instance, called `titleVO`, is used to populate the `preparedStatement` object. Once the `preparedStatement` object has been populated, it executes the INSERT statement:

```
preparedStatement.setLong(1, titleVO.getTitleId());
preparedStatement.setString(2, titleVO.getTitleDescr());
preparedStatement.setFloat(3, titleVO.getTitleCost());
preparedStatement.setLong(4,1);
preparedStatement.execute();
```

After the record has been inserted into the `title` table, there needs to be a relationship established with the `editor` table. The `insert()` method will retrieve a `HashMap` containing all the editor records that are to be linked with the title record:

```
HashMap editorHash = titleVO.getEditors();
Collection editorCol = editorHash.values();
IteratoreditorIterator = editorCol.iterator();
```

It will then walk through each of the `EditorVO` objects in the `editorIterator` object, adding an entry in the `title_editor` table as it goes:

```
    while (editorIterator.hasNext()){
      EditorVO editorVO = (EditorVO) editorIterator.next();
      preparedStatement = conn.prepareStatement(sqlTitleEditor);
      preparedStatement.setLong(1,titleVO.getTitleId());
      preparedStatement.setLong(2,editorVO.getEditorId());
      preparedStatement.execute();
    }
  } catch(SQLException e) {
    //Aborting the transaction
    ctx.setRollbackOnly();
    throw new DataAccessException(
        "Error in TitleDAO.findByPrimaryKey()", e);
  } catch(RemoteException e) {
    //Aborting the transaction
    ctx.setRollbackOnly();
    throw new DataAccessException(
          "Error in TitleDAO.findByPrimaryKey()", e);
  } catch(CreateException e) {
    //Aborting the transaction
    ctx.setRollbackOnly();
    throw new DataAccessException(
          "Error in TitleDAO.findByPrimaryKey()", e);
  } finally {
    try {
      if (rs != null) rs.close();
      if (conn != null) conn.close();
    } catch(SQLException e) {
      System.out.println("I am unable to close a resultset, " +
                    "statement, or connection " +
                    "TitleDAO.findByPrimaryKey().");
    }
    return titleVO;
  }
}
```

If everything works successfully, the `finally{}` block of the code is executed and the `preparedStatement` and resulting database connection are closed. If any exception is encountered during the course of the insert, like an `SQLException`, then it will be caught and re-wrapped as a `DataAccessException`.

Looking at the code for the `insert()` method, you might have two questions:

❑   How and where is the primary key for the record generated?

❑   How is the transaction being committed to the database?

The primary key for a record in the `title` table is the `title_id`. We see that the value inserted for this code comes from the `getTitleId()` method on the `titleVO` object. How the actual primary key value is generated will be discussed in the *Primary Key Generation Strategies* section later on in this chapter.

A database commit is not taking place in the following code. This is because the `TitleDAO` session EJB is using container-based transaction management. The application server is handling all data commits. The only thing the code worries about is notifying the application when an exception has been raised and the transaction has to be rolled back. This is done by the `setRollbackMethod()` on the `ctx` object. The `ctx` object is the `SessionContext` for the `TitleDAO` EJB:

```
ctx.setRollbackOnly();
```

The whole issue of transaction management will be covered in the *Transaction Management Strategies* section of this chapter.

The createValueObject() Method

The `createValueObject()` method found in our DAO implementation is used to create a `ValueObject` that can be populated with data and then passed to the `insert()` method of the DAO from which it was created. The `createValueObject()` method acts in many ways like a constructor. It gives the DAO developer the opportunity to properly initialize a `ValueObject` before it is inserted into a data source.

Remember, in *The insert() Method* section above, a question was raised as to where a primary key was generated for a record. The answer is in the `createValueObject()` method. Here is the `createValueObject()` implementation for the `TitleDAO`:

```
public ValueObject createValueObject()
    throws DataAccessException, ServiceLocatorException {

  TitleVO titleVO = new TitleVO();

  try {
    //Creating a counter instance. We will use this counter instance
    //to retrieve a primary key for the new record being used.
    ServiceLocator serviceLocator = ServiceLocator.getInstance();

    CounterHome counterHome = (CounterHome)
        serviceLocator.getEJBHome(ServiceLocator.COUNTER);
    Counter counter = counterHome.create();
    titleVO.setTitleId(counter.getNextVal("title_pk"));

    //Populating the rest of the value object with data
    titleVO.setTitleDescr("");
    titleVO.setTitleCost(0);
    titleVO.setRowVersion(1);
    titleVO.resetFlags();
  } catch(CreateException e){
    //Aborting the transaction
    ctx.setRollbackOnly();
    throw new DataAccessException(
            "Error in TitleDAO.createValueObject()", e);
  } catch(RemoteException e){
    //Aborting the transaction
    ctx.setRollbackOnly();
```

```
            throw new DataAccessException(
                    "Error in TitleDAO.createValueObject()",e);
        } finally {
        return titleVO;
        }
    }
```

In the code above, a new `TitleVO` object is created and prepopulated with data. The interesting part of the code shows how the primary key is generated for the new `TitleVO` value object.

The primary key for the `ValueObject` is being generated by creating a session EJB called `Counter` and calling its `getNextVal()` method:

```
    ServiceLocator serviceLocator = ServiceLocator.getInstance();

    CounterHome counterHome = (CounterHome)
      serviceLocator.getEJBHome(ServiceLocator.COUNTER);
    Counter counter = counterHome.create();
    titleVO.setTitleId(counter.getNextVal("title_pk"));
```

The `Counter` EJB, which will be covered in greater detail in the *Primary Key Generation Strategies* section, is used to generate all of the primary keys for the subscription database. The `createValueObject()` method has a completely database-independent mechanism for generating primary keys. This is important because almost every database platform available has its own mechanism for generating primary keys. The `Counter` EJB decouples how the primary key generation is carried out from the rest of the application and persistence-framework code.

Move your application to another database platform and you only have to change the primary key generation for your applications in one location, rather than several. This simple abstraction can save a significant amount of work if you ever move your DAOs from one database platform to another.

> *The `createValueObject()` method has a database-independent mechanism for generating primary keys. The `Counter` EJB that generates these primary keys can still very much be database dependent.*

The update() Method

The `update()` method for the `TitleDAO` is shown below. This method updates the `title` table with the data contained within the `ValueObject` passed into it:

```
    public void update(ValueObject pValueObject)
        throws DataAccessException, OptimisticLockException,
            ServiceLocatorException {

        //Getting my SQL Code for updating all of the titles
        SQLCode sqlCode = SQLCode.getInstance();
        String sql = sqlCode.getSQLStatement("titledao.update().update");

        TitleVO titleVO = (TitleVO) pValueObject;
```

```
ServiceLocator serviceLocator = ServiceLocator.getInstance();
Connection conn =
  serviceLocator.getDBConn(ServiceLocator.SUBSCRIPTIONDB);

PreparedStatement preparedStatement = null;

try {
  //Retrieving a row version number via the Counter session bean
  CounterHome counterHome =
    (CounterHome) serviceLocator.getEJBHome(ServiceLocator.COUNTER);
  Counter counter = counterHome.create();
  long nextRowVersion = counter.getNextVal("title_rv");

  //Populating the prepared statement's parameters
  preparedStatement = conn.prepareStatement(sql);
  preparedStatement.setString(1, titleVO.getTitleDescr());
  preparedStatement.setFloat( 2, titleVO.getTitleCost());
  preparedStatement.setLong( 3, nextRowVersion);
  preparedStatement.setLong( 4, titleVO.getTitleId());
  preparedStatement.setLong( 5, titleVO.getRowVersion());

  //Check to see if we were successful in updating the record.
  // If the queryResult does not equal 1, then we have run
  // into an optimistic lock situation.
  int queryResults = preparedStatement.executeUpdate();
  if (queryResults != 1) {
    ctx.setRollbackOnly();
    throw new OptimisticLockException("Stale data for title record: "
                                    + titleVO.getTitleId());
  }
  //Cyclr through all of the editors and seeing if an editor
  //needs to be updated.
  Collection col = titleVO.getEditors().values();
  Iterator iterator = col.iterator();

  EditorDAOHome editorDAOHome = (EditorDAOHome)
      serviceLocator.getEJBHome(ServiceLocator.EDITORDAO);
  EditorDAO editorDAO = editorDAOHome.create();

  while (iterator.hasNext()) {
    EditorVO editorVO = (EditorVO) iterator.next();
    //If the updateFlag has been set to true then update the editor
    // vo record by invoking update on the editorDAO.
    if (editorVO.getUpdateFlag()) {
      editorDAO.update(editorVO);
    }
  }
} catch(SQLException e) {
  //Aborting the transaction
  ctx.setRollbackOnly();
  throw new DataAccessException("Error in TitleDAO.update()", e);
} catch(CreateException e) {
  //Aborting the transaction
```

```
       ctx.setRollbackOnly();
       throw new DataAccessException("Error in TitleDAO.update()", e);
     } catch(RemoteException e) {
     //Aborting the transaction
     ctx.setRollbackOnly();
     throw new DataAccessException("Error in TitleDAO.update()", e);
   } finally {
   try {
     if (preparedStatement!=null) preparedStatement.close();
     if (conn!=null) conn.close();
   } catch(SQLException e) {
     System.out.println("I am unable to close a resultset, " +
                        "statement, or connection TitleDAO.update().");
   }
   }
 }
```

The code for the update() method starts by getting SQL code for executing the update to the title table and retrieving a JDBC connection to the subscription database:

```
SQLCode sqlCode = SQLCode.getInstance();
String sql = sqlCode.getSQLStatement("titledao.update().update");

TitleVO titleVO = (TitleVO) pValueObject;

ServiceLocator serviceLocator = ServiceLocator.getInstance();
Connection conn =
    serviceLocator.getDBConn(ServiceLocator.SUBSCRIPTIONDB);
```

Next, the update() method uses the Counter EJB to retrieve the next row version number that is going to be applied when updating the targeted title table record:

```
CounterHome counterHome =
    (CounterHome) serviceLocator.getEJBHome(ServiceLocator.COUNTER);
Counter counter = counterHome.create();
long nextRowVersion = counter.getNextVal("title_rv");
```

The update() method uses an optimistic locking strategy to handle multiple users trying to update the same database record at the same time. An optimistic locking strategy does not apply an explicit database lock to a record when a user retrieves it from the database. Instead, an optimistic locking strategy lets each user retrieve a copy of the same record. The record is versioned and when the user tries to update the record in the database, this version number is checked to make sure that the data the user is trying to update has not already been updated by another user.

There are a number of different ways of implementing an optimistic locking strategy. For the purpose of this chapter's implementation, the optimistic locking strategy requires that every table in the database have a column called row_version.

The row_version column contains a number that indicates the version number of the row. In the data-persistence framework built in this chapter, when a record is retrieved from the database, it is retrieved into a ValueObject. As part of the data put into the ValueObject, a row_version is retrieved.

When a user wishes to commit any changes that they have made to a record, a `ValueObject` containing the data is passed into the `update()` method. The `update()` method will then use the `row_version` as part of the `WHERE` for the `UPDATE` statement. The `UPDATE` statement used in the `TitleDAO` EJB is shown below:

```
UPDATE title SET title_descr=? , title_cost=?, row_version=? WHERE title_id=? AND
row_version=?
```

In the `UPDATE` statement above, the `row_version` is being updated as part of the `UPDATE` SQL statement. The updating of the row's version number is used to indicate that the row has changed and other users who are using a copy of this record now have stale data. The generation of a `row_version` number for each row in the `title` table is done by the `Counter` EJB. Each table in the `subscription` database has its own entry in the `counter` table that keeps track of the current row version number for that table.

Once the row version number has been generated, a prepared statement is populated with the data from the `TitleVO` object passed in and the newly generated row version. This `preparedStatement` is then executed:

```
preparedStatement = conn.prepareStatement(sql);
preparedStatement.setString(1, titleVO.getTitleDescr());
preparedStatement.setFloat( 2, titleVO.getTitleCost());
preparedStatement.setLong( 3, nextRowVersion);
preparedStatement.setLong( 4, titleVO.getTitleId());
preparedStatement.setLong( 5, titleVO.getRowVersion());
```

So, what happens when two users try to update the same record in the `title` table at the same time? Both users will have received the same version of the record via a `ValueObject` they retrieved from the `TitleDAO`'s `find()` method. User one issues an update by calling the `update()` method on the `TitleDAO` EJB. User one's record will successfully update the database because the `UPDATE` statement will find a match on a record in the database. In the process of updating the record, the `row_version` number will change for the record that user one just updated.

User two's data is now stale. When this user tries to update the database via the `TitleDAO.update()` method, it will fail because the `UPDATE` statement will not be able to find a record whose `title_id` and `row_version` match that of the `ValueObject` passed into the `update()` method. The `update()` method checks to see if the update has been successfully executed by looking at the number of rows updated by the `UPDATE` statement:

```
int queryResults = preparedStatement.executeUpdate();
if (queryResults != 1) {
  throw new OptimisticLockException("Stale data for title record: "
                                    + titleVO.getTitleId());
}
```

If the number of rows returned by the `UPDATE` SQL call does not equal 1, then the user trying to update the `title` table will know they have stale data.

If an optimistic lock situation does occur, an OptimisticLockException is thrown. The OptimisticLockException is a user-defined exception that extends the DataAccessException. The OptimisticLockException is thrown to the application calling the update so it can make a decision on what to do with the data. If the application using the DAO is a user interface, the end user might be informed that someone has changed the data they are working on and that they must submit their changes again.

> *Different implementations of the optimistic locking strategy are discussed later in the chapter in the* Concurrency Strategies *section.*

After the record in the title table is updated, the update() method will create an EditorDAO EJB:

```
EditorDAOHome editorDAOHome = (EditorDAOHome)
    serviceLocator.getEJBHome(ServiceLocator.EDITORDAO);
EditorDAO editorDAO = editorDAOHome.create();
```

After the EditorDAO EJB is created, the update() method will walk through each of the EditorVO's objects associated with the TitleVO. If an EditorVO's update flag is set to true, determined by calling the EditorVO.getUpdateFlag() method, the data for the EditorVO is updated by passing that EditorVO into the EditorDAO.update() method:

```
while (iterator.hasNext()) {
  EditorVO editorVO = (EditorVO) iterator.next();
  if (editorVO.getUpdateFlag()){
    editorDAO.update(editorVO);
  }
}
```

The insert, update, and delete flags are used when a DAO is going to allow the users of the DAO to insert, update, or delete ValueObjects contained within the ValueObject passed into the DAO. In the case of TitleDAO, we are giving an application the ability to update not only a TitleVO, but also any EditorVOs contained within that particular TitleVO. The user tries to retrieve them with the HashMap contained with the TitleVO, change any values they want changed, and then set the update flag to true for that EditorVO. When the update() method is then called on the TitleDAO, that EditorVO will also be updated in the subscription database.

The delete() Method

The delete() method not only deletes the record from the title table, it also deletes all entries associated with the targeted title record from the title_editor table. This extra delete is done to ensure referential integrity between the title table and the title_editor table:

```
public void delete(ValueObject pValueObject)
    throws DataAccessException, ServiceLocatorException {

  //Build the SQL Code for deleting a record from the title table.
  SQLCode sqlCode = SQLCode.getInstance();
  String sqlTitle =
    sqlCode.getSQLStatement("titledao.delete().deletetitle");
  String sqlTitleEditor =
```

```
    sqlCode.getSQLStatement("titledao.delete().deletetitleeditor");

TitleVO titleVO = (TitleVO) pValueObject;

ServiceLocator serviceLocator = ServiceLocator.getInstance();
Connection conn =
  serviceLocator.getDBConn(ServiceLocator.SUBSCRIPTIONDB);

PreparedStatement preparedStatement = null;

try {
  //Delete the row from the title table
  preparedStatement = conn.prepareStatement(sqlTitle);
  preparedStatement.setLong(1, titleVO.getTitleId());
  preparedStatement.executeQuery();

  //Delete all rows from the title_editor table that match the
  //title_id
  preparedStatement = conn.prepareStatement(sqlTitleEditor);
  preparedStatement.setLong(1, titleVO.getTitleId());
  preparedStatement.executeQuery();
} catch(SQLException e) {
  //Aborting the transaction
  ctx.setRollbackOnly();
  throw new DataAccessException("Error in TitleDAO.delete()", e);
} finally{
  try {
    if (preparedStatement!=null) preparedStatement.close();
    if (conn!=null)          conn.close();
  } catch(SQLException e) {
    System.out.println("I am unable to close a resultset, " +
                       "statement, or connection. TitleDAO.delete()");
  }
}
}
```

DAOs and Relationships

Capturing and modeling relationships between entities in your persistence framework can be a difficult task. In the TitleDAO code, there is a many-to-many relationship between the TitleVO and the EditorVO. It is up to the developer of the persistence framework to determine how much control they are going to allow applications to modify either the data entities or the data relationships that exists between items represented in the framework.

In its implementation in this chapter, the TitleDAO only manages the relationship between the title table and the editor table. It does not allow the developer to add new editors that are absent in the editor table nor delete any editors from the editor table by marking them for deletion (that is, setting the deleteFlag to true on an EditorVO object). The only thing that the TitleDAO does is to:

❑   Add entries to the title_editor table when a new title record is inserted. It will walk through the TitleVO's editors HashMap and add an entry for each EditorVO to the HashMap. However, the code assumes that the editor record exists in the editor table already.

120

❑ Delete entries from the `title_editor` table when an existing title is deleted from the `title` table.

❑ Allow for updates of `EditorVO` objects contained within a `TitleVO` passed into a `TitleDAO.update()` method.

One of the core design decisions you will have to make in your persistence framework is at what level you want to give a DAO control and management of records belonging to another data entity in your database.

The management of data relationships is more than a code issue; it is a data management issue. How much control you give a DAO to add, update, and delete records outside of its immediate scope, as is the case with the `TitleDAO` being allowed to update records in the `editor` table, should be given careful consideration. Managing data relationships in code is extremely difficult. Poorly written code can corrupt your database by breaking the referential integrity that exists between data entities in the database.

The Value Object Pattern

The Value Object pattern first came into use as a business-tier J2EE design pattern that helps minimize the number of remote calls that are needed when using entity EJBs. Before the EJB 2.0 specification, any time a client made a call on an EJB's methods, a remote call would take place. This remote method call could have a significant amount of network overhead even if the client calling the EJB was located in the same application server hosting the EJB.

The Value Object pattern helped mitigate network overhead by having the entity EJB populate a plain Java class with all of the data requested by the user. The value object would then be sent back to the application calling the entity bean. The calling application could then work with the value object and then pass it back to the entity it originated from. By having the calling application getting and setting data on the value object, rather then the EJB, the amount of potential network traffic associated with using an entity EJB is significantly reduced. We'll be looking at this use of the Value Object pattern in the next chapter.

However, the Value Object pattern can be extended for significant use in our persistence framework. One could even argue that the Value Object pattern could be considered a core data-tier pattern. There are two reasons why this argument can be made:

❑ Firstly, a value object can be used to represent a logical view of data contained within your databases. The Value Object pattern can be used to abstract away the data relationships (such as whether or not there exists a one-to-many or many-to-many relationship between entities). The value object can even be used to present a single interface for data pulled from multiple data sources. As far as the client application using the value object is concerned, it has no idea where the data came from or how it is going to be managed.

❑ The second reason is that a value object is the glue that holds all tiers of n-tier architecture together. Value objects can be used to pass data back and forth across the presentation, business-logic, and data tiers. When a user keys data into a user interface, that data can be put into a value object, passed to the business-logic tier and then forwarded to the data tier. Conversely, when a user requests information, the data tier can return a value object (or a set of value objects) back up to the business-logic tier, which can then forward these value objects to the presentation tier.

All value objects in this chapter's data-persistence framework descend from a single abstract class called `ValueObject`, which is shown below:

```java
package valueobject;

import java.io.Serializable;

/*
 * The ValueObject is the abstract class that all ValueObjects in our
 * data persistence framework descend off of. It provides a number of
 * methods, including get/set methods for the VO status flags and the
 * rowVersion method.
 */
public abstract class ValueObject implements Serializable {

  /*Below are the VO status flags*/
  private boolean insertFlag = false;
  private boolean updateFlag = false;
  private boolean deleteFlag = false;
  private long    rowVersion = 0;

  /*
   * Retrieves the insertFlag. The insertFlag is used to tell the DAO that
   * data in the ValueObject should be inserted into the database.
   */
  public boolean getInsertFlag() {
    return insertFlag;
  }

  /*
   * Retrieves the deleteFlag. The deleteFlag is used to tell the DAO that
   * the data in the ValueObject should be deleted from the database.
   */
  public boolean getDeleteFlag() {
    return deleteFlag;
  }

  /*
   * Retrieves the updateFlag. The updateFlag is to tell the DAO that the
   * data in the ValueObject should be updated in the database.
   *
  public boolean getUpdateFlag() {
    return updateFlag;
  }

  /*
   * Retrieves the rowVersion. The rowVersion holds the current rowVersion
   * of the record and is used by the DAO.update() method to enforce
   * optimistic locking exceptions.
   */
  public long getRowVersion() {
    return rowVersion;
  }
```

```
/*Sets the insertFlag and sets all other status flags to false*/
public void setInsertFlag(boolean pFlag) {
  insertFlag = pFlag;
  deleteFlag = false;
  updateFlag = false;
}

/*Sets the updateFlag and sets all other status flags to false*/
public void setUpdateFlag(boolean pFlag) {
  insertFlag = false;
  deleteFlag = false;
  updateFlag = pFlag;
}

/*Sets the deleteFlag and sets all other status flags to false*/
public void setDeleteFlag(boolean pFlag) {
  insertFlag = false;
  deleteFlag = pFlag;
  updateFlag = false;
}

/*Sets the rowVersion property*/
public void setRowVersion(long pRowVersion) {
  rowVersion = pRowVersion;
}

/*Resets all VO status flags to false*/
public void resetFlags() {
  insertFlag = false;
  deleteFlag = false;
  updateFlag = false;
}
}
```

The ValueObject class has three status properties with their own get() or set() methods:

- ❑ insertFlag

- ❑ updateFlag

- ❑ deleteFlag

These three flags are used to give hints as to what a DAO should do with a value object. Earlier in the chapter, we saw how the TitleDAO bean could update the editor table when the TitleDAO.update() method was called.

Remember, in the TitleDAO.update() method, the update flag was used to give a "hint" to the TitleDAO as to what it should do with EditorVOs contained within the TitleVO. The TitleDAO will only perform an update on an editor record when the update flag for the EditorVO is set.

Only one of these flags can be set at any given time. A call to any one of the set methods of these status flags will automatically set the other status flags to false. For instance, if the setInsertFlag() method is called, the insertFlag for the record is set to whatever value is passed in by the calling application. The updateFlag and deleteFlag will automatically be set to false:

```
public void setInsertFlag(boolean pFlag) {
   insertFlag = pFlag;
   deleteFlag = false;
   updateFlag = false;
}
```

The `ValueObject` class also provides a `reset()` method. This method will automatically reset the value of the insert, update, and delete status flags to be `false`.

As you will see shortly, the `TitleVO` automatically sets the `updateFlag` to `true` every time a call to any of its set methods is made. This can be problematic when a DAO is creating a `ValueObject` for the first time and populating it with data. Before the `ValueObject` can be sent back to the end user, its update status has already been set to `true`. The `reset()` method can be used to take this populated `ValueObject` and make sure all of its status flags have been set back to `false`:

```
public void resetFlags(){
    insertFlag = false;
    deleteFlag = false;
    updateFlag = false;
  }
```

Finally, the `ValueObject` class provides `get()` and `set()` method for the `rowVersion` attribute. The `rowVersion` attribute was put in the `ValueObject` class to ensure that every `ValueObject` in our persistence framework participates in the framework's optimistic locking strategy.

We have seen the `ValueObject` class at abstract level. Let's look at a more concrete example of it by looking at the `TitleVO` value object:

The TitleVO Value Object

The `TitleVO` class returns all of the information associated with the `title` table. It also captures the relationship that exists between the `title` table and the `editor` table via the `getEditors()` or `setEditors()` methods. However, the `TitleVO` class does not reveal to the application using it what the relationship between the `title` and the `editor` table is. This is an important abstraction because the relationship between the `title` and the `editor` table can be changed. This change has to be updated in the `TitleDAO`, but the `TitleVO` does not have to change. This means applications consuming data from the `TitleVO` are protected from the underlying database change.

All the application code needs to know is that it can find all of the editor records associated with a title record simply by calling the `TitleVO.getEditors()` method. This is a powerful abstraction, particularly, if at some point the database relationship between the `title` and the `editor` tables needs to be restructured:

```
package valueobject;

import java.util.HashMap;

/*
 * The TitleVO class represents data retrieved from the ValueObject.
 * It is an implementation of the ValueObject pattern.
```

```
*/
public class TitleVO extends ValueObject {
  private long    titleId;
  private String  titleDescr;
  private float   titleCost;
  private HashMap editors;

  /*Constructor: Initializes the properties of the class to be empty*/
  public TitleVO() {
    titleId     = 0;
    titleDescr  = "";
    titleCost   = 0;
    editors     = new HashMap();
  }

  /*Retrieves the title id*/
  public long getTitleId() {
    return titleId;
  }

  /*Retrieves the title description*/
  public String getTitleDescr() {
    return titleDescr;
  }

  /*Retrieves the title cost*/
  public float getTitleCost() {
    return titleCost;
  }

  /*Returns all the editors associated with a title*/
  public HashMap getEditors() {
    return editors;
  }

  /*Sets the title id*/
  public void setTitleId(long pTitleId) {
    setUpdateFlag(true);
    titleId = pTitleId;
  }

  /*Sets the title descr*/
  public void setTitleDescr(String pTitleDescr) {
    setUpdateFlag(true);
    titleDescr = pTitleDescr;
  }

  /*Sets the title cost*/
  public void setTitleCost(float pTitleCost) {
    setUpdateFlag(true);
    titleCost = pTitleCost;
  }
```

```
/*Sets a hashmap with all of the editors*/
public void setEditors(HashMap pEditors) {
  setUpdateFlag(true);
  editors = pEditors;
}
}
```

When designing your value object layer keep in mind the following:

❏ **Your value objects should be lightweight**
A value object is nothing more than a wrapper for data going in and out of a database. This means there should be little to no code inside your value object implementation. If you find that you are placing business logic inside your value object, consider re-factoring your value object to take the logic out. The logic is better placed in either the business tier or the database in the DAO.

❏ **Value objects are a view of data within your database**
There is nothing wrong with having your DAO's find() method return different variations or views of a value object. This is particularly true when a DAO is servicing many types of applications. For instance, one find() method might return a single TitleVO fully populated with editor information. Another find() method might return a HashMap of TitleVOs that do not have their editor values populated. You can even have a single DAO return completely different types of value objects.

❏ **Keep your value object's object hierarchy simple**
If you need to build a complex object hierarchy to return to an application, do it in the business-logic layer. Have your business object take value objects from several different DAOs and assemble them into its hierarchy. This will significantly reduce the complexity of the database code being developed in your DAOs.

❏ **Watch out for the number of value objects in your persistence framework**
A common mistake of developers is to make their value objects too fine grained. The result is an explosion of small value objects that become unwieldy to use and maintain.

The Service Locator Pattern

Throughout the examples in this chapter, you have seen several occasions where EJBs and JDBC database connections were retrieved for use by the persistence framework. These two items were retrieved using the JNDI (Java Naming Directory Interfaces) API. How JNDI lookups are accomplished can vary from vendor to vendor. In addition, repeated JNDI lookups can be expensive.

Each time a user needs a service retrieved from JNDI, they must populate the appropriate JNDI environment information, make a connection to the JNDI server and then look up the service. What is needed is a single point for creating and retrieving various services from JNDI. This is where the Service Locator pattern is useful.

The Service Locator pattern abstracts away all JNDI lookups behind a simple-to-use interface. The Service Locator implementation used in this chapter provides methods for retrieving EJBHome interface and JDBC database connections. In addition, this Service Locator minimizes the number of JNDI lookups required by caching EJBHome interfaces and the DataSource objects used to created JDBC connections the first time a user requests a specific EJB or JDBC connection.

The code for the Service Locator pattern is shown below:

```
package dataaccess;

import java.sql.*;
import javax.sql.DataSource;
import java.util.Hashtable;
import javax.naming.*;
import javax.ejb.*;
import javax.rmi.PortableRemoteObject;
import session.counter.CounterHome;
import session.title.TitleDAOHome;
import session.editor.EditorDAOHome;

/*
 *  The Service Locator pattern is abstracts away the JNDI
 *  logic necessary for retrieving a JDBC Connection or EJBHome
 *  interface
 */
public class ServiceLocator{
  private static ServiceLocator serviceLocatorRef = null;
  private static Hashtable      ejbHomeCache      = null;
  private static Hashtable      dataSourceCache   = null;

  /*Enumerating the different services available from the
   * Service Locator
   */
  public static final int COUNTER       = 0;
  public static final int TITLEDAO      = 1;
  public static final int EDITORDAO     = 2;
  public static final int SUBSCRIPTIONDB = 3;

  /*The JNDI Names used to lookup a service*/
  private static final String COUNTER_JNDINAME="counter/Counter";
  private static final String TITLEDAO_JNDINAME="title/TitleDAO";
  private static final String EDITORDAO_JNDINAME="editor/EditorDAO";
  private static final String
     SUBSCRIPTIONDB_JNDINAME="java:/subscriptionDS";

  /*References to each of the different EJB Home Interfaces*/
  private static final Class COUNTERCLASSREF = CounterHome.class;
  private static final Class TITLECLASSREF   = TitleDAOHome.class;
  private static final Class EDITORCLASSREF  = EditorDAOHome.class;

  static {
    serviceLocatorRef = new ServiceLocator();
  }

  /*Private Constructor for the ServiceLocator*/
  private ServiceLocator(){
    ejbHomeCache    = new Hashtable();
    dataSourceCache = new Hashtable();
  }
```

```
/*
 * The ServiceLocator is implemented as a Singleton. The getInstance()
 * method will return the static reference to the ServiceLocator stored
 * inside of the ServiceLocator Class.
 */
public static ServiceLocator getInstance(){
  return serviceLocatorRef;
}


/*
 * The getServiceName will retrieve the JNDI name for a requested
 * service.  The service is indicated by the ServiceId passed into
 * the method.
 */
static private String getServiceName(int pServiceId)
    throws ServiceLocatorException {

  String serviceName = null;

  switch (pServiceId) {
    case COUNTER:
        serviceName = COUNTER_JNDINAME;
        break;
    case TITLEDAO:
        serviceName = TITLEDAO_JNDINAME;
        break;
    case EDITORDAO:
        serviceName = EDITORDAO_JNDINAME;
        break;
    case SUBSCRIPTIONDB:
        serviceName = SUBSCRIPTIONDB_JNDINAME;
        break;
    default:
        throw new ServiceLocatorException(
                "Unable to locate the service requested in " +
                "ServiceLocator.getServiceName() method.  ");
  }
  return serviceName;
}


/*
 * Returns the EJBHome Class reference for a requested service.
 * If the method can not make a match, it will throw a
 * ServiceLocatorException.
 */
static private Class getEJBHomeRef(int pServiceId)
    throws ServiceLocatorException {
  Class homeRef = null;

  switch (pServiceId){
    case COUNTER:
        homeRef = COUNTERCLASSREF;
        break;
    case TITLEDAO:
```

```
            homeRef = TITLECLASSREF;
            break;
       case EDITORDAO:
            homeRef = EDITORCLASSREF;
            break;
       default:
            throw new ServiceLocatorException(
                    "Unable to locate the service requested in " +
                    "ServiceLocator.getEJBHomeRef() method.  ");
   }
   return homeRef;
}


/*
 * The getEJBHome method will return an EJBHome interface for a
 * requested service.  If it can not find the requested EJB, it will
 * throw a servicelocator exception.
 *
 * The getEJBHome interface caches a requested EJBHome so that the first
 * time an EJB is requested, a home interface will be retrieved but then
 * be placed into a cache.
 */
public EJBHome getEJBHome(int pServiceId)
       throws ServiceLocatorException {
   //Trying to find the JNDI Name for the requested service
   String serviceName = getServiceName(pServiceId);
   EJBHome ejbHome    = null;

   try {
       //Checking to see if I can find the EJBHome interface in cache
       if (ejbHomeCache.containsKey(serviceName)) {
           ejbHome = (EJBHome) ejbHomeCache.get(serviceName);
           return ejbHome;
       } else {
           //If I could not find the EJBHome interface in the cache, look it
           // up and then cache it.
           Context ctx = new InitialContext();
           Object jndiRef = ctx.lookup(serviceName);

           Object portableObj =
             PortableRemoteObject.narrow(jndiRef, getEJBHomeRef(pServiceId));

           ejbHome = (EJBHome) portableObj;

           ejbHomeCache.put(serviceName, ejbHome);
           return ejbHome;
       }
   } catch(NamingException e) {
       throw new ServiceLocatorException(
            "Naming exception error in ServiceLocator.getEJBHome()" ,e);
   } catch(Exception e) {
       throw new ServiceLocatorException(
            "General exception in ServiceLocator.getEJBHome",e);
   }
```

```
    }

    /*
     * The getDBConn() method will create a JDBC connection for the
     * requested database.  It too uses a cachin algorithm to minimize
     * the number of JNDI hits that it must perform.
     */
    public Connection getDBConn(int pServiceId)
        throws ServiceLocatorException {
      //Getting the JNDI Service Name
      String      serviceName = getServiceName(pServiceId);
      Connection conn         = null;

      try {
        //Checking to see if the requested DataSource is in the Cache
        if (dataSourceCache.containsKey(serviceName)) {
          DataSource ds = (DataSource) dataSourceCache.get(serviceName);
          conn = ((DataSource)ds).getConnection();
          return conn;
        } else {
          // The DataSource was not in the cache.  Retrieve it from JNDI
          // and put it in the cache.
          Context ctx = new InitialContext();
          DataSource newDataSource = (DataSource) ctx.lookup(serviceName);
          dataSourceCache.put(serviceName, newDataSource);
          conn = newDataSource.getConnection();
          return conn;
        }
      } catch(SQLException e) {
        throw new ServiceLocatorException(
            "A SQL error has occurred in ServiceLocator.getDBConn()", e);
      } catch(NamingException e) {
        throw new ServiceLocatorException(
            "A JNDI Naming exception has occurred "+
            " in ServiceLocator.getDBConn()", e);
      } catch(Exception e) {
        throw new ServiceLocatorException(
            "An exception has occurred in ServiceLocator.getDBConn()", e);
      }
    }
  }
```

Let's start our discussion with the getEJBHome() method. This method is used to retrieve an EJBHome interface from the ServiceLocator:

```
public EJBHome getEJBHome(int pServiceId)
    throws ServiceLocatorException {
```

When a user wants a specific EJB, they call this method, passing in a service ID. These service IDs are defined as `static final int` variables in the `ServiceLocator` class:

```
public static final int COUNTER        = 0;
public static final int TITLEDAO       = 1;
public static final int EDITORDAO      = 2;
public static final int SUBSCRIPTIONDB = 3;
```

When one of these values is passed into the `getEJBHome()` method it is converted to a JNDI name. The JNDI name is what is passed to a JNDI context's `lookup()` method to retrieve an item from the naming directory. The conversion of the service ID to the JNDI name is accomplished by calling the `getServiceName()` method:

```
String serviceName = getServiceName(pServiceId);
```

The `getServiceName()` method is nothing more then a `switch/case` statement that will match a JNDI name with the service ID passed into it. If a match is not found, the `getServiceName()` method will throw a `ServiceLocatorException`. This exception is raised whenever an abnormal situation occurs within the `ServiceLocator`.

After the JNDI name is retrieved, the cache will be checked to see if there is already an `EJBHome` interface that has already been retrieved from JNDI. The cache for this `ServiceLocator` implementation is a `Hashtable` that uses the JNDI name for the EJB as the key:

```
if (ejbHomeCache.containsKey(serviceName)){
   ejbHome = (EJBHome) ejbHomeCache.get(serviceName);
   return ejbHome;
}
```

If a match is made on the cache, the `EJBHome` interface is retrieved out of the cache and returned to the application calling it. If the `EJBHome` interface is not in the cache, then a JNDI lookup will be performed:

```
} else {
  Context ctx = new InitialContext();
  Object jndiRef = ctx.lookup(serviceName);
```

The `ctx.lookup()` method above will return a reference to the item looked up via JNDI. The code then tries to cast the abstract interface returned from the JNDI lookup to its appropriate type. This is done by using the `PortableRemoteObject.narrow()` call, passing in the item to be checked with the `Class` type we want to cast it to:

```
Object portableObj =
   PortableRemoteObject.narrow(jndiRef, getEJBHomeRef(pServiceId));
```

The actual `Class` type that is going to be passed into the `narrow()` method will be retrieved by a call to `getEJBHomeRef()`. This method will retrieve a class reference for the particular EJB requested. The `getEJBHomeRef()`, like the `getServiceName()`, uses a switch/case statement to map a service name to a `Class` type.

Once the `EJBHome` has been retrieved, it is put into the cache and then returned to the application requesting it:

```
ejbHomeCache.put(serviceName, ejbHome);
return ejbHome;
```

The `getDBConn()` method works in the same manner as the `getEJBHome()` method. This method uses JNDI to retrieve a `DataSource` object representing the database connection requested by the user. It then uses that `DataSource` to create a database connection. Like the `getEJBHome()` method, the `getDBConn()` method caches a `DataSource` object when it first retrieves it from JNDI. After the `DataSource` is cached, any requests for it will cause the `DataSource` to be pulled out of the cache rather than a new JNDI lookup.

One final thing to note about this `ServiceLocator` implementation is that it implemented as a Singleton pattern. As you have seen throughout all of the examples in the chapter, users never create a `ServiceLocator` by calling its constructor. Instead, they use the `ServiceLocator`'s `getInstance()` method to retrieve a reference to the static `ServiceLocator` stored within the `ServiceLocator` class:

```
public static ServiceLocator getInstance() {
    return serviceLocatorRef;
}
```

Implementing the `ServiceLocator` as a Singleton pattern is extremely efficient because the class is heavily used and does not need to maintain instance information.

The use of non-final static methods in the `ServiceLocator` is actually in violation of the EJB specification (see section 21.4.2). However, we can get away with this because we're not dependent on our cache being consistent across Java Virtual Machines, which is the reason that the restriction exists. You must also verify that your factory classes can be used by multiple threads concurrently without synchronization; this issue is not addressed in the specification. These two issues make our solution perform better but also make it slightly less portable. We could trade some performance back for portability by doing the caching in the bean instance instead.

The Persistence Framework in Action

Let's now walk through two examples of how to use the data-persistence framework we have built to retrieve and insert `title` data. These examples consist of two JSP pages called:

- ❏ `selectExample.jsp`
  The `selectExample.jsp` shows how to retrieve a single title record from the `TitleDAO.find()` method. It will also show how to retrieve a `TitleVO`'s editor information by using the `getEditors()` method on the `TitleVO` object retrieved from the `TitleDAO`.

- ❏ `insertExample.jsp`
  The `insertExample.jsp` will demonstrate how to use a `TitleDAO` to insert a record into the `title` table. It will also use the `EditorDAO` to retrieve `EditorVOs` that can then be associated with the `title` record being inserted.

> You should *never* have your JSP pages directly accessing your DAO layer. Instead, your JSP pages should use a Session Façade to access the DAOs on behalf of the page. However, for purposes of demonstrating the DAO, to build this extra layer of abstraction would significantly increase the amount of code needed to demonstrate the actions of inserting and retrieving data with a DAO. In addition, the Session Façade is more relevant to the next chapter so we'll leave its discussion until then.

For more information on how to properly layer your presentation, business, and data tiers refer to the *Migration Strategies* section at the end of the chapter.

The selectExample.jsp Page

```jsp
<%@page import="java.util.*"%>
<%@page import="javax.naming.*"%>
<%@page import="dataaccess.*"%>
<%@page import="valueobject.*"%>
<%@page import="session.title.*"%>

<!--
    Remember this JSP is for example purposes only.
    In a real-world application you should never allow a JSP to directly
    access the DAO.
-->
<H1>Example 1 - Using a DAO to retrieve a title</H1>
<BR/>
<BR/>
<P>
    This JSP page will retrieve a single record from the Title table using
    a TitleDAO <BR/>
    and TitleVO object. It will also display all of the editors associated
    with this <BR/>
    Title by calling the getEditors() method on the TitleVO.
</P>
<BR/>
<%
    try {
```

The `selectExample` page retrieves a single record from the `title` table. It does this by retrieving a `TitleDAO` EJB:

```java
ServiceLocator serviceLocator = ServiceLocator.getInstance();
TitleDAOHome titleDAOHome = (TitleDAOHome)
            serviceLocator.getEJBHome(ServiceLocator.TITLEDAO);

TitleDAO titleDAO = titleDAOHome.create();
```

A `TitleDAO` EJB, called `titleDAO`, is retrieved by using a `ServiceLocator` to find the `TitleDAO`'s `EJBHome` interface and then uses the `EJBHome` interface to retrieve the `TitleDAO`'s remote interface.

Once a `TitleDAO` is retrieved, the `find()` method on the DAO is invoked, passing in the primary key of the record to be retrieved:

```
/*Calling the find method and retrieving a Title by title ID.*/
TitleVO titleVO  = (TitleVO) titleDAO.findByPrimaryKey("1");
```

After the `TitleVO` is retrieved via the `TitleDAO.find()` method, it is used to print information about the title record requested:

```
out.println("<P>Title id    : " + titleVO.getTitleId()    + "<br/>");
out.println("<P>Title descr : " + titleVO.getTitleDescr() + "<br/>");
out.println("<P>Title cost  : " + titleVO.getTitleCost()  + "<br/>");

out.println("<P>Editor(s) Working on the Title  : <br/>");
```

Remember, there is a many-to-many relationship between titles and editors. The editors associated with the title record retrieved can be accessed by calling the `getEditors()` method on `titleVO`:

```
/*
 * Retrieving the editors that the user currently has.  We will
 * then grab an iterator off of the HashMap and then display the
 * names of each editor.
 */
HashMap hashMap = titleVO.getEditors();
```

Once a `HashMap` is retrieved from the `getEditors()` call, it is less work to cycle through the HashMap and retrieve an `EditorVO` for each editor record. Each retrieved `EditorVO` object can be queried for the editor's name:

```
Collection col = hashMap.values();

Iterator iterator = col.iterator();

while (iterator.hasNext()) {
  EditorVO editorVO = (EditorVO) iterator.next();

  out.println(editorVO.getFirstName() + " " +
            editorVO.getMiddleName() + " " +
            editorVO.getLastName() + "<br/>");
}
} catch(Exception e) {
out.println("error--> " + e.getMessage());
}
%>
```

The JSP page example used in this section is very simplistic, but it should drive home a simple point. Through the judicious use of persistence design patterns, we have been able to completely decouple any knowledge of the subscription database from the JSP page. The `selectExample.jsp` page has no idea where the title data is coming from or even how it is being retrieved.

When the `selectExample.jsp` page is run successfully, you should see the following results:

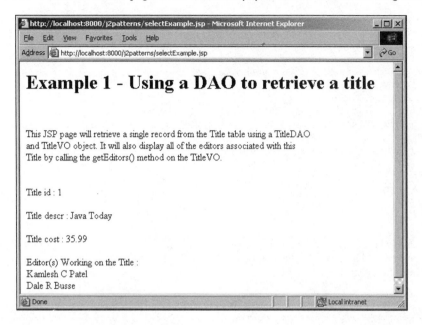

The insertExample.jsp Page

The `insertExample.jsp` page builds upon what was shown in the `selectExample.jsp` page. The `insertExample.jsp` will insert a new record into the `title` table using a `TitleDAO`. In the process of inserting this record, the `insertExample.jsp` page will also use the `EditorDAO` to retrieve editors that are then associated with the title record being inserted. The code for the `insertExample.jsp` page is shown below:

```
<%@page import="java.util.*"%>
<%@page import="javax.naming.*"%>
<%@page import="javax.transaction.*"%>
<%@page import="dataaccess.ServiceLocator"%>
<%@page import="valueobject.*"%>
<%@page import="session.title.*"%>
<%@page import="session.editor.*"%>

<!--
    Remember this JSP is for example purposes only.  In a real-world
    Application you should never allow a JSP to directly access the DAO.
    You would instead access the DAO from a session EJB.
```

135

```
-->

<H1>Example 2 - Using a DAO to insert a title</H1>
<BR/>
<BR/>
<P>
    This JSP page will insert a single record from the Title table using a
    TitleDAO <BR/>
    and TitleVO object.
    It will also establish relationships between the title <BR/>
    and the editor by retrieving 3 editorVO's and then adding them to the
    HashMap returned <BR/>
    by the getEditors() method on the TitleVO.<BR/>
</P>
<BR/>

<%
    try {
```

The first thing the `insertExample.jsp` page does is to retrieve a `TitleDAO` and `EditorDAO` from the application server. These two DAOs will be used to build the `TitleVO` object that is going to be inserted into the `subscription` database:

```
/*Getting a TitleDAO for manipulating title information*/
ServiceLocator serviceLocator = ServiceLocator.getInstance();
TitleDAOHome titleDAOHome = (TitleDAOHome)
            serviceLocator.getEJBHome(ServiceLocator.TITLEDAO);
TitleDAO titleDAO = titleDAOHome.create();

/*Getting an EditorDAO to retrieve Editor information*/
EditorDAOHome editorDAOHome = (EditorDAOHome)
            serviceLocator.getEJBHome(ServiceLocator.EDITORDAO);
EditorDAO editorDAO = editorDAOHome.create();
```

After the two DAOs are created, three editor records are retrieved from the `subscription` database (later, in the `insertExample.jsp` code, these records will be associated with the title record after it has been created):

```
/*
 * Looking up three editors.  I am going to associate these editors
 * to the new title record
 */
EditorVO editorVO1 = (EditorVO) editorDAO.findByPrimaryKey("1");
EditorVO editorVO2 = (EditorVO) editorDAO.findByPrimaryKey("2");
EditorVO editorVO3 = (EditorVO) editorDAO.findByPrimaryKey("3");
```

Now, the real work begins. A new `TitleVO` object, called `newTitleVO`, will be created by calling the `createValueObject()` method on the `titleDAO` EJB:

```
/*Creating a new title vo by calling the TitleVO's
 * createValueObjectMethod
 */
TitleVO newTitleVO = (TitleVO) titleDAO.createValueObject();
```

The `newTitleVO` object is an empty `TitleVO` object. The only property that is set on this object is the `titleId`. This property holds a primary key value that was generated inside the `createValueObject()` method. If you remember from earlier discussions, the `TitleDAO.createValueObject()` method uses the `Counter` EJB to generate a primary key.

After the `newTitleVO` has been created, the JSP page populates it with data:

```
/*Populate the new TitleVO with data*/
newTitleVO.setTitleDescr("Geek World");
newTitleVO.setTitleCost(100);
```

The JSP page also associates the three `EditorVO`s retrieved earlier by the `EditorDAO`. Each `EditorVO` retrieved is added to a `HashMap` stored inside the `newTitleVO` object:

```
/*Add the editors I retrieved from the EditorDAO to the TitleVO*/
newTitleVO.getEditors().put(
  new Long(editorVO1.getEditorId()), editorVO1);
newTitleVO.getEditors().put(
  new Long(editorVO2.getEditorId()), editorVO2);
newTitleVO.getEditors().put(
  new Long(editorVO3.getEditorId()), editorVO3);
```

An entry in the `title_editor` table will be created for each of the `EditorVO`s added to the `newTitleVO` object:

```
/*Insert the record into the DAO*/
titleDAO.insert(newTitleVO);

/*Retrieving the record I just inserted into the database*/
TitleVO  titleVO  = (TitleVO) titleDAO.findByPrimaryKey(
                     new Long(newTitleVO.getTitleId()).toString());

/*Printing out the TitleVO data just inserted*/
out.println("<B><P>Record just inserted:</P></B><BR/>");

out.println("<P>Title id    : " + titleVO.getTitleId()    + "<br/>");
out.println("<P>Title descr : " + titleVO.getTitleDescr() + "<br/>");
out.println("<P>Title cost  : " + titleVO.getTitleCost()  + "<br/>");

out.println("<P>Editor(s) Working on the Title  : <br/>");
HashMap hashMap = titleVO.getEditors();

Collection col = hashMap.values();
```

```
      Iterator iterator = col.iterator();

    while (iterator.hasNext()) {
      EditorVO editorVO = (EditorVO) iterator.next();

      out.println(editorVO.getFirstName() + " " +
                  editorVO.getMiddleName() + " " +
                  editorVO.getLastName() + "<br/>");
    }
  } catch(Exception e) {
    out.println("error--> " + e.getMessage());
  }
%>
```

Once the `insertFlag` for the `newTitleVO` object is set, the actual insertion of the record takes place by calling `insert()` on the `titleDAO` EJB. The rest of the code in the `insertExample.jsp` page retrieves the record (just inserted) back from the `subscription` database and displays it.

When the `insertExample.jsp` page runs successfully, you should see the following output on your web browser:

Persistence Framework Strategies

Providing a common interface for applications to work with databases within your organization is a powerful construct. However, in order to build a powerful persistence framework, you have to make sure that a number of issues are addressed. These issues include:

❑ Generating primary keys for records going into your database

❑ Handling concurrent updates by multiple users to the same database record in your application

❑ Identifying the best approach for transaction management within your persistence framework

❑ Optimizing the performance of your persistence framework

❑ Migrating your current Java data access code to a persistence framework

In the following sections, we will look at different strategies for addressing these issues.

Primary Key Generation Strategies

A primary key uniquely identifies a record with a database table. Primary keys are usually numeric values. Almost all databases provide some kind of mechanism for generating primary keys. From an application developer's perspective, there are a number of different approaches for generating primary keys for a database insert. Some of these approaches include:

❑ Using a database trigger to automatically generate a primary key when a record is inserted into the database. The trigger would use a sequence object (if the database supports it) to get the primary key.

❑ Using an auto-increment column construct to automatically insert a value when a record is inserted into the database. All leading vendors (for example, MySQL and Microsoft SQL*Server) offer auto-incrementing columns for generating primary keys.

❑ Directly using a database sequence generator to generate a primary key that can then be used for the insert into the database. An example of this would be Oracle's sequence object that can be queried for the next value in a sequence. This value can then be used when the insert occurs.

❑ Writing a stateful session EJB or entity EJB combination to maintain a cache of pre-generated sequences that can be invoked to retrieve a sequence number. The entity EJB would retrieve a sequence number from a table in the database and then update the counter value stored in the table. The session EJB would grab a block of these sequence numbers and cache them. The session EJB would then hand out these sequences to anyone requesting the EJB. When more sequence numbers are needed, the entity EJB would retrieve another set of numbers from the database. This way, the entity EJB is not constantly being hit with requests for sequences.

These four different approaches have their advantages and disadvantages. Using a database construct like a trigger, auto-increment column, or a sequence object is very easy to implement. Using these approaches ensures that the user never has to worry about generating a primary key. However, there are also some problems in using these approaches.

First, by using a database trigger to perform the primary key generation, there is no way of returning the primary key generated back to the code performing the database insert. This is a big problem if you need to establish a parent-child relationship in the data you are manipulating. For example, if your code is inserting an order and then order detail line items into the table, you will need the primary key of the order being inserted so that you can insert the order's detail line items.

Auto-incrementing database columns can offer the same challenges as a database trigger. How do you look up the primary key value after the insert? Before JDK1.3, this was a problem. However, with the release of JDK1.4, the JDBC Statement object now allows you to indicate whether you want an auto-generated value to be returned from an insert. However, since this feature has just been released in JDK1.4, check your JDBC driver documentation carefully to see if the driver supports this feature.

Database sequence objects are extremely powerful because they can be queried and the value can be returned before a database insert occurs. Oracle provides a sequence object that can be defined and then queried for primary key values. MySQL offers the LAST_INSERT_ID() function. Database sequences are very powerful, but they are also database specific. If database sequences are haphazardly scattered throughout the database code and not centralized into a single service, this can become a porting nightmare if your application has to be moved to a new database platform.

The last approach, the stateful session bean caching primary key values, is a popular implementation because it is very fast and can be written to be database independent. Cached primary keys require fewer calls to the database, which can offer a significant performance improvement in a high-transaction environment. However, there are a few things to keep in mind with this approach:

❑ The use of a stateful session EJB to cache primary key values can be very difficult to implement in a clustered environment. Each EJB in the cluster must ensure that the keys it has cached are not duplicated in any of the other EJBs.

❑ A stateful session EJB will lose all of the primary keys in its cache if the application server it is running in goes down. This can result in "gaps" in the primary keys stored in a database table. This is usually not a major problem, but for some database administrators, there is a level of discomfort when this situation occurs.

❑ There can be data corruption issues if there are other applications inserting data into the database that are not using the stateful session bean. Using database-specific constructs like triggers, auto-increment columns, and sequences is far less likely to encounter the problem.

What is the right approach? All of the approaches have been successfully implemented. Using database sequence objects is usually the easiest primary key generation mechanism. Since database sequences are database specific, it is important to write "wrapper" code that:

❑ Provides a single point of service for generating primary keys for your applications

❑ Decouples how primary keys are generated from the code actually using the primary keys

❑ Hides the database-specific features behind a façade

In the persistence framework presented in this chapter, the primary key generation was done via the Counter EJB. The Counter EJB is responsible for generating a unique number based on the counter ID passed into its getNextVal() method. The Counter EJB is used to generate both primary keys and row version numbers for the TitleDAO application.

The `Counter` EJB uses a combination of a database table to track sequences and the `LAST_INSERT_ID()` function of the MySQL database to generate primary keys in the subscription database. Let's walk through how the `Counter` EJB is implemented so that you can understand how to apply the concepts within this EJB to your own persistence framework.

The Counter EJB Database Structures

As there might be multiple counters in the subscription database, a table called `counter` was created. The `counter` table has two columns:

- `seq_num` – This column represents the current value for a counter

- `counter_name` – This column is the primary key for the counter table and represents a unique counter within the database

The `Counter` EJB is a standard session EJB with a home interface, a remote interface, and a bean class. The home and remote interfaces for the `Counter` EJB are shown below:

```
package session.counter;

import javax.ejb.EJBObject;
import java.rmi.RemoteException;
import dataaccess.DataAccessException;
import dataaccess.ServiceLocatorException;

public interface Counter extends EJBObject {
  public long getNextVal(String pCounterName)
    throws DataAccessException, ServiceLocatorException, RemoteException;
}
```

```
package session.counter;

import java.io.Serializable;
import javax.ejb.CreateException;
import java.rmi.RemoteException;
import javax.ejb.EJBHome;

public interface CounterHome extends EJBHome {
  Counter create() throws CreateException, RemoteException;
}
```

Now let's look at the bean implementation class:

```
package session.counter;

import javax.ejb.SessionBean;
import javax.ejb.SessionContext;
import java.sql.*;
import dataaccess.*;

public class CounterBean implements SessionBean{
  SessionContext ctx = null;
```

```
/*
 *   The getNextVal method will retrieve the next sequence number
 *   of the sequence the user requests.  The sequence values are stored
 *   in a database table called counter.
 */
public long getNextVal(String pCounterName)
  throws DataAccessException, ServiceLocatorException {

    long                valueReturned   = 0;
    Connection          conn            = null;
    PreparedStatement   updateStatement = null;
    ResultSet           rsCounter       = null;

    try {
      //Getting a connection to the subscription database
      ServiceLocator serviceLocator = ServiceLocator.getInstance();
      conn = serviceLocator.getDBConn(ServiceLocator.SUBSCRIPTIONDB);
```

The process of retrieving a primary key starts when the user calls the getNextVal() method on the Counter EJB and passes in a String value representing the counter the application wants to increment.

The code below will update the sequence number for the counter being requested:

```
//Building a SQL statement that will update the counter
SQLCode sqlCode = SQLCode.getInstance();
String sql = sqlCode.getSQLStatement("counter.nextval.update");

//Executing the SQL statement
updateStatement = conn.prepareStatement(sql.toString());
updateStatement.setString(1, pCounterName);
updateStatement.execute();
```

The SQL code class is used to retrieve the SQL statement shown below:

```
UPDATE counter SET seq_num = LAST_INSERT_ID(seq_num+1)
WHERE counter_name = ?
```

You will notice that the UPDATE statement will call the MySQL LAST_INSERT_ID() function passing in the value of the current seq_num column, incremented by one. The LAST_INSERT_ID() function is behaving as a sequence generator, returning the expression passed into the function. The value returned by the LAST_INSERT_ID() function will be unique to each client issuing the above SQL statement. Since we are using a MySQL-specific function to implement the Counter EJB, we would have to rewrite the counter class if it were to run against a different database platform.

Once the update has completed, the code will immediately retrieve the incremented seq_num value by issuing a SELECT statement that invokes the LAST_INSERT_ID() function:

```
sql = sqlCode.getSQLStatement("counter.nextval.select");
```

```
        //Executing the sql statement
        updateStatement = conn.prepareStatement(sql.toString());
        updateStatement.setString(1, pCounterName);
        rsCounter = updateStatement.executeQuery();
```

The SQL code associated with the `counter.nextval.select` key is:

```
SELECT LAST_INSERT_ID() seq_num FROM counter WHERE counter_name = ?
```

Using the `LAST_INSERT_ID()` function in the `SELECT` statement above will cause the `seq_num` value that was updated in the `UPDATE` call earlier to be returned. The value retrieved from the `SELECT` statement is returned to the application calling the `getNextVal()` method:

```
        //Pulling the new sequence id
        if (rsCounter.next()){
          valueReturned = rsCounter.getLong("seq_num");
        }
      } catch(SQLException e) {
        //Marking the session bean for rollback
        ctx.setRollbackOnly();
        throw new DataAccessException(
            "Error has occurred in CounterBean.getNextVal()", e);
      } finally {
        try {
          //Close my database connections
          if (updateStatement != null) updateStatement.close();
          if (rsCounter!=null) rsCounter.close();
          if (conn!=null) conn.close();
        } catch(SQLException e) {
          System.out.println("Unable to close resultset, database " +
                    "connection or statement in Counter.getNextVal");
        }
      }
      return valueReturned;
    }

    public void ejbCreate(){}
    public void ejbRemove() {}
    public void ejbActivate() {}
    public void ejbPassivate() {}
    public void setSessionContext(SessionContext pCtx){
      ctx = pCtx;
    }
  }
```

Remember, this is only one way of implementing a primary key generation strategy. The power of this approach comes from the fact that you can completely rewrite how primary keys are generated within your application and the DAOs using the primary key generator will never have to be rewritten.

Concurrency Strategies

Imagine the following scenario: Two users are trying to update the same record. They both have retrieved copies of the record and User 1 submits some changes and commits. User 2 then submits some changes on the same record and commits. User 2's changes have now overwritten the data just saved by User 1.

The problem here is that the two users' transactions are going on concurrently. Neither user knows that they have both retrieved and are working on copies of the same record. Furthermore, User 1 will never know that User 2 made a change to record they just committed. What is needed is a locking strategy that will prevent one user from overwriting another user's record when both users are working on the same record concurrently. Two different strategies can be applied here:

❑ The first user to retrieve the record can explicitly place a database lock on the record and prevent all other users from retrieving or manipulating that record until they have explicitly released the lock. This strategy is called a **pessimistic locking strategy** because it says no one can touch the database record, even if they only want to read it, until the first user is done with. Pessimistic locking is the safest way to isolate one user's transactions from another. However, it is a performance killer in a high transaction volume application because one user locking a record can quickly cause other users to have to wait. As each user has to wait, they may be locking other records other users might need and you can quickly end up in a deadlock.

❑ The second strategy is to allow both users to retrieve a copy of the record. Their retrieved copy will include some kind of version information. This version information on the retrieved record will be compared against the version number stored in the database. If the version information indicates that an update has not occurred on a record a user is trying to update, then the update can occur. This strategy is called optimistic locking. Each user is allowed to access data and make their modifications to data without the overhead of placing an explicit database lock.

Optimistic locking is best suited for high transaction environments where a small amount of data is going to be retrieved and then quickly updated.

As stated earlier, the persistence framework built in this chapter uses an optimistic locking strategy. Optimistic locking strategies can be very easy or very difficult to implement depending on whether the optimistic locking approach is only going to be used for new application development, or will be used for existing applications.

There are a number of different ways of implementing an optimistic locking strategy for a brand new application. Two of the more common mechanisms for implementing an optimistic locking strategy are:

❑ Having a row version column on each row in a table. Before a record is updated, the row version of the record being updated is compared with the row version of the record in the database.

❑ Having a date/timestamp column that holds the timestamp of when a record was last updated. Before an update is allowed to occur, the date/timestamp of the record in the database and the date/timestamp of record that is going to be used for the update are compared. If the date/timestamp on the record in the database is newer than the record being used for the update, then record being used for the update is considered stale.

For the subscription database, a row_version number-based optimistic locking strategy was implemented. The row_version optimistic locking strategy requires that a row_version column be added to each table in a database. This row_version column will be updated on a specific record every time the record is updated. The actual checking for whether or not data being updated is "stale" can be implemented in one of two ways:

❑ Put the code that checks to see if there is stale data for an update inside your DAO layer. This was demonstrated in the update() method of the TitleDAO EJB earlier in the chapter. The update() method attempts to update a record in the title table by using the primary key and the row version in the WHERE clause of the UPDATE statement.

❑ Use database triggers to implement your optimistic locking strategy. Each table in your database has a database trigger that will fire whenever an update on a record occurs. The trigger compares the row version of the record being updated against the record currently in the database. If they are the same, the record is updated. If the row version numbers differ, the trigger raises an exception and the record is not updated.

Using database triggers to manage an optimistic locking strategy is actually the easier of the two methods to implement. You do not have to clutter up your DAOs with optimistic locking code. All of this is done at the trigger level. Furthermore, you do not have to worry whether all applications that update data in your application are also implementing optimistic locking code.

The disadvantage of using the trigger-based approach is that database triggers can be very database specific and this makes it more difficult to support your application across multiple databases. However, a well-designed case tool, like ER-WIN, can help mitigate this by providing the ability to generate triggers for multiple databases through the tool. This simplifies things tremendously.

For this chapter, the optimistic locking code was put inside of the DAO layer simply because the MySQL database does not support triggers.

For existing applications, implementing an optimistic locking strategy can be a significant amount of work. If you have ownership of the application source code, implementing an optimistic locking strategy often involves walking through the entire code base and changing all database selects and updates to implement the optimistic locking strategy. Furthermore, the application code must be changed to handle any optimistic locking exceptions raised during the course of a transaction. This is not an easy task.

If you do not own the application source code, as is often the case with products bought from third-party vendors, you will need to work with the vendor to see if an optimistic locking strategy can be implemented. If the vendor is not willing to implement one, you are in a bind. However, if you are currently in the process of selecting a package that you know you are going to have to integrate with other applications within your organization, ask how they are implementing a locking strategy for the application in question.

If the vendor is using pessimistic locking, locking a database resource via issuing a lock on a row or table in the database can lead to performance problems in a high transaction environment. If they are not using any kind of locking strategy (you would be surprised at the number of application vendors who do not), this can lead to "corrupt" data when you need to integrate that package with applications in your organization. Asking questions like this, at the package selection phase, can save a significant amount of headaches later on when you are trying to perform application integration.

Transaction Management Strategies

J2EE offers two different approaches for managing database transactions: bean-managed or container-managed demarcation. For bean-managed transactions, the application developer must place transaction code in their DAO (assuming the JDBC code is placed directly inside the DAO) or entity bean (if bean-managed persistence entity beans are used). The developer is responsible for beginning the transaction and then committing or rolling back the transaction.

The developer controls the transaction by using the Java Transaction API (JTA). If the developer forgets to commit or rollback a transaction before leaving a method call on a bean-managed transaction EJB, an exception will be thrown by the EJB container. The exact exception thrown is specific to the container the EJB is running in.

In container-managed transactions, also called declarative transaction management, the container the EJB is running in manages the transaction. The application developer declares in the EJB's deployment descriptor how the container is supposed to manage transactions. There are six different transaction types that can be declared inside an EJB's deployment descriptor:

❏ NotSupported
With the NotSupported transaction type, the EJB in question cannot be involved in any transactions. If an EJB starts a transaction and then calls another EJB with a transaction type of NotSupported, then the calling EJB will have its transaction suspended. Since the DAO pattern is used for handling database transactions, this transaction type should never be used for declaring a DAO EJB.

❏ Supports
The Supports transaction type tells the container to run the EJB in the transaction if a transaction has already been started. If a transaction has not been started, the EJB will not run in a transaction. Since a DAO can insert, update, or delete database records it should always run in a transaction. Since Supports transaction type does not guarantee that an EJB will be run in a transaction it is highly recommend you do not use it for building the DAO EJBs seen in this chapter.

❏ Required
The Required transaction type forces the EJB to run within a transaction. If a transaction already exists, the EJB will run in the context of that transaction. If a transaction does not exist, a new one will be started and the EJB will run in that transaction.

❏ RequiresNew
The RequiresNew transaction causes the EJB to run in a transaction independent of any transactions currently running. This transaction type is used when you want to run database transactions independently of one another.

❏ Mandatory
The Mandatory transaction type requires that the EJB run in the context of an already running transaction. If no transaction is already running, then a javax.ejb.TransactionRequiredException is thrown back to the calling application.

❑ Never

The Never transaction type tells the EJB container that the EJB should never run in a transaction. If it is called by code that is currently running within a transaction, an exception will be thrown. The exception thrown will vary depending on whether or not the EJB is called as a local EJB or a remote EJB. The exception thrown will be `javax.ejb.EJBException` or `javax.ejb.RemoteException` respectively.

In terms of writing a data-persistence framework for your applications, it highly recommended that you use container-managed transactions. There are several reasons for this:

❑ A persistence framework written with container-managed transactions is significantly easier. All transaction management is done declaratively and you do not have to clutter up your DAO code with transaction code. Transaction code can be extremely difficult to write and debug when you have to write transactions that span multiple components.

❑ Container-managed transactions are more flexible. If you want to change the transaction behavior of an EJB, it is a simple matter of changing the EJB's deployment descriptor and re-deploying the bean. For instance, suppose you wanted to ensure that commits made by the Counter EJB always run in a new transaction. If the Counter EJB is currently set to transaction type of Required, it is a simple matter to change the transaction type in Counter's deployment descriptor to be RequiresNew and then redeploy the EJB. No changes have to be made to the Counter code for this to take place.

❑ Poorly written transaction code can cripple the performance of an application. Remember, that while a transaction is in progress, application server and database resources are used to track the progress of the transaction. Too often, developers writing bean-managed transaction code keep a transaction open for longer than needed. In high-volume, transaction-processing applications, like most e-commerce web sites, poor coding of transaction management can result in abysmal performance.

Keep in mind that bean-managed persistence offers a high degree of flexibility and ultimately gives the persistence framework developer the highest degree of transaction control and isolation that can be obtained. However, this level of control is rarely needed for most applications. This section only gives a brief overview of EJB transaction management.

Performance Strategies

Abstraction and encapsulation all come at the cost of performance. Building a data-persistence framework will rarely be as high performance as going directly after the data. However, the reuse and the lower cost of maintenance associated with implementing a data-persistence framework often outweighs the performance costs associated with it.

However, there are some very common mistakes when implementing data-persistence patterns that can severely limit the performance and scalability of these applications. Some of the more common performance issues can range from design errors to a misunderstanding of how EJB's function:

❑ The wrong level of granularity for the DAOs in your persistence framework

❑ A large number of value objects returned from DAO find() method calls

❑ Common EJB implementation pitfalls

Persistence framework developers often fall into the trap of trying to map their data model directly to DAO classes. The result is a data-persistence framework that has too many DAO classes and retrieves large numbers of fine-grained value objects.

A persistence framework should be built on the concept of coarse-grained objects. The DAO in your persistence framework should not be returning large numbers of value objects. So when designing your data-persistence framework keeps in mind the following:

❑   **Watch the breadth of the objects being returned by the DAOs in your framework**
    Returning too many value objects from a call on a find() method will result in your application quickly running into Java Virtual Machine (JVM) memory issues. Persistence frameworks that do not have the right level of granularity will have problems with frequent garbage collection or running out of memory in the JVM.

❑   **Watch the depth of the objects being returned by the DAOs in your framework**
    A common mistake in applying persistence patterns is making the object hierarchy for your value objects too deep. This too is a granularity issue. Every value object returned should not have more then three levels of other objects contained within it. Otherwise, even the act of retrieving or updating a few value objects can represent a significant amount of overhead.

The persistence patterns presented in this chapter work well when writing OLTP (Online Transaction Processing) applications where your application is working with a relatively small data set that is going to be manipulated by an end user. However, you can run into serious scalability and performance issues implementing these patterns in an OLAP (Online Analytical Processing) environment like a reporting database or a data warehouse.

In these situations, you are far better off going directly after the data using JDBC to directly retrieve a ResultSet. In order to get a ResultSet, the application must get a JDBC connection and then issue a SQL query and retrieve a ResultSet. In doing this, it would appear that every abstraction principle the persistence framework works so hard to establish is now violated. However, architecture is never a pure thing and occasional exceptions must be made.

However, there are some more choices provided by the Optional Package (and now in JDK 1.4):

The JDBC Optional Package (found in J2EE) introduced the concept of a RowSet. A RowSet extends the JDBC ResultSet with one important difference. A RowSet, can be disconnected from the database connection, so even if the JDBC connection is closed, the RowSet can still be used to read and manipulate data. Later the RowSet can re-establish a connection to the database and update it with any changes that were made to the data contained within it.

If you only need to retrieve large amounts of data infrequently, you can integrate and add a find() method to your DAO that returns a RowSet. Remember, a DAO pattern will abstract away how data is actually retrieved. This means you can have one find() method returning a RowSet using JDBC and another find() method returning a value object that was read from an entity EJB. For bulk updates, inserts, or deletes you can even pass the RowSet back into the DAO and have DAO perform the updates, inserts or deletes on behalf of the application using the RowSet.

Another common performance issue involved with implementing a J2EE-based persistence framework is that the framework developer falls into common pitfalls associated with writing EJB-based applications. Since persistence frameworks often involve many small transactions executed against a database, there are two things to keep in mind:

❏ Be aware that every time a JNDI lookup is performed, there is overhead associated with it. If you have a situation where one heavily used DAO is using several other DAOs to carry out a transaction, consider using a Service Locator with a caching strategy, such as the one demonstrated in this chapter, to cut down on the number of JNDI lookups performed. In a high transaction environment, this can significantly cut down on the number of JNDI lookups being performed.

❏ Use local and remote EJB interfaces appropriately. If your DAO layer is only going to be used by application code running within your application server, consider using local interfaces for your DAO implementation. Local interfaces are part of the EJB 2.0 specification and significantly reduce the amount of network traffic that has traditionally been the bane of any EJB application development.

Always, design your persistence framework with performance in mind from the beginning. It is much easier to implement the performance strategies discussed above while the framework is still being developed and the code is fluid than after several applications have been built on top of the framework:

> **Good architecture starts from the beginning and not as an afterthought when a project has been deployed.**

Migration Strategies

Most IT developers would love to spend their careers writing applications from scratch. However, the reality is that the majority of a developer's time is spent supporting existing code for integrating applications together.

Persistence frameworks are always easiest to implement for new applications. How do you implement a persistence framework for J2EE applications that have already been written? The answer: start small and slow. Most J2EE applications have leveraged session EJBs to build the business logic for their applications. However, they have intermixed data access code all through their session EJB layer.

The key is to start small and identify a few key data entities that you want represented in a persistence layer. Usually, the entities that work best are going to be data entities that are used throughout all of the applications in your organization. For most companies, customer data is the most critical piece of information in their databases. Take that data entity and use that as the foundation for building your persistence framework.

Before you begin any implementation of the persistence framework, whether the implementation is for new application development or a migration of existing applications, it is critical that you have a conceptual road map to build your entire framework. This road map is a diagram that lays out all of the tiers in your framework and how the different pieces are going to interact together.

Shown below is an example of a framework road map:

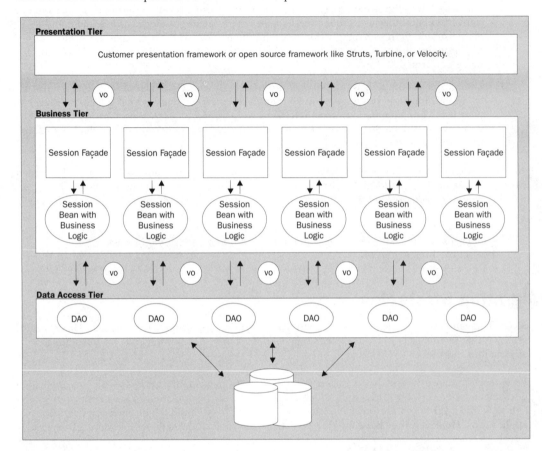

The framework shown above is n-tiered architecture using a closed-layer approach. It is a closed-layer approach because each tier can only talk to the tiers directly above and below it. The presentation tier can only talk to the business tier, the business tier can only talk to the presentation and data tiers, and the data tier is the sole point of access to all corporate data sources.

The business tier in the above road map is split into two pieces: Session Façades and session beans. The Session Façades are Java classes that sit between the presentation tier and the session EJBs. Session Façades wrap session EJBs and keep the presentation layer from being exposed to which EJBs are being used to process business logic. The session beans are using the DAO in the data access tier to retrieve and manipulate data. Value objects are the only pieces of the architecture that can move data back and forth between the tiers.

Once the conceptual road map for your framework has been established and you understand how your applications are going to communicate with the data tier, you can begin the process of migrating your existing application base over to a persistence framework.

Some of the steps involved with this migration include:

- Look through all of the applications that are currently using customer data. Identify core data elements of the customer that are repeatedly used throughout the applications. Also, identify how different business processes are using these data elements.

- Build the base classes of your persistence framework. Identify the data sources you are going to need and wrap them in a `DataSourceFactory`.

- Identify how primary keys in your framework are to be generated. Look at the underlying databases you are going to be accessing and develop a centralized mechanism for generating primary keys that is consistent with how customer records are currently stored.

- Identify whether or not you need to implement an optimistic locking mechanism. Remember, if you start small, you do not need to implement optimistic locking on every table in your database.

- Build the DAO and VO classes that you are going to use. If the majority of the code is written as JDBC code, look at starting out with using JDBC directly in your session EJB.

- Walk through each of the applications that use the customer data and convert them over to the new persistence framework.

It is highly recommended that you do not go for a big bang with your migration strategy. Your migration strategy should start with a small number of data entities that will be built and no radical shifts in database access technology.

This means that if your application code uses JDBC, then stick with that during your persistence framework implementation. Do not jump to container-managed persistence or some other radically different approach. That can come later in other iterations of your persistence framework. Otherwise, you are going to find yourself not only debugging the patterns you are implementing, but also trying to support a new data access technology your team might not be familiar with.

Summary

The J2EE platform offers a flexible platform for building a persistence framework. Its component-based architecture and multiple database APIs provide readymade tools for crafting a persistence framework that can be leveraged for most of, if not all, your application development needs.

Data is the only thing that remains consistent within an organization's IT infrastructure. Applications come and go. However, the data used by them rarely disappears. It might be migrated to another database platform or transformed to a different format or structure, but it is still fundamentally the same. After all, when an organization implements a new Customer Relationship Management application does it throw out all of its customer data? No, it migrates that data to the new system, often massaging it into a new data structure.

Herein lies the power of a data-persistence framework. All application development frameworks provide a degree of code reuse. However, persistence frameworks go beyond letting developers reuse code. A data-persistence framework defines a standard set of interfaces for retrieving and manipulating data entities that are important to your organization.

The underlying technology of the persistence framework might change, but you get reusability because not all of the applications using the framework have to change when those data entities migrate or move. Only the implementation of the framework changes, not the public interfaces the applications uses to retrieve and manipulate data:

> **The power of a persistence framework comes from its ability to abstract away the underlying data source implementation.**

This chapter has provided the three basic patterns that lay a foundation for a data-persistence framework. The patterns are:

- The Data Access Object pattern that hides how data for a particular business data entity is retrieved, inserted, updated, and deleted

- The Value Object pattern that abstracts away the physical relationships that exist between data entities residing in a corporate data source

- The Service Locator pattern that abstracts away how EJB and JDBC connections are retrieved from the database

In addition to these core patterns, this chapter also provided a number of strategies for dealing with such issues as:

- Primary key generation

- Concurrency management

- Transaction management

- Performance strategy

- Migration strategies for moving your existing applications to a persistence framework

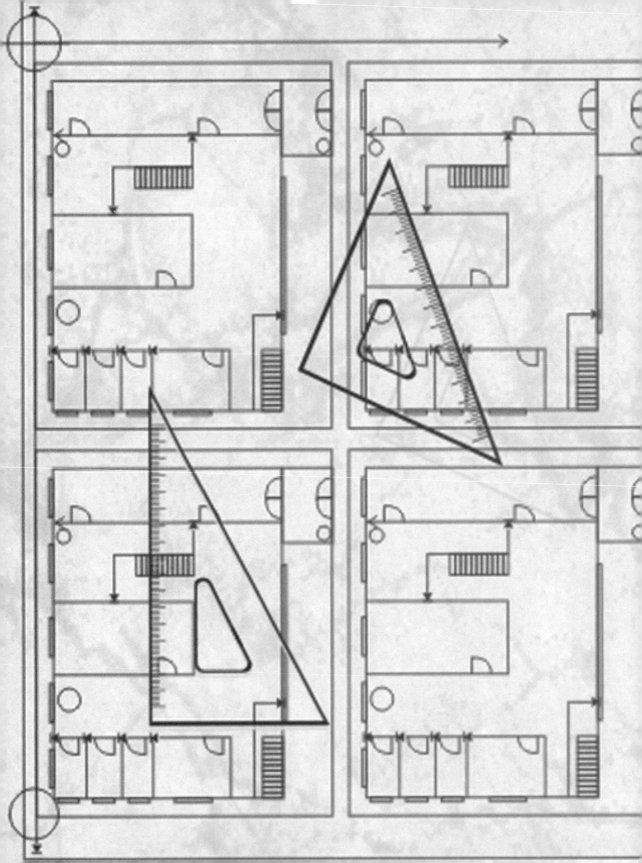

4

Patterns Applied to Improve Performance and Scalability

There are many design considerations that must be made when using the J2EE platform. Some of these, like performance and scalability, are not specific to J2EE but are typical of any distributed system. They are elements of design that can be significantly improved by the use of appropriate idioms and patterns. Conversely, an ill-conceived design can result in a system that performs so poorly that no amount of additional hardware will improve the situation.

None of the pattern catalogs explicitly identify a category for performance or scalability. However, there are patterns that address performance and scalability concerns. The choice of a pattern may not be purely for performance reasons, but it is helpful to understand those patterns that can provide performance improvements.

In this chapter we'll look at a number of patterns that lead to a better performing and more scalable design – most of which we have already seen in the earlier chapters.

What Causes Performance Problems?

One of the significant differences (from a performance viewpoint) between a standalone application and one built using the J2EE framework is the number of virtual machines (VMs) involved. A simple standalone application runs in a single VM. An application deployed on a J2EE framework can have many VMs (the web server, servlet container, application server, and so on). What's more, all of these VMs could be on completely separate physical machines. Even if they are not physically distributed, a J2EE application will need to communicate between these different VMs, and this can cause some significant performance problems.

Remote Method Invocation

The Java language itself does not provide a mechanism for making method invocations between VMs. However, there are a number of language extensions available that provide the necessary plumbing to forward a method invocation from an object in one VM to an object in another VM.

The base extension that provides this functionality is **Remote Method Invocation (RMI)**. RMI provides a set of classes and interfaces that allow us to transparently call remote objects (an object executing in a different JVM from its client). RMI also requires a low-level transport that allows objects to be marshaled into a request for transmission across the network. In J2EE, this protocol is called the **Internet Inter ORB Protocol (IIOP)**.

RMI hides the location of an object from a calling client. The remote object is accessible through an interface, which is implemented by a stub or a proxy. The proxy forwards any method calls to the remote object, blocks waiting for a reply, and then returns the result to the calling object. So the client application can treat the remote object as if it were local, by using a local reference to a local proxy that communicates with the remote object.

Of course it's not quite this simple. Each remote call has to go through three layers of abstraction:

❑ **The Stubs/Skeletons Layer**
This layer intercepts method calls made by the client to the interface reference and redirects these calls to a remote object. It is worth remembering that stubs are specific to the client side, whereas skeletons are found on the server side.

❑ **The Remote Reference Layer**
This layer handles the details relating to interpreting and managing references made by clients to remote objects. It connects clients to remote objects that are running and exported on a server by a one-to-one connection link. In the Java 2 SDK, this layer was enhanced to support the activation framework (discussed later).

❑ **The Transport Layer**
This layer is based on TCP/IP connections between machines in a network. It provides basic connectivity, and some firewall penetration strategies.

The following diagram shows these three layers, along with the breakup of the transport layer. The descriptions on the right-hand side represent the OSI layers (OSI is concisely described at http://www.webopedia.com/TERM/O/OSI.html/):

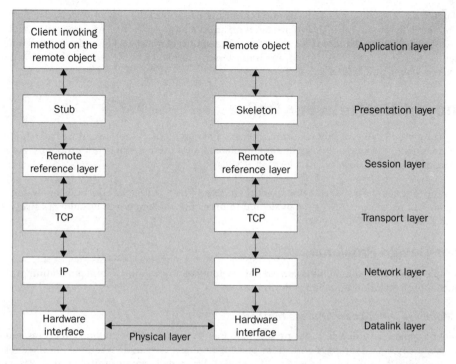

So you can see that although, from a development perspective, using a remote call seems quite simple, in reality there is lot of behind-the-scenes action taking place to make our remote calls seem local.

All EJB remote home interfaces (which extend `EJBHome`) and remote component interfaces (which extend `EJBObject`) use this mechanism for invoking method calls on remote objects. They are constrained by the RMI implementation requirements. The remote interface must extend `java.rmi.Remote` interface. This is done through extension of `EJBHome` and `EJBObject` both of which extend `java.rmi.Remote` interface. In addition, all method calls in the remote interface must also throw the `java.rmi.RemoteException`. The arguments and return types of remote methods are required to be Java primitives, serializable, or remote references. RMI normally passes arguments by value using object serialization, unlike in-VM method calls where object references are passed.

The proxy objects that are used by a remote client are not lightweight. They are complex resource-consuming objects. Their creation is resource intensive and happens usually as a result of some network call. If the client is truly remote (and not in the same VM as the target object), then a network socket will have been created connecting the client and target VMs.

Similarly, the server-side target object is also a complex resource-consuming animal. It is more complex than the client-side proxy. In a traditional RMI server, a remote object has its own equivalent of the client proxy. The server-side 'proxy' retrieves the requests sent from the client proxy, unpacks them, and invokes the appropriate method on the target object. With the advent of the application server, this may no longer be true since optimized server implementations can use a dispatching mechanism to field the incoming requests, and forward them to the target object. The server also provides caching mechanisms to handle large numbers of client requests by pooling object instances.

Although various caching mechanisms and optimizations support the server objects, the client often does not have the luxury of such sophisticated management mechanisms. An application that requires the client to hold many hundreds (or thousands) of remote references will be placing a significant burden on the client resources. One of the important performance bottlenecks with RMI is the effort involved in passing objects by value.

Latency of the Network Call

An in-VM method call typically takes microseconds to complete. A remote call will take milliseconds to complete, possibly seconds, and might not complete at all if there are network problems. A remote call is orders of magnitude slower than a local in-VM call.

Whenever remote interfaces are being used, there should be a conscious effort during design to reduce the number of network calls that are made and to maximize the amount of useful work that is being done as a result of the remote call.

Common Design Problems

Let's explore that last point in a bit more detail by looking at a couple of implementation problems that produce more network traffic than is desirable.

Private Members with Access/Mutate Methods

Consider a typical Java object. It has private data members and get/set methods to access and modify those data members. Mapping the methods of such an object directly to a remote interface results in many method calls to retrieve the state of the object. A remote client must first retrieve a remote reference to the object and then call multiple getXXX() access methods to transport the state data into the local VM. This model is not a problem with local intra-VM calls. However, when made remotely, the latency of the multiple getXXX() method calls become significant. In other words, each getXXX() call requires a network round trip that is vulnerable to network latency problems.

Chatty Objects

A common style of development uses a controller to implement a use case. The controller object containing business logic holds references to many other objects, and it mediates the interaction between these other objects. It typically implements some form of workflow. If this controller is implemented as a client-side object and the client is remote, many remote references are needed by the client. The client-side controller also makes numerous remote calls to the server-based objects. This type of chatty client should be avoided.

> Each time you need to make a remote call you incur a performance hit, as you are subject to network latency problems. Therefore to improve performance you need to reduce the number of remote calls.

What Causes Scalability Problems?

What characterizes a scalable system? Given some measurable range of a system's acceptable performance (the response time to a request, for example) and a measure of the system's workload (the number of concurrent users, for example), a system can be considered scalable if, as the workload increases, the performance measurement stays within the acceptable range of measure. Clearly, this increase cannot go on indefinitely.

At some point the system will become overloaded and the performance measurement will no longer remain within the acceptable range. Any given system will have some upper limit on its capacity. This is often measured as the number of concurrent connected users for a primarily web-oriented system. Another useful measure of capacity is the number of transactions per second that the system can perform.

Tightly-Coupled Systems

Consider a user interacting with a system using a web browser. The underlying protocol will be HTTP or HTTPS, which are connection-based. The client browser opens a connection to the web server, sends a request, and then blocks waiting for a reply. When the reply is received, the browser presents the page to the user.

The request/reply model of interaction is the norm for browser-based activity. Slow web servers are an accepted part of the Internet. Moreover, since a person's ability to assimilate information is magnitudes slower than that of a computer system, it is considered an acceptable model of interaction. However, for system-to-system interaction, delays of seconds should not be tolerated.

There are two basic problems with the blocking request/reply model:

- ❏ The first is the blocking client. If the response is too slow, the client may simply give up or go elsewhere.

- ❏ The second problem is the constraint that the blocking client places on the server. The server must react immediately and send the reply as soon as possible.

The number of connected clients thus dictates the load on the server. The server doesn't have any choice about how or when to schedule requests. Each request must be responded to as quickly as possible. These types of connection-oriented systems are said to be tightly-coupled. To improve scalability, we need to reduce the amount of coupling between the different interacting components in the system.

We can reduce this coupling through a number of strategies, which in turn can lead to better performance and better scalability of the system.

Synchronous vs. Asynchronous Behavior

In a system built on the J2EE platform, much of the distributed communication is of a synchronous blocking-call nature. This is true for both client-side interactions such as browser access to the web server, and inter-component interaction such as a servlet invoking methods on a session bean. Such behavior is a natural extension of the intra-VM method call. Technologies such as CORBA and RMI present remote references in such a way that the remote object appears to be local. This means that we also get the blocking behavior of intra-VM calls, but because we know there will be network latency, we know that we will be blocking for all this time. However, it doesn't have to be this way.

159

Asynchronous Calls

In an asynchronous model of interaction, the client sends a request and then forgets about it and carries on with the next operation. Sometime later, the request is delivered to a server that processes the request. If the client needs confirmation that the request has been processed, or needs to receive information as a result of the processing, a second interaction between client and server can take place.

Obviously, this model of interaction will not be appropriate for all business processes but the more calls you make asynchronously, the less strain you put on the server resources.

Indirection

One of the more obvious ways to improve scalability is to simply throw more hardware at the problem. This can be done either horizontally (clustering resources across a tier) or vertically (increasing the resources such as memory, CPUs, and so on). However, if our components are tightly-coupled such that they are explicitly linked to the location of each other, it becomes considerably more difficult to add hardware resources because we will need to update clients with the additional network configurations for the new hardware resources.

Therefore, what we need to do is reduce the coupling through indirection such that clients do not know or care about the server resources they are utilizing. We can then add more server resources without affecting our client.

The City Break Booking Application

To demonstrate the application of patterns in this chapter, we shall be using a city break booking application that coordinates the booking of hotels and flights for a particular city vacation. The main use cases that we shall be concentrating on are:

- **View available vacations**
  See a list of all cities contained in the database for vacationing

- **Get a City Break vacation quote**

  - Choose the city

  - Choose the hotel

  - Choose the flights (outbound and inbound)

- **Book a City Break vacation**

  - Either register as a new customer or login as an existing customer

  - Book the vacation using the previously constructed quote

- **Register as a new customer**

  - Send new customer details

- **Login as an existing customer**

  - Send e-mail and password details to login to the system

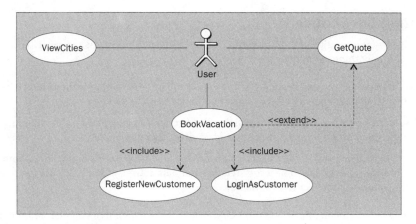

Our entity domain objects will consist of:

❑ **City**
Contains information on the city including description and airport

❑ **Hotel**
Contains information on the available hotels in each city including name, description, and the number of available rooms

❑ **Flight**
Contains information on all flights including flight times, destinations, and available seats

❑ **Customer**
Contains the basic customer information that can be used for logins and for tracking bookings

❑ **Booking**
Collates the various information on flights, hotels, and customers

We will be implementing these entities as entity beans with container-managed persistence (2.0):

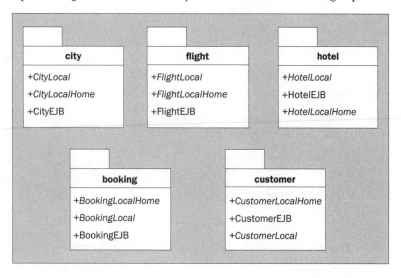

Implementing the Entities

All our entity beans are quite straightforward. They all use container-managed persistence and local interfaces. The only things of note are:

❑ We're using a `Counter` session bean to create the unique ID that is the primary key for each entity. This `Counter` bean is the same as the one used in Chapter 3.

❑ The `Counter` bean is itself located using the Service Locator pattern. Its implementation is a modification of the `ServiceLocator` class described in Chapter 3.

❑ We will be using the Value Object pattern over the course of this application. Some of the entity beans use a value object for creation and data retrieval. We'll discuss the benefits of using value objects later in the chapter.

We'll only provide the bean implementation classes here for each entity. You can find the home and component interfaces in the download source code for this chapter (available from http://www.wrox.com/).

These entity beans are somewhat simplified versions of what a full scale implementation of such a system would require, to reduce the complexity of demonstrating the patterns in action.

The City Entity Bean

The `City` entity bean contains three properties: the city name, a description of the city, and the name of the airport that services this city. This is used in conjunction with the `Flight` entity later to choose flights to and from the city:

```
package entity.city;

import javax.ejb.*;
import common.*;
import common.counter.*;

public abstract class CityEJB implements EntityBean {

  public abstract Long getId();
  public abstract void setId(Long id);

  public abstract String getName();
  public abstract void setName(String name);

  public abstract String getDescription();
  public abstract void setDescription(String desc);

  public abstract String getAirport();
  public abstract void setAirport(String airport);

  public Long ejbCreate(String name, String desc, String airport)
      throws CreateException {

    try {
      ServiceLocator locator = ServiceLocator.getInstance();
      CounterHome home = (CounterHome)
```

```
            locator.getEJBHome(ServiceLocator.COUNTER);
        Counter counter = home.create();
        setId(counter.getNextVal("CITY"));
        setName(name);
        setDescription(desc);
        setAirport(airport);
    } catch (ServiceLocatorException sle) {
        throw new EJBException(sle);
    } catch (java.rmi.RemoteException re) {
        throw new EJBException(re);
    }

    return null;
}

  public void ejbPostCreate(String name, String desc, String airport)
    throws CreateException {}

public void ejbActivate() {}
public void ejbPassivate() {}
public void ejbLoad() {}
public void ejbRemove() {}
public void ejbStore() {}
public void setEntityContext(EntityContext ctx) {}
public void unsetEntityContext() {}

}
```

The Flight Entity Bean

The Flight entity bean contains eight properties: destination and originating airports, departure and arrival times, airline, price of flight, the number of seats available to the operator on this flight, and the date of the flight:

```
package entity.flight;

import javax.ejb.*;
import vo.FlightVO;
import common.*;
import common.counter.*;

public abstract class FlightEJB implements EntityBean {

    public abstract Long getId();
    public abstract void setId(Long id);

    public abstract String getFrom();
    public abstract void setFrom(String from);

    public abstract String getTo();
    public abstract void setTo(String to);

    public abstract String getDepartureTime();
    public abstract void setDepartureTime(String time);
```

```
    public abstract String getArrivalTime();
    public abstract void setArrivalTime(String time);

    public abstract String getAirline();
    public abstract void setAirline(String airline);

    public abstract int getAvailableSeats();
    public abstract void setAvailableSeats(int seats);

    public abstract String getDate();
    public abstract void setDate(String date);

    public abstract double getPrice();
    public abstract void setPrice(double price);

    public Long ejbCreate(String from, String to, String dept,
                          String arrival, String airline, int seats,
                          String date, double price)
        throws CreateException {

      try {
        ServiceLocator locator = ServiceLocator.getInstance();
        CounterHome home = (CounterHome)
            locator.getEJBHome(ServiceLocator.COUNTER);
        Counter counter = home.create();

        setId(counter.getNextVal("FLIGHT"));
        setFrom(from);
        setTo(to);
        setDepartureTime(dept);
        setArrivalTime(arrival);
        setAirline(airline);
        setAvailableSeats(seats);
        setDate(date);
        setPrice(price);
      } catch (ServiceLocatorException sle) {
        throw new CreateException();
      } catch (java.rmi.RemoteException re) {
        throw new CreateException();
      }

      return null;
    }

    public void ejbPostCreate(String from, String to, String dept,
                              String arrival, String airline, int seats,
                              String date, double price)
        throws CreateException {}

    public void ejbActivate() {}
    public void ejbPassivate() {}
    public void ejbLoad() {}
    public void ejbRemove() {}
    public void ejbStore() {}
```

```
public void setEntityContext(EntityContext ctx) {}
public void unsetEntityContext() {}
```

This bean can return its data as a `FlightVO` value object and also has a business method that reduces the number of available seats when a booking is made:

```
public FlightVO getFlightInfo() {

    FlightVO vo = new FlightVO();

    vo.flightId = getId();
    vo.from = getFrom();
    vo.to = getTo();
    vo.departure = getDepartureTime();
    vo.arrival = getArrivalTime();
    vo.airline = getAirline();
    vo.availableSeats = getAvailableSeats();
    vo.date = getDate();
    vo.price = getPrice();

    return vo;
}

public void bookSeats(int seats) {
    setAvailableSeats(getAvailableSeats() - seats);
}
}
```

This entity bean also requires a finder method that allows us to search for flights by date, destination airport, and originating airport (`findByFlightDateToFrom()`). The EJB QL needed is:

```
SELECT OBJECT(f) FROM flight f WHERE f.date=?1 AND f.from=?2 AND f.to=?3
```

The Hotel Entity Bean

The `Hotel` entity bean has five properties: hotel name, hotel description, location that maps to a city, number of available rooms, and price per room per night:

```
package entity.hotel;

import javax.ejb.*;
import common.*;
import common.counter.*;
import vo.HotelVO;

public abstract class HotelEJB implements EntityBean {

    public abstract Long getId();
    public abstract void setId(Long id);

    public abstract String getName();
    public abstract void setName(String name);
```

```
public abstract String getLocation();
public abstract void setLocation(String location);

public abstract int getAvailableRooms();
public abstract void setAvailableRooms(int rooms);

public abstract String getDescription();
public abstract void setDescription(String desc);

public abstract double getPricePerNight();
public abstract void setPricePerNight(double price);

public Long ejbCreate(String name, String location, int noRooms,
                String description, double price)
   throws CreateException {

   try {
      ServiceLocator locator = ServiceLocator.getInstance();
      CounterHome home = (CounterHome)
         locator.getEJBHome(ServiceLocator.COUNTER);
      Counter counter = home.create();

      setId(counter.getNextVal("HOTEL"));
      setName(name);
      setLocation(location);
      setAvailableRooms(noRooms);
      setDescription(description);
      setPricePerNight(price);
   } catch (ServiceLocatorException sle) {
      throw new CreateException();
   } catch (java.rmi.RemoteException re) {
      throw new CreateException();
   }

   return null;
}

 public void ejbPostCreate(String name, String location, int noRooms,
                String description, double price)
    throws CreateException {}

public void ejbActivate() {}
public void ejbPassivate() {}
public void ejbLoad() {}
public void ejbRemove() {}
public void ejbStore() {}
public void setEntityContext(EntityContext ctx) {}
public void unsetEntityContext() {}
```

As with the Flight entity bean, the hotel data can be returned as a value object and there is a business method that reduces the number of available rooms when a booking is made:

```
public HotelVO getHotelInfo() {

    HotelVO vo = new HotelVO();

    vo.id = getId();
    vo.name = getName();
    vo.description = getDescription();
    vo.location = getLocation();
    vo.noAvailableRooms = getAvailableRooms();
    vo.pricePerNight = getPricePerNight();

    return vo;
}

public void bookRooms(int rooms) {
    setAvailableRooms(getAvailableRooms() - rooms);
}

}
```

There is also a finder method on this bean that allows us to search for all hotels within a specific city, in other words by location (findByLocation()). The EJB QL is:

```
SELECT OBJECT(h) FROM hotel h WHERE h.location=?1
```

The Booking Entity Bean

The Booking entity bean has eight properties that correspond to the data that is needed to book a city break vacation: the ID of the customer, the ID of the hotel, the number of rooms required at that hotel, the ID for the outbound and inbound flights, the number of seats required on those flight, the price of the vacation, and the starting and end date:

```
package entity.booking;

import javax.ejb.*;
import vo.BookingVO;
import common.*;
import common.counter.*;

public abstract class BookingEJB implements EntityBean {

    public abstract Long getId();
    public abstract void setId(Long id);

    public abstract Long getCustomerId();
    public abstract void setCustomerId(Long id);

    public abstract Long getFlightIdOut();
    public abstract void setFlightIdOut(Long id);

    public abstract Long getFlightIdIn();
    public abstract void setFlightIdIn(Long id);
```

```
public abstract Long getHotelId();
public abstract void setHotelId(Long id);

public abstract double getPrice();
public abstract void setPrice(double price);

public abstract int getNoRooms();
public abstract void setNoRooms(int rooms);

public abstract int getNoSeats();
public abstract void setNoSeats(int seats);

public abstract String getFromDate();
public abstract void setFromDate(String from);

public abstract String getToDate();
public abstract void setToDate(String to);
```

A booking can only be made through the use of a BookingVO value object:

```
public Long ejbCreate(BookingVO vo) throws CreateException {

   try {
      ServiceLocator locator = ServiceLocator.getInstance();
      CounterHome home = (CounterHome)
         locator.getEJBHome(ServiceLocator.COUNTER);
      Counter counter = home.create();

      setId(counter.getNextVal("BOOKING"));
      setCustomerId(vo.customerId);
      setFlightIdOut(vo.flightIdOut);
      setFlightIdIn(vo.flightIdIn);
      setHotelId(vo.hotelId);
      setPrice(vo.price);
      setNoRooms(vo.noRooms);
      setNoSeats(vo.noSeats);
      setFromDate(vo.fromDate);
      setToDate(vo.toDate);
   } catch (ServiceLocatorException e) {
      throw new EJBException(e);
   } catch (java.rmi.RemoteException re) {
      throw new EJBException(re);
   }

   return null;
}

public void ejbPostCreate(BookingVO vo) throws CreateException {}
public void ejbActivate() {}
public void ejbPassivate() {}
public void ejbLoad() {}
public void ejbRemove() {}
public void ejbStore() {}
```

```
      public void setEntityContext(EntityContext ctx) {}
      public void unsetEntityContext() {}
}
```

The Customer Entity Bean

The Customer entity bean has eight fields for a customer (although it could easily have many more): the name of the customer, several fields for the address, state, zip code, e-mail address and password for future logins, and a record of previous bookings made:

```
package entity.customer;

import javax.ejb.*;
import vo.CustomerVO;
import common.*;
import common.counter.*;

public abstract class CustomerEJB implements EntityBean {

    public abstract Long getId();
    public abstract void setId(Long id);

    public abstract String getName();
    public abstract void setName(String name);

    public abstract String getAddress1();
    public abstract void setAddress1(String addr1);

    public abstract String getAddress2();
    public abstract void setAddress2(String addr2);

    public abstract String getState();
    public abstract void setState(String state);

    public abstract String getZip();
    public abstract void setZip(String zip);

    public abstract String getEmail();
    public abstract void setEmail(String email);

    public abstract String getPassword();
    public abstract void setPassword(String pwd);

    public abstract String getBookings();
    public abstract void setBookings(String id);
```

As with the Booking entity, a new Customer can only be created using a CustomerVO value object:

```
      public Long ejbCreate(CustomerVO vo) throws CreateException {

          try {
             ServiceLocator locator = ServiceLocator.getInstance();
             CounterHome home = (CounterHome)
                locator.getEJBHome(ServiceLocator.COUNTER);
```

169

```
        Counter counter = home.create();

        setId(counter.getNextVal("CUSTOMER"));
        setName(vo.name);
        setAddress1(vo.addr1);
        setAddress2(vo.addr2);
        setState(vo.state);
        setZip(vo.zip);
        setEmail(vo.email);
        setPassword(vo.pwd);
    } catch (ServiceLocatorException e) {
      throw new CreateException();
    } catch (java.rmi.RemoteException re) {
      throw new CreateException();
    }
    return null;
  }

  public void ejbPostCreate(CustomerVO vo) throws CreateException {}

  public void ejbActivate() {}
  public void ejbPassivate() {}
  public void ejbLoad() {}
  public void ejbRemove() {}
  public void ejbStore() {}
  public void setEntityContext(EntityContext ctx) {}
  public void unsetEntityContext() {}
```

The bean can also return the customer information as a value object (used after successful login):

```
  public CustomerVO getCustomer() {

    CustomerVO vo = new CustomerVO();

    vo.customerId = getId();
    vo.name = getName();
    vo.addr1 = getAddress1();
    vo.addr2 = getAddress2();
    vo.state = getState();
    vo.zip = getZip();
    vo.email = getEmail();
    vo.pwd = getPassword();

    return vo;
  }
```

Finally, there is an additional business method that allows us to record what bookings this customer has placed, by recording the booking ID as pipe-delimited string:

```
  public void addBooking(Long id) {
    setBookings(getBookings() + "|" +id.toString());
  }
}
```

There is also one finder that takes the e-mail address and password and uses them to check if an existing customer can login to the system (findByEmailAndPassword()). The EJB QL we need is:

```
SELECT OBJECT(c) FROM customer c WHERE c.email=?1 AND c.password=?2
```

Now that our basic entity beans are in place, let's take a look at what design patterns we can use to implement our use cases.

Identifying Patterns to Improve Performance

Within the context of the J2EE platform, the number of VMs and the potential for network calls is dependent on the physical deployment of the system. A fully distributed application incorporating a web server, servlet container, EJB container, and database may have up to four separate VMs.

However, many application server vendors provide an optimized installation that executes the servlet container and EJB container in the same VM. Further optimizations that circumvent the pass-by-value semantics of the remote interface may be done. This avoids the parameters of a method call being copied but is contrary to the specification.

However, these optimizations can result in significant performance benefits circumventing some of the issues described above. But it is not compliant with the specification and is therefore not guaranteed to be available from all application-server vendors, nor will it lead to a portable solution. Furthermore, it may not be possible to physically locate the servlet container and EJB container together, particularly where complex load balancing and firewall mechanisms are in place.

A typical deployment utilizes a separate servlet container and EJB container with the database running on a dedicated machine. A web-based client thus accesses the system via the servlet container. Non-web-based clients (other systems for example) will access the system via the EJB container. In both cases, the remote calls are between a remote client and the EJB container, as access to the EJBs will be through remote interfaces (EJBHome and EJBObject). So, it is in this area that the performance patterns are the most effective.

The Service Locator Pattern

A client obtains a resource reference either by retrieving it from the JNDI naming service or by receiving it as a return value from another method call. In any reasonably complex J2EE application, there are going to a fair number of resources that need to be accessed. However, looking up and retrieving a resource reference can be fairly labor-intensive process, especially if it occurs across tiers.

In addition, in the case of EJB references, a client first needs access to the EJBHome (a remote call) and then, to do something useful with the home object, subsequent remote calls are required.

The Service Locator pattern, if used with the Singleton pattern, can be used to implement a caching mechanism to store initial context objects and references to the factory objects (EJBHome, JMS connection factories, JDBC data sources, and so on), thus reducing intensive JNDI lookup and the number of remote calls required:

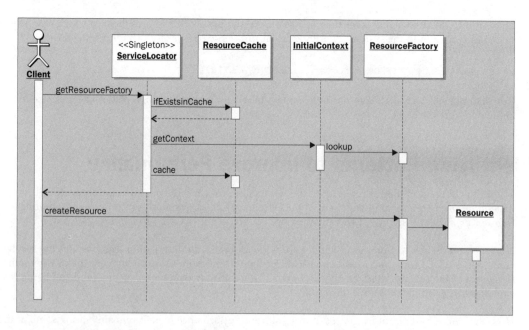

Implementing Service Locator in the City Break Application

We've already seen a Service Locator implementation in the previous chapter. Here we simply extend it so that we can cache EJBLocalHomes as well as JMS resources (we'll see why later), and obviously update the constants to be appropriate for the beans in this application.

The full source can be found in the download for this chapter (available from http://www.wrox.com/).

To get the performance improvements through using the Service Locator, we need to cache any resource factories:

```
private static Hashtable ejbHomeCache                    = null;
private static Hashtable dataSourceCache                 = null;
private static Hashtable queueConnectionFactoryCache     = null;
private static Hashtable queueCache                      = null;
private static Hashtable ejbLocalHomeCache               = null;
```

Then whenever we use the ServiceLocator to get a resource factory, we can first check to see if we have already cached it. For example:

```
if (ejbLocalHomeCache.containsKey(serviceName)){
    ejbLocalHome = (EJBLocalHome) ejbLocalHomeCache.get(serviceName);
    return ejbLocalHome;
} else {
```

If it's the first time we've requested the resource, we look it up and then place the reference in the cache:

```
                  Context ctx = new InitialContext();
                  Object jndiRef = ctx.lookup(serviceName);
                  ejbLocalHome = (EJBLocalHome) jndiRef;
                  ejbLocalHomeCache.put(serviceName, ejbLocalHome);
                  return ejbLocalHome;
              }
```

Now let's quickly examine the new methods. Firstly, the getLocalHome() method is nearly identical to getEJBHome() except that obviously it uses the EJBLocalHome interface instead of the remote EJBHome:

```
...
...
   public EJBLocalHome getEJBLocalHome(int pServiceId)
     throws ServiceLocatorException{

     //Trying to find the JNDI Name for the requested service
     String serviceName = getServiceName(pServiceId);
     EJBLocalHome ejbLocalHome    = null;

     try {
       //Checking to see if I can find the EJBLocalHome interface in cache
       if (ejbLocalHomeCache.containsKey(serviceName)){
           ejbLocalHome = (EJBLocalHome) ejbLocalHomeCache.get(serviceName);
           return ejbLocalHome;
       } else {
       //If I could not find the EJBLocalHome interface in the cache,
       //look it up and then cache it
         Context ctx = new InitialContext();
         Object jndiRef = ctx.lookup(serviceName);
         ejbLocalHome = (EJBLocalHome) jndiRef;
         ejbLocalHomeCache.put(serviceName, ejbLocalHome);
         return ejbLocalHome;
       }
     } catch(NamingException e){
         throw new ServiceLocatorException(
           "Naming exception error in ServiceLocator.getEJBLocalHome()" + e);
     } catch(Exception e){
         throw new ServiceLocatorException(
           "General exception in ServiceLocator.getEJBLocalHome" + e);
     }
   }
...
...
```

Then we have two methods that return and cache a JMS QueueConnection and Queue respectively:

```
...
...
   public QueueConnection getJMSQueueConn(int pServiceId)
       throws ServiceLocatorException {

     //Getting JNDI Service Name
```

173

```
      String serviceName = getServiceName(pServiceId);
      QueueConnection qc = null;

      //Check to see if requested service is in cache
      try   {
         if (queueConnectionFactoryCache.containsKey(serviceName)) {
            QueueConnectionFactory qcf = (QueueConnectionFactory)
               queueConnectionFactoryCache.get(serviceName);
            qc = qcf.createQueueConnection();
         } else {
            Context ctx = new InitialContext();
            QueueConnectionFactory qcf = (QueueConnectionFactory)
               ctx.lookup(serviceName);
            queueConnectionFactoryCache.put(serviceName, qcf);
            qc = qcf.createQueueConnection();
         }

      } catch(JMSException e){
         throw new ServiceLocatorException(
            "A JMS exception has occurred in ServiceLocator.getJMSQueueConn()"
            + e);
      } catch(NamingException e){
         throw new ServiceLocatorException(
            "A JNDI Naming exception has occurred in " +
            "ServiceLocator.getJMSQueueConn()" + e);
      } catch(Exception e){
         throw new ServiceLocatorException(
            "An exception has occurred in ServiceLocator.getJMSQueueConn()"
            + e);
      }
      return qc;
   }

   public Queue getJMSQueue(int pServiceId) throws ServiceLocatorException {

      String serviceName = getServiceName(pServiceId);
      Queue newQ = null;

      try   {
         if (queueCache.containsKey(serviceName)) {
            newQ = (Queue) queueCache.get(serviceName);
         } else {
            Context ctx = new InitialContext();
            newQ = (Queue) ctx.lookup(serviceName);
         }
      } catch(NamingException e){
         throw new ServiceLocatorException(
            "A JNDI Naming exception has occurred in " +
            "ServiceLocator.getJMSQueue()" + e);
      } catch(Exception e){
         throw new ServiceLocatorException(
            "An exception has occurred in ServiceLocator.getJMSQueue()" + e);
      }
```

```
      return newQ;
  }
  ...
  ...
```

We'll be seeing this `ServiceLocator` class used quite a lot over the rest of the application.

The Value Object Pattern

Entity beans mix persistence and remoteness with many individual get/set methods (for persistence) exposed in the component interface. This forces the developer into a situation where a client has to make many fine-grained calls to retrieve and update the state data of the entity. As we just discussed, this form of get/set methods is far from ideal as each will require a remote call. The number of remote calls should be reduced as much as possible.

The Value Object pattern can reduce the remote calls to just one. A value object (VO) packages all the state data into a single serializable object that is then passed between the client and entity. The VO must be serializable because it will be used as an RMI parameter or return value. The VO provides the remote client with a local object graph that is representative of what is on the server:

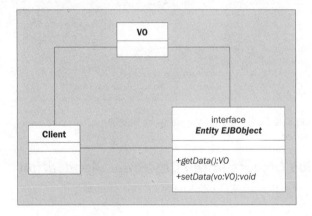

Local Interfaces

At this point, you are probably thinking, "What about local interfaces?". The EJB 2.0 specification included a significant addition in the form of the local interface. Local interfaces provide a means to implement the home and component interfaces without using RMI. In other words, they don't implement `java.rmi.Remote`. Consequently, we could simply specify our get/set methods on a local interface and thus avoid the remote overhead. In addition, local interfaces avoid the performance bottleneck of pass-by-value objects. Using local interfaces, we can pass by reference instead.

However, local interfaces are not quite the same as a standard intra-VM method call. Local interfaces avoid the overhead of an RMI call but the EJB container still has to interpose itself between your client call and the EJB object to provide the various services that are the point of EJBs. So each local interface call has an overhead of its own. In addition, local interfaces are only callable from within the EJB container. Therefore, at some point in our design, we are going to need to make the remote call as our clients will be remote. Either way, the use of the Value Object pattern will help simplify and improve the performance of our design.

Composite Value Objects and the Value Object Assembler

A problem with the above approach is that the information needed by the client is unlikely to map directly to the entity bean structure. A client will typically need information from several entity beans. In this case, a VO can be used that includes what the client needs to fulfill its goal. This sort of workflow-specific VO may include data from different sources packaged together for transport to the client. To put together these domain-specific value objects, we are going to need the Value Object Assembler design pattern.

The Value Object Assembler pattern allows us to further reduce remote calls by amalgamating access to a number of entities into one access point. Typically the assembler would be implemented as a session bean that accesses the entity beans through local interfaces – see the Session Façade pattern:

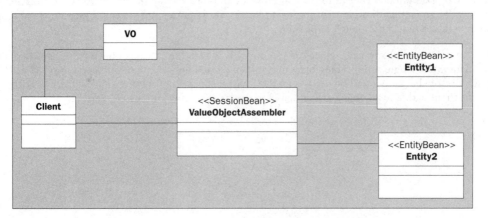

Rather than making repeated trips across the network, it's better to make a single remote call that returns everything needed.

Implementing Value Objects in the City Break Application

For our City Break application we will be using five value objects:

- ❑ CustomerVO
- ❑ BookingVO
- ❑ FlightVO
- ❑ HotelVO
- ❑ CityBreakVO

Most of these value objects map directly to the entity to which they relate. However, the CityBreakVO is actually an amalgamation of a couple of entities (City and Hotel) so we will need to implement the Value Object Assembler pattern to put this object together.

The implementation of these value objects is very straightforward. Note that they need to implement Serializable so that they can be passed to and from our EJBs.

Hotel Value Object

The following is the Hotel Value Object interface:

```
package vo;

public class HotelVO implements java.io.Serializable {
    public Long id;
    public String name;
    public String location;
    public int noAvailableRooms;
    public String description;
    public double pricePerNight;
}
```

Flight Value Object

The following is the Flight Value Object interface:

```
package vo;

public class FlightVO implements java.io.Serializable {
    public Long flightId;
    public String from;
    public String to;
    public String departure;
    public String arrival;
    public String airline;
    public int availableSeats;
    public String date;
    public double price;
}
```

Booking Value Object

The following is the implementation of the Booking Value Object:

```
package vo;

public class BookingVO implements java.io.Serializable {
    public Long hotelId;
    public Long flightIdOut;
    public Long flightIdIn;
    public Long customerId;
    public String fromDate;
    public String toDate;
    public int noSeats;
    public int noRooms;
    public double price;
}
```

Customer Value Object

The following is the Customer Value Object interface:

```
package vo;

public class CustomerVO implements java.io.Serializable {
   public Long customerId;
   public String name;
   public String addr1;
   public String addr2;
   public String state;
   public String zip;
   public String email;
   public String pwd;
}
```

City Break Value Object

The `CityBreakVO` is a little more complicated because it contains a collection of `HotelVO` objects:

```
package vo;

import java.util.Collection;
import java.util.LinkedList;

public class CityBreakVO implements java.io.Serializable {

   public String cityName;
   public String cityDesc;
   public String airport;

   private LinkedList hotels_list = new LinkedList();

   public Collection getHotels() {
      return hotels_list;
   }

   public void addHotel(HotelVO vo) {
      hotels_list.add(vo);
   }
}
```

The Value Object Assembler

As our `CityBreakVO` is assembled from the `City` and `Hotel` entities, we are going to need an assembly routine that handles the connection to the `City` and `Hotel` entity beans and constructs the `HotelVO` value objects:

```
private CityBreakVO assembleCityBreakValueObject(Long cityId) {

   CityBreakVO cbvo = new CityBreakVO();
   try {
      //First get info on the city
```

```
        ServiceLocator locator = ServiceLocator.getInstance();
        CityLocalHome chome = (CityLocalHome)
                        locator.getEJBLocalHome(ServiceLocator.CITY);
        CityLocal city = chome.findByPrimaryKey(cityId);
        cbvo.cityName = city.getName();
        cbvo.cityDesc = city.getDescription();
        cbvo.airport = city.getAirport();

        //Then get hotels for this city
        HotelLocalHome hhome = (HotelLocalHome)
                        locator.getEJBLocalHome(ServiceLocator.HOTEL);
        Collection hotels = hhome.findByLocation(cbvo.cityName);

        //For each hotel create a Hotel value object
        Iterator iter = hotels.iterator();
        while (iter.hasNext()) {
           Object ref = iter.next();
           HotelLocal hotel = (HotelLocal) ref;
           HotelVO hvo = hotel.getHotelInfo();
           cbvo.addHotel(hvo);
        }
    } catch (Exception e) {
      throw new EJBException(e);
    }
}
```

Note that we're using the Service Locator pattern to look up our EJBLocalHome objects. The following is the code for creating an instance of the Service Locator and getting the CityLocalHome object:

```
        ServiceLocator locator = ServiceLocator.getInstance();
        CityLocalHome chome = (CityLocalHome)
                        locator.getEJBLocalHome(ServiceLocator.CITY);
```

You'll see where the code fits into the greater application in a just a moment.

The Session Façade Pattern

The controller style of implementation results in interfaces that require a client to make several calls to business-tier EJBs collecting context and storing workflow or session information between calls. If this interaction is moved to the server, the multiple network calls can be reduced. The Session Façade pattern introduces a coarse-grained interface to do just this.

The client has a single remote reference to the Session Façade rather than many remote references to each of the underlying EJBs (typically entity beans). The client has a single object to deal with, and as the Session Façade provides coarse-grained methods (typically mapped to use cases), it should only make occasional remote calls to the façade:

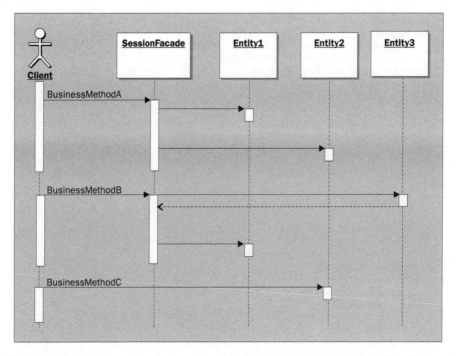

Calls from the remote client to the Session Façade will be remote by nature but the calls from the façade to the supporting EJBs can take advantage of container-provided optimizations for intra-VM calls, and in EJB 2.0, through local interfaces. This can be improved further by using value objects in conjunction with the façade.

Implementing Session Façade in the City Break Application

The Session Façade provides a coarse-grained representation of the business interface for clients to use. Therefore, the general strategy is to implement each use case, or related use cases as separate Session Façades.

In our City Break, we have five use cases that our client uses:

❑ View available vacations

❑ Get a City Break vacation quote

❑ Book a City Break vacation

❑ Register as a new customer

❑ Log in as an existing customer

We could implement five session beans, one for each use case, but on closer examination we can see that a number of use cases are related. Therefore, we will construct only two Session Façades:

❑ CityBreakFacade

    ❑ View available vacations

- ❑   Get a City Break vacation quote
- ❑   Book a City Break vacation
❑   `CustomerFacade`
- ❑   Register as a new customer
- ❑   Log in as an existing customer

Each of these will be a stateless session bean that uses the Service Locator pattern to look up the relevant entity beans and will use value objects to pass the data back and forth between the session layer and the entity layer:

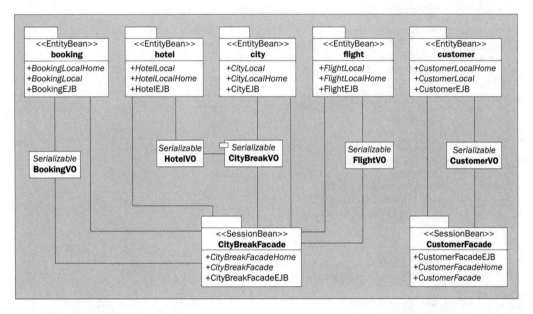

The CustomerFacade Session Bean

Here is the implementation for our `CustomerFacade` bean. We need to implement two use cases; therefore, our remote interface will contain a business method for each:

```
package facade.customer;

import javax.ejb.*;
import java.rmi.RemoteException;
import vo.CustomerVO;

public interface CustomerFacade extends EJBObject {

    public void registerNewCustomer(CustomerVO vo) throws RemoteException;

    public CustomerVO loginCustomer(String email, String pwd)
        throws RemoteException;
}
```

The following is the implementation of each business method:

```
package facade.customer;

import javax.ejb.*;
import common.*;
import vo.CustomerVO;
import entity.customer.*;

public class CustomerFacadeEJB implements SessionBean {

    public void ejbCreate() throws CreateException {}
    public void ejbRemove() {}
    public void ejbActivate() {}
    public void ejbPassivate() {}
    public void setSessionContext(SessionContext ctx) {}
    public void unsetSessionContext() {}

    //Create a new customer from Customer value object
    public void registerNewCustomer(CustomerVO vo) {

        try {
            ServiceLocator locator = ServiceLocator.getInstance();
            CustomerLocalHome home = (CustomerLocalHome)
                locator.getEJBLocalHome(ServiceLocator.CUSTOMER);
            home.create(vo);
        } catch (Exception e) {
            throw new EJBException (e);
        }
    }

    //Return customer details from a customer's email and password
    public CustomerVO loginCustomer(String email, String pwd) {

        CustomerVO vo = null;

        try {
            ServiceLocator locator = ServiceLocator.getInstance();
            CustomerLocalHome home = (CustomerLocalHome)
                locator.getEJBLocalHome(ServiceLocator.CUSTOMER);
            CustomerLocal cust = home.findByEmailandPassword(email, pwd);
            vo = cust.getCustomer();
        } catch (Exception e) {
            throw new EJBException(e);
        }

        return vo;
    }
}
```

The CityBreakFacade Session Bean

Our `CityBreakFacade` bean is somewhat more complex in that it needs three of the use cases:

```
package facade.citybreak;

import javax.ejb.*;
import java.util.Hashtable;
import java.util.ArrayList;
import vo.CityBreakVO;
import java.rmi.RemoteException;

public interface CityBreakFacade extends EJBObject {

    public Hashtable getCityList() throws RemoteException;

    public CityBreakVO getInfoOnCity(Long cityId) throws RemoteException;

    public ArrayList getFlightInfoForFlight(String date, String from,
                                            String to)
        throws RemoteException;

}
```

In addition, in our bean implementation class, we also need to use the Value Object Assembler pattern that we saw earlier:

```
package facade.citybreak;

import javax.ejb.*;
import common.*;
import entity.city.*;
import entity.hotel.*;
import entity.flight.*;
import vo.*;
import java.sql.*;
import java.util.Collection;
import java.util.Hashtable;
import java.util.Iterator;
import java.util.ArrayList;
import javax.rmi.PortableRemoteObject;

public class CityBreakFacadeEJB implements SessionBean {

    public void ejbCreate() throws CreateException {}
    public void ejbRemove() {}
    public void ejbActivate() {}
    public void ejbPassivate() {}
    public void setSessionContext(SessionContext ctx) {}
    public void unsetSessionContext() {}

    //Return a CityBreak Value object for a specific city
    public CityBreakVO getInfoOnCity(Long cityId) {
```

```
        CityBreakVO cbvo = assembleCityBreakValueObject(cityId);

      return cbvo;
   }

   private CityBreakVO assembleCityBreakValueObject(Long cityId) {
      ...
   }

   //Get flights that match a specific date between one airport and another
   public ArrayList getFlightInfoForFlight(String date, String from,
                                           String to) {

      ArrayList flights = new ArrayList();

      try   {
         ServiceLocator locator = ServiceLocator.getInstance();
         FlightLocalHome fhome = (FlightLocalHome)
            locator.getEJBLocalHome(ServiceLocator.FLIGHT);
         Collection flightmatchs =
            fhome.findByFlightDateToFrom(date, from, to);

         Iterator iter = flightmatchs.iterator();
         while (iter.hasNext()) {
            Object ref = iter.next();
            FlightLocal flight = (FlightLocal) ref;
            flights.add(flight.getFlightInfo());
         }

      } catch (Exception e) {
         throw new EJBException(e);
      }

      return flights;
   }
}
```

We are also using JDBC for Reading pattern here, to implement the getCityList() business method. (See the ServerSide.com patterns or the book *EJB Design Patterns*, Wiley (ISBN: 0-471-20831-0) for more on this pattern.) This is because we only require a list of all the cities in the datastore for read access. To use a findAll() method would be wasteful of server resources as there's no reason that we need to create a whole load of entity beans just for this once-only read-access. Therefore, we're going to use straight JDBC from the session bean itself to query the datastore. We use the Service Locator to get the datasource lookup:

```
   //Return a list of cities in database
   public Hashtable getCityList() {

      Hashtable tbl = new Hashtable();

      try {
         //Get connection to db
         ServiceLocator locator = ServiceLocator.getInstance();
```

```
        Connection conn = locator.getDBConn(ServiceLocator.CITYDB);
        String sql = "SELECT * FROM \"CityEJBTable\"";

        /*Executing the sql statement*/
        Statement statement = conn.createStatement();
         ResultSet rsCities = statement.executeQuery(sql);

        while (rsCities.next()) {
           Long id = new Long(rsCities.getLong("id"));
           tbl.put((Object)id, (Object)rsCities.getString("name"));
         }

      } catch (Exception e) {
         throw new EJBException(e);
      }

      return tbl;
   }
```

You will note that our implementation of the `CityBreakFacade` is actually short of one of the use cases (`BookVacation`). We are going to implement this slightly differently as you'll see in a moment.

Identifying Patterns to Improve Scalability

The J2EE platform provides support for asynchronous processing through the use of the Java Message Service (JMS). Although optional in J2EE 1.2 servers, it is mandatory according to the 1.3 specifications because of the introduction of a new EJB type: the message-driven beans. These are session beans that are only accessed through a queue (Point-to-Point messaging) or a topic (Publish/Subscribe messaging).

The Message Façade Pattern

The Message Façade pattern is a version of the Session Façade pattern. It fulfills the same objectives as the Session Façade (hides the system complexity behind a coarse-grained interface) with the added advantage that it executes asynchronously by being implemented as a message-driven bean:

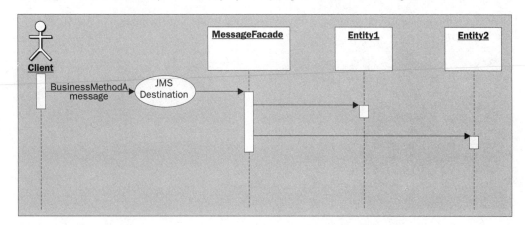

A further scalability enhancement provided by the Façade pattern is that it also serves to provide a layer of indirection between the components. As the client only interacts with a single façade object, it doesn't know anything about the location and implementation of the objects and resources behind the façade.

Implementing Message Façade in the City Break Application

The process of making a booking is quite complex in that it requires the creation of a new Booking entity as well as updating values in the Hotel, Customer, and Flight entities. It makes sense to place all these interactions behind a façade because these updates can take place asynchronously.

To place a new booking, we need to construct a `BookingVO` value object with the relevant data and then send the object to a JMS queue (`newBookingQ`):

```
BookingVO vo = new BookingVO();
vo.hotelId = 1;
vo.flightIdOut = 2;
vo.flightIdIn = 3;
vo.customerId = 4;
vo.fromDate = "01-01-02";
vo.toDate = "03-01-02";
vo.noSeats = 2;
vo.noRooms = 1;
vo.price = 200;

try {
    InitialContext ctx = new InitialContext();
    QueueConnectionFactory qf = (QueueConnectionFactory)
        ctx.lookup("jms/QueueConnectionFactory");
    QueueConnection qc = qf.createQueueConnection();
    QueueSession qs = qc.createQueueSession(false, Session.AUTO_ACKNOWLEDGE);
    Queue q = (Queue) ctx.lookup("jms/newBookingQ");
    QueueSender qSender = qs.createSender(q);
    ObjectMessage msg = qs.createObjectMessage(vo);
    qSender.send(msg);
} catch (Exception e) {
    System.out.println(e);
}
```

Listening on this queue will be a message-driven bean that is our implementation of the Message Façade pattern:

```
package facade.bookingmsg;

import javax.ejb.*;
import javax.jms.*;
import vo.BookingVO;
import common.*;
import entity.booking.*;
import entity.flight.*;
import entity.hotel.*;
import entity.customer.*;
```

```
public class BookingMsgFacadeEJB implements MessageDrivenBean,
    MessageListener {

  public void ejbCreate() {}
  public void ejbRemove() {}
  public void setMessageDrivenContext(MessageDrivenContext ctx) {}
```

All the action in this bean takes place in the onMessage() method that is called by the server when a new message arrives in the queue. This method first of all updates all the entities as relevant:

```
public void onMessage(Message msg) {

  QueueConnection qc = null;

  try {
    ObjectMessage omsg = (ObjectMessage) msg;
    BookingVO booking = (BookingVO) omsg.getObject();
    ServiceLocator locator = ServiceLocator.getInstance();

    //Make booking
    BookingLocalHome bhome = (BookingLocalHome)
      locator.getEJBLocalHome(ServiceLocator.BOOKING);
    BookingLocal bookingejb = bhome.create(booking);

    //Set available seats on flight Out
    FlightLocalHome fhome = (FlightLocalHome)
      locator.getEJBLocalHome(ServiceLocator.FLIGHT);
    FlightLocal flightOut =
      fhome.findByPrimaryKey(booking.flightIdOut);
    if ((flightOut.getAvailableSeats() - booking.noSeats) > 0) {
      flightOut.bookSeats(booking.noSeats);
    } else {
      throw new  Exception("Not enough seats for flight: " +
                  booking.flightIdOut.toString());
    }

    //Set available seats on flight in
    FlightLocal flightIn = fhome.findByPrimaryKey(booking.flightIdIn);
    if ((flightIn.getAvailableSeats() - booking.noSeats) > 0) {
      flightIn.bookSeats(booking.noSeats);
    } else {
      throw new
        Exception("Not enough seats for flight: " +
                        booking.flightIdIn.toString());
    }

    //Set available rooms in hotel
    HotelLocalHome hhome = (HotelLocalHome)
      locator.getEJBLocalHome(ServiceLocator.HOTEL);
    HotelLocal hotel = hhome.findByPrimaryKey(booking.hotelId);
    if ((hotel.getAvailableRooms() - booking.noRooms) > 0) {
      hotel.bookRooms(booking.noRooms);
    } else {
```

187

```
        throw new Exception("Not enough rooms for: " +
                            booking.hotelId.toString());
    }

    //Add booking id to customer
    CustomerLocalHome chome = (CustomerLocalHome)
        locator.getEJBLocalHome(ServiceLocator.CUSTOMER);
    CustomerLocal customer =
        chome.findByPrimaryKey(booking.customerId);
    customer.addBooking(bookingejb.getId());
```

Then, to acknowledge the successful booking, our bean sends the booking ID (the primary key of the new `Booking` entity) back to the client via another queue (`bookingCompleteQ`):

```
    //Send booking id
    qc = locator.getJMSQueueConn(ServiceLocator.QUEUECONNFACTORY);
    Queue q = locator.getJMSQueue(ServiceLocator.BOOKING_COMPLETE);
    QueueSession qs = qc.createQueueSession(false,
                                    Session.AUTO_ACKNOWLEDGE);
    QueueSender qSender = qs.createSender(q);
    TextMessage txtMsg = qs.createTextMessage(
        "Booking complete: id = " + bookingejb.getId());
    qSender.send(txtMsg);

} catch (Exception e) {
    throw new EJBException(e);
} finally {
    if (qc != null)   {
        try   {
            qc.close();
        } catch (JMSException jmse)   {}
    }
}

    }
}
```

The Business Delegate Pattern

One of the greatest areas of coupling in J2EE components is through the resource location mechanism. Although the use of JNDI means we do not need to know specific network locations, our clients must still know what resources they need to use and consequently look up. As a result, our clients (on the presentation tier) must handle the complexity of working with the remote objects themselves. By interposing a delegate object between the presentation tier and the business objects, our clients are able to invoke business-specific calls without any knowledge of the operation and whereabouts of the business objects themselves. This is the Business Delegate pattern:

Client	BusinessDelegate	
		BusinessObjects

The performance and decoupling of the Business Delegate pattern can be further improved by combining it with the Service Locator pattern to handle the lookup of the business objects from the delegate:

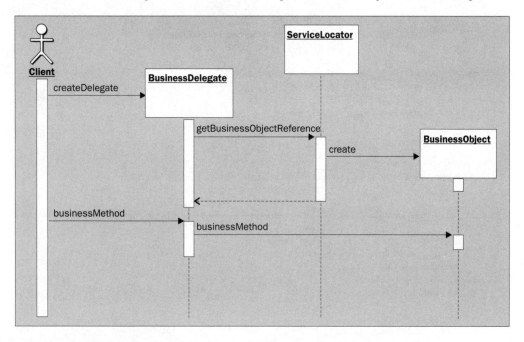

Implementing Business Delegates in the City Break Application

We have already added a layer of indirection through the use of the Session Façade and Message Façade patterns. However, for our client tier to interact with our Session Façade, it needs to look up the session beans (`CityBreakFacade` and `CustomerFacade`).

To further decouple our client tier through the use of the Business Delegate pattern, we will create two vanilla Java classes to act as delegates between our client tier and the Session Façade. We therefore need two delegates: `CustomerDelegate` for the `CustomerFacade`, and `CityBreakDelegate` for the `CityBreakFacade`.

The implementation of these delegate classes is straightforward because all they need to expose is the business interfaces that they then forward to the façades. First the `CustomerDelegate`:

```
package delegate;

import common.*;
import facade.customer.*;
import vo.CustomerVO;

public class CustomerDelegate {

    private static CustomerFacade cFacade = null;

    //Get the remote interface to the CustomerFacade session bean
```

```
private static void setCustomerFacade() {

    try {
       ServiceLocator locator = ServiceLocator.getInstance();
       CustomerFacadeHome cfhome = (CustomerFacadeHome)
          locator.getEJBHome(ServiceLocator.CUSTOMERFACADE);
       cFacade = cfhome.create();
    } catch (ServiceLocatorException sle) {
       System.out.println("ServiceLocator exception thrown: " + sle);
    } catch (Exception e) {
       System.out.println(e);
    }
}

//Create a new customer
public void registerNewCustomer(String name, String addr1,
                                String addr2, String state,
                                String zip, String email,
                                String password) {

    //Construct Customer Value Object
    CustomerVO vo = new CustomerVO();
    vo.name = name;
    vo.addr1 = addr1;
    vo.addr2 = addr2;
    vo.state = state;
    vo.zip = zip;
    vo.email = email;
    vo.pwd = password;

    //Connect to facade and pass on value object
    try {
       if (cFacade == null) {
          setCustomerFacade();
       }
       cFacade.registerNewCustomer(vo);

    } catch (Exception e) {
        throw new Exception(e);
    }
}

//Send email and password info to get customer id
public Long loginCustomer(String email, String pwd) {

    CustomerVO vo = null;

    try {
       if (cFacade == null) {
          setCustomerFacade();
       }

       vo = cFacade.loginCustomer(email, pwd);
    } catch (Exception e) {
```

```
          System.out.println(e);
       }

       return vo.customerId;
    }
}
```

As you can see the delegate can also hide the complexity of working with value objects from the client – although it might be appropriate to extend the value object architecture to the web tier to facilitate connection across the tiers.

Finally the `CityBreakDelegate`:

```
package delegate;

import common.*;
import facade.citybreak.*;
import javax.jms.*;
import vo.*;
import java.util.Hashtable;
import java.util.ArrayList;

public class CityBreakDelegate {

    private static CityBreakFacade cbFacade = null;

    //Get the remote interface to the CityBreakFacade session bean
    private static void setCityBreakFacade() {

       try {
          ServiceLocator locator = ServiceLocator.getInstance();
          CityBreakFacadeHome cbfhome = (CityBreakFacadeHome)
             locator.getEJBHome(ServiceLocator.CITYBREAKFACADE);
          cbFacade = cbfhome.create();
       } catch (ServiceLocatorException sle) {
          System.out.println("ServiceLocator exception thrown: " + sle);
       } catch (Exception e) {
          System.out.println(e);
       }
    }

    //Return the cities available in the database
    public Hashtable getListOfCities() {

       Hashtable htble = null;

       try {
          if (cbFacade == null) {
             setCityBreakFacade();
          }
          htble = cbFacade.getCityList();

       } catch (Exception e) {
```

```
            throw new Exception(e);
        }
        return htble;
    }

    //Get a CityBreak Value Object for a specfic city
    public CityBreakVO getInfoOnCity(Long cityId) {

        CityBreakVO vo = null;

        try {
            if (cbFacade == null) {
                setCityBreakFacade();
            }

            vo = cbFacade.getInfoOnCity(cityId);

        } catch (Exception e) {
            throw new Exception(e);
        }

        return vo;
    }

    //Get all flights for a specific date from one airport to another
    public ArrayList getFlightInfoForFlight(String date, String from,
                                            String to) {
        ArrayList flights = null;
        try    {
            if (cbFacade == null) {
                setCityBreakFacade();
            }
            flights = cbFacade.getFlightInfoForFlight(date, from, to);
        } catch (Exception e) {
            throw new Exception(e);
        }
        return flights;
    }

    //Send a Booking Value Object to book a city break
    public void bookCityBreak(Long hotelId, Long flightIdOut,
                              Long flightIdIn, Long customerId,
                              String fromDate, String toDate,
                              int noSeats, int noRooms, double price) {

        //Create value object and load with parameters
        BookingVO vo = new BookingVO();
        vo.hotelId = hotelId;
        vo.flightIdOut = flightIdOut;
        vo.flightIdIn = flightIdIn;
        vo.customerId = customerId;
        vo.fromDate = fromDate;
        vo.toDate = toDate;
        vo.noSeats = noSeats;
```

```
vo.noRooms = noRooms;
vo.price = price;

QueueConnection qc = null;

//Create a connection to the booking queue and send the value object
try {
    ServiceLocator locator = ServiceLocator.getInstance();
    qc = locator.getJMSQueueConn(ServiceLocator.QUEUECONNFACTORY);
    QueueSession qs = qc.createQueueSession(false,
                                            Session.AUTO_ACKNOWLEDGE);
    Queue q = locator.getJMSQueue(ServiceLocator.NEW_BOOKINGS);
    QueueSender qSender = qs.createSender(q);
    ObjectMessage msg = qs.createObjectMessage(vo);
    qSender.send(msg);

} catch (ServiceLocatorException sle) {
    throw new Exception("ServiceLocator exception thrown: " + sle);
} catch (JMSException jmse) {
    throw new Exception("JMS Exception thrown: " + jmse);
} catch (Exception e) {
    throw new Exception(e);
} finally {
    if (qc != null)   {
        try   {
            qc.close();
        } catch (JMSException jmse)   {}
    }
}
    }
}
```

The Complete City Break Architecture

Let's look back at the application architecture we have designed for our complete City Break application. We'll break it down by basic process to simply the diagrams.

The Customer Processes

For creating a new customer and logging-in as an existing customer we used:

❑   The Business Delegate pattern (CustomerDelegate)

❑   The Session Façade pattern (CustomerFacade)

❑   The Value Object pattern (CustomerVO)

❑   The Service Locator pattern (ServiceLocator)

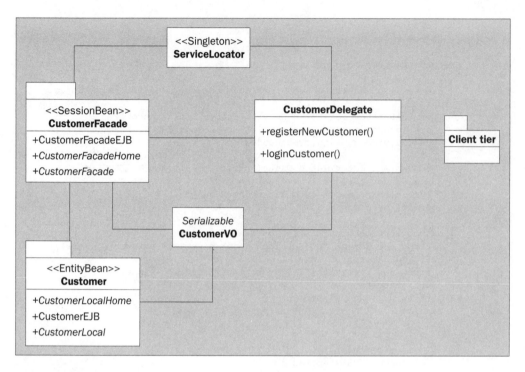

The Quote Process

To put together a City Break vacation, we have a similar architecture to that used in the Customer processes except somewhat more complicated because there are more entities involved. We used:

- ❑ The Business Delegate pattern (CityBreakDelegate)
- ❑ The Session Façade pattern (CityBreakFacade)
- ❑ The Value Object pattern (HotelVO, FlightVO, and CityBreakVO)
- ❑ The Value Object Assembler pattern (CityBreakFacade.assembleCityBreakValueObject())
- ❑ The JDBC for Reading pattern (CityBreakFacade)
- ❑ The Service Locator pattern (ServiceLocator)

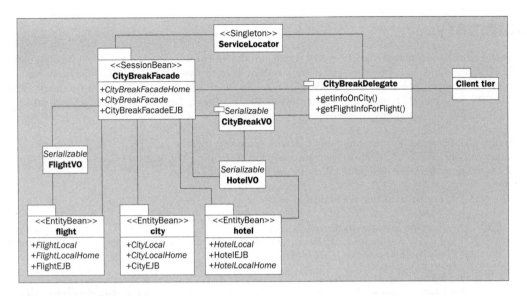

The Booking Process

For the booking process we used:

- ❑ The Business Delegate pattern (`CityBreakDelegate`)
- ❑ The Message Façade pattern (`BookingMsgFacade`)
- ❑ The Value Object pattern (`BookingVO`)
- ❑ The Service Locator pattern (`ServiceLocator`)

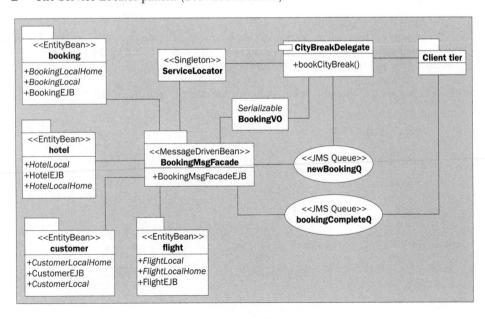

Summary

Performance and scalability are two very significant design considerations not only while designing J2EE applications, but also in any distributed system development. A badly designed system can perform so poorly that no amount of additional hardware can improve the situation. Although none of the patterns in the J2EE pattern catalog explicitly identify these, there are patterns that address performance and scalability concerns.

In this chapter we've seen how to apply patterns to address these in our applications. We began by analyzing the various problems for performance and scalability. We then looked at the application of these design patterns by designing a City Break Booking application.

The performance patterns that we looked at were:

- ❑ **The Service Locator pattern**
  This pattern uses a cache mechanism to store initial context object references to the factory objects to avoid intensive JNDI lookup

- ❑ **The Value Object pattern**
  This pattern reduces the number of remote calls by packaging all the state data into a single serializable object

- ❑ **The Session Façade pattern**
  This pattern introduces a course-grained interface to reduce multiple network calls

The patterns that address the scalability issues were:

- ❑ **The Message Façade pattern**
  This pattern is similar to the Session Façade pattern, with an additional advantage that it executes asynchronously by being implemented as a message bean

- ❑ **The Business Delegate pattern**
  This pattern handles the complexity of working with delegate objects by interposing between the presentation tier and the business objects; this helps in reducing the overhead of the client knowing the whereabouts of the business objects

In the next chapter we'll discuss the design patterns that address security issues.

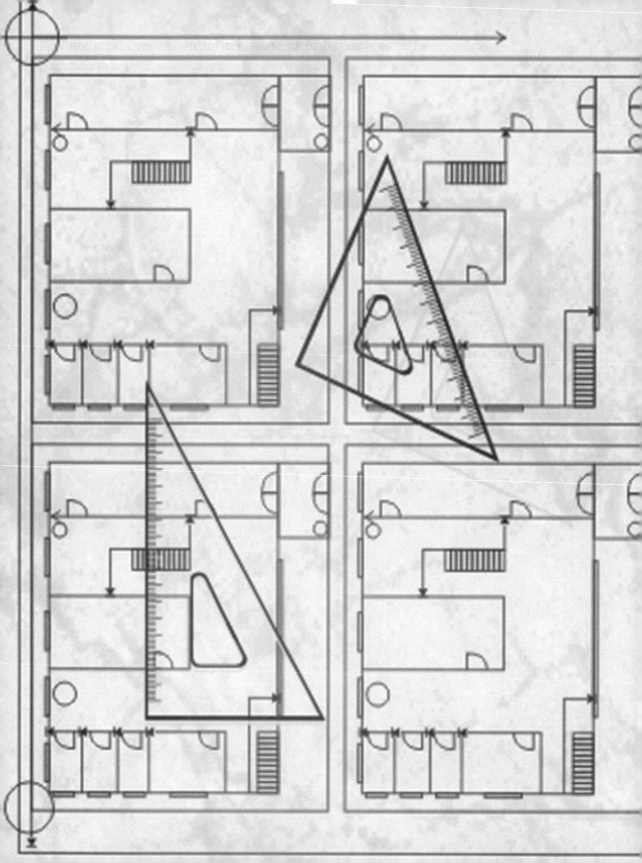

Patterns Applied to Manage Security

In this chapter, we introduce security patterns and their benefits throughout the design of our case study, a J2EE Web Banking application. We will define the scope and requirements of this application, identify relevant security patterns, and apply them to the design of both the application and its operating environment. We will develop use cases, and finally present code for a few of the major Java classes.

What are Security Patterns?

Security patterns provide techniques for addressing known security issues, in the same manner as J2EE and other object-oriented patterns provide proven techniques for solving known programming problems.

Security patterns work together to form a collection of best practices, whose ultimate goal is to support an organization's security policy – a policy that addresses not just application security, but host and network security, as well. Thus they can (and ideally should) be applied to the design and development of applications, and to the configuration and management of the hosts, and the network within which these applications operate. Security patterns, however, do not define specific technologies, coding styles, or programming languages. They do not identify industry vendors, application version numbers, or patch levels.

Benefits of Using Security Patterns

Similarly to standard object-oriented patterns, security patterns provide the following benefits:

- ❑ They can be revisited and implemented at anytime to improve the design of a system
- ❑ Less experienced practitioners can benefit from the experience of more advanced practitioners
- ❑ They provide a common language of discussion, testing, and development
- ❑ They can easily be categorized, searched, and refactored
- ❑ They provide reusable, repeatable, and documented security practices

When to Use Security Patterns

Security patterns can provide guidance when dealing with the following issues:

- ❑ Whenever data is being sent to or received from an external system, application, or object:
  - ❑ Will it validate the information based on length, value, or type?
  - ❑ Is the communication channel secure? Does it need to be?
  - ❑ What is the origin of the data, is it a trusted or non-trusted source?
- ❑ Whenever an application is accessible by trusted or non-trusted users:
  - ❑ Who is trying to access the application?
  - ❑ Is their request legitimate? Should it care?
  - ❑ Does it know how to process their request? What should it do if it doesn't?
  - ❑ Does it know about every attempt to access the system? How can it be sure?
- ❑ Whenever data is considered confidential or sensitive:
  - ❑ How is the data being protected?
  - ❑ Are these means sufficient or unwarranted?
  - ❑ Is the data being stored or backed up elsewhere? Is this adequate?

Secure Programming

As mentioned previously, security patterns are essentially best practices and can assist in the design of secure applications. However, they are not a replacement for secure programming techniques. Following proper coding standards in all languages is essential for developing resilient software. The following are few examples of proper coding:

- ❑ Data validation
- ❑ Code, design reviews
- ❑ Scoping
- ❑ Synchronized operations
- ❑ Secure (dynamic) class loading
- ❑ Proper exception handling, error reporting, logging

The Web Banking Case Study

The goal of this case study is to apply security patterns to the design of a web banking application. The application will be a J2EE web-based one, which will act as a front end to an existing banking system. We will identify the features of the application, and then define the key business and technical requirements.

High-level Overview

The Wrox Bank is a national bank with branch offices and ATMs (Automated Teller Machines) located across the country, and operates on an existing computing (mainframe) infrastructure. The bank is being pressured by customers to provide banking services online. A recent survey revealed the following three services as most important to the customers:

❏   View account balance

❏   View account activity

❏   Transfer funds between accounts

Assumptions

The following assumptions can be made about this case study:

❏   The existing banking infrastructure consists of a trusted mainframe system, which will be capable of supporting all activity generated by this web-based application

❏   Connectivity to the back-end mainframe occurs over a dedicated, high-speed network

❏   The creation of web-based accounts (including usernames and passwords) is performed at branch locations and is outside the scope of this online application

Business Requirements

Business requirements define the features or services of an application.

The Wrox Web Banking application will be web-based and accessible over the Internet by standard web browsers (wireless devices will not be supported at this time). It will be a front end to the existing banking infrastructure, that is, it will not duplicate the core account information of the mainframe.

There will be three types of users of this application:

❏   Anonymous users are those who access only the public pages of the web site and cannot log in and thus cannot perform any banking activities.

❏   Regular customers are those who perform the following activities:

   ❏   Log in to the application: after successful form-based authentication, the application will create a user session, allowing the customer to access other services

   ❏   Log out of the application: this will terminate the user session

   ❏   View account balance: immediately after login, the application will display a list of the customer's active accounts and their balances

❏   Preferred customers are those who perform all the activities of Regular customers in addition to the following:

❑ View account activity: beginning with the most recent transaction, this will display transactions as of the last statement period (30 days). At this time, the customer will not have the ability to view activity previous to this period. The following table specifies the fields that will be displayed for each transaction:

Field	Description
Date	Specifies the time and date the transaction was processed by the back-end system.
Description	Provides a description of the transaction.
Type	This field should contain one of the following values: ATM, Cheque, Web, Service Charge, or Other. ATM implies that the transaction was processed at an ATM. Cheque implies that a credit or debit was made using a cheque. Service Charge implies that the bank made the transaction. Other specifies all other types of transactions.
Reference Number	Specifies the cheque number if the transaction type was a Cheque, otherwise the reference number (as generated by the back-end system).
Amount	Specifies the amount of money that was withdrawn (shown as negative value) or deposited (shown as a positive value).

❑ Transfer funds between active accounts: This service will allow Preferred customers to transfer money from one active account to another. There will be no limit on the amount of money that can be transferred as long as the sending account has sufficient funds to support the transfer. Funds transfer can only occur between two active accounts.

By default, only the primary chequing and/or saving account will be active. Other accounts, such as credit card or line of credit accounts will be made available (active) only at the request of the customer at a branch location. Customers will only be allowed to view account information for which they are authorized and will not have access to other customer's account information. Confidential information will not be sent unprotected over an untrusted network. User accounts will be locked until the next business day if an incorrect password has been entered three consecutive times within 24 hours. User sessions will expire after 10 minutes of inactivity.

Technical Requirements

Technical requirements, also known as non-functional requirements, define issues such as performance, scalability, and availability. The application consists of the following tiers, each of which will exist on a separate network segment protected with a firewall restricting all but essential network activity:

❑ Presentation (web): Consists of a load balancer and web servers

❑ Application: Supports a cluster of application servers

❑ Data tier: The user (data) store will contain at least the following information:

    ❑ Customer ID: a unique customer identification number as assigned by the back-end mainframe system

    ❑ Username: as provided by the application to the customer

    ❑ Full name: first and last name as listed in the mainframe system

❑ Password: as provided to the customer by the application

❑ Role assignment: as assigned by the back-end system

❑ The list of active accounts: a list of those accounts accessible by the customer of the web banking application

The back-end banking system will be the authoritative source of data for all remaining customer information including (but not limited to) the following:

❑ Personal customer information (full name, address, and so on.)

❑ Customer account numbers

❑ Customer account balances and history

All confidential information sent to the customer over HTTP will be transmitted in a secure fashion using 128 bit SSL. The web-based infrastructure will support high availability (HA) via load-balancing, clustered web, application, and database servers. Each network device and application will be hardened and configured with the latest patches. A testing and staging environment will be configured to match the production environment as closely as possible. Only authorized personnel will have access to production, and staging servers.

Security Patterns

Let us now identify and discuss security patterns as they apply to this case study. Given the scope, business, and technical requirements of this application, we will identify relevant security patterns that will help us develop a more secure application.

The Single Access Point Pattern

The Single Access Point pattern describes a system with a single point of entry; an entry that is common to all incoming requests, and is the only way to gain an entry into a system. All users (or other applications) requesting access must first pass through this entryway. By employing the Single Access Point pattern, the application is assured (as best it can) that any given user has achieved basic authentication and not bypassed any identification checkpoints. For example, unauthorized requests for protected resources can be automatically redirected to this access point for proper validation.

This pattern is typically represented by a single login prompt to an organization's network or individual server. Another example is an application that provides a single login page versus separate login prompts for each service.

Larger, more complex applications can benefit more from this. J2EE applications, for example, by virtue of their extensibility, tend to incorporate many disparate applications such as messaging, rules engines, and reporting applications, each of which may require some form of user authentication. Rather than developing login pages for each ancillary application, the Single Access Point is used to gather user information once, and forward it along.

The J2EE security model provides a simple mechanism to implement the Single Access Point pattern. By employing declarative security in the J2EE web tier, the designer is able to specify the web resources (URLs, URL patterns, and HTTP methods) that are to be protected. When an anonymous user requests a protected resource, the application (web container) will attempt to authenticate the user via a number of mechanisms. The J2EE platform natively supports basic authentication, forms-based authentication, and client-side certificates. Our Wrox Web Banking application employs forms-based authentication.

The Check Point Pattern

The Check Point is a pattern that centralizes and enforces authentication and authorization. It is the responsibility of this mechanism to determine if a user has sufficient privileges to grant access to a requested resource. By centralizing this logic, the Check Point pattern also affords easier management of application policies and business rules. Designers are able to modify and extend these rules without altering the remaining application. The Check Point pattern can apply to any of the following situations:

❑ Consider a system with multiple security levels. To initially gain access, a user enters a basic username and password. The Check Point grants them access to all resources matching this level of security. To achieve higher security clearance and access more sensitive information, the user would be required to provide stronger credentials such as a digital certificate. Another stronger authentication mechanism could be biometric identification. The Check Point pattern manages the security requirements of the resources, determines their security level, and provides the users access according to predefined security policies.

❑ Consider a system with multiple user stores, where the authentication credentials of some users are stored in an LDAP directory, some in a RDBMS, and others still in a mainframe system. It is the function of the Check Point to communicate with, and validate users against, any and all of those user stores.

❑ Consider an application that is currently only accessible via HTTP browsers but must extend services to end-user devices like IVR, cellular phones, or PDAs. A gateway can be created to forward requests from these devices to the application but the security will be assured if the requests from the devices are cleared through the Check Point.

Note that a simple application may only employ one or two of these scenarios in a single Check Point whereas a much more complex system may have multiple Check Points and may use each of these scenarios multiple times. For example, a multi-national organization may employ a Check Point at each national border to enforce the security policy of that country. Even then, it may incorporate regional Check Points to support local end-user devices.

Much of the functionality of the Check Point pattern can be supported natively in the J2EE security architecture with the Java Authentication and Authorization Service (JAAS). JAAS provides both pluggable and stackable authentication. The pluggable authentication module (PAM) framework abstracts the application from the underlying authentication code, thereby removing dependencies and allowing for greater flexibility and selection of authentication mechanisms.

PAM also provides stackable authentication that defines where and when any particular mechanism is 'optional', 'required', or 'sufficient'. In the above discussion of a system with multiple security levels, a user's successful authentication would be 'required' to achieve higher security clearance. To access resources of lower security levels, no further authentication would be required because they already possess 'sufficient' privileges.

The Role Pattern

The Role pattern describes the disassociation of a user from their privileges. A user is assigned one or more roles and each role is granted one or more privileges. A user can be assigned to, or removed from, a role whenever their responsibilities change and roles can be granted new privileges as new resources or objects become available. This approach provides two very important benefits:

❑ No modification to the underlying access control objects is necessary when updating role definitions or user privilege assignment

❑ Permissions are more intuitive to manage since roles closely represent a company's organizational structure or the types of users of an application like developer, administrator, manager, Silver, Gold, or Platinum Customer, and so on

More sophisticated implementations of the Role pattern, commonly known as Role-Based Access Control (RBAC) extend the basic Role pattern by applying the following concepts:

❑ Inheritance (or Role Hierarchy): when the sum total of privileges granted to a role, equals the privileges for that role as well as privileges of lesser, associated roles.

❑ Separation of duties: Static, Dynamic, and Organizational separation of duties represent real-world conditions where individuals cannot belong to two roles at the same time. Additionally, they cannot belong to a given set of roles. For example, a bank manager cannot also be an auditor or a bank customer cannot also be a teller.

The business requirement for the Wrox Web Banking application has identified three roles; Anonymous User, Regular Customer, and Preferred Customer, each with their associated privileges. Specifically, an Anonymous user can view all public pages. A Regular Customer has access to all public pages and can view their account balances. A Preferred Customer has all the privileges of the Regular Customer plus the ability to transfer funds between their accounts and view their account history.

The J2EE platform incorporates roles into its architecture by way of a declarative security model. Simple role-based access control can be achieved by defining roles (in declarative syntax) within the `ejb-jar.xml` and `web.xml` deployment descriptors. When a protected resource is requested, and the user is authenticated, the web container or enterprise bean references the role declarations and either permits or denies access to the web resource.

Risk Assessment and Management

Security equals risk management. Risk assessment and management speak of the "reasonable" and "appropriate" effort required to protect an application and its resources and are the first step in a security analysis. The goal is to perform a task in a secure manner, not to consume resources, over-engineer code, or unnecessarily encrypt publicly available information. It can be said that risk is proportional to the following thee factors:

❑ Threat: the frequency of attempts or successes

❑ Vulnerability: the likelihood of success

❑ Cost: cost of successful breach, or value of the resource

The greater any of these factors, the greater the overall risk will be. A proper risk assessment ensures that not only the application is being properly protected, but also each system with which it has direct or ultimately indirect contact. For example, the web servers of the Wrox Web Banking application are a target for attack, not because they necessarily contain sensitive information themselves, but because they can be used to launch a more rewarding or malicious attack against targets like the back-end banking system. (Of course, information could certainly be harvested from the web servers and used in other attacks.)

Clearly, the threat for these front-line applications is high. Their vulnerability depends on the extent to which the application has been securely written – it could be quite low. The cost of a breach in the application can include everything from the value placed on stolen code and customer data, to time lost detecting and repairing damage.

Authoritative Source of Data

When an application blindly accepts data from any given source then it is at risk of processing potentially outdated or fraudulent data. Therefore, an application needs to recognize which, of many possible sources, is the single authority for data. Understanding the authoritative source of data means recognizing where your data is coming from and knowing to what extent you can trust the validity of such information. In short, never make assumptions about the validity of unverified data or its origin.

In most cases, determining the authoritative source of data will lie with the owner of the business process. The owner understands better than the application designer or developer the purpose of the information in a larger context. Information security groups and application designers, however, should still advise the business owner on the volatility and integrity of the data source(s) under consideration.

While the interface of the Wrox Web Banking application may differ (from an ATM or teller), the account information is retrieved from a single data source – the back-end mainframe system. Attempting to duplicate customers' personal and account information locally would present unnecessary technical and procedural issues at this stage.

The banking application will therefore be designed to access the mainframe system for all customer account information. Only the information that is relevant to the web banking system, for example, web banking usernames, passwords, and role assignments need be stored in a local data store. The authoritative source of data for customer account information is the back-end mainframe, whereas the authoritative source of data for web banking usernames and passwords is the local user store.

Authoritative source of data also embodies the premise of validating information received from a user or system. In our case study, user input is the form, which contains the username, password, monetary amount; each of these data fields must be validated at least for character type and length. At a minimum, this validation should be performed on the server side by the processing servlet. Additionally, client-side validation (within JavaScript, for example) will offer a first check of the information before it is submitted to the server.

Wrox Web Banking Use Cases

Functional and technical requirements have been identified and a number of security patterns have been discussed. These will aid us in properly defining the use cases for this application.

Actors

Based on the functional requirements, Anonymous users, Regular Customers, and Preferred Customers are the identified actors.

Use Cases

The following use cases have been identified:

- ❏ View public pages
- ❏ Log in to the application
- ❏ Log out of the application
- ❏ View account balances
- ❏ View account activity
- ❏ Transfer funds between Wrox accounts

Given the aforementioned use cases, consider the following use case diagram:

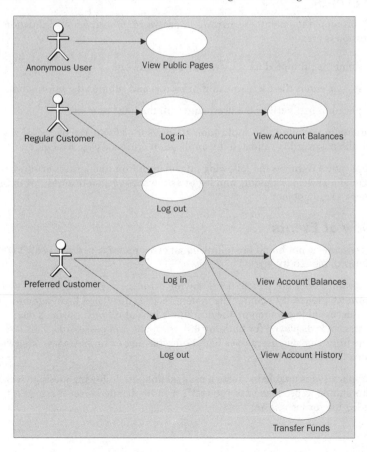

The diagram attempts to demonstrate how the Preferred Customer has access to all the services of the Regular Customer with the addition of View account activity and Transfer funds.

View Public Pages

This is the trivial use case, which describes any unauthenticated user browsing the public pages of the web site.

Main Flow of Events

❑   The public pages represent the sections of the web site where no authentication is required

❑   An anonymous user accesses the public web site

Login Use Case

The Regular or Preferred Customers utilize this use case when they wish to access any of the Wrox Web Banking services.

Main Flow of Events

The customer is prompted to enter a username and password. On successful validation of their credentials, a session is created:

❑   The customer is prompted for a username and password.

❑   The customer enters the username and password and submits the information.

❑   The application first verifies the username with the local user store.

❑   If the username is found, the application attempts to validate the password with the local user store. If the password is validated the application creates a user session.

❑   The application retrieves the following information from the local user store: username, first and last name, role designation, and list of active accounts, and stores this information in the customer's session object.

Alternative Flow of Events

❑   If the username is not found the following an error message is displayed: "Invalid username or password, please try again".

❑   If the password does not match, the following error message is displayed: "Invalid username or password, please try again". The system records this failed login attempt. If this was the third unsuccessful login attempt, the account is locked till next business day. (Note the same error message is displayed for both invalid username and passwords. This is done to prevent attackers from guessing usernames based on returning error messages, otherwise known as username harvesting.)

❑   If the application is unable to create a user session, the following message will be displayed, "We are unable to process your request". A more detailed error message is logged to the system log file for inspection.

Logout Use Case

A Regular or Preferred Customer uses this use case when they are done using the application.

Main Flow of Events

The use case starts when a customer has successfully authenticated to the application. The customer selects the logout button and exits the application:

❑ A customer selects the logout operation

❑ The application terminates the user session

❑ The customer is redirected to a page confirming that the logout was successful

Alternative Flow of Events

Ten minutes of inactivity lapses. At this time, the application terminates the user session.

View Account Balances Use Case

A Regular or Preferred Customer utilizes this use case to view the account balances of their active accounts.

Main Flow of Events

The use case starts when a customer has successfully authenticated to the application. The application retrieves and displays the account balances for all active accounts:

❑ The application verifies that the customer has a valid session. If not, the user is redirected to the login page.

❑ The application retrieves a list of the customer's active accounts from the user session object and verifies their role assignment.

❑ The application requests account balance information from the back-end system.

❑ If the user is a Preferred Customer the application will provide hyperlinks to view account history.

❑ The application displays the information to the customer.

Alternative Flow of Events

❑ If the customer does not have any active accounts the application will display the following message, "You do not currently have any active accounts".

❑ If the application is unable to retrieve a list of the customer's active accounts, the following error message will be displayed, "The application is currently unable to process your request, please try again shortly". A more detailed error message is logged to the system log file for inspection.

View Account Activity Use Case

The Preferred Customer utilizes this use case to view account activity.

Main Flow of Events

This use case starts when the Preferred Customer selects an account from the list of account balances. The application retrieves account activity and displays the information:

- ❏ The customer selects an account from the list of account balances.

- ❏ The application verifies that the customer has a valid session. If not, the customer is redirected to the login page.

- ❏ The application verifies that the customer is part of the Preferred role. If they are not, the following error is displayed, "You are currently not allowed to perform this function". A more detailed message is logged. The application requests the account activity from the back-end system. This information is displayed to the customer.

Alternative Flow of Events

- ❏ If the customer does not have any active accounts, the application will display the following message, "You do not currently have any active accounts".

- ❏ If the application is unable to retrieve the customer's account history, the following error message will be displayed, "The application is currently unable to process your request, please try again shortly". A more detailed error message is logged to the system log file for inspection.

Transfer Funds Use Case

The Preferred Customer utilizes this use case to transfer money between accounts.

Main Flow of Events

This use case begins when the Preferred Customer sees a list of account balances. The Preferred Customer selects to transfer funds between a sending and a receiving account. The application verifies that sufficient funds exist in the sending account. The amount is debited from the sending account and credited to the receiving account. The back-end system records the transaction and generates a transaction number:

- ❏ The customer requests to transfer funds between active accounts.

- ❏ The application verifies that the customer has a valid session. If not, the customer is redirected to the login page.

- ❏ The application verifies that the customer belongs to the Preferred role.

- ❏ The customer selects the sending and receiving account, and the amount of funds to transfer.

- ❏ The application verifies that sufficient funds exist in the sending account.

- ❏ The application sends a request to the back-end system to perform the transfer.

- ❏ The back-end system performs the transfer and returns a status code and optionally, a transaction record.

- ❏ The application displays a confirmation message and the transaction record to the customer.

Alternative Flow of Events

❏ If the user is not a Preferred Customer, the following error message is displayed, "You are currently not allowed to perform this function". A more detailed message is logged.

❏ If the Preferred Customer does not have sufficient funds in the sending account, the following message is displayed, "Sorry, you do not have sufficient funds to perform this transfer".

❏ If the back-end system encountered an error and returned an error message, that message will be displayed and a more detailed message is logged.

Implementing the Case Study

In the next few sections, we will have a look at implementing the case study, using standard J2EE components:

❏ The web tier will be implemented using a controller servlet, a set of JSP pages, and helper classes

❏ The business tier will be implemented using Enterprise JavaBean components

❏ The web tier will interface with the EJB tier using business delegate components

Designing the Database

The domain objects that are identified in the system are:

❏ User
This represents a user who is authorized to use the system.

❏ User Role
This entity represents the various roles that are assigned to the user. In this case the roles will represent Regular and Preferred Customers.

❏ Account
This represents the account details that are held by the users.

❏ Account Detail
This represents the transaction details associated with each account.

The diagram below depicts the domain model of the system:

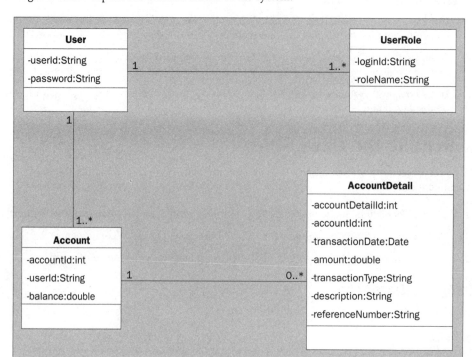

The diagram above shows the following details:

❑ A user has a user ID and password and may have one or more roles and one or more accounts

❑ An account can inform a user of its closing balance and may have zero or more transactions associated with it

❑ An account detail has the transaction date, amount involved, transaction type, description, and a reference number

The domain objects will persist in relational database tables. The script below shows the SQL commands for creating the tables and adding some sample data:

```
DROP TABLE WR_ACCOUNT;
CREATE TABLE WR_ACCOUNT (
   id NUMBER PRIMARY KEY,
   user_id NUMBER,
   balance NUMBER);

DROP TABLE WR_ACCOUNT_DETAIL;
CREATE TABLE WR_ACCOUNT_DETAIL (
   id NUMBER PRIMARY KEY,
   account_id NUMBER,
   transaction_date DATE,
```

```
    amount NUMBER,
    transaction_type VARCHAR(30),
    description VARCHAR(60),
    ref_num VARCHAR(30));

DROP TABLE WR_USER;
CREATE TABLE WR_USER (
   id NUMBER PRIMARY KEY,
   login_id VARCHAR2(30),
   pwd  VARCHAR2(30));

DROP TABLE WR_USER_ROLE;
CREATE TABLE WR_USER_ROLE (
   id NUMBER PRIMARY KEY,
   login_id VARCHAR2(30),
   role_name VARCHAR2(30),
   role_group VARCHAR2(30));

INSERT INTO WR_USER VALUES (1, 'zola', 'striker');
INSERT INTO WR_USER VALUES (2, 'gallas', 'defender');

INSERT INTO WR_USER_ROLE VALUES (1, 'zola', 'standard', 'Roles');
INSERT INTO WR_USER_ROLE VALUES (2, 'gallas', 'preferred', 'Roles');

INSERT INTO WR_ACCOUNT VALUES (1, 1, 1000.00);
INSERT INTO WR_ACCOUNT VALUES (2, 2, 20000.00);

INSERT INTO WR_ACCOUNT_DETAIL VALUES (1, 1, '12-Dec-2000', 1000.00, 'Paid in by
cheque', 'No Description', '012345');
INSERT INTO WR_ACCOUNT_DETAIL VALUES (2, 2, '12-Dec-2000', 20000.00, 'Paid in by
cheque', 'No Description', '123456');
INSERT INTO WR_ACCOUNT_DETAIL VALUES (3, 2, '12-Dec-2000', 1000.00, 'Paid in by
cash', 'No Description', '234567');
INSERT INTO WR_ACCOUNT_DETAIL VALUES (4, 2, '12-Dec-2000', -1000.00, 'Paid out by
cheque', 'No Description', '345678');

COMMIT;
```

Application Architecture

When the users access the system through their browsers, the system will authenticate their security credentials. Once authentication is performed, the system will display the transaction details for Preferred Customers and the account balance for Standard Customers. The Preferred Customers will also be able to view the account balance.

The component diagram shown below depicts the high-level application architecture:

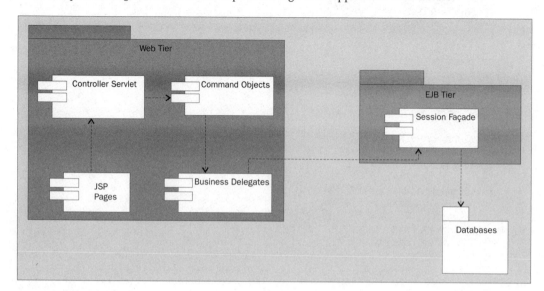

- ❏ All the HTTP requests originating from the client browsers will be intercepted by a Controller servlet

- ❏ This servlet, based on some information present in the request, will choose a Command object that will process the request

- ❏ If processing the request involves utilizing the services provided by the EJB tier, the Command object will access the Session Façade providing the business services using Business Delegates

- ❏ The Session Façade returns the data from the relational data store using JDBC

- ❏ The Command objects will store this data as request scope beans and inform the Controller servlet about the JSP page that will render the next view

- ❏ The JSP pages will extract the data from the request scope beans and display it

Application Security

One of the most important aspects of application development using J2EE is that these applications can rely on the container in which they run for a whole host of system-level services. Among these system-level services defined by the J2EE, EJB, and Servlet specifications are security services. J2EE enables applications to define security policies declaratively using deployment descriptors. The Servlet and EJB APIs also provide features for accessing various aspects related to security. Hence it is possible to implement most of the patterns explained earlier using standard J2EE API and deployment descriptor features.

Single Access Point and Check Point Patterns

In the application all public requests will be mapped to a Controller servlet and access to the Controller servlet will be restricted to authenticated users only.

The application will use form-based login for authenticating users.

❑ **API Feature:**

getRemoteUser() method on javax.servlet.http.HttpServletRequest returns the currently authenticated user.

getAuthType() method on javax.servlet.http.HttpServletRequest identifies whether the authentication scheme used is BASIC, FORM, DIGEST or CLIENT_CERT.

getCallerPrincipal() method of javax.ejb.EJBContext returns the principal associated with the security credentials of the currently executing thread.

getRemoteUser() method on javax.servlet.http.HttpServletRequest returns the currently authenticated user.

❑ **Deployment Descriptor Feature:**

The <login-config> element in the web deployment descriptor is used to specify the login scheme.

The <method-permission> element in the EJB deployment descriptor can be used to restrict access to the EJB methods to authenticated threads only.

The Role Pattern

The Command object that handles the initial login will decide the JSP that will display the next view to the user based on the role of the authenticated user.

All the JSP pages are stored in the WEB-INF directory and are not available for direct access from the browser.

❑ **API-Feature:**

isUserInRole() method on javax.servlet.http.HttpServletRequest identifies whether the currently authenticated user belongs to the specified role.

isCallerInRole() method on javax.ejb.EJBContext provides the same functionality.

❑ **Deployment Descriptor Feature:**

The <security-constraint>, <auth-constraint>, and <security-role> elements in the web deployment descriptor can be used to specify role-based access to URI patterns.

The <method-permission> and <security-role> elements in the EJB deployment descriptor can be used to specify role-based access to EJB methods.

The <security-role-ref> and <role-link> elements in EJB and web deployment descriptors can be used to map roles defined in the container environment to coded roles in the EJB and web components.

Sessions

We'll be relying on the server-provided features to manage sessions in the application.

❑ **API-Feature**

The web components can use `javax.servlet.http.HttpSession` for session-based functionality.

The EJB components can use stateful session beans for implementing session-based functionality.

❑ **Deployment Descriptor Feature**

The `<session-config>` element in the web deployment descriptor can be used for setting maximum inactive intervals for sessions.

In addition to the features explained above, J2EE also provides JAAS (Java Authentication and Authorisation Service) for implementing pluggable security modules. Later in the chapter we will see how we can use the RDBMS-based JAAS module provided by the container provider to implement the security policies defined in the deployment descriptor.

Roles Used in the System

The system basically utilizes the following roles:

❑ Standard: users with this role can only view the current balance of their accounts

❑ Preferred: users with this role can view their current balances as well as their transaction statements

Request URIs

The table below depicts the request URIs that are served by the system and the roles required to access those URIs:

URI	Role	Description
index.jsp	Standard, Preferred	The first page that is accessed
home.do	Standard, Preferred	The URI that serves the home page
balance.do	Standard, Preferred	The URI that serves the current balance
statement.do	Preferred	The URI that serves the current statement

Web Deployment Descriptor

Now we will look at how the security policies are defined in the web tier using the deployment descriptor:

```
<?xml version="1.0" encoding="ISO-8859-1"?>

<!DOCTYPE web-app
    PUBLIC "-//Sun Microsystems, Inc.//DTD Web Application 2.3//EN"
    "http://java.sun.com/dtd/web-app_2_3.dtd">
```

```
<web-app>

    <display-name>WROX Internet Banking Application</display-name>

    <!-- Define the controller servlet -->
    <servlet>
        <servlet-name>Controller</servlet-name>
        <servlet-class>web.ControllerServlet</servlet-class>
        <!-- Map roles to coded values -->
        <security-role-ref>
            <role-name>PRF</role-name>
            <role-link>preferred</role-link>
        </security-role-ref>
        <security-role-ref>
            <role-name>STD</role-name>
            <role-link>standard</role-link>
        </security-role-ref>
    </servlet>

    <!-- Map all the *.do requests to the controller servlet -->
    <servlet-mapping>
<servlet-name>Controller</servlet-name>
        <url-pattern>*.do</url-pattern>
    </servlet-mapping>

    <!-- Set the maximum inactive interval to thirty minutes -->
    <session-config>
        <session-timeout>30</session-timeout>
    </session-config>

    <!-- Define the home page -->
    <welcome-file-list>
        <welcome-file>index.jsp</welcome-file>
    </welcome-file-list>
```

This security constraint identifies the resources that can be accessed by users belonging to either Standard or Preferred roles:

```
<security-constraint>
    <display-name>WROX Bank Security</display-name>
    <web-resource-collection>
        <web-resource-name>Standard\Preferred Customers</web-resource-name>
        <description>Resource to get bakance and login</description>
        <url-pattern>/balance.do</url-pattern>
        <url-pattern>/home.do</url-pattern>
        <url-pattern>/index.jsp</url-pattern>
        <http-method>GET</http-method>
        <http-method>POST</http-method>
    </web-resource-collection>
    <auth-constraint>
        <role-name>preferred</role-name>
        <role-name>standard</role-name>
    </auth-constraint>
</security-constraint>
```

This security constraint identifies the resources that can be accessed only by users belonging to the Preferred role:

```
<security-constraint>
    <display-name>WROX Bank Security</display-name>
    <web-resource-collection>
        <web-resource-name>Preferred Customers</web-resource-name>
        <description>Resource to get statements</description>
        <url-pattern>/statement.do</url-pattern>
        <http-method>GET</http-method>
        <http-method>POST</http-method>
    </web-resource-collection>
    <auth-constraint>
        <role-name>preferred</role-name>
    </auth-constraint>
</security-constraint>

<!-- Define form login configuration -->
<login-config>
    <auth-method>FORM</auth-method>
    <realm-name>WROX Bank Authentication</realm-name>
    <form-login-config>
        <form-login-page>/Login.jsp</form-login-page>
        <form-error-page>/LoginError.jsp</form-error-page>
    </form-login-config>
</login-config>

<!-- Define the security roles -->
<security-role>
    <description>Preferred Customers</description>
    <role-name>preferred</role-name>
</security-role>
<security-role>
    <description>Standard Customers</description>
    <role-name>standard</role-name>
</security-role>

</web-app>
```

EJB Deployment Descriptor

The use cases to get the balance and statement are implemented as methods on a stateless Session Façade. Now we will have a look at how access to these methods is controlled based on roles defined in the EJB deployment descriptor:

```
<?xml version="1.0" encoding="UTF-8"?>
<ejb-jar>

    <enterprise-beans>

        <session>

            <ejb-name>AccountBean</ejb-name>
```

```
            <home>ejb.AccountHome</home>
            <remote>ejb.Account</remote>
            <ejb-class>ejb.AccountEJB</ejb-class>
            <session-type>Stateless</session-type>
            <transaction-type>Container</transaction-type>

        </session>

    </enterprise-beans>

    <assembly-descriptor>

        <!-- Define the security roles -->
        <security-role>
            <description>Preferred Customer</description>
            <role-name>preferred</role-name>
        </security-role>
        <security-role>
            <description>Standard Customer</description>
        <role-name>standard</role-name>
        </security-role>

        <method-permission>
            <description>
                Permissions for preferred and standard customers
            </description>
            <role-name>preferred</role-name>
            <role-name>standard</role-name>
            <method>
                <ejb-name>AccountBean</ejb-name>
                <method-name>create</method-name>
            </method>
            <method>
                <ejb-name>AccountBean</ejb-name>
                <method-name>getBalance</method-name>
            </method>
        </method-permission>

        <method-permission>
            <description>Permissions for preferred customers</description>
            <role-name>preferred</role-name>
            <method>
                <ejb-name>AccountBean</ejb-name>
                <method-name>getStatement</method-name>
            </method>
        </method-permission>

    </assembly-descriptor>

</ejb-jar>
```

Application Classes

In this section, we will have a look at the various classes and interfaces used in the application:

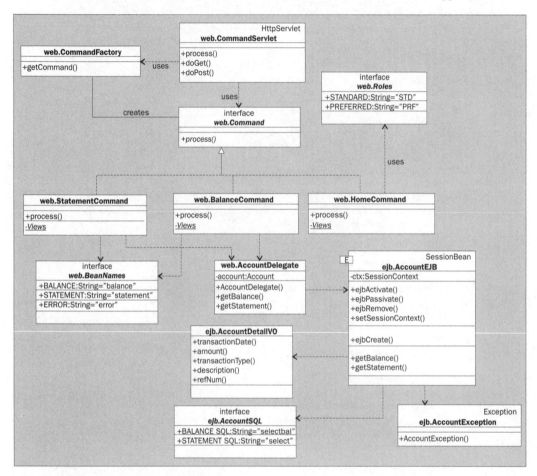

The ControllerServlet Servlet

This servlet acts as the front-end controller:

```
package web;

import javax.servlet.http.HttpServlet;
import javax.servlet.http.HttpServletRequest;
import javax.servlet.http.HttpServletResponse;

import javax.servlet.RequestDispatcher;
import javax.servlet.ServletException;

import java.io.IOException;
```

```
public class ControllerServlet extends HttpServlet {

    public void process(HttpServletRequest req, HttpServletResponse res)
        throws ServletException, IOException {

        try {
```

Get the command from the factory based on the servlet path:

```
        Command com = CommandFactory.getCommand(req.getServletPath());
```

Get the command to process the request and retrieve the JSP page for the next view:

```
        String view = com.process(req, res);
```

Forward the request to the JSP page using request dispatcher:

```
            RequestDispatcher rd = getServletContext().getRequestDispatcher(view);
            rd.forward(req, res);

        } catch(Throwable th) {
            throw new ServletException(th);
        }
    }

    public void doGet(HttpServletRequest req, HttpServletResponse res)
        throws ServletException, IOException {
        process(req, res);
    }

    public void doPost(HttpServletRequest req, HttpServletResponse res)
        throws ServletException, IOException {
        process(req, res);
    }
```

The Command Interface

This interface defines the contract for all the Command objects used in the system:

```
package web;

import javax.servlet.http.HttpServletRequest;
import javax.servlet.http.HttpServletResponse;

public interface Command {
```

This method should be implemented by all the Command objects:

```
    public String process(HttpServletRequest req, HttpServletResponse res);

}
```

The Roles Interface

This interface enumerates the coded role values used in the web tier:

```
package web;

public interface Roles {
```

The coded role used in the web tier for Standard users:

```
    public static final String STANDARD = "STD";
```

The coded role used in the web tier for Preferred users:

```
    public static final String PREFERRED = "PRF";
}
```

The BeanNames Interface

This interface enumerates the bean names used in the JSP pages:

```
package web;

public interface BeanNames {
```

Bean name under which the balance is stored:

```
    public static final String BALANCE = "balance";
```

Bean name under which the statement is stored:

```
    public static final String STATEMENT = "statement";
```

Bean name under which the error message is stored:

```
    public static final String ERROR = "error";
}
```

The StatementCommand Command Object

This Command object handles the statement requests:

```
package web;

import javax.servlet.http.HttpServletRequest;
import javax.servlet.http.HttpServletResponse;

import ejb.AccountException;

public class StatementCommand implements Command {
```

The inner interface that defines the possible views for the command:

```
    private static interface Views {

        public static final String STATEMENT = "/WEB-INF/Statement.jsp";
        public static final String ERROR = "/WEB-INF/Error.jsp";

    }

    public String process(HttpServletRequest req, HttpServletResponse res) {

        try {
```

Use the account delegate to get the balance and store it as a request scope bean and return the name as the JSP page that will display the balance:

```
            AccountDelegate delegate = new AccountDelegate();
            req.setAttribute(BeanNames.STATEMENT, delegate.getStatement());
            return Views.STATEMENT;

        } catch(AccountException ex) {
```

If an error occurs, store the error message as a request scope bean and return the error JSP name:

```
            req.setAttribute(BeanNames.ERROR, ex.getMessage());
            return Views.ERROR;
        }
    }
}
```

The BalanceCommand Command Object

This Command object handles the balance requests:

```
package web;

import javax.servlet.http.HttpServletRequest;
import javax.servlet.http.HttpServletResponse;

import ejb.AccountException;

public class BalanceCommand implements Command {
```

The inner interface that defines the possible views for the command:

```
    private static interface Views {

        public static final String BALANCE = "/WEB-INF/Balance.jsp";
```

```
        public static final String ERROR = "/WEB-INF/Error.jsp";

    }
    public String process(HttpServletRequest req, HttpServletResponse res) {

        try {
```

Use the account delegate to get the statement and store it as a request scope bean and return the name of the JSP page that will display the statement:

```
        AccountDelegate delegate = new AccountDelegate();
        req.setAttribute(BeanNames.BALANCE, delegate.getBalance());
        return Views.BALANCE;

    } catch(AccountException ex) {
```

If an error occurs, store the error message as a request scope bean and return the error JSP page name:

```
        req.setAttribute(BeanNames.ERROR, ex.getMessage());
        return Views.ERROR;
    }
    }
}
```

The HomeCommand Command Object

This Command object decides which page to display after the initial login based on the role of the authenticated user:

```
package web;

import javax.servlet.http.HttpServletRequest;

import javax.servlet.http.HttpServletRequest;
import javax.servlet.http.HttpServletResponse;

public class HomeCommand implements Command {
```

The inner interface that defines the possible views for the command:

```
    private static interface Views {

        public static final String STATEMENT = "/statement.do";
        public static final String BALANCE = "/balance.do";

    }

    public String process(HttpServletRequest req, HttpServletResponse res) {
```

Return the URI to display statement for preferred customers:

```
        if(req.isUserInRole(Roles.PREFERRED)) return Views.STATEMENT;
```

Return the URI to display balance for standard customers:

```
        else if(req.isUserInRole(Roles.STANDARD)) return Views.BALANCE;
        else throw new IllegalArgumentException("Unexpected Role.");
    }
  }
```

The CommandFactory Factory

This class implements a factory based approach to create Command objects:

```
package web;

public class CommandFactory {

    public static Command getCommand(String path) {
```

Return a Command object based on the specified servlet path:

```
        if(path.equals("/home.do")) return new HomeCommand();
        else if(path.equals("/balance.do")) return new BalanceCommand();
        else if(path.equals("/statement.do")) return new StatementCommand();
        else throw new IllegalArgumentException("Invalid path:" + path);
    }

  }
```

The Account Remote Interface

This is the component interface for the Session Façade that implements the use cases:

```
package ejb;

import javax.ejb.EJBObject;
import java.rmi.RemoteException;

import java.util.ArrayList;

public interface Account extends EJBObject {
```

Business method to get the balance:

```
    public Double getBalance() throws RemoteException, AccountException;
```

Business method to get the statement:

```
    public ArrayList getStatement() throws RemoteException, AccountException;

}
```

The AccountHome Home Interface

```
package ejb;

import javax.ejb.CreateException;
import javax.ejb.EJBHome;
import java.rmi.RemoteException;

public interface AccountHome extends EJBHome {

    public Account create() throws RemoteException, CreateException;

}
```

The AccountEJB Bean Class

This is the bean class for the Session Façade that implements the use cases:

```
package ejb;

import javax.sql.DataSource;
import java.sql.Connection;
import java.sql.PreparedStatement;
import java.sql.ResultSet;
import java.sql.SQLException;

import javax.naming.InitialContext;
import javax.naming.NamingException;

import javax.ejb.SessionBean;
import javax.ejb.EJBException;
import javax.ejb.SessionContext;

import java.util.ArrayList;

public class AccountEJB implements SessionBean {

    private SessionContext ctx;

    public void ejbCreate() {}
    public void ejbActivate() {}
    public void ejbPassivate() {}
    public void ejbRemove() {}
    public void setSessionContext(SessionContext ctx) {
        this.ctx = ctx;
    }
```

```
    public Double getBalance() throws AccountException {

        Connection con = null;
        PreparedStatement stmt = null;
        ResultSet rs = null;
        InitialContext iCtx = null;
        DataSource ds = null;

        try {
```

Get the login ID of the currently authenticated user. The security context is propagated to the EJB container from the web container:

```
            String loginId = ctx.getCallerPrincipal().getName();
```

Look up the datasource:

```
            iCtx = new InitialContext();
            ds = (DataSource)iCtx.lookup("java:/AccountDS");
```

Issue the SQL to get the balance for the authenticated user:

```
            con = ds.getConnection();
            stmt = con.prepareCall(AccountSQL.BALANCE_SQL);
            stmt.setString(1, loginId);

            rs = stmt.executeQuery();
```

Return the balance:

```
            if(rs.next())
                return new Double(rs.getDouble(1));

            throw new AccountException("Account not found.");
        } catch(NamingException ex) {
            throw new EJBException(ex);
        } catch(SQLException ex) {
            throw new EJBException(ex);
        } finally {

            try {
                if(iCtx != null) iCtx.close();
                if(rs != null) rs.close();
                if(stmt != null) stmt.close();
                if(con != null) con.close();
            } catch(Throwable th) {
                th.printStackTrace();
            }
        }
    }
```

```
public ArrayList getStatement() throws AccountException {

    Connection con = null;
    PreparedStatement stmt = null;
    ResultSet rs = null;
    InitialContext iCtx = null;
    DataSource ds = null;

    try {
        String loginId = ctx.getCallerPrincipal().getName();

        iCtx = new InitialContext();
        ds = (DataSource)iCtx.lookup("java:/AccountDS");
```

Issue the SQL to get the statement for the authenticated user:

```
        con = ds.getConnection();
        stmt = con.prepareCall(AccountSQL.STATEMENT_SQL);
        stmt.setString(1, loginId);

        rs = stmt.executeQuery();

        ArrayList statement = new ArrayList();
        AccountDetailVO vo;
        while(rs.next()) {
            vo = new AccountDetailVO();
            vo.transactionDate = rs.getTimestamp(1);
            vo.amount = rs.getDouble(2);
            vo.transactionType = rs.getString(3);
            vo.description = rs.getString(4);
            vo.refNum = rs.getString(5);

            statement.add(vo);
        }
```

Return the statement:

```
        if(statement.size() > 0)
            return statement;

        throw new AccountException("Account not found.");

    } catch(NamingException ex) {
        throw new EJBException(ex);
    } catch(SQLException ex) {
        throw new EJBException(ex);
    } finally {
        try {
            if(iCtx != null) iCtx.close();
            if(rs != null) rs.close();
            if(stmt != null) stmt.close();
            if(con != null) con.close();
```

```
              } catch(Throwable th) {
                  th.printStackTrace();
              }
         }
    }
}
```

The AccountSQL Interface

This interface enumerates the SQL commands used in the system:

```
package ejb;

public interface AccountSQL {
```

SQL to get the balance:

```
    public static final String BALANCE_SQL =
       "SELECT balance " +
       "FROM WR_ACCOUNT, WR_USER " +
       "WHERE WR_ACCOUNT.user_id = WR_USER.id " +
       "AND WR_USER.login_id = ?";
```

SQL to get the statement:

```
    public static final String STATEMENT_SQL =
       "SELECT transaction_date, amount, transaction_type, description, ref_num " +
       "FROM WR_ACCOUNT, WR_USER, WR_ACCOUNT_DETAIL " +
       "WHERE WR_ACCOUNT.user_id = WR_USER.id " +
       "AND WR_ACCOUNT.id = WR_ACCOUNT_DETAIL.account_id " +
       "AND WR_USER.login_id = ?";

    }
```

The AccountDetailVO Value Object

This is the value object used to transfer account detail data from the EJB tier to the presentation tier:

```
package ejb;

import java.sql.Timestamp;

public class AccountDetailVO {

    public Timestamp transactionDate;
    public double amount;
    public String transactionType;
    public String description;
    public String refNum;

}
```

The AccountException Exception

This is the business exception used by the Session Façade:

```
package ejb;

public class AccountException extends Exception {

    /* Creates a new instance of AccountException */
    public AccountException() {
    }

    public AccountException(String message) { super(message); }

}
```

The AccountDelegate Delegate Class

```
package web;

import ejb.Account;
import ejb.AccountHome;
import ejb.AccountException;

import javax.rmi.PortableRemoteObject;

import javax.naming.InitialContext;
import javax.naming.NamingException;

import java.rmi.RemoteException;

import javax.ejb.CreateException;

import java.util.ArrayList;

public class AccountDelegate {
```

A reference to the Session Façade:

```
    private Account account;

    /* Creates a new instance of AccountDelegate */
    public AccountDelegate() {

        try {
```

Look up the home reference for the Session Façade and use it to create the remote reference:

```
            InitialContext ctx = new InitialContext();
            Object obj = ctx.lookup("AccountBean");
            AccountHome home =
                (AccountHome)PortableRemoteObject.narrow(obj, AccountHome.class);
```

```
            account = home.create();

      } catch(NamingException ex) {
          ex.printStackTrace();
          throw new RuntimeException(ex.getMessage());
      } catch(RemoteException ex) {
          ex.printStackTrace();
          throw new RuntimeException(ex.getMessage());
      } catch(CreateException ex) {
          ex.printStackTrace();
          throw new RuntimeException(ex.getMessage());
      }


   }

   public Double getBalance() throws AccountException {

      try {
```

Delegate the method call to the Session Façade:

```
            return account.getBalance();

      } catch(AccountException ex) {
          throw ex;
      } catch(Throwable ex) {
          ex.printStackTrace();
          throw new RuntimeException(ex.getMessage());
      }
   }
   public ArrayList getStatement() throws AccountException {

      try {
```

Delegate the method call to the Session Façade:

```
            return account.getStatement();

      } catch(AccountException ex) {
          throw ex;
      }catch(Throwable ex) {
          ex.printStackTrace();
          throw new RuntimeException(ex.getMessage());
      }
   }
 }
```

JSP Pages Used in the Application

Now, we will have a look at the various JSP pages that are used in the application:

The index.jsp Page

This is the welcome JSP page. This simply forwards the request to the URI `home.do`:

```
<%@page contentType="text/html"%>
 <jsp:forward page="/home.do"/>
```

The Login.jsp Page

This JSP page is used by the container to perform authentication when an unauthenticated user tries to access the system:

```html
<html>
    <head>
        <title>Login Page for Examples</title>
    </head>
    <body bgcolor="white">
        <form method="POST" action='<%= response.encodeURL("j_security_check") %>'
        >
            <table border="0" cellspacing="5">
                <tr>
                    <th align="right">Username:</th>
                    <td align="left"><input type="text" name="j_username"></td>
                </tr>
                <tr>
                    <th align="right">Password:</th>
                    <td align="left"><input type="password"
                    name="j_password"></td>
                </tr>
                <tr>
                    <td align="right"><input type="submit" value="Log In"></td>
                    <td align="left"><input type="reset"></td>
                </tr>
            </table>
        </form>
    </body>
</html>
```

The LoginError.jsp Page

This JSP page is used by the container if authentication fails:

```html
<html>
    <head>
        <title>Error Page For Examples</title>
    </head>
    <body bgcolor="white">
        Invalid username and/or password,
    </body>
</html>
```

The Statement.jsp Page

This JSP is used for displaying the statement:

```jsp
<%@page contentType="text/html" import="java.util.*,ejb.AccountDetailVO"%>
<html>
    <head>
        <title>Account Statement</title>
    </head>
    <body>

        <jsp:useBean id="statement" scope="request" type="java.util.ArrayList" />
        <table>
            <tr>
                <th>Date</th>
                <th>Amount</th>
                <th>Type</th>
                <th>Description</th>
                <th>Reference</th>
            </tr>
            <%
                Iterator it = statement.iterator();
                while(it.hasNext()) {
                    AccountDetailVO vo = (AccountDetailVO)it.next();
            %>
            <tr>
                <td><%= vo.transactionDate %></td>
                <td><%= vo.amount %></td>
                <td><%= vo.transactionType %></td>
                <td><%= vo.description %></td>
                <td><%= vo.refNum %></td>
            </tr>
            <%
                }
            %>
        </table>

        <a href="balance.do">View Balance</a>
    </body>
</html>
```

The Error.jsp Page

This JSP page is used to display error messages:

```jsp
<%@page contentType="text/html" isErrorPage="true" import="web.BeanNames" %>
<html>
<head><title>JSP Page</title></head>
<body>

    <%= request.getAttribute(BeanNames.ERROR) %>

</body>
</html>
```

Summary

In this chapter, we have seen the following patterns associated with security:

- ❑   The Single Access Point pattern
- ❑   The Check Point pattern
- ❑   The Role pattern

We have also implemented these patterns in the case study Wrox Web Bank Application using the standard J2EE API and deployment descriptor features. These patterns can be applied to the design and development of applications, to configuration and management of hosts, and so on; however, these patterns do not define specific technologies nor coding styles. The ultimate goal of these patterns is to support not only the application security but also the host and network security.

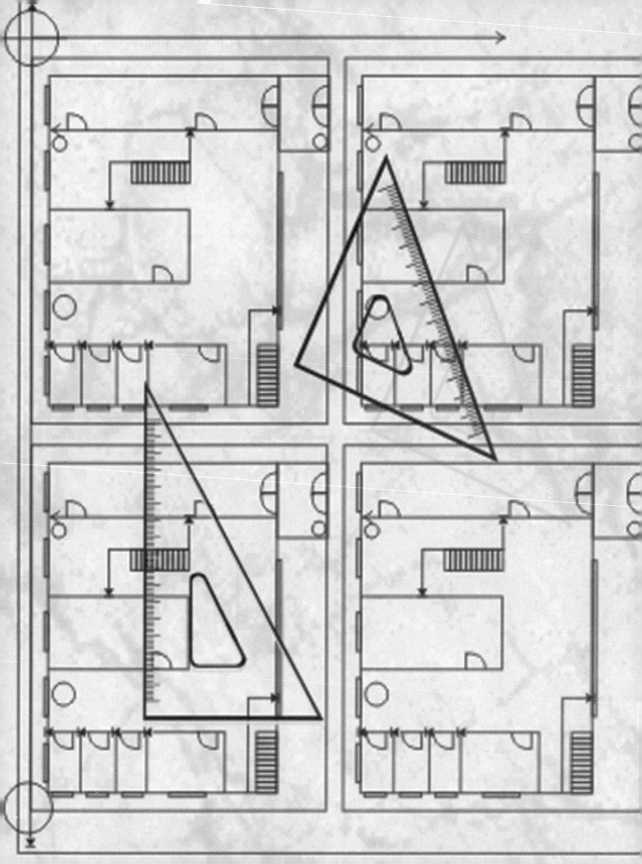

6

Patterns Applied to Enable Enterprise Integration

Enterprise integration is the key success factor for information systems. With the growing requirements for information access and e-business, the need for integrated applications is higher than ever. However, the fact is that most companies have standalone existing applications developed in a variety of technologies, languages, and architectures. These companies cannot afford to write off or replace them overnight because they are mission critical. On the other hand, they need to introduce new applications.

Today, it is particularly important that companies provide support for e-business, which includes B2B (Business-to-Business) and B2C (Business-to-Consumer), and also CRM (Customer Relationship Management), PRM (Partner Relationship Management), SCM (Supply Chain Management), and so on.

The fact is that companies cannot be successful in introducing these new applications without a well-integrated back-end enterprise information system (EIS). Enterprise Application Integration (EAI) has become one of the most difficult problems facing enterprise application development in the last few years. First, it is necessary to allow for application integration within a company, which we call intra-EAI. Second, there are growing needs to ensure inter-EAI or "business-to-business" integration.

At first glance, concrete integration problems and the corresponding solutions are seldom identical. However, after working on several integration projects, we can see that problems and solutions can be classified into common categories. We will call these integration patterns. Integration patterns will help us to understand the different solutions and methods for integration and allow us to choose the best solution for our problem. They allow us to look at integration problems from a certain level of abstraction. Still, these patterns provide sound solutions for intra-EAI as well as inter-EAI.

In this chapter, we will discuss the most important integration patterns and show how to apply them in J2EE standards. We will cover the following:

❑　What is Enterprise Application Integration (EAI)?

❑　Integration patterns for J2EE

    ❑　Integration Broker pattern

    ❑　Integration Wrapper pattern

    ❑　Integration Mediator pattern

    ❑　Virtual Component pattern

    ❑　Data Mapping pattern

    ❑　Process Automator pattern

    ❑　Relationships between integration patterns

❑　Simple integration scenario

❑　Design with pattern identification

❑　Implementing the integration patterns

❑　Using integration patterns for B2B

What is Enterprise Application Integration?

EAI seems to be one of the most strategic priorities for business processes, mainly because new innovative business solutions demand integration of different business units, enterprise data, applications, and business systems. Integrated information systems improve the competitive advantage with unified and efficient access to the information. Integrated applications make it much easier to access relevant, coordinated information from a variety of sources. In effect, the total becomes more than the sum of its parts.

From a business perspective, EAI is the competitive advantage that a company gets when all applications are integrated into a unified information system, capable of sharing information and supporting business work flows. Information must often be gathered from several domains and integrated into a business process. Although the required information may well be available, and might exist in some form somewhere in an application, as a rule, for typical users it is practically inaccessible without EAI.

From a technical perspective, EAI refers to the process of integrating different applications and data to enable sharing of data and integration of business processes among any and all involved applications without having to modify existing applications. EAI uses methods and activities that enable it to be effective in terms of costs and time.

Although these definitions sound simple, many people believe that EAI is one of the most chaotic fields. They believe that identifying problems and selecting solutions can be time consuming and requires a lot of knowledge, and that often even a sixth sense is necessary, to succeed with the integration. Although we will not be able to neglect the fact that integration requires a lot of knowledge and is complex, we will show that with a disciplined and systematic approach, and particularly with application of integration patterns, we can perform integration in a controlled manner with a very good chance of success.

Integration Architecture

The major challenge with EAI is that companies are faced with a disparate mix of heterogeneous existing systems on which they depend. Unfortunately, this mix of different architectures has not been designed in any unified manner; it just grew, and will continue to grow. Heterogeneity thus drains the development resources. The heterogeneity is manifested through:

- ❑ Combinations of monolithic, client-server, and multi-tier applications

- ❑ Mix of procedural and object-oriented solutions

- ❑ Mix of programming languages

- ❑ Different types of database management systems (relational, hierarchical, object)

- ❑ Different middleware solutions for communication (message-oriented middleware, object request brokers, remote procedure calls)

- ❑ Multiple information transmission models, including publish and subscribe, request/reply, and conversational

- ❑ Different transaction and security management middleware

- ❑ Different ways of sharing data

- ❑ Possible usage of EDI, XML, and other formats for data exchange

The answer to the demands of EAI is to build robust and scalable integration architecture. There are five most important integration levels:

- ❑ Data-level integration

- ❑ Application interface integration

- ❑ Business method integration

- ❑ Presentation integration

- ❑ Inter-EAI integration

Application interface and business method integration combined together are sometimes referred to as business-level integration because they share some concepts. Let's now examine these layers of application integration individually.

Data-Level Integration

Data-level integration is often the starting point of application integration. It enables access to the data shared by other applications and allows it to be moved between different data stores. This might sound simple but it can become quite difficult to manage when several hundreds of data stores are involved.

239

Typical difficulties include understanding the schemas, identifying the data, mapping the data between different systems, guaranteeing data consistency, problems with distributed databases, latency with updating them, and so on. In addition, it is necessary to unify the data model, solve the redundancies and other semantic abnormalities that have been introduced in the information systems during their development over the years, which is a difficult task. We also call this schema integration. Compared to other integration levels, data-level integration is relatively easy to implement, because it often does not require changes in the source code of existing applications.

Application Interface Integration

Application interface integration enables a higher level form of integration, where an application can use some functionality of the other applications. This is achieved using the application programming interfaces (APIs) that the applications expose. Often, a form of middleware like message-oriented middleware (MOM), remote method invocation (RMI), or remote procedure call (RPC) is involved for transferring the requests and results.

It is very important to understand that application interface integration solves just technical aspects of integration. In other words, the applications are using technology-oriented, low-level interfaces to achieve interoperability. Application interface integration, however, solves several problems that we have identified by the data-level integration; particularly, it enables the reuse of functionality without duplicating it.

Business Method Integration

Business method integration exposes the high-level methods as abstractions of business methods through interfaces where existing solutions take part in distinctive steps of the business process. Business method integration presents the enterprise-wide information system as we would like to have it or, as we would build it if we could build it anew, with clear requirements on what we would like to get from the integrated system and with the knowledge and support of modern technologies. This means that the information system interfaces are based on a newly designed architecture.

However, the functionalities are not re-implemented; rather, they use existing applications. Those existing applications are remodeled in such a way that they expose the functionality of the business process tier and fit into the modern application architecture.

Achieving business method integration is often connected with business process re-engineering and is not solely a technical problem. It requires the implementation of several technical layers as the foundation and integrates applications at a higher level of abstraction.

Presentation Integration

Presentation integration is about the development of a unified presentation tier, which hides the fact that in the background different applications, some legacy and other newly developed applications are being executed. This way, we improve the efficiency of end users and provide a way to replace parts of legacy systems in the future without influencing the other parts of the system. The figure shows how the user interface components from the presentation tier access the business-logic components. Some of them implement their operations through reuse of existing systems; the others are new developments. Both look exactly the same to the presentation tier components:

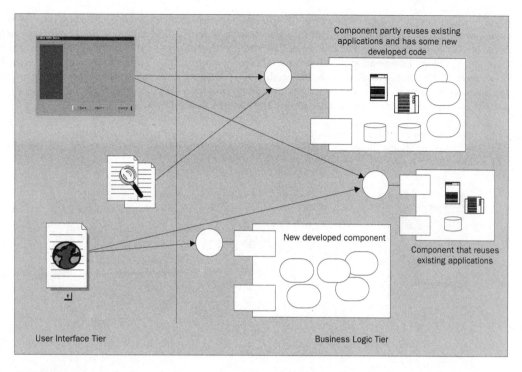

Inter-EAI

Today, even the integration of applications inside a company is not sufficient. There are growing needs to enable inter-enterprise integration, often referred to as B2B integration, or e-business. E-business places particular new challenges before an information system. The requirements today are very high and gone are the days when a company could just publish offline catalogs on its web pages. What is expected is online, up-to-date information, efficiency, reliability, and quality. Even well known names from traditional business cannot expect their position to be maintained in an e-business environment without effort.

Of course, the prerequisite for efficient e-business or B2B integration is an integrated enterprise information system, possibly at the business-process level. Only this level of integration enables on-demand processing of requests. Customers today expect immediate response and are not satisfied with batch processing and several days of delays in confirming orders. However, this is often the case when e-business is not backed by an efficiently integrated enterprise information system. Immediate responsiveness, achieved by highly coupled integration of back-end (enterprise information systems) and front-end (presentation) systems is a key success factor.

Although this sounds obvious, research from leading consulting companies like the Gartner Group shows that today there are very few front-end systems that are efficiently integrated with the backend. Most of these non-integrated applications will fail to meet the business expectations. The primary reason is the lack of enterprise integration, which is the most important prerequisite for both – a successful e-business and an efficient company.

Another important fact is that most front-end applications can use the existing and legacy systems as back-end solutions. Making the integration between such systems efficient will be the key success factor. In particular, immediate response and immediate propagation of data to all related applications will be the major problem. Front-end applications not efficiently supported by back-end systems will certainly fail to meet all requirements. Although this prediction is reasonable, even by 2005 more than a half of the front-end systems will not be adequately integrated, according to prognoses from industry research and advisory organizations, like Gartner Group (http://www.gartner.com/).

To achieve a seamless B2B integration, companies will have to base the inter-EAI connectivity on intra-EAI. The following figure shows the B2B integration layer, implemented as web services, on top of J2EE EAI architecture:

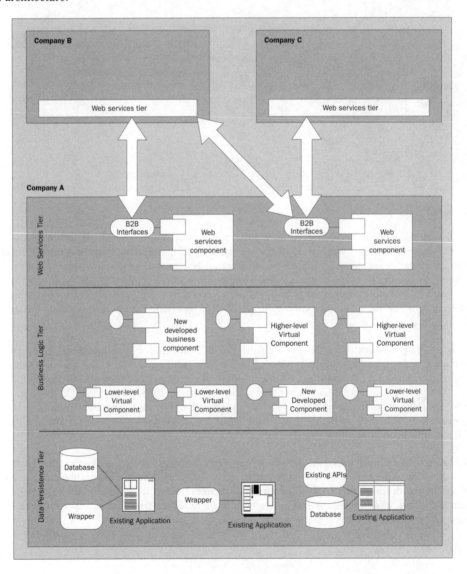

Now that we are familiar with the most important integration levels, let's have a look at J2EE platform in terms of EAI.

EAI with J2EE

As we know, J2EE is built upon the multi-tier application model. The building blocks of each tier are components:

- The components for the client tier are application clients and applets.

- The web-component tier components are servlets and JSP pages, which provide the ability to service thin clients. They respond to HTTP requests and generate thin client user interfaces using HTML, XML, and other technologies.

The components for the business-logic tier are Enterprise JavaBeans (EJB). These often use support services such as transactions, security, and persistence.

The only tier that does not consist of components is the EIS tier. In this tier we find the existing enterprise infrastructure, like ERP systems, TP monitors, database management systems, and other existing systems.

J2EE supports several open standards for communication between tiers. These include HTTP(S) and IIOP protocols, and middleware APIs. The most important Java APIs for integration are:

- Data access middleware: JDBC

- Message-oriented middleware: JMS

- Object request brokers: RMI-IIOP and Java IDL

- Transaction processing: JTA with JTS

- Security: JAAS, and the security APIs from J2SE

- Java Connector Architecture (JCA) for accessing existing EIS system in a universal manner

- XML support through JAXP

- JNDI for integrating different naming and directory services

- Web Services support, although not part of J2EE version 1.3, is available as separate packages

> **The fact that J2EE supports open standards for communication between tiers allows us to include components that have not been developed in Java on any of the tier, thus providing a way to integrate existing applications.**

On the business-logic tier, we can deploy not only EJB components, but also CORBA (and RMI-IIOP) distributed objects and components communicating through a JMS-compliant MOM. This is one of the most important facts for integration. We can see that for developing virtual components on the business-logic tier, we are not limited to EJBs, but can use CORBA, RMI-IIOP, and MOM components too.

Note that CORBA and MOM components do not have to be developed in Java, rather we can use a variety of programming languages. Both CORBA and leading MOM products support all popular programming languages, including C++, C, Smalltalk, Ada, COBOL, Delphi, and even Visual Basic.

These non-Java components do not reside inside the EJB container, and as such cannot take advantage of the managed environment provided by containers. However, they can still take part in transaction and security mechanisms. For this, they have to use the corresponding APIs. We will come to this later.

On the web-component tier we can also deploy other non-Java components. These can include any components that can respond to HTTP(S) requests. Again, we cannot execute them within the J2EE application server provided web container. However, we will not be accessing existing applications directly from the web-component tier, but rather via the business-logic tier.

Similarly, for the client tier, the application clients need not necessarily be Java applications. They can be developed in other languages and use the identified protocols to communicate with the other tiers. Examples include web browsers, CORBA clients, MOM clients, and so on.

All this brings us to the extended J2EE integration architecture that we will use to achieve J2EE EAI, which is conceptually shown in the following figure:

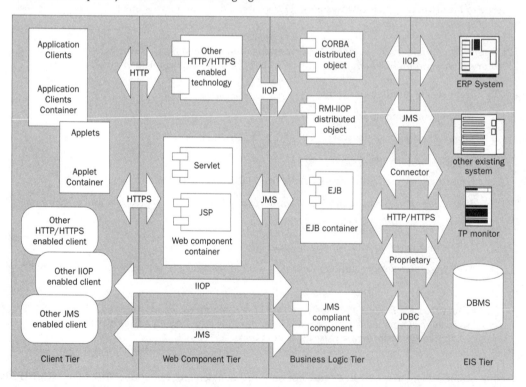

We can see that the extended J2EE integration architecture cleanly separates the tiers and places a limited set of protocols that can be used for communication between the tiers. The business logic tier separates the web-component and the client tier from the EIS tier. The client and web-component tier should not access the EIS tier.

Therefore, the only way to access the EIS tier is from the business-logic tier. Here the EJB, CORBA, RMI-IIOP, and JMS-compliant components use a variety of protocols and technologies to access the EIS tier. Only here we are faced with the heterogeneity of the existing applications that are located in the EIS tier.

To access and exchange the data between applications, we have to define formats for such exchange. In the last few years, XML has established itself as the de facto standard for data exchange. The power of XML lies in the possibility that we can define the tags ourselves. This allows us to describe any data in any structure (although XML is perhaps best suited to hierarchical data structures). However, freely defined tags can cause semantic problems during data exchange. It is impossible for a computer to guess the meaning of the data from the tags.

A vocabulary agreement must be achieved between the parties, where each party has to support the same set of tags, in the form of a clearly defined DTD or Schema. Achieving an agreement on vocabulary inside the company is not as difficult as it is between companies. Therefore, great effort is put into the definition of standardized vocabularies for different industries.

Integration Patterns for J2EE

Integration patterns describe proven methods and processes used for integration within an enterprise or beyond. They emerge from classifications of common integration solutions. Each integration pattern defines a common integration problem and a sound solution. Integration patterns covered in this chapter are focused on J2EE; therefore the examples and application of these patterns are specific to J2EE. However, the patterns themselves are usable on other architectures as well.

In this chapter, we will cover the following architectural integration patterns:

- ❑ Integration Broker pattern (also known as Integration Messenger)
- ❑ Wrapper pattern (Integration Adapter, Integration Connector)
- ❑ Integration Mediator pattern
    - ❑ Single step application integration
    - ❑ Multi step application integration
- ❑ Virtual Component (Integration Façade)
- ❑ Data Access Object (DAO) (Data Exchange pattern) pattern
- ❑ Data Mapping pattern
    - ❑ Direct Data Mapping
    - ❑ Multi-Step Data Mapping
- ❑ Process Automator pattern

Of these, the Data Access Object (DAO) pattern is well known, as it is included in J2EE Design Patterns catalog. Therefore, we will not describe it here. The other patterns are introduced specifically for J2EE integration. The author is not aware that these patterns are described (in this form) in any of the pattern catalogs. Therefore, we will give a short introduction into these patterns, to ease their selection later in the case study, where we will show how to apply them on an example integration scenario. For more information on EAI with J2EE refer to the book *Professional J2EE EAI* from Wrox Press (ISBN-1-861005-44-X).

Integration Broker Pattern

First, we will now look in detail at the Integration Broker pattern.

Context

When integrating applications within a company or between companies, we are usually required to achieve integration between several different applications. Connecting each application with each other is not a valuable solution, because it increases the dependencies – complexity. Thus the maintenance becomes very difficult.

Problem

In point-to-point integration, the application interaction logic is coupled with both the integrated applications. This makes both applications highly dependent on each other, which makes their maintenance complicated and time consuming. Small changes to one application could require modifications to all the other connected applications.

In fact, the maintenance of an integrated system will be more time consuming and costly than the maintenance of the applications themselves, which will make the benefits of integration less obvious. Considering that in a typical integration scenario we are faced with many such applications (often more than fifty), the point-to-point approach becomes unusable, because it leads to an exponential increase in complexity.

Forces

These are as follows:

❑ Separation of responsibilities for different operations is required between applications that need to be integrated

❑ An application should provide a common integration interface, which solves the complexity and does not require building interoperability interfaces for each integration scenario

❑ The integration logic should be separated for easier maintenance

❑ The clients should not see the details of integration

❑ The clients should not see the internal structure of applications being integrated

❑ The communication model should not be limited; rather, the best solution should be used for each application

Solution

The Integration Broker describes the architectural approach to integration of many different applications. It overcomes the disadvantages of point-to-point integration. This pattern minimizes the dependencies between integrated applications and provides one or more communication mechanisms between applications. The Integration Broker is an abstraction for middleware technologies and is realized with a combination of middleware technologies offered by the J2EE platform. It provides the necessary services, such as transaction, security, naming, lifecycle, scalability, management, rules, routing, brokering, and so on.

The Integration Broker will be used by applications that need to be integrated to achieve integration on different levels. Applications will access the integration broker transparently through interfaces in programmatic or declarative ways. The programmatic ways mean that applications will have to implement code to use the infrastructure services. The declarative ways on the other hand enable us to mark specific applications and declare which services they should use and the infrastructure takes care of the details of invoking a service.

The transparency of the provided services for the applications will depend on the selected technology. Communication, brokering, and routing services can be, for example, implemented transparently with the use of object request brokers, which mask remote method invocations to the level that they look like local method invocation to the developers. A message-oriented middleware on the other hand will require that the application creates a message and that it parses incoming messages and reacts to them accordingly. Declarative transaction and security services can provide services to applications without adding any code to the application, and so on.

The Integration Broker opens the path to build the integration layers step-by-step and reuse the previous results. It is not based on the point-to-point communication between applications. Thus, it can reduce the n-to-n multiplicity to n-to-1, which reduces the complexity and simplifies the maintenance. The structure is shown in the following figure:

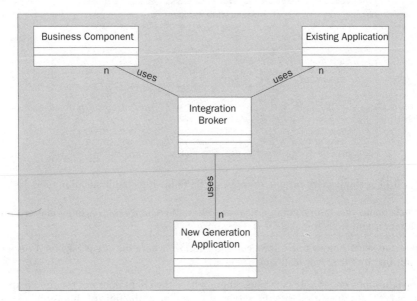

The Integration Broker defines the roles of each application for a certain integration interaction. For each interaction, one or more applications require certain services from a certain application. The applications that require services are called client applications. The application that provides the service is called the server application. Please note that the client and server roles are defined for a certain interaction only and can change during the execution. Usually, all applications will have both roles – they will be server applications for certain interactions and client applications for the other interactions.

The Integration Broker not only connects the applications, but bases the integration on contracts between applications. These contracts are usually expressed as interoperability interfaces. The interoperability interfaces define what services the client applications can request from server applications.

Interoperability interfaces define relations between applications on which they depend. Interfaces as long-living contracts define the coupling between integrated applications. They provide a façade through which client applications access the interoperability services, and encapsulate the applications. As long as the interfaces stay unchanged we can replace parts or whole server applications without influencing any client application. Therefore, great efforts have to be put into the definition of interoperability interfaces.

This is shown in the following figure, where the integration broker schematically connects five applications all with interoperability interfaces, which we will use later for our case study:

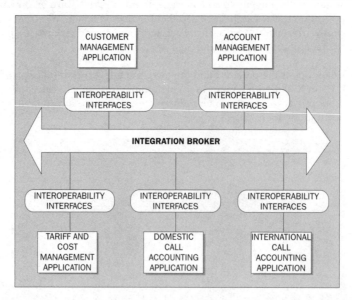

The Integration Broker should support one or more of the following communication models:

❑ Synchronous one-to-one communication, where the client requires immediate response from the server and waits (blocks) for the response.

❑ Deferred synchronous one-to-one communication, where the client asks for a response later or is notified by the server (callback or event).

❑ Asynchronous one-to-one communication, where the client does not require an answer from the server, nor does it require the server to be online at the time of submitting the request.

❑ Asynchronous one-to-many communication, where a single client can communicate with more than one server. This model is also called publish and subscribe.

Typical representatives of this pattern are common middleware technologies, particularly remote method invocations (object request brokers) and message-oriented middleware.

Usually, the Integration Broker pattern is implicitly used in integration. This pattern requires one or more middleware products, which implement the functionality. Today, as a high level of abstraction is achieved, this pattern is not modeled at design time. However, the architecture has to be aware of this pattern and should adapt the communication requests between components.

Consequences

❑ The number of connections between application is reduced, which also reduces the level of coupling between integrated applications

❑ The dependencies between applications are defined as contracts in the form of interoperability interfaces

❑ If the interfaces are carefully designed, we can replace parts or whole applications without influencing other involved applications

❑ The location transparency is achieved

❑ Maintenance effort and costs are therefore reduced to an acceptable level

Related Patterns

This pattern is related to all other integration patterns covered in this chapter. It's also related to the GoF Mediator pattern.

Applying Pattern

In J2EE, either one or the combination of the following technologies can realize the Integration Broker:

❑ **RMI-IIOP**
RMI (Remote Method Invocation) is the primary J2EE technology for synchronous inter-process communication based on interoperability interfaces. Due to the use of IIOP, it enables interoperability with CORBA.

❑ **CORBA**
CORBA offers synchronous, differed synchronous, and asynchronous communication between components and is based on interoperability interfaces. It is not bound to the Java language, thus enabling the integration of applications in different programming languages. Moreover, because RMI-IIOP clients are compatible with CORBA, the EJB and RMI-IIOP components also look like CORBA components. This fact allows us to put components that are not actual EJBs on the business-logic tier. The CORBA implementation included with J2EE (and J2SE) is called Java IDL.

❑ **JMS (MOM)**
The Java Message Service (JMS) enables asynchronous communication based on sending and receiving messages. It supports the point-to-point, and publish/subscribe models. Through JMS, we can use any JMS-compliant MOM product (assuming that we have the MOM client product installed with JMS). JMS provides the abstraction layer and makes applications easily portable between different MOM products. This is very important because MOM middleware has traditionally been used in companies to enable partial integration between applications. Through JMS, we can easily reuse this integration and attach it to the communication paths of existing applications on the EIS tier.

❑ **JDBC**
To access data from a DBMS, we can use the JDBC API that provides a unified interface to access different relational DBMS products through a common interface. JDBC provides four different types of drivers (JDBC-ODBC bridge, JDBC-native driver bridge, JDBC network bridge, and pure Java driver).

❑ **JCA**
The Java Connector Architecture (JCA) solves the problem of custom solutions required today to access different EIS systems. JCA defines system-level contracts for connection management, security, and transactions between an application server and a connector. The connector for each EIS system implements these contracts in an EIS-specific way. J2EE components access the EIS through a standard API called the Common Client Interface (CCI). The CCI hides the differences of EIS systems. In other words, the JCA is for EIS systems what JDBC is for databases.

Integration Wrapper Pattern

We will now look in detail at the Integration Wrapper pattern.

Context

Providing programmatic access to existing applications is important for reusing the functionality of existing applications and developing new solutions. Existing applications may not provide APIs, or the provided APIs might not be sufficient.

Problem

If we want to reuse the functionality of existing applications, we have to access them somehow. The most obvious possibility is to access them through APIs that existing applications provide.

Sometimes, however, existing applications will either not provide any APIs to access their functionality, not even proprietary ones, or they will provide only a subset of functionality through APIs, but we would need access to other functions as well.

Forces

These are as follows:

❑ For integrating and reusing existing applications we need to access them programmatically

❑ Through API access, we can reuse data and functionality of existing applications

❑   Accessing the application through APIs is better than going into the database directly, because we do not avoid business logic

Solution

The Integration Wrapper pattern is a layered approach to adding APIs to existing applications. This means that the services and functionality of existing applications are exported to other applications thus enabling interoperability and integration. Its motivation lies in the Adapter pattern (GoF); however, the goal of the Integration Wrapper is to provide reusable interfaces for multiple clients to access simultaneously.

To develop wrappers, we will build a layer around the existing application and add the necessary interfaces. We will call the added application interfaces wrappers and the modified existing application will be called a wrapped existing application.

The Integration Wrapper has two major objectives:

❑   It should provide open and reusable interoperability interfaces

❑   It should convert the calls to reuse the services and functionality of existing application

For the latter, the Integration Wrapper can either reuse the APIs already provided or add such APIs. The structure of the Integration Wrapper is shown in the following figure:

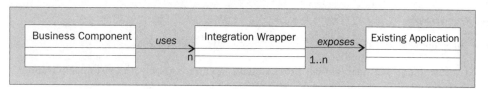

Generally, the wrapper can add APIs in an intrusive or non-intrusive way. There are two possibilities to add wrappers to existing applications:

❑   We can modify existing applications and provide the missing access to the functionality

❑   We can use screen scraping or terminal emulation to access the functionality though user interfaces

One criterion that will influence the decision between modifying the existing applications and using screen scrapping or terminal emulation will be the availability of source code and the required tools. We have to make sure that the versions of source code are complete and reflect the current executable code. If we do not have the source code and all tools and libraries necessary to build the working executable of the existing application, our only choice will be to utilize user interface wrapping (discussed a little later in the chapter).

Even if we have the source code and all required tools, we may choose not to modify existing applications and rather use screen scraping or terminal emulation. The reason can be that we don't want to risk introducing bugs into the existing application, that we are not familiar with the technology of existing application, and so on.

Even before we select one of these choices we have to identify the operations through which we will access the existing application functionality. We will figure this out with the existing application analysis. We have to analyze the application, and must focus on what we actually need. The wrapper is schematically shown in the following figure:

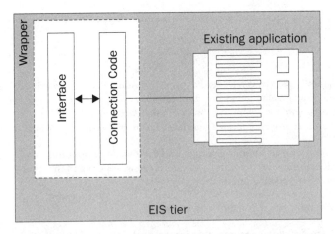

The Integration Wrapper pattern is related to the Integration Broker pattern. Depending on the type of communication, the structure of the wrapper differs. If we use synchronous communication style, such as remote method invocation, then the infrastructure will force typed communication and will check the operation signatures. When using asynchronous communication, the wrapper is responsible for decomposing the messages.

Consequences

The consequences are as follows:

❏ Integration Wrapper enables programmatic communication with existing applications

❏ It enables reuse of services and functionality of existing applications

❏ It hides the details of the internal structure of existing applications, their technologies, programming model, and communication details

❏ It reduces the complexity and decouples the clients

Related Patterns

The related patterns are Integration Broker, Virtual Component, and GoF Adapter.

Applying the Pattern

There are a variety of technologies suitable for developing wrappers. In general, we can choose from the following:

❏ ORB-style communication, using CORBA or COM+

❏ MOM communication using one of the products like IBM MQseries (one that supports JMS mapping)

❏ Implementing communication at the protocol level (SOAP, HTTP, TCP/IP, and so on)

❏ RPC style communication using a distributed computing environment (DCE)

❏ Direct communication through Java Native Interface (JNI)

The fact is that Integration Wrappers will rarely be implemented in Java, because existing applications are usually not in Java. Therefore we will focus on technologies that are interoperable with J2EE on one side and support other programming languages on the other. The most important are CORBA, JMS (MOM), and SOAP. Later, we will demonstrate how to develop a wrapper in CORBA.

Integration Mediator Pattern

We will now look in detail at the Integration Mediator pattern.

Context

When integrating applications, the integration logic often needs to be separated from all involved applications and also to be encapsulated to minimize dependencies, increase reuse, and simplify maintenance.

Problem

For existing applications that need to be integrated with each other, or where a common functionality is distributed among several applications and/or duplicated in several existing applications we often need integration logic, which will solve these problems and represent a service or functionality in a common way to its clients. The clients should be unaware of the complexity, hidden inside the mediator.

Forces

These are as follows:

❑   Existing applications often need to be integrated with each other

❑   Certain functionality is often distributed among more than one existing application

❑   Certain functionality is often duplicated in more than one existing application

❑   The interaction between applications is complex

❑   Clients should be unaware of this complexity

Solution

The Integration Mediator acts like a controller for involved existing applications and provides an interface for clients. It should be aware of the existing applications and include the interaction logic to fulfill certain higher-level operations, which require complex interaction with existing and/or new developed applications. The integration logic contained inside the Integration Mediator can be used for different integration levels, such as data-level integration or function- and method-level integration. The Integration Mediator should not access the existing applications directly. Rather it should use integration wrappers.

The structure of the Integration Mediator shows the client, integration wrappers, and the mediator in the following figure:

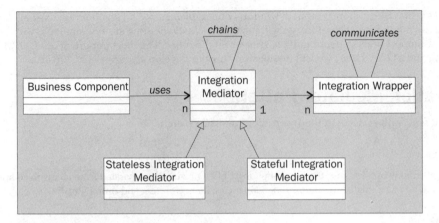

Generally, there are two forms of integration mediators:

❑ Single-step or Stateless

❑ Multi-step or Stateful

Stateless mediators are used for integration scenarios where the maintenance of state during interaction with existing applications is not necessary. This means that the way the mediator acts depends only on the response from the existing applications. Examples are routing and brokering, and vocabulary transformation. A typical example of stateless mediator is an XSLT engine.

Stateful Integration Mediator is used when we have to keep track of previous interactions with applications. The mediator then accumulates the data about previous interactions and uses this information for further interactions. Stateful Integration Mediators are also those based on events, that remember events and after all required events have been triggered perform a certain action.

Stateful Integration Mediator requires that the state is managed and sometimes even persisted. State persistence might be needed for interactions with existing applications, which take a longer time to survive system shutdowns. Such long-lasting interactions might be very complex, lasting from a few minutes to hours or even days.

Consequences

These are as follows:

❑ Application dependencies are minimized

❑ The integration logic is encapsulated and decoupled from the participating existing applications and new clients

❑ Maintenance is simplified as integration logic is centralized rather than distributed among existing applications

❑ Services can be built on top of the functionality provided by the mediator, thus they don't have to be aware of the complexity of existing applications

Related Patterns

The related patterns are Integration Wrapper, Virtual Component, GoF Mediator, and GoF Façade.

Applying the Pattern

For developing integration mediators in J2EE we have a variety of technology choices, including EJBs, CORBA components, RMI-IIOP distributed objects, JMS, and JCA. However, the most common choice is EJB, which maps directly with different types of mediators. For Stateless Mediators, we will use stateless session beans or message-driven beans. For Stateful Mediators, we will choose between stateful session beans and entity beans, depending on the persistence type we require.

Virtual Component Pattern

We will now look in detail at the Virtual Component pattern.

Context

Accessing the services of an integrated information system can vary, particularly if the integration system uses a variety of existing applications implemented in different technologies. Accessing these services directly would require that the clients possesses knowledge of the internal structure of the information system. The Virtual Component provides a common, unified access point for services, thus acting as a façade to existing applications.

Problem

Clients accessing the integrated information system should not be aware of the complexity of existing applications and should not access them directly. An integrated information system is also more than just connected existing applications. It should provide new services and functionalities. These should be exposed to the clients in a common, uniform way. If clients accessed existing applications directly, they would be highly coupled with them, making maintenance and replacement very difficult.

Forces

These are as follows:

- ❑   Existing applications do not provide the high-level services and functionalities required by clients
- ❑   Clients should not be aware of the complexity of the information system
- ❑   Client should use high-level services

Solution

The Virtual Component pattern provides a solution for integrating existing applications with clients. The pattern has its motivation in the Façade pattern; however, it is targeted towards integration and provides reusability and the ability to re-engineer and replace the applications behind the virtual component with actual, modern implementation. An integrated information system based on the Virtual Component pattern is a system that looks like a newly developed information system when, in fact, it reuses the functionality of existing applications.

Virtual components do not differ from new developed components from the perspective of the clients. Both provide the functionality through the interfaces. The concept of virtual components will therefore allow us to make existing applications look like newly developed components and to mix existing and new applications in any and every possible way.

The Virtual Component pattern encapsulates the details that existing applications contribute to satisfying requests and the methods by which they are satisfied. On one side, it presents the existing application through abstract interoperability interfaces. On the other side, the Virtual Component communicates with Integration Wrapper and Integration Mediator. This is shown in the following figure:

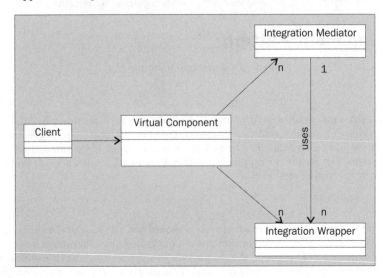

The Virtual Component might be, for example, an order placing component, which provides a simple interface to place an order and internally accesses existing systems like the payment system, inventory system, and so on.

The Virtual Component together with abstract interoperability interfaces presents an application view that is implementation independent. If we keep the abstract interface constant, the other applications would not be aware of any changes that are made to the original application. Thus, there is no need for modifying other applications that depend on the original application when a change is made. In other words, client virtual components are unable to determine how the server virtual components are implemented.

The Integration Broker pattern influences exactly how a virtual component will be implemented. In each case the Virtual Component masks the complexity of the existing applications that implement the high-level business functionality in the background.

The Virtual Components are deployed on the business-logic tier. They are built in several stages during integration. The different virtual components expose interfaces that offer different abstraction levels to access the functionality. Therefore, we will organize the virtual components into several sub-tiers on the business-logic tier.

We will build the following virtual-tier components:

❑ Lower-level virtual components to access the existing databases. These virtual components will be developed in data-level integration.

❑ Lower-level virtual components to access functionality of existing applications. These virtual components will be developed in application interface-level integration.

❑ Higher-level virtual components that will expose high-level business methods. These virtual components will be developed in business-method-level integration.

The virtual components on a lower level will take care of technology adoption, and will be built on data level and application interface-level integration. The virtual components on higher levels will transform the high-level business request into a series of lower-level calls to different lower-level virtual components for existing applications. The high-level virtual components will also do some data conversions and adaptions to finally reach the goal of implementing the functionality through reuse of existing applications.

The organization of virtual components into multiple sub-tiers inside the business-logic tier is shown in the following diagram, where a higher-level virtual component accesses three lower-level virtual components, which access existing systems. The arrows show the communication in the following diagram:

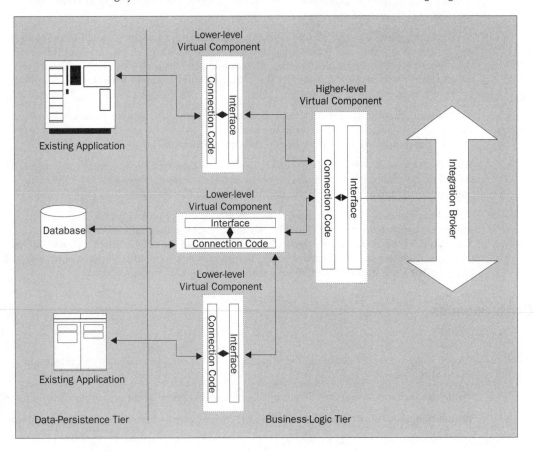

We will typically use virtual components for one or a combination of the following functions:

❑ Virtual components encapsulate the functionality of existing applications and present it in the same way, or some rearranged way. Virtual components can, for example, present exactly the same functionality that can be found in the existing application APIs. In this case, they just mask the technology differences and are called lower-level virtual components.

❑ Lower-level virtual components implement code that translates the method invocations into one or more calls to APIs of existing applications and databases accesses. This code will often have to do parameter transformations, alignment of data types, and other transformations to mask the technology differences between the J2EE technologies and technologies used by existing applications. In more simple terms, the lower-level virtual components will act as adapters between the new and the existing applications.

❑ Virtual components can provide a different, higher-level interface and thus mask the way existing applications implement their APIs, too. Such virtual components are called higher-level virtual components and their interfaces should be defined based on a global design model, which we will discuss later in this chapter.

❑ Virtual components can encapsulate several existing applications and help in maintaining transaction integrity and security.

❑ Virtual components are also useful to encapsulate or abstract persistent data. For this purpose, the virtual components can access EIS databases directly or through provided protocols. In this case, they often also implement the validation logic. This is an extra level of security, which might not have been handled by the old application, that will keep the database in a consistent state.

❑ Virtual components can provide a unified access to several EIS databases and can handle different combinations of databases in the background. Alternatively, they can use APIs to access data, if those APIs are provided by existing applications.

❑ Virtual components will often be layered, thus higher-level virtual components will aggregate the behaviors of lower-level virtual components and provide the higher level of abstraction required for multiple levels of abstraction of EIS application functionality.

❑ Virtual components can also be used to map technical differences. A particularly useful scenario is using them to adapt synchronous and asynchronous communication models. Through the J2EE technologies, particularly JMS, they will be able to adapt different MOM products. Adapting the ORB products will, in most cases, not be difficult because they are all based on the IIOP protocol (and are therefore interoperable).

Consequences

These are as follows:

❑ Virtual components provide a unified view on the services and functionality of integrated information system

❑ Virtual components abstract the details of the information system, thus providing a sort of façade

❑ Virtual components provide high-level, business-process-oriented interfaces for interoperability

❏ Virtual components enable easy replacement with new components as long as the interfaces stay unchanged

Related Patterns

The related patterns to the Virtual Component pattern are Façade, Integration Wrapper, Integration Mediator, and Integration Broker.

Applying the Pattern

When developing virtual components, we should follow these guidelines:

❏ We should design virtual components such that they can be used in different scenarios. The high-level virtual components should support different combinations of low-level virtual components. Low-level virtual components should be easily adjustable to different EIS systems.

❏ A higher-level virtual component should not rely on the environment in which it is executing, and should also not make assumptions about the environment. This will make replacement with a new component easier.

❏ A virtual component should be capable of cooperating in the transaction and security models used by the J2EE integration architecture. Furthermore, it should be capable of mapping those transactions and security models to existing applications, if they support transactions and/or security. If they do not, the virtual component will have to provide this functionality, depending on the particular requirements of the project in hand.

We have also already identified that the virtual components will be deployed on the business-logic tier. In J2EE integration architecture, we can use the following appropriate technologies: EJB, RMI-IIOP, CORBA, JMS, JCA, JAX/RPC (including SOAP), and JAXM. The latter two technologies are still under development, therefore currently not very common, but this might change in the future.

Selecting the appropriate technology will not be a particularly difficult task. The first three technologies are EJB, RMI-IIOP, and CORBA, based on the IIOP protocol, making the choice rather simple. They provide synchronous, ORB-like communication interfaces. The virtual components built in to all three technologies look similar, exposing their functionality for remote method invocation to Java-based and other IIOP-compliant clients. Due to the similarity, we can exchange the implementations in any of these technologies without the need to alter the clients (clients would not even note the difference).

CORBA and RMI-IIOP

We will use CORBA and RMI-IIOP particularly for lower-level virtual components, which will often have to communicate with existing applications in other programming languages. We will use CORBA virtual components when they have to use proprietary mechanisms to access existing application APIs that cannot be invoked from Java. For this purpose, we'll consider using CORBA together with the programming language of the existing application. To access these CORBA virtual components, we will often use RMI-IIOP.

The lower-level virtual components will often communicate directly with existing applications on the EIS tier. They will use any or a combination of protocols and technologies to access the EIS tier. This includes the use of JMS, Connectors, IIOP, HTTP, JDBC, or proprietary mechanisms to access the APIs or databases of existing applications.

JMS

We'll use JMS particularly for lower-level virtual components when we will have to achieve asynchronous message-oriented communication, through one or a combination of MOM products. Often, we will use the MOM on one side through JMS, and on the other side we will usually use a MOM product natively.

EJB

We will use EJBs particularly for developing higher-level virtual components. These virtual components will often communicate with lower level virtual components, developed in other technologies.

If we need to provide synchronous access over RMI-IIOP to APIs or wrappers, we will use session beans to implement virtual components. They will often have to call several methods and will also have to transform and adapt the results. If the virtual component does not need to store any client-dependent data between method invocations (from the client and web-component tier) we will select stateless session beans; otherwise, we will implement them with stateful session beans.

If we would like to provide asynchronous access to APIs or wrappers then we can use message-driven beans to provide the functionality to the clients. We implement the connection with existing systems in a similar way to session beans. The fact that message beans are stateless does not cause problems with asynchronous requests, as it is highly unlikely that the bean would need to memorize client-dependent information.

To represent persistent data, we can use entity beans. If we implement direct access to the database using JDBC we can use container-managed persistence. If we access data over proprietary protocols or over APIs or wrappers we will have to use bean-managed persistence.

J2EE Connector Architecture

The J2EE Connector Architecture (JCA) is solving the problem of custom solutions required today to access commercial EIS systems. JCA defines system-level contracts for connection management, security, and transactions between an application server and a connector. The connector for each EIS system implements these contracts in EIS-specific way. J2EE components access the EIS through a standard API, called the Common Client Interface (CCI). The CCI hides the differences of EIS systems.

JAX/RPC and JAXM

Sometimes, particularly when integrating newer systems or even new generation systems developed on other enterprise architectures, we will consider using modern XML-based protocols, like SOAP. For this purpose, we will use the same architecture as the one presented for wrapping different existing systems. The only difference will be that we will use JAX/RPC or JAXM interfaces to access those systems through XML-based interfaces. Using XML-based protocols (such as SOAP) moves the integration towards B2B integration.

Later, we will show an example of how to develop a virtual component.

Data Mapping Pattern

We will now look in detail at the Data Mapping pattern.

Context

When integrating existing applications, the data often needs to be moved from one application to another. Access to the databases of existing applications varies from the type of data store (relational, object, hierarchical, flat files, and so on) and the way data is accessed (directly to the database, through an application, and so on).

Problem

The data mapping logic can get complex, therefore it is preferable if it is encapsulated and decoupled for existing applications. This way the data mapping logic is less coupled with existing applications, which improves maintenance.

Forces

These are as follows:

❑   Data needs to be moved between existing applications

❑   Data is stored in different formats in existing applications

❑   Accessing this data varies with the type of storage and access technologies

❑   The data mapping logic should be separated and should not be complicated with technical details

Solution

The Data Mapping pattern is used to encapsulate and abstract the data mapping logic for transferring, replicating, and updating data between related integrated existing applications. This pattern accesses the data store, either directly, through DAO, or using wrappers.

The Data Mapping pattern comes in two variations:

❑   Direct Data Mapping

❑   Multi-Step Data Mapping

The Direct Data Mapping pattern handles the mapping where data needs to be moved from a certain data store to another without transformations. The Multi-Step Data Mapping also transforms the data. The structure of the pattern is shown in the following diagram:

261

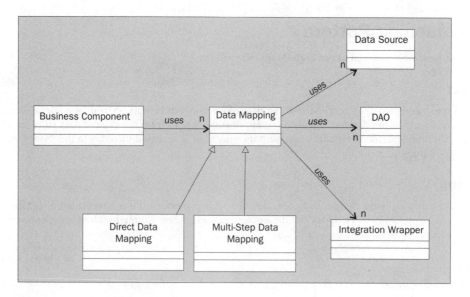

Consequences

The consequences are as follows:

- ❑ The data mapping logic is encapsulated and decoupled from the participating existing applications and their data stores

- ❑ Data dependencies are minimized

- ❑ Maintenance is simplified as the data mapping logic is centralized rather than distributed among existing applications

- ❑ Business components can use the functionality provided by the Data Mapping pattern, thus they don't have to be aware of the data complexity of existing applications

Related Patterns

The related patterns to the Data Mapping pattern are Integration Wrapper, Integration Mediator, and Data Access Object.

Applying the Pattern

The Data Mapping pattern can be implemented using entity EJBs. For single-step application integration, we can choose between bean- and container-managed persistence (BMP, CMP). For Multi-Step Data Mapping, the only choice is to use BMP, because CMP currently does not provide the required functionality. An option is to use third-party relational mapping tools and XSLT engines.

Now that we are familiar with architectural integration patterns, let's have a quick look at the Process Automator pattern.

Process Automator Pattern

We will now look in detail at the Process Automator pattern.

Context

System interactions should often be hidden and abstracted by the process controller. The dependencies between business process controllers and system logic of the information system should also be minimized.

Problem

The services of an integrated information system should be exposed to clients through high-level methods that reflect their business processes. A typical business process method will require interaction with different virtual components and integration mediators. This interaction should not be delegated to the clients, because this enhances the complexity, increases the maintenance effort, and does not allow us to use declarative transaction management.

Forces

These are as follows:

❑ Services of the integrated system should be exposed as high-level business-process methods

❑ The business-process interaction logic should be abstracted and encapsulated on the middle tier

❑ Clients should not be responsible for making the necessary operation invocations

❑ Business-process logic should often be performed inside transactions

❑ The dependencies between process automation control and the information system technology should be minimized

Solution

The Process Automator pattern helps to gather and encapsulate business-process logic and thus minimizes the dependencies between business-process automation logic and information technology system logic. The Process Automator controller hides all interactions. This pattern helps to improve the quality of business processes, reduce process execution costs, and reduce development. Therefore this pattern is highly appropriate for defining integration process within and between companies.

The Process Automator pattern sequences the activities of a business process and delegates steps to the corresponding parts of the information system. It does this using virtual components and integration mediators, through which the automator components access the functionality of existing applications. The Process Automator can, however, access newly developed components as well. The structure is shown in the following figure:

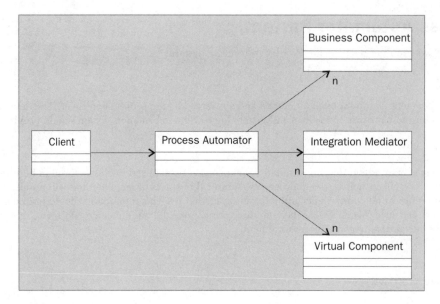

The common uses for the Process Automator pattern are the definition of business activities, timers, and for process-context information. It comes in two variations:

❑   Closed Process Automator

❑   Open Process Automator

The difference is exclusively in the semantic understanding of both types of processes. The Closed Process Automator implements a process that is managed internally and externalizes the key process activities only through the data exchange. The clients are able to monitor the activities within the process, but cannot actively participate in their execution.

The Open Process Automator enables sharing business process between clients. Such processes are managed by more than one client and are particularly useful for inter-EAI or B2B integration where more than one company shares a single process.

Consequences

These are as follows:

❑   The architecture allows easy analysis of business processes, their bottlenecks, utilization, downtime, and so on

❑   Flexibility is achieved for redefining the business process

❑   The Process Automator components are aligned with the business manager's view, which reduces the semantic gap between IT and management

❑   With the connection to virtual components and integration mediators, highly flexible integration architecture can be defined

Related Patterns

The related patterns to the Process Automator pattern are Virtual Component and Integration Mediator.

Applying the Pattern

Applying the Process Automator pattern to J2EE requires the selection of appropriate technology. In J2EE, the most appropriate components are:

❑   Session beans

❑   Message-driven beans

❑   Web services

The selection depends on the interaction model that we require. We will use session beans when we require synchronous communication and expect an immediate response on our requests. The use of stateless or stateful session beans depends on the nature of the process. We will use stateless beans when the process will not require storing any intermediate, client-dependent state. On the other hand, when the process will require maintaining the state, we will use stateful session beans.

If we want to model long-lasting, update-type processes where we will not require an immediate answer, we should select message-driven beans. These can model process automators, which do not require to store client-dependent state and which do not require immediate notification to the client.

Web services, in J2EE built on top of EJBs, are particularly useful for implementing inter-EAI (B2B) process automators. Later in this chapter, we will demonstrate how to use both types of EJBs to implement the process automator component.

Before we discuss the application of the patterns, let's have a look at the relations between the presented integration patterns.

Relationships Between Integration Patterns

To understand the integration patterns, it is very important to understand the relationships between them. Therefore, in the following figure, we present the most important dependencies between the presented patterns. We can see that the Process Automator usually depends on one or more Virtual Components, which use Integration Mediators to support the communication with Integration Wrappers and Data Mappings. Usually, Data Mappings use Data Access Objects. Integration Wrapper, Integration Mediator, and Virtual Component depend on Integration Broker pattern:

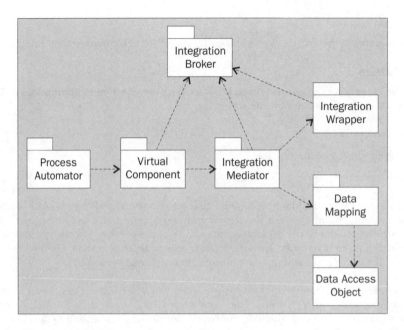

To understand how to apply these patterns, we will introduce a case study where we will show a practical example, in which these patterns are implemented.

Simple Integration Scenario

Now that we have become familiar with integration patterns, let's take a look at the simple integration scenario where we will demonstrate how to apply those patterns. The scenario for integration is simplified and is based on a hypothetical mobile operator company. The mobile phone operator provides services for digital (GMS) mobile telephony. It started its business many years ago with the analog services and through the years subsequently expanded. Today, it offers digital telephony only. The main services are two types of mobile accounts:

❑   **Subscriber account** is an account where the customer receives an invoice each month and has to pay it later

❑   The **prepaid account** is an account where the customer has to put money on the account in advance and cannot use more that the current balance

The architecture of the information system did not follow the evolution of the company. The mobile operator does not have an integrated information system and uses a set of non-connected or partially connected applications (existing applications in our terminology). The primary applications that the operator uses are the following:

❑   **Mobile phone customer information application**
    This enables management of phone customers. This includes entering new customers, updating existing customers, and adding data about the phone account that they have.

❑ **Application that manages the account balance for mobile phone users**
This manages both types of accounts. It allows data to be entered regarding the consumption of money and about the deposits on the accounts (they can be either the payments of the invoices or the advance deposits, depending of the account type). It also enables searching for accounts that have a negative balance (for the subscribers). For the prepaid accounts, it allows a search for accounts that have had zero balance for a specified period of time. This is because those accounts are then automatically disconnected. Finally, it allows searching for money deposits on accounts based on the age. Please notice that this and the previous application are not connected and require manual input.

❑ **Application that prints the invoices each month**
This is a simple one that goes through the subscriber accounts and prints the invoices for the consumptions for the specified month.

❑ **Application that evaluates the domestic mobile phone calls**
This calculates the consumption for each account based on the data transferred from the mobile phone exchange, but only for domestic calls.

❑ **Application that calculates the international mobile phone calls**
This has a similar function to the domestic application. However, it does not have a direct connection with the mobile phone exchange. Rather, it receives input data formatted from each roaming partner.

❑ **Application that manages the mobile phone calls tariff information**
This includes functions to enter and display the tariff information. This includes tariff policies, tariff classes, and costs-per-minute for voice and data communication.

Some of the primary applications are not integrated at all. Therefore the users have to manually enter the data several times into different applications. The other primary applications facilitate simple data exchange based on sharing of files with data, formatted in proprietary format. The following diagram shows the applications and dependencies. Those denoted Manual require manual data entry, while those denoted Automatic are performed as occasional data transfers:

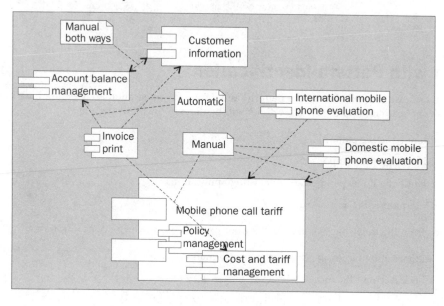

Such a set of applications cannot fulfill several needs and does not provide the efficiency that could be achieved with an integrated information system. We can, however, also see that we will not be able to cover all the requirements for the integrated system in this chapter. Rather, we will focus on the two most important functionalities, which are not provided by the existing system, and on which we will demonstrate the integration patterns:

❑   Mobile phone users should be able to check their account balance at any time online, using the mobile phone (WAP or SMS), or a PC (Internet browser). The information provided should be accurate and include all domestic and international calls, as well as any discounts (based on the monthly usage of the phone and on the average use during the last six months, for example).

❑   Mobile phone users should be able to deposit money on the mobile phone account using the mobile phone (WAP or SMS), or a PC (Internet browser). Money should be charged to the credit card that the user enters. The money deposit should be performed only if the credit card authorization is successful.

We can also easily identify that both use cases perform authorization and selection of the account. The use case diagram will then look like this:

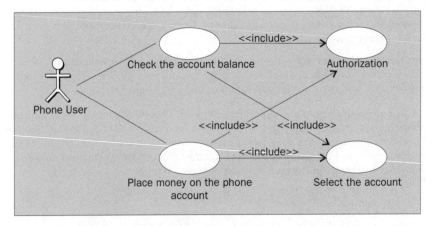

Design with Pattern Identification

For each use case, we will identify the patterns and design the integration architecture based on these patterns. The main tasks of the design activity will be done in the following steps:

❑   Identifying the patterns

❑   Identifying the components

❑   Identifying the dependencies on existing applications

❑   Determining the architecture

Let us focus on the following two use cases for our example now, which are as follows:

❑   Authorization (accessing the customer information)

❑   Check Account Balance

Authorization (Accessing the Customer Information)

From the perspective of integration, the authorization will be connected with accessing the information about customers. Therefore, we will look at how to present the customers' information stored in the existing applications.

We will use the following integration patterns:

- ❑ Virtual Component pattern
- ❑ Data Mapping pattern
- ❑ Data Access Object (DAO) pattern
- ❑ Integration Wrapper pattern

Note that here we focus solely on integration patterns. As these patterns will be implemented using J2EE technologies, we could apply general J2EE design patterns covered in previous chapters as well.

Next, we have to identify the components. The high-level components can be identified from the analysis model. The problem is that although this task sounds easy, it is not. Selecting the right components will have a long-lasting influence on the information system as a whole. The selection will also determine how suitable the integration architecture will be to re-engineer existing applications and replace them with newly developed solutions.

Our example of the mobile phone operator is relatively simple. Therefore the identification of virtual components will also be simple. We will use the CustomerVC virtual component to represent the customers to the J2EE clients.

Now, let's identify the dependencies on existing applications and databases. We can see that the required data is stored in the account balance management database and in the customer information application. This is shown in the following figure:

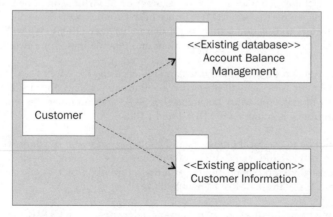

We can see that we need to access the account balance management application. For this, we will use the Integration Wrapper pattern. As we will access data only, we will abstract this interaction with a DAO. We will also use DAO to access the existing customer information database. To extract, compare, and join the data from the two applications, we will use the Data Mapping pattern. This brings us to the following design:

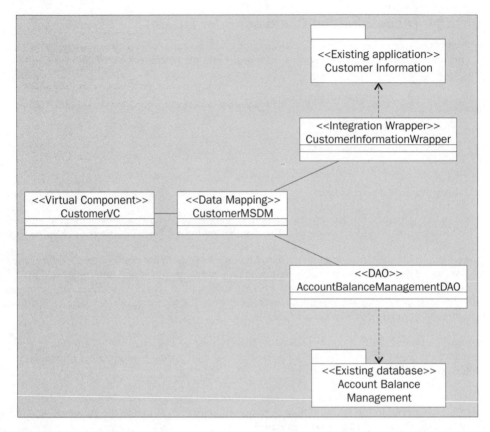

Next, we have to select the technologies. For the `CustomerVC` virtual component we will use entity beans with bean-managed persistence (BMP). Entity beans are best suited to represent entity components, which store transaction state and are shared between clients. We will use BMP and not CMP because we have to access existing applications and map the data from two different applications.

We will access the date and do the required data mappings using the Multi-Step Data Mapping pattern, which we will implement as dependent objects. We will use dependent objects for both DAO objects as well. With this, we will make the entity bean coarse-grained and minimize the remote method invocation. This approach is suitable for EJB 1.1 and EJB 2.0.

An alternative would be to use local interfaces and container-managed relations. However, this solution would be limited to EJB 2.0 and would offer a slightly lower performance, because the container would be still involved in local method invocations. For more information on this, please refer to the book *Professional EJB* from Wrox Press (ISBN 1-861005-08-3).

Finally, we will implement the `CustomerInformationWrapper` as a CORBA integration wrapper. Using CORBA will allow us to develop the wrapper in a different programming language and we need synchronous access to the existing application. CORBA is suitable for this task.

Next, let's look at the Check Account Balance use case.

Check Account Balance

In the previous description, we have seen that checking the account balance requires interaction with several existing applications. Therefore we would have to access these applications in the right way and coordinate the whole interaction logic. We also have to present this functionality as a high-level service, accessible by other J2EE clients.

We will use the following patterns:

- ❏ Process Automator
- ❏ Virtual Component
- ❏ Integration Mediator
- ❏ Integration Wrapper

Next, we have to identify the high-level components, where we recapitulate the analysis class diagram (not shown here). We can identify the following components:

- ❏ The `CheckBalance` component will implement the Process Automator pattern
- ❏ The `AccountVC` (Account entity component from the analysis) will implement the Virtual Component pattern

To identify other components, we first have to identify the related existing applications. We will focus on the operation that allows checking the account balance of a certain mobile account. The existing applications will certainly support this functionality; however, the functionality is not gathered inside a single existing application. Therefore, this component will have to depend on more than one existing application.

To calculate the current balance of a mobile account, the component will have to interact with existing applications. The dependencies are shown in the following diagram:

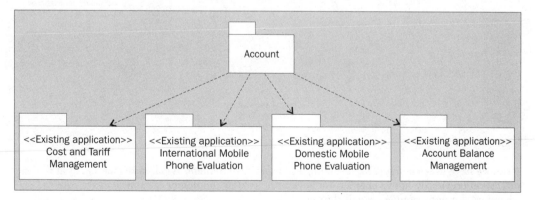

These dependencies will allow us to identify the other required components. To interact with existing applications we will use integration wrappers, which will provide programmatic access to them. For domestic and international mobile phone evaluation, we will also use an Integration Mediator pattern, which will coordinate the interaction logic with both existing applications.

This brings us to the following design:

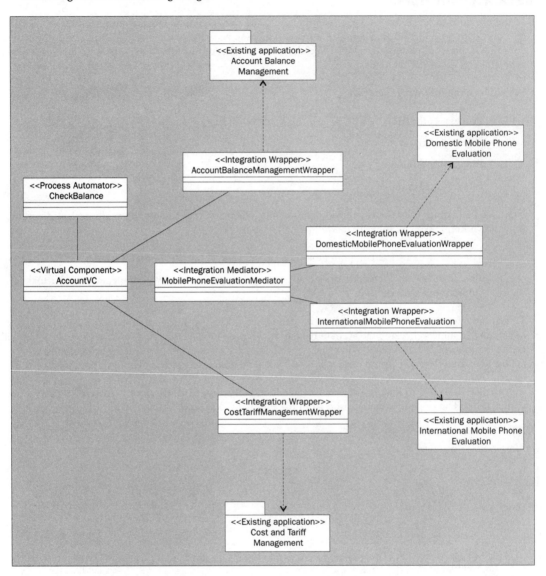

Next, we have to select the J2EE technologies for each component. As already mentioned in the pattern discussion previously in this chapter, we have a choice of technologies for almost every pattern. Therefore, for our example we will choose:

❑   A session bean for the CheckBalance Process Automator pattern. A session bean is well suited for stateless as well as stateful Process Automator components. Our scenario requires synchronous request/response communication; that's why a session bean is the optimal choice. Alternatively, we could use message-driven beans if we needed asynchronous communication.

❑ An entity bean with BMP for `AccountVC` Virtual Component pattern. We will use entity beans, because `AccountVC` should represent shared, transaction state. Entity beans are best suited for this. The `AccountVC` will have to gather data from different existing applications. Therefore we cannot rely on CMP.

❑ A RMI-IIOP distributed object for `MobilePhoneEvaluationMediator` Integration Mediator pattern. We have chosen RMI-IIOP, because we do not need the container overhead of the session beans and might, in more complex scenarios, require thread control and synchronization. Alternatively, we could use session beans or CORBA, but we believe this is a good interoperability demonstration as well.

❑ CORBA wrappers for all four integration wrappers. We will use CORBA, because we need synchronous communication. CORBA provides interoperability with RMI-IIOP and is not limited to the Java language, which is important for developing wrappers.

Particularly, the selection of integration wrapper technology depends on the architecture of existing applications. However, we have chosen CORBA, because it is widely used for these purposes and supports a variety of programming languages, operating systems, and platforms. Next, we'll take a look at how to implement these patterns.

Implementing the Integration Patterns

Unfortunately, for the implementation of the integration patterns, we are somewhat limited because we do not have access to the existing applications. Therefore we will demonstrate prototypes, which will show the concept to develop particular types of components and apply the described patterns in J2EE. We will, however, not implement the interaction with existing applications, but will place comments in the code.

Implementing the Integration Wrapper Pattern

In this section, we will show how to develop the customer integration wrapper using CORBA. Building a CORBA integration wrapper (or component wrapper) is similar to building a general-purpose CORBA distributed object. We will build a simple component wrapper using the Java IDL bundled with the Java SDK 1.3.

Define the Interface

To build the integration wrapper we will use the same API as provided by the existing application. The CORBA IDL looks like this:

```
module CustomerManagement {

  interface Customer {

    enum statusType {normal, silver, gold};

    enum typeOfAccounts {subscription, prepaid};

    struct dateType {
      short date;
```

```idl
        short month;
        short year;
    };

    exception customerNotFound {
        string reason;
        short errorCode;
    };

    exception customerNotUpdated {
        string reason;
        short errorCode;
    };

    exception accountNotAdded {
        string reason;
        short errorCode;
    };

    exception accountNotDeleted  {
        string reason;
        short errorCode;
    };

    void getCustomer ( in long customerId,
                       out wstring firstName,
                       out wstring lastName,
                       out wstring address,
                       out short numberOfPhoneAccounts,
                       out statusType status)
        raises (customerNotFound);

    long setCustomer ( in wstring firstName,
                       in wstring lastName,
                       in wstring address,
                       in short numberOfPhoneAccounts,
                       in statusType status)
        raises (customerNotUpdated);

    void newAccount ( in wstring phoneNumber,
                      in wstring startDate,
                      in typeOfAccounts typeOfAccount)
        raises (accountNotAdded);

    void deleteAccount ( in wstring phoneNumber)
        raises (accountNotDeleted);

    };
};
```

The IDL compiler maps the IDL to the programming language. This is part of every CORBA implementation. To compile the IDL interface that we have defined, we will use the `idlj` compiler, which is a part of JDK 1.3 (and also higher versions). To generate both mappings, for the client and the server side, we use the -fall option, which generates all the bindings.

Connect with Existing Application

Now we have to connect the operations that we have defined in the interface with those of the existing application. The same example is suitable for accessing the existing application through a proprietary API, or through source code modification, screen scraping, or terminal emulation. To implement the component wrapper, we have to define a class that will implement the functionality of the IDL interface. We will name the class `CustomerImpl`, which will inherit (extend) the `_CustomerImplBase` class, provided by the IDL compiler. The example connection code looks like this:

```
package CustomerManagement;

public class CustomerImpl extends _CustomerImplBase {

  public void getCustomer(int customerId, org.omg.CORBA
          .StringHolder firstName, org.omg.CORBA.StringHolder lastName, org
          .omg.CORBA.StringHolder address, org.omg.CORBA
            .ShortHolder numberOfPhoneAccounts, CustomerManagement
              .CustomerPackage.statusTypeHolder status)
                throws CustomerManagement.CustomerPackage
                  .customerNotFound {

    // Connect to the existing applicaiton
    // Locate the customer and retrieve the data
    Boolean successful = true;    // Determined from existing application

    if (successful) {

      // Fill in the data
      firstName.value = "Jack";
      lastName.value = "B. Good";
      address.value = "Warwick Road";
      numberOfPhoneAccounts.value = 2;
      status.value = CustomerManagement.CustomerPackage.statusType.silver;
    } else {
      throw new CustomerManagement.CustomerPackage
        .customerNotFound("Bad customerID", (short) 1);
    }
  }

  public int setCustomer(String firstName, String lastName, String address,
      short numberOfPhoneAccounts, CustomerManagement
          .CustomerPackage.statusType status)
            throws CustomerManagement.CustomerPackage.customerNotUpdated {

    // Connect to the existing application
    // Generate the customerID
    // Add the customer data
    int customerId = 1;
    Boolean successful = true;

    if (successful) {
      return customerId;
    } else {
      throw new CustomerManagement.CustomerPackage
```

```
            .customerNotUpdated("DB error", (short) 1);
    }
}

public void newAccount(String phoneNumber, String startDate,
    CustomerManagement.CustomerPackage.typeOfAccounts typeOfAccount)
        throws CustomerManagement.CustomerPackage.accountNotAdded {

    // Similar to above example
}

public void deleteAccount(String phoneNumber)
        throws CustomerManagement.CustomerPackage.accountNotDeleted {

    // Similar to above example
}
}
```

Implement the Server Process

At this stage, we have almost implemented the component wrapper. However, we still have to implement the process where the CORBA distributed object will execute; and we have to create at least one instance of the object. We will define a class with the name `Server`. We have to obtain the reference to the ORB, create a new instance of the `Customer` wrapper, and connect the instance with the ORB. This is quite straightforward and the code to achieve it looks like this:

```
package CustomerManagement;

import org.omg.CosNaming.*;
import org.omg.CosNaming.NamingContextPackage.*;
import org.omg.CORBA.*;

public class Server {

  public static void main(String[] args) {

    try {
        ORB orb = ORB.init(args,null);

        Customer c = new CustomerImpl();

        orb.connect(c);
```

However, this is not enough. More specifically, we have to provide a way for the client to obtain the initial reference. We will use the Naming Service. The code continues as follows:

```
        org.omg.CORBA.Object objRef =
            orb.resolve_initial_references("NameService");
        NamingContext ncRef = NamingContextHelper.narrow(objRef);

        NameComponent nc;
        NameComponent path[] = {
```

```
        Null
      };

      nc = new NameComponent("CustomerWrapper", "");
      path[0] = nc;
      ncRef.rebind(path, c);

      System.out.println("Server is ready...");
```

We should remember not to allow the server process to end. So we have to persuade the process to stay alive. One of the ways to do is this:

```
      java.lang.Object sync = new java.lang.Object();
      synchronized (sync) {
        sync.wait();
      }
```

Finally, we have to catch any possible exceptions:

```
      } catch (Exception e) {
        System.out.println(e);
      }
    }
  }
}
```

Implement the Client to Test the Component Wrapper

Although we have finished the development of the component wrapper, it is still a good idea to test it. For this purpose, we can develop a small CORBA client that will invoke some of the methods. In the example that we present here, we catch CORBA user exceptions, CORBA systems exceptions, and all other exceptions:

```
package CustomerManagement;

import org.omg.CosNaming.*;
import org.omg.CORBA.*;

public class Client {
  public static void main(String args[]) {
    try {

      // Connect to the wrapper
      ORB orb = ORB.init(args, null);

      org.omg.CORBA.Object objRef =
        orb.resolve_initial_references("NameService");
      NamingContext ncRef = NamingContextHelper.narrow(objRef);

      NameComponent nc = new NameComponent("CustomerWrapper", "");
      NameComponent path[] = {
        nc
      };
```

```
        Customer c = CustomerHelper.narrow(ncRef.resolve(path));

        // test the functionality
        StringHolder firstName = new StringHolder();
        StringHolder lastName = new StringHolder();
        StringHolder address = new StringHolder();
        ShortHolder numberOfPhoneAccounts = new ShortHolder();
        CustomerManagement.CustomerPackage.statusTypeHolder status =
          new CustomerManagement.CustomerPackage.statusTypeHolder();

        c.getCustomer((int) 1, firstName, lastName, address,
                    numberOfPhoneAccounts, status);
        System.out.println("First name: " + firstName.value);
        System.out.println("Last name:  " + lastName.value);
        System.out.println("Address:    " + address.value);
        System.out.println("No. of phone accounts: "
                        + numberOfPhoneAccounts.value);

        int customerId =
          c.setCustomer("Jack", "B. Good", "Birmingham", (short) 1,
                    CustomerManagement.CustomerPackage.statusType.gold);
        System.out.println("Setting new customer... id: " + customerId);

    } catch (UserException e) {
      System.out.println("User exception: " + e);

    } catch (SystemException e) {
      System.out.println("System exception: " + e);

    } catch (Exception e) {
      System.out.println("Exception: " + e);
    }
  }
}
```

To run the example, we first have to start the Name Service. Java SDK 1.3 provides a transient name service, called the tnameserv. Then, after setting the appropriate classpath, we simply start the Server.java and the Client.java, each in its own process, as shown below:

```
C:\WINDOWS\System32\cmd.exe                                           _ □ ×

C:\Chapter06\Integration\Wrapper\boa>javac CustomerManagement/*.java

C:\Chapter06\Integration\Wrapper\boa>start tnameserv

C:\Chapter06\Integration\Wrapper\boa>start java CustomerManagement.Server

C:\Chapter06\Integration\Wrapper\boa>java CustomerManagement.Client
First name: Jack
Last name:  B. Good
Address:    Warwick Road
No. of phone accounts: 2
Setting new customer... id: 1

C:\Chapter06\Integration\Wrapper\boa>_
```

If we decide to start the client and the server on different machines, we have to provide the address of the naming service using the -ORBIntialHost switch. We can also select the port manually, using the -ORBInitialPort switch.

In the next section, we will show how to implement the Integration Mediator pattern.

Implementing the Integration Mediator Pattern

In this section, we will show how to implement the Mobile Phone Evaluation mediator pattern, identified earlier in this chapter. We will implement it using RMI-IIOP. The other choice would be to use session beans. We have decided to use RMI-IIOP, because we do not need the container overhead here. We will develop the MobilePhoneEvaluation mediator, which will have a single operation, evaluateConsumption(). The mediator will connect to the existing domestic and international mobile phone evaluation applications and perform the necessary tasks to calculate and evaluate the phone consumption.

Define the Interface and Connect with Existing Application

First, we have to define the corresponding RMI-IIOP interface. To make a Java interface accessible from remote clients, the interface has to inherit from the java.rmi.Remote interface:

```
import java.rmi.Remote;
import java.rmi.RemoteException;
import java.util.Date;

public interface MobilePhoneEvaluation extends Remote {

  double evaluateConsumption (Date fromDate, Date toDate)
                 throws RemoteException;

}
```

The next step is to implement the functionality for the interface – that is to connect the interface methods to the existing application. For this we will use wrappers, as discussed previously. To do this, we will declare a class that will implement the previously defined MobilePhoneEvaluation interface. To make this class an RMI-IIOP class (to connect it with the RMI-IIOP object request broker) the implementation class has to inherit from javax.rmi.PortableRemoteObject and implement the interface. The implementation class looks as follows:

```
import java.rmi.RemoteException;
import javax.rmi.PortableRemoteObject;
import java.util.Date;

public class MobilePhoneEvaluationImpl extends PortableRemoteObject
     implements MobilePhoneEvaluation {

  public MobilePhoneEvaluationImpl() throws RemoteException {
  }

  public double evaluateConsumption (Date fromDate, Date toDate)
  throws RemoteException {
```

```
        double cost = 0;
        // Connect to the domestic mobile phone evaluation existing application
        // Connect to the international mobile phone evaluation existing
        // application

        cost = 55;

        return cost;
    }
}
```

When using this mediator component in the real world, we have to add the code that actually connects it with the existing application. This will differ from one existing application to the other. But we have not finished the development yet. Next, we have to make instances of this component and register them so that clients will be able to locate them.

The RMI-IIOP components need a process where they will execute. Therefore, we have to provide a server application that will create a server process in which we instantiate an instance (or several) of the RMI-IIOP component implementation class. The code looks like this:

```
import java.rmi.RemoteException;
import javax.rmi.PortableRemoteObject;
import javax.naming.*;

public class Server {

  public static void main(String[] args) {

    try {

      Context iNamingContext = new InitialContext();

      MobilePhoneEvaluation mpe = new MobilePhoneEvaluationImpl();

      iNamingContext.rebind("MobilePhoneEvaluation", mpe);

      System.out.println("Server ready...");

    } catch (Exception e) {
      System.out.println(e);
      e.printStackTrace(System.out);
    }
  }
}
```

This is almost all that we have to implement. However, we still have to develop a simple client to test the functionality of the RMI-IIOP virtual component.

Develop the Client

To test the functionality of the virtual component we have to develop a simple RMI-IIOP client. The client will connect to the Naming Service, resolve the name, and invoke the remote operation. The code for the client is as follows:

```
import java.util.*;
import javax.naming.*;
import javax.rmi.PortableRemoteObject;

public class Client {

  public static void main(String[] args) {

    MobilePhoneEvaluation mpe = null;

    try {
      Context inc = new InitialContext();
      mpe = (MobilePhoneEvaluation)
              PortableRemoteObject.narrow(inc.lookup(
                "MobilePhoneEvaluation"),MobilePhoneEvaluation.class);
    } catch (Exception e) {
      System.out.println(e);
    }

    try {

      double r = mpe.evaluateConsumption(
                     (new GregorianCalendar(2,4,1)).getTime(),
                     (new GregorianCalendar(2,4,1)).getTime());
      System.out.println(r);

    } catch (Exception e) {
      System.out.println(e);
    }
  }
}
```

After compiling the source code, we have to generate the stubs and skeletons using the Java RMI Compiler, or `rmic`. For more information on `rmic`, please refer to the Java SDK documentation. For our example, we will use the `-iiop` switch.

Before starting the server object and the client, we have to activate the naming service provider. For this we can use the transient CORBA Naming Service, `tnameserv`. Finally, we are ready to start the server classes that will instantiate the RMI-IIOP component. We have to specify the initial naming factory and the naming provider URL. To start the client we also have to provide the initial naming factory and the naming provider URL (note that to run the example on different computers we have to modify this URL accordingly), which gives the following amazing results:

Next, we will demonstrate how to develop the Data Mapping pattern.

Implementing the Data Mapping Pattern

We will use entity EJBs in the implementation of the Data Mapping pattern. We will show both the single-step and multi-step scenarios. For the single-step data mapping, we will use CMP, for the multi-step, we will use BMP.

Define the Interface

The remote component interface of our example looks like the following:

```
package cmp1;

import javax.ejb.EJBObject;
import java.rmi.RemoteException;

public interface Customer extends EJBObject {

  public String getCustomerPrimaryKey() throws RemoteException;
  public String getCustomerName() throws RemoteException;
  public void setCustomerName(String name) throws RemoteException;
  public String getCustomerAddress() throws RemoteException;
  public void setCustomerAddress(String address) throws RemoteException;
  public int getCustomerNoOfPhoneAccounts() throws RemoteException;
  public void setCustomerNoOfPhoneAccounts(int noOfPhAcc)
                                        throws RemoteException;
  public CustomerData getCustomerData() throws RemoteException;
  public void setCustomerData(CustomerData custData) throws RemoteException;
}
```

We also need to declare the value object `CustomerData`. The declaration looks like this:

```
package cmp1;

public class CustomerData implements java.io.Serializable {

    private String customerId = null;
    private String name = null;
    private String address = null;
    private int noOfPhoneAccounts = 0;

    public CustomerData () {
    }
```

```
    public CustomerData (String id, String nm, String ad, int na) {
       customerId = id;
       name = nm;
       address = ad;
       noOfPhoneAccounts = na;
    }

    public String getCustomerId() {
      return customerId;
    }
    public void setCustomerId(String id) {
      if (customerId==null)
         customerId = id;
    }

    public String getName() {
      return name;
    }
    public void setName(String nm) {
      name = nm;
    }

    public String getAddress() {
      return address;
    }
    public void setAddress(String ad) {
      address = ad;
    }

    public int getNoOfPhoneAccounts() {
      return noOfPhoneAccounts;
    }
    public void setNoOfPhoneAccounts(int pa) {
      noOfPhoneAccounts = pa;
    }

}
```

Next, we define the home interface, which provides methods to create and find entity beans. For our example, we define two create methods, one that takes the parameters one by one as arguments, and one that takes the four constituents of the value object (CustomerData) as arguments. We also define two finder methods: one locates entity beans by the primary key, and the other locates them by name. The latter one returns a Collection because it can happen that several customers have the same name. The remote home interface is presented below:

```
package cmp1;

import javax.ejb.CreateException;
import javax.ejb.EJBHome;
import javax.ejb.FinderException;
import java.util.Collection;
import java.rmi.RemoteException;
```

```
public interface CustomerHome extends EJBHome {

  public Customer create(String customerId, String name, String address,
                         int noOfPhAcc)
      throws RemoteException, CreateException;

  public Customer create(CustomerData custData)
      throws RemoteException, CreateException;

  public Customer findByPrimaryKey(String primaryKey)
      throws RemoteException, FinderException;

  public Collection findByName(String name)
      throws RemoteException, FinderException;

}
```

For our example, we will use the Social Security Number (SSN) as the primary key for the customer (CustomerId).

Develop Implementation Class for CMP

The implementation class is the place where we provide implementations for all the methods from the component interface. In the implementation class, we also implement the methods from the home interface and the required container callback methods. These include: ejbLoad(), ejbStore(), ejbActivate(), ejbPassivate(), setEntityContext(), unsetEntityContext(), ejbCreate(), ejbRemove(), and ejbFindXXX() methods.

If we use CMP we will not have to implement all the mentioned methods; the container will provide implementations for ejbLoad(), ejbStore(), and ejbFindXXX() methods. However, we have to specify additional information in the deployment descriptor. In addition to that, we also have to define the attributes. If we use CMP in EJB 2.0, we have to define abstract getter and setter methods for all persistent attributes, as we will see soon.

To implement the class for our Customer bean, we will define the CustomerBean abstract class that implements the EntityBean interface. The class has to be abstract because the container will implement several methods, as we will see a little later. We will declare a private attribute to store the context and an empty constructor:

```
package cmp1;

import javax.ejb.*;

abstract public class CustomerBean implements EntityBean {

  private EntityContext ctx;

  public CustomerBean() {
  }
```

To continue with the implementation of our entity bean implementation class, we have to define the container-managed attributes. In EJB 2.0, using CMP, we have to define pairs of getter and setter methods for each attribute. At bean deployment the container will provide implementations for these methods. This is why we have to declare these methods abstract. This is also the reason why the whole class is declared abstract:

```
// Container-managed fields
abstract public String getCustomerId();
abstract public void setCustomerId(String customerID);
abstract public String getName();
abstract public void setName(String name);
abstract public String getAddress();
abstract public void setAddress(String address);
abstract public int getNoOfPhoneAccounts();
abstract public void setNoOfPhoneAccounts(int noOfPhAcc);
```

In the next step, we have to provide the implementations of the methods from the component interface. As our entity bean is relatively simple, the implementation of these methods will also be simple. The fine-grained methods for get and set attributes will be implemented with simple method calls to the abstract getter and setter methods defined earlier:

```
// Component interface
public String getCustomerPrimaryKey() {
  return getCustomerId();
}
public String getCustomerName() {
  return getName();
}
public void setCustomerName(String name) {
  setName(name);
}
public String getCustomerAddress() {
  return getAddress();
}
public void setCustomerAddress(String address) {
  setAddress(address);
}
public int getCustomerNoOfPhoneAccounts() {
  return getNoOfPhoneAccounts();
}
public void setCustomerNoOfPhoneAccounts(int noOfPhAcc) {
  setNoOfPhoneAccounts(noOfPhAcc);
}
```

In addition, we have also defined two coarse-grained methods, which use the value object CustomerData. Their implementation is as follows:

```
public CustomerData getCustomerData() {
  CustomerData cd = new CustomerData();
  cd.setCustomerId(getCustomerId());
  cd.setName(getName());
  cd.setAddress(getAddress());
```

```
    cd.setNoOfPhoneAccounts(getNoOfPhoneAccounts());
    return cd;
}

public void setCustomerData(CustomerData cd) {
  setCustomerId(cd.getCustomerId());
  setName(cd.getName());
  setAddress(cd.getAddress());
  setNoOfPhoneAccounts(cd.getNoOfPhoneAccounts());
}
```

Then we have to implement the methods from the home interface. We do not need to implement the `ejbFindXXX()` methods, but we do need to implement the `ejbCreate()` methods. As mentioned above in our example we have two different methods: one that takes arguments one by one, and one that takes the four constituents of the value object (`CustomerData`) as arguments. The implementation is like this:

```
// home methods
public String ejbCreate(String customerId, String name, String address,
                        int noOfPhAcc) throws CreateException {
  setCustomerId(customerId);
  setName(name);
  setAddress(address);
  setNoOfPhoneAccounts(noOfPhAcc);
  return null;
}

public void ejbPostCreate(String customerId, String name,
                          String address, int noOfPhAcc) {
}

public String ejbCreate(CustomerData cd) throws CreateException {
  setCustomerId(cd.getCustomerId());
  setName(cd.getName());
  setAddress(cd.getAddress());
  setNoOfPhoneAccounts(cd.getNoOfPhoneAccounts());
  return null;
}

public void ejbPostCreate(CustomerData cd) {
}
```

We also have to declare other EJB-related methods that we have mentioned before. Luckily, we can leave them blank because we use CMP and the container will do this for us:

```
public void setEntityContext(EntityContext ctx) {
  this.ctx = ctx;
}

public void unsetEntityContext() {
  this.ctx = null;
}
```

```
    public void ejbActivate() {
    }

    public void ejbPassivate() {
    }

    public void ejbLoad() {
    }

    public void ejbStore() {
    }

    public void ejbRemove() throws RemoveException {
    }
}
```

This makes the bean implementation complete. In the next step, we have to define a suitable deployment descriptor. In the deployment descriptor we have to provide all the necessary additional information required to deploy the enterprise bean in the container. The deployment descriptor is included with the source code files for this chapter.

Before we can deploy the bean we have to compile the classes that we have created and pack the EJB to the JAR file. As we have mentioned, the further steps in the deployment are application-server specific. EJB developers should always refer to the appropriate application-server documentation for instructions on how to deploy a bean. Typically, this procedure will include invoking an EJB compiler or going through GUI interfaces.

Client Application for the Entity Bean

After a successful deployment we have to test the entity bean. For this we have to write a simple client. Here we present a client application that invokes some of the methods on the remote component interface of the entity bean. To test the local interface we have to develop another enterprise bean and deploy it in the same container:

```
package cmp1;

import java.rmi.*;
import javax.rmi.*;
import java.util.*;

import javax.ejb.*;
import javax.naming.*;

public class Client {

  public Client() {
  }

  public static void main(String[] args) {
    System.out.println("EAI CMP1 client");
    System.out.println();

    try {
```

```
    // Creates a new instance
    Client client = new Client();

    // Invokes the example() method
    client.example();

  } catch (Exception e) {
    System.out.println(e);
  }
}

public void example() {
  try {
    // Creates initial naming context
    Context ctx = new InitialContext();

    // Resolves to the home object and narrows
    CustomerHome home = (CustomerHome)PortableRemoteObject.narrow(
      (CustomerHome)ctx.lookup("eai-CustomerHome"), CustomerHome.class);

    // Creates a new bean
    Customer c = home.create("1","Matjaz","Wrox",5);

    // Invokes a method and writes the result to console
    System.out.println("Customer name is: "+c.getCustomerName());

    // Removes the bean
    c.remove();

  } catch(Exception e) {
    System.out.println(e);
  }
  }
}
```

We get the following result:

Implement the Multi-Step Data Mapping Using BMP

Container-managed persistence cannot satisfy all the needs of integration. We quickly hit the limits of CMP particularly when using more complex relational schemes and data stored in non-relational formats. Then we are forced to use bean-managed persistence. With BMP, we do not use the container persistence service, but implement the necessary methods ourselves. This goes particularly for ejbLoad() and ejbStore() methods, and we also have to implement the finder methods manually.

However, there is no difference in the component or home interface definitions, so the majority of changes will focus on the implementation class and on the deployment descriptor. So, let's see how to write the BMP implementation class `CustomerBean` for our example. As with the previous example, we use the value object `CustomerData`. Our BMP implementation class thus looks like this:

```
package bmp;

import javax.ejb.*;
import java.util.*;

public class CustomerBean implements EntityBean {

  private EntityContext ctx;

  public CustomerBean() {
  }


  private CustomerData cd;
```

Then we define the component interface methods:

```
  // Component interface
  public String getCustomerPrimaryKey() {
    return cd.getCustomerId();
  }
  public String getCustomerName() {
    return cd.getName();
  }
  public void setCustomerName(String name) {
    cd.setName(name);
  }
  public String getCustomerAddress() {
    return cd.getAddress();
  }
  public void setCustomerAddress(String address) {
    cd.setAddress(address);
  }
  public int getCustomerNoOfPhoneAccounts() {
    return cd.getNoOfPhoneAccounts();
  }
  public void setCustomerNoOfPhoneAccounts(int noOfPhAcc) {
    cd.setNoOfPhoneAccounts(noOfPhAcc);
  }

  public CustomerData getCustomerData() {
    return cd;
  }
  public void setCustomerData(CustomerData cd) {
    this.cd = cd;
  }
```

Next, we define the home methods. The `ejbCreate()` methods are very similar to the CMP example:

```
// home methods
public String ejbCreate(String customerId, String name,
                String address, int noOfPhAcc) throws CreateException {
  // Connect to the existing database
  // and create a new record
  // Store this record in the value object
  cd = new CustomerData();
  cd.setCustomerId(customerId);
  cd.setName(name);
  cd.setAddress(address);
  cd.setNoOfPhoneAccounts(noOfPhAcc);
  return customerId;
}

public void ejbPostCreate(String customerId, String name, String address,
                        int noOfPhAcc) {
}

public String ejbCreate(CustomerData cd) throws CreateException {
  // Connect to the existing database
  // and create a new record
  // Store this record in the value object
  this.cd = new CustomerData();
  this.cd = cd;
  return cd.getCustomerId();
}

public void ejbPostCreate(CustomerData cd) {
}
```

However, we also have to implement the `ejbFindXXX()` methods, so we have to declare and implement both methods – the `ejbFindByPrimaryKey()` and `ejbFindByName()`. Here we will have to access the database using any appropriate mechanism, the most common of which is the use of JDBC. On the other hand, to access existing data we sometimes have to use other approaches, including access to other types of databases or calling wrappers or DAOs for data access.

We will not show the code to access a database using JDBC here, because it is rather trivial. It is worth noting, however, that from the performance perspective it is always good to use prepared statements with JDBC. The skeletons of the necessary methods look like this (the full working code is included with the download package):

```
public String ejbFindByPrimaryKey(String pk)
    throws ObjectNotFoundException {
  // Access the existing database
  // Locate the record by primary key
  // Return the primary key
  return "1";
}

public Collection ejbFindByName(String name) {
  Vector v = new Vector();
```

```
      // Access the existing database
      // Locate the records
      // Add primary keys to the vector
      v.addElement("1");
      // Return the vector
      return v;
    }
```

Then we implement the `ejbLoad()` and `ejbStore()` methods where we load and update the state to the database, respectively, using the same mechanism as the finder methods:

```
    public void ejbLoad() {
      cd = new CustomerData();

      // Access the existing databases and applications and load the data

      // Store the data to the value object
      cd.setCustomerId("1");
      cd.setName("Matjaz");
      cd.setAddress("Wrox");
      cd.setNoOfPhoneAccounts(5);
    }

    public void ejbStore() {
      // Access the existing databases and applications
      // Update the data from the bean to the database
    }
```

Finally, we provide other EJB-related methods:

```
    public void setEntityContext(EntityContext ctx) {
      this.ctx = ctx;
    }

    public void unsetEntityContext() {
      this.ctx = null;
    }

    public void ejbActivate() {
    }

    public void ejbPassivate() {
    }

    public void ejbRemove() throws RemoveException {
    }
  }
```

For a BMP entity bean we also have to define a deployment descriptor that differs a little from the CMP bean deployment descriptor. We do not have to specify all the details of container managed attributes and the finder methods that we had to for the CMP bean so the deployment descriptor is actually rather simple. We will not show it here, but it is included with the source code for this chapter.

Next, we will show how to implement the Virtual Component pattern.

Implementing the Virtual Component Pattern

In this section, we will demonstrate how to develop a virtual component using EJBs. We will develop the Customer virtual component and show how to access the wrapper, developed previously in CORBA. Due to the nature of the Customer component we will use entity beans with BMP. We will build on the example from the previous section, and thus keep the home and the remote interfaces the same.

To develop the Customer virtual component entity bean (the `CustomerBean` class), we have imported the `org.omg.CosNaming` and `org.omg.CORBA` packages, and declared a private attribute `cust` of type `CustomerManagement.Customer`. The `cust` attribute stores the reference to the CORBA component wrapper `Customer`. Here's how the code starts:

```java
package bmp2;

import javax.ejb.*;
import java.util.*;
import org.omg.CosNaming.*;
import org.omg.CORBA.*;

public class CustomerBean implements EntityBean {

    private EntityContext ctx;
    private CustomerData cd;
    private CustomerManagement.Customer cust;
```

Next, we implement the component interface. We do this the same way as in the previous examples:

```java
    // Component interface
    public String getCustomerPrimaryKey() {
        return cd.getCustomerId();
    }
    public String getCustomerName() {
        return cd.getName();
    }
    public void setCustomerName(String name) {
        cd.setName(name);
    }
    public String getCustomerAddress() {
        return cd.getAddress();
    }
    public void setCustomerAddress(String address) {
        cd.setAddress(address);
    }
    public int getCustomerNoOfPhoneAccounts() {
        return cd.getNoOfPhoneAccounts();
    }
    public void setCustomerNoOfPhoneAccounts(int noOfPhAcc) {
        cd.setNoOfPhoneAccounts(noOfPhAcc);
    }

    public CustomerData getCustomerData() {
        return cd;
```

```
    }
    public void setCustomerData(CustomerData cd) {
      this.cd = cd;
    }
```

Next, we provide the EJB-related methods. In the setEntityContext(), we acquire the connection to the ORB and connect to the component wrapper, which in our case is a stateless wrapper. If it were a stateful wrapper then we would use ejbActivate() method. In our case ejbActivate() is empty. We also release the resources in unsetEntityContext() and ejbPassivate(), respectively (in our case ejbPassivate() is empty):

```
    public void setEntityContext(EntityContext ctx) {
      this.ctx = ctx;
      try {
         // Connect with the ORB
         String args[] = new String[1];
         args[0] = "";
         ORB orb = ORB.init(args, null);

         // Connect with the component wrapper if stateless
         org.omg.CORBA.Object objRef =
                           orb.resolve_initial_references("NameService");
         NamingContext ncRef = NamingContextHelper.narrow(objRef);

         NameComponent nc = new NameComponent("CustomerWrapper", "");
         NameComponent path[] = {nc};
         cust = CustomerManagement.CustomerHelper.narrow(ncRef.resolve(path));
      } catch (Exception e) {
        System.out.println(e);
      }
    }

    public void unsetEntityContext() {
      // Disconnect with the component wrapper if stateless
      cust = null;

      this.ctx = null;
    }

    public void ejbActivate() {
      // Connect with the component wrapper if stateful
    }

    public void ejbPassivate() {
      // Disconnect with the component wrapper if stateful
    }
```

In all cases where we communicate with the wrapper we should handle the CORBA-related exceptions and react appropriately. We can forward them to the client, but we should only forward the relevant exceptions. The client should not be aware that we communicate with the CORBA wrapper, therefore we should not forward any CORBA-related exceptions to the client. Rather, we should translate them to EJB-related exceptions – we should throw an appropriate exception, as we will see in the ejbCreate() method.

293

The other possibility is to first try to deal with the exceptions, before forwarding them to the client. If, for example, we cannot invoke methods on CORBA wrapper we might consider reconnecting to it first before notifying the client of an error.

Now we'll continue with the implementation of the entity bean by implementing the `ejbLoad()` and `ejbStore()` methods. We load and store the persistent state using the wrapper:

```java
public void ejbLoad() {
   cd = new CustomerData();

   try {
      // Acquire the data from component wrapper
      StringHolder firstName = new StringHolder();
      StringHolder lastName = new StringHolder();
      StringHolder address = new StringHolder();
      ShortHolder numberOfPhoneAccounts = new ShortHolder();
      CustomerManagement.CustomerPackage.statusTypeHolder status =
               new CustomerManagement.CustomerPackage.statusTypeHolder();

      String cId = (String) ctx.getPrimaryKey();
      int ciId = (new Integer(cId)).intValue();

      cust.getCustomer (ciId, firstName, lastName,
                  address, numberOfPhoneAccounts, status);

      cd.setCustomerId(cId);
      cd.setName(lastName.value);
      cd.setAddress(address.value);
      cd.setNoOfPhoneAccounts(numberOfPhoneAccounts.value);
   } catch (Exception e) {
     System.out.println(e);
   }
}

public void ejbStore() {
   // Store the data in the component wrapper
   try {
      int r = cust.setCustomer(cd.getName(), "",
                  cd.getAddress(),
                  (short)cd.getNoOfPhoneAccounts(),
                  CustomerManagement.CustomerPackage.statusType.gold);
   } catch (Exception e) {
     System.out.println(e);
   }
}
```

Then we implement the home methods. First, the `ejbCreate()` methods:

```java
// home methods
public String ejbCreate(String customerId, String name, String address,
                  int noOfPhAcc) throws CreateException {
   cd = new CustomerData();
```

```
        try {
            // Store to the bean
            cd.setCustomerId(customerId);
            cd.setName(name);
            cd.setAddress(address);
            cd.setNoOfPhoneAccounts(noOfPhAcc);

            // Create the corresponding record
            // in the existing system though wrapper
            int r = cust.setCustomer(cd.getName(), "",
                        cd.getAddress(),
                        (short)cd.getNoOfPhoneAccounts(),
                        CustomerManagement.CustomerPackage.statusType.gold);

            // Return the primary key
            return customerId;
        } catch (Exception e) {
          System.out.println(e);
          throw new CreateException();
        }
    }

    public void ejbPostCreate(String customerId, String name,
                                            String address, int noOfPhAcc) {
    }

    public String ejbCreate(CustomerData cd) throws CreateException {
        try {
            this.cd = new CustomerData();
            this.cd = cd;

            // Create the corresponding record
            // in the existing system though wrapper
            int r = cust.setCustomer(cd.getName(), "",
                    cd.getAddress(),
                    (short)cd.getNoOfPhoneAccounts(),
                    CustomerManagement.CustomerPackage.statusType.gold);

            return cd.getCustomerId();
        } catch (Exception e) {
          System.out.println(e);
          throw new CreateException();
        }
    }

    public void ejbPostCreate(CustomerData cd) {
    }

    public void ejbRemove() throws RemoveException {
    }
```

295

Finally, we have to implement the finder methods. The implementation of the `ejbFindByPrimaryKey()` is straightforward:

```
public String ejbFindByPrimaryKey(String pk)
                                throws ObjectNotFoundException {
    cd = new CustomerData();

    try {
        StringHolder firstName = new StringHolder();
        StringHolder lastName = new StringHolder();
        StringHolder address = new StringHolder();
        ShortHolder numberOfPhoneAccounts = new ShortHolder();
        CustomerManagement.CustomerPackage.statusTypeHolder status =
                new CustomerManagement.CustomerPackage.statusTypeHolder();

        int ciId = (new Integer(pk)).intValue();

        cust.getCustomer (ciId, firstName, lastName,
                            address, numberOfPhoneAccounts, status);

        cd.setCustomerId(pk);
        cd.setName(lastName.value);
        cd.setAddress(address.value);
        cd.setNoOfPhoneAccounts(numberOfPhoneAccounts.value);

        return pk;
    } catch (Exception e) {
    System.out.println(e);
    throw new ObjectNotFoundException();
    }
}
```

The implementation of the `ejbFindByName()` requires some further thoughts because the current component does not provide a suitable method. The solution might be to iterate through all customers comparing each name, but this would require several remote method invocations, which would negatively influence the network traffic and would place additional load on the EJB server and component wrapper.

A better solution would be to modify the component wrapper (assuming that you have access to the code, and the authority to modify it) and add the necessary method to locate customers by name. Such a method would then return a list of primary keys, exactly what we need for the entity bean. We won't go into the fine details here, because it is a relatively easy task:

```
public Collection ejbFindByName(String name) {
    Vector v = new Vector();

    // Delegate the search to the wrapper
    return v;
}
```

The deployment descriptor of this entity bean is almost exactly the same as the deployment descriptor of the BMP entity bean that we developed in the previous example. To build the entity bean in the correct order, we should first generate the client-side mapping from the `CustomerInt.idl`, using an IDL compiler, for example Sun's `idlj`. Then we should compile the source code files, including the generated interfaces and classes to access the CORBA wrapper. Finally, we should pack these classes, together with the usual content (deployment descriptors) to the JAR file, which we will deploy in the container.

We also need to start the CORBA wrapper. First, we should run the CORBA Naming Service (`tnameserv`) and then the CORBA wrapper server-side object. To test the entity bean we will use a simple client, almost the same as in previous example. The major differences will be the correct JNDI name of the entity bean (`eai3-CustomerHome`) and that we use the `bmp2` package here.

After compiling the client source code, we should run it with command shown below. Here's what the output looks like:

```
C:\WINNT\System32\cmd.exe                                    _ □ ×

C:\WROX\J2EEPatterns\Ch06\Integration\VirtualComponent>java -classpath %j2ee_hom
e%\lib\j2ee.jar;VCClient.jar;. bmp2.Client
EAI BMP2 client

Customer name is: B. Good

C:\WROX\J2EEPatterns\Ch06\Integration\VirtualComponent>
```

Finally, we will look at how to implement the Process Automator pattern.

Implementing the Process Automator Pattern

In this section, we will demonstrate how to develop the Process Automator component. We will show two examples. First, we will develop the Check Balance component, identified previously in the design phase. For the Check Balance component, we will use a stateless session bean. Next, we will show how to use message-driven beans.

Let's first take a look at the Check Balance session bean. To implement it, we first have to define the component interface for our session bean (`CheckBalance`), which can be remote or local. We will use the remote interface because it is very likely that the Process Automator will be accessed remotely. We will define a single method, `calculateBalance()`. The remote component interface for our session bean is presented in the next listing:

```
package session1;

import java.rmi.RemoteException;
import javax.ejb.EJBObject;

public interface CheckBalance extends EJBObject {

  public double calculateBalance(int accountNo) throws RemoteException;

}
```

After we have defined the remote interface we have to define the home interface. The home interface provides the methods for the session bean lifecycle. The session beans do not expose their identity to clients, so the home interface will have only `create()` methods – in our case only a single `create()` method. As with component interfaces, home interfaces can also be remote or local. A remote home interface declaration is shown in the next listing:

```
package session1;

import java.rmi.RemoteException;
import javax.ejb.CreateException;
import javax.ejb.EJBHome;

public interface CheckBalanceHome extends EJBHome {

  public CheckBalance create() throws CreateException, RemoteException;

}
```

After we have defined both interfaces we can continue with the development of the implementation class. In the implementation class, we have to provide implementations for all methods declared in the component and home interfaces. We also have to implement certain container callback methods: `ejbActivate()`, `ejbPassivate()`, `setSessionContext()`, `ejbCreate()`, and `ejbRemove()`.

Session beans are simpler than entity beans and therefore require less EJB-related methods. We will declare the `CheckBalanceBean` class, which will have to implement the `SessionBean` interface. The implementation class including all the necessary methods is very simple. We will start with the declaration:

```
package session1;

import javax.ejb.*;
import javax.naming.*;
import javax.rmi.PortableRemoteObject;
import java.util.*;

public class CheckBalanceBean implements SessionBean {
```

The session bean will call the `MobilePhoneEvaluation` mediator, developed on the RMI-IIOP component that we have developed earlier in this section. Notice that in real-world scenarios the Process Automator would have to call more than one component. Here, we show a simplified solution because our objective is to demonstrate the technical aspects.

If we call the RMI-IIOP component, it would be wise to connect to the component when the session bean instance is created, and store the connection. Making the connection requires a lookup in the naming service and narrowing the reference. These are costly operations and from the performance perspective it would not be efficient to make the connection each time before a method invocation.

It is reasonable to partition the resources to those that are client-dependent and those that are not. With stateless session beans we will not have this problem, because the beans themselves are stateless and therefore cannot store any client-related state. If we need to store client-related state we should use stateful session beans, which we will discuss later.

We will continue our session bean implementation class with declaring private attributes. One will store the session context, the other the connection to the `MobilePhoneEvaluation` component. Notice that stateless session beans can store client-independent state. Therefore we can store the connection to the virtual component in the bean. We will also declare several EJB-related methods that we do not need to implement in this simple example:

```
private SessionContext ctx;
private MobilePhoneEvaluation mpe;

public void ejbActivate() {
}

public void ejbRemove() {
}

public void ejbPassivate() {
}

public void setSessionContext(SessionContext ctx) {
  this.ctx = ctx;
}
```

Next we will implement the create method from the home interface. The `ejbCreate()` method is called by the container after calling the `setSessionContext()`, which is after the bean instance has been created in the container. Therefore, the `ejbCreate()` method is an appropriate place where we can establish a connection to the `MobilePhoneEvaluation` RMI-IIOP component:

```
// home
public void ejbCreate() throws CreateException {
  System.out.println("create: Connecting to the mediator");
  try {
    Properties h = new Properties();
    h.put(Context.INITIAL_CONTEXT_FACTORY,
          "com.sun.jndi.cosnaming.CNCtxFactory");
    h.put(Context.PROVIDER_URL, "iiop://localhost:900");
    Context inc = new InitialContext(h);
    Object a = inc.lookup("MobilePhoneEvaluation");
    mpe = (MobilePhoneEvaluation)
          PortableRemoteObject.narrow(
          inc.lookup("MobilePhoneEvaluation"),
          MobilePhoneEvaluation.class);
  } catch (Exception e) {
    System.out.println(e);
    throw new CreateException();
  }
}
```

With this setting, we do not have to modify the RMI-IIOP server that was developed earlier.

We would also have to modify the RMI-IIOP server to use the same naming service to register it. We should also manage the exceptions. In the above example, we have decided to forward any exceptions that may occur during the connection to the RMI-IIOP server as create exceptions. In production systems, we would build in a more sophisticated exception management mechanism.

Finally, we have to implement our business method, that is, the `calculateBalance()` method. As already mentioned, this method would normally call several existing systems. Here, to keep things simple so that we can focus on the technical issues, we will call only a single RMI-IIOP component:

```
// business method
public double calculateBalance(int accountNo) {
  double result = 0;
  System.out.println("calculateBalance: invoking remote " +
                     "method on the mediator");
  try {

    result = mpe.evaluateConsumption(
                         (new GregorianCalendar(2,4,1)).getTime(),
                         (new GregorianCalendar(2,4,1)).getTime());

  } catch (Exception e) {
  System.out.println(e);
  }

  return result;
  }
}
```

With this, we have finished the implementation class for our stateless session bean. Next, we have to define the deployment descriptor and build the example into a JAR file, and then proceed to deploy and test it. The deployment descriptor (`ejb-jar.xml`) for stateless session beans is relatively straightforward and is included with the code for this chapter.

Finally, we can compile the source files and gather all the necessary files into the JAR file. In addition to the usual files we must not forget to include the RMI-IIOP interface `MobilePhoneEvaluation` (`MobilePhoneEvaluation.class`) and the necessary stub (`_MobilePhoneEvaluation_Stub.class`). We can use the same stub that we built previously, or can build the stub again using `rmic`. We have to deploy the session bean to the application server. We should follow the specific steps relating to the particular application server we choose to deploy on.

Client

To be able to test the session bean we will write a simple client that will test the functionality through the remote interface. The client code that is shown below assumes that we have registered the session bean with JNDI under the name `eaiSS-CheckBalanceHome`:

```
package session1;

import java.rmi.*;
import javax.rmi.*;
import java.util.*;

import javax.ejb.*;
import javax.naming.*;

public class Client {
```

```
    public Client() {
    }

    public static void main(String[] args) {
      System.out.println("EAI process automator client");
      System.out.println();

      // Create a new instance and invoke the example() method
      try {
        Client client = new Client();
        client.example();
      } catch (Exception e) {
        System.out.println(e);
      }
    }

    public void example() {

      try {
        // Obtain a reference to the initial naming context
        Context ctx = new InitialContext();

        // Resolve the JNDI home name and narrow
        CheckBalanceHome home = (CheckBalanceHome)PortableRemoteObject.narrow
                  ((CheckBalanceHome)ctx.lookup("eaiSS-CheckBalanceHome"),
                                            CheckBalanceHome.class);

        // Create a new session bean instance
        CheckBalance cb = home.create();

        // Invoke the method
        System.out.println("The balance of account no. 1 is: "
                                    +cb.calculateBalance(1));

        // Remove the session bean instance
        cb.remove();

      } catch(Exception e) {
        System.out.println(e);
      }
    }
  }
```

Running the Example

To run the session bean we should perform the following steps:

❑   Deploy the bean to the application server

❑   Run the naming service tnameserv

❑   Run the RMI-IIOP server-side object – the MobilePhoneEvaluation mediator component
    that we have developed earlier in this chapter

❑   Finally, we can run the EJB client using the following command:

```
C:\WINNT\System32\cmd.exe                                              _ □ ×

C:\WROX\J2EEPatterns\Ch06\Integration\ProcessAutomator>java -classpath %j2ee_hom
e%\lib\j2ee.jar;PAClient.jar;. session1.Client
EAI process automator client                                      .

The balance of account no. 1 is: 55.0

C:\WROX\J2EEPatterns\Ch06\Integration\ProcessAutomator>
```

Using Stateful Session Beans for Process Automators

We have already identified that we should use stateful session beans if we need to preserve the conversational state between different method invocations from the client. Using a stateful session bean as Process Automator is very similar to using the stateless one. The major difference is that in the implementation class we declare public attributes in which the stateful session bean will preserve the conversational state.

The container will preserve the state of these public attributes and will temporarily store them, if it needs to reuse the same bean instance. The container will use serialization to store the state, so, as we emphasized earlier, all attributes that maintain conversational state should be serializable.

Furthermore, stateful session beans can be passivated and activated, which means that we should partition the resources that we use in the bean in a similar way to with entity beans. The resources that are client dependent should be acquired in the `ejbActivate()` method and released in `ejbPassivate()` whereas client-independent resources should be acquired in `ejbCreate()` and released in `ejbRemove()`.

Using Message-Driven Beans for Process Automators

Session beans are appropriate for Process Automators, which require synchronous RMI-IIOP communication with remote clients, which means that the client that invokes a method on a session bean waits for a response. This synchronous nature has several consequences. Since the client is blocked, it would be nice if the operation were performed relatively quickly. With certain operations, this is not possible, or requires too many resources from the EJB tier. In many information systems we face peak usage times where we have a large number of simultaneous clients.

The solution is to use message-driven beans (MDB) that communicate asynchronously, using JMS. With asynchronous communication we can store the requests and process them in off-peak hours. The fact, however, is that we cannot return results to clients, therefore message-driven beans will be appropriate for update operations that do not need to return the results to clients, or can use some other mechanism to report them.

Here, we will demonstrate how to develop a simple Process Automator with MDB. We will develop a `DisableAccountsBean`, a message-driven bean that will search for and disable accounts that have zero balance for three months or longer. Searching for and disabling accounts will be done using the existing Account Balance Management application. This is usually a task that requires a lot of time, and does not require that a result be sent to the client who initiated the operation immediately. A message-driven bean is therefore the perfect choice.

302

A message-driven bean has to implement two interfaces: MessageDrivenBean and MessageListener. The first interface requires the implementation of EJB container callback methods, like setMessageDrivenContext() and ejbRemove(), that enable the container instance pooling. The second interface requires the implementation of the onMessage() method. This method is how the message-driven bean gets requests. More specifically, the message-driven bean will get a message through the onMessage() method and will then have to parse and react to the message accordingly.

We can see that message-driven beans are loosely coupled and that they can react on different messages with the onMessage() method. There is no compile-time type checking and the parsing of the messaging must be done by hand.

Implementation of the message-driven bean will therefore have only the implementation class. In our example we'll define the DisableAccountsBean implementation class that will implement the abovementioned interfaces. In the bean, we will implement the onMessage() method that will perform the search for old accounts and disable them:

```java
package msg;

import javax.ejb.*;
import javax.jms.*;

public class DisableAccountsBean implements MessageDrivenBean,
        MessageListener {

  private MessageDrivenContext mctx;

  public void ejbRemove() {
  }

  public void setMessageDrivenContext(MessageDrivenContext ctx) {
    mctx = ctx;
  }

  public void ejbCreate () throws CreateException {
  }

  // Implementation of MessageListener

  public void onMessage(Message msg) {
    try {
      // Extract the message
      TextMessage tm = (TextMessage) msg;
      String text = tm.getText();
      System.out.println("Received request: " + text);

      // Process the request
      System.out.println("Processing the request: disabling accounts...");

      // Contact the existing application
      // Search for accounts and disable them
    }
    catch(JMSException ex) {
      ex.printStackTrace();
```

```
      }
    }
  }
```

After we have defined the implementation class, we need to write the deployment descriptor, which is included with the source code for this example. Next, we have to compile the source files and prepare the JAR file that will include the `DisableAccountsBean.class` and the deployment descriptors. Then we have to deploy the JAR file to the application server. However, we also have to create a JMS `Topic` with the name `disableAccounts`.

Client

The client for the message-driven bean can be any client that delivers messages to a certain topic (or queue if we use `Queue` instead of `Topic`). This can be a Java client using JMS, or an existing application that uses a compliant MOM. Hence, message-driven beans are suitable to process requests from existing applications.

Here, we will show a simple JMS client in Java, which will create a topic connection and start it, create a new topic session, create a topic publisher, create a text message, and publish it:

```java
package msg;

import java.rmi.RemoteException;
import java.util.Properties;
import javax.jms.*;
import javax.naming.*;
import javax.ejb.CreateException;
import javax.ejb.RemoveException;
import javax.rmi.PortableRemoteObject;

public class Client {
  // The name of the topic the client and the message bean use
  static private String TOPIC_NAME = "disableAccounts";

  public Client() {
  }

  public static void main(String[] args) {
    System.out.println("EAI message client");
    System.out.println();

    try {
      Client client = new Client();
      client.example();
    } catch (Exception e) {
      System.out.println(e);
    }
  }

  public void example() {
    try {
      // Create a message context
```

```
        Context mctx = new InitialContext();

        // Create the topic connection and start it
        TopicConnectionFactory cf = (TopicConnectionFactory)
          mctx.lookup("javax.jms.TopicConnectionFactory");
        TopicConnection mTopicConn = cf.createTopicConnection();
        mTopicConn.start();

        Topic newTopic = null;
        TopicSession session = null;

        try {
          // Create a new topic session
          session = mTopicConn.createTopicSession(
                            false,    // non transacted
                            Session.AUTO_ACKNOWLEDGE);

          // Lookup the topic name (if exist, otherwise exception)
          newTopic = (Topic) mctx.lookup(TOPIC_NAME);

        } catch(NamingException ex) {

          // If the topic doesn't exist create it
          newTopic = session.createTopic(TOPIC_NAME);
          mctx.bind(TOPIC_NAME, newTopic);
        }

        // Create a topic publisher
        TopicPublisher sender = session.createPublisher(newTopic);

        // Create a text message
        TextMessage tm = session.createTextMessage();
        tm.setText("EAI-dissableAccounts");

        // Publish the message
        sender.publish(tm);

      } catch(Exception ex) {
        ex.printStackTrace();
      }
    }
  }
}
```

To run the client, we have to compile it first. We have to run it specifying the initial naming factory and the naming provider URL (as in previous examples). Please notice that the client will not output any result, because the operation that it requested is not finished yet. The client has, however, returned the control to the operating system (the client is not blocked for the duration of performing the operation). We have to look into the application server window to see that our message-driven bean is actually performing the work:

```
C:\WINDOWS\System32\cmd.exe - C:\j2sdkee1.3\bin\j2ee -verbose          _ □ X
Application MessageApp deployed.

Received request: EAI-dissableAccounts
Processing the request: disabling accounts...
```

With this demonstration, we have completed the implementation of integration patterns. In the next section, we will talk about using these patterns for B2B integration.

Using Integration Patterns for B2B

The presented integration patterns are useful for intra-EAI as well as for inter-EAI and B2B integration. We have followed the principle that successful inter-EAI and B2B integration can be built on a well defined intra-EAI only. Therefore we say that the presented patterns have to be applied step by step to enable intra-EAI integration. Then we should build B2B interactions on top of an integrated architecture. In this context, all the presented patterns are important. However, the Process Automator pattern is the one that deserves special consideration. Typically, we apply this pattern to implement business processes. These will differ depending on the type of interaction.

Summary

In this chapter, we have discussed the patterns for enterprise integration. First, we have made a brief overview of Enterprise Application Integration and identified the most important phases: the data-level integration, the application interface integration, business method, presentation, and inter-EAI or B2B integration. Then we discussed EAI with J2EE. We have seen that J2EE supports several open standard technologies and protocols, which enable integration with existing applications as well as the development of web services.

Next, we introduced the most important integration patterns, where we covered the following patterns:

❑   Integration Broker pattern

❑   Integration Wrapper pattern

❑   Integration Mediator pattern

❑   Virtual Component pattern

❑   Data Mapping pattern

❑   Data Access Object (DAO) pattern

❑   Process Automator pattern

Of these, only the DAO pattern is well known, as it is a part of J2EE Design Patterns catalog. Therefore we have described the other patterns. We have shown which integration patterns to select and how to apply them into the overall integration architecture. We have based our discussion on our mobile phone operator case study and shown the use of the patterns for a few use cases.

Finally, we have shown how to apply these patterns in J2EE. We have discussed the selection of appropriate technologies and shown the actual implementations. We have shown how to develop Integration Wrappers using CORBA and Integration Mediators using RMI-IIOP, how to implement Data Mapping pattern using entity beans, and how to implement Virtual Components and Process Automators using various types of EJBs.

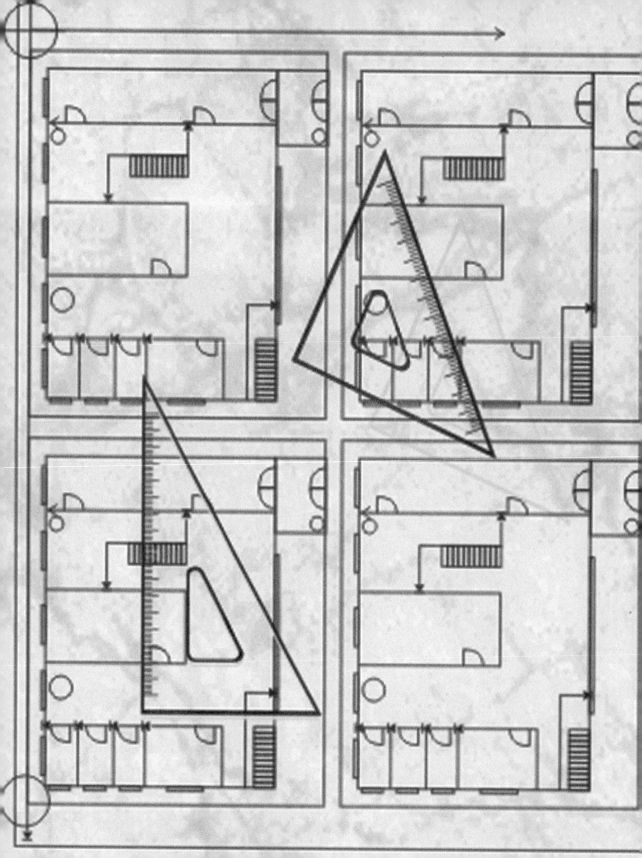

7

Patterns Applied to Enable Reusability, Maintainability, and Extensibility

In this chapter, we shall discuss the application of design patterns for the specific purpose of reusing software and developing more maintainable and extensible software. Here, we shall introduce the aspects of reusability, maintainability, and extensibility. We shall then focus on a group of patterns that demonstrate these aspects in a general framework, which is composed of a series of components in the context of a J2EE framework. The patterns discussed in this chapter are:

❑   The Façade pattern

❑   The Abstract Factory pattern

❑   The Decorator pattern

❑   The Template Method pattern

❑   The Builder pattern

Object-oriented analysis (OOA) and object-oriented design (OOD) were developed to address modern software because it is very large and complex. The three main advantages of adopting an object-oriented method are reusability, maintainability, and extensibility. These ideas should be applied on multiple levels like classes, components, services, or patterns:

- One or more individual classes can be designed to address a specific task. A typical example is a utility class such as the Debug class, or set of classes designed to work together. Normally, these are packaged and deployed together.

- Components are reusable software models, which publish and register their interfaces. A component could also be re-deployed within its environment (for example, a J2EE-component like an Enterprise JavaBean).

- Services are the reuse of a framework and a contract interface. A provider of a service can publish its services and an interested potential client of that service registers an interest in it; for example, an application server environment, which provides privileged services like transaction management, security provision, and database pooling to client components within its domain.

- Patterns mean a description of communicating objects and classes that are customized to solve a general problem in a particular context. There are some patterns that encourage decoupling, closure, and (in effect) the potential to reuse and extend code. In theory, the reuse of patterns makes the reusability, maintainability, and extendibility of classes, components, and services easier to achieve.

Good quality object-oriented software should be:

- Well-encapsulated
- Modular
- Loosely-coupled
- Designed to be generic so that it can be used in different contexts

Why Write Reusable Software?

Software reusability has not met its potential expectations in the commercial world. There has been less success in GUI tool-kit products, than in business component products.

Software reuse plays a big role in moving the "software thinking" forward. The innovative corporations start new trends by exploiting a hole in the market, for example, the application server market. A successful application server product is reused and extended to support hundreds of different products developed for different business services by different businesses every day.

Another example is the JDK itself. From the early days, Java has had a reputation for its extensive set of libraries and packages. The basic Java language classes have been reused again and again by different Java programmers in their applications. The Hashtable class is a good example of a reusable class. This class accepts Object types as parameters and as return types. Potentially, any class implemented in Java can reuse this class. The class is also cleanly decoupled from other classes. It is easy to understand how to use its methods and a deep knowledge of its implementation is not required.

There are other recent smaller stories of success such as Log4J and Ant. Therefore, writing good object-oriented reusable software remains a very important part of Java software development, provided that this is treated as a business objective and is marketed as such.

The benefits of software reusability are summarized as follows:

❑ **Time-to-market**
Instead of writing an application from scratch, it is much quicker to reuse existing code

❑ **Quality**
The reuse of code that has already been extensively tested reduces the risk of bugs and leads to an increase in quality

❑ **Ease of learning**
The use of the same code reduces the learning curve for developers, ensuring that time can be spent where it is most needed (for example, in tackling new areas)

Why Write Maintainable Software?

In software terms, maintainability is ensuring that a piece of software or system continues to function correctly throughout its lifecycle.

Software needs to be maintained; failure to maintain it can have potentially catastrophic consequences. It is an expensive exercise to write a piece of software. However, development only represents 20% of the cost of a piece of software over its lifetime; the remaining 80% is spent on its maintenance.

Software products are becoming increasingly complex with large teams of developers working on a single project. People come and go over the lifetime of a project, and unless great care is taken, the time and difficulty in maintaining a piece of software can escalate dramatically. To make life easier, a couple of simple rules can be applied:

❑ **Structure**
A clearly-defined and easy-to-read structure needs to be applied at all levels. The application should have easily identifiable sections dealing with distinct aspects of the application, such as the GUI and data processing. This makes it easier to find a piece of code among thousands of lines. Methods should be kept small, as it is easy to get lost in a very large method.

❑ **Legibility**
Individual lines of code, if well formatted, become quicker and easier to read. Comments should be concise and meaningful. It is very easy to do something clever and then, months later, forget why something has been done in that particular way.

Why Write Extensible Software?

Given the very large cost incurred in developing a software product, it is only natural to try to extend the useful life of a product as far as possible. However, we live in an ever-changing world, and the demands that are placed on a software product also change.

Extending the capabilities software or adding new capabilities can increase the useful life of a product. All this can be done at a significantly lower cost than developing a new product. Modularity and loose coupling ensures that only those aspects of a product that need to be altered are changed, and that the possible knock-on effects are minimized.

In the next section, we shall look into designing and developing a generic case study scenario to demonstrate the three objectives described earlier.

A Component-Based Case Study

Let's imagine that we have been asked by a company to develop a set of extensible and reusable components to reduce the development iteration for each project that is undertaken. These components can be shared internally between projects.

The systems interact with a proprietary data source, which has its own proprietary query language. The components, which we have been asked to develop, support the structuring and the building of these queries in a J2EE context.

The basic components that we shall be developing are as follows:

❑ A set of extensible value object classes that can transport the content parameters for each query

❑ A set of basic query classes that can be extended into a larger query family

❑ A set of factory and building classes to create and construct the value objects and the query objects

The Interface

An important aspect of the component set that we are developing is the interface, which client classes use to gain access to the services we are building. This interface should be easy to use and easy to understand. It should also be unified and singular. The learning curve to use the interface should be small. Developers using the component set can then focus on developing the business logic for their own applications.

There are a number of patterns that could be used for the purpose of hiding the complexities of a subsystem and providing decoupling for client classes:

❑ **Façade** – provides a higher abstraction to a group of classes and interfaces in a subsystem, making it easier to use

❑ **Session Façade** – is an enterprise bean that hides the complexities of interaction between the presentation tier and the business-logic tier, and provides coarse-grained access to business objects in the J2EE framework

❑ **Business Delegate** – decouples the client tier from the business tier and hides underlying business services details like EJB lookups in the J2EE context

The three patterns are similar, but positioned differently to achieve subtly different purposes. Both Session Façade and Business Delegate are specializations of the Façade pattern for a specific purpose in the J2EE context. While Session Façade is an enterprise bean, which provides coarse-grained access, the latter hides the underlying business services of the business tier. The Façade design pattern is less specific and, therefore, can be adapted to different situations. Hence, it is more suitable for our study.

The Façade Design Pattern

The Façade pattern provides a higher-level interface or a higher level of abstraction to a group of interfaces in a subsystem. This makes the subsystem easier to use.

The main motive behind the use of this pattern is to reduce complexity exposed to client classes and also the number of classes that a client deals with. The Façade pattern has two main advantages. First, it protects a client from the internal details of the subsystem it is using, making it easier to use. Second, it promotes low coupling between the client classes and the subsystem classes, making it easier to change or extend the functionality internal to the subsystem without affecting the client code that uses the subsystem. The following diagram shows the structure of the Façade design pattern:

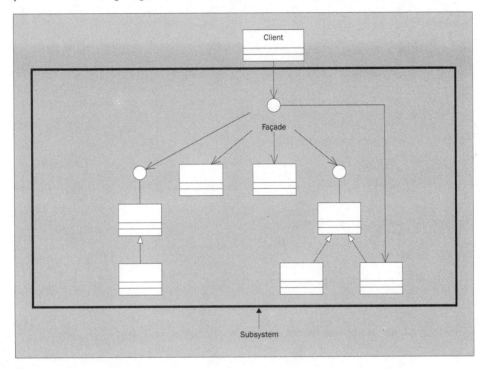

Participants of the Façade pattern are as follows:

- **Façade** – a higher-level interface to a group of interfaces and classes in a subsystem

- **Subsystem classes** – the internal classes and interfaces of the subsystem

- **Client classes** – classes external to the subsystem, which require the subsystem services

Implementing Façade in the J2EE Context

In the J2EE context, Façade can be used as a support pattern to other J2EE patterns to hide some of the internal complexity of a subsystem.

Unlike C++, Java defines public classes and package classes. Classes declared as public are exposed to packages outside to the package where they belong, but those declared with package access are only visible to classes in the package where they belong. This feature can be utilized to implement the Façade pattern by only making some of the implementation class packages visible. Enforcing this rule will make it possible to change the implementation of a class without affecting classes outside the scope of its package.

One recurring problem in a J2EE system is servicing value objects to client classes. In this chapter, we have developed a sample `Facade` interface and its implementation to show the Façade pattern in this context. In addition, we have defined a `ValueObject` interface and its implementation. The code in this chapter is used to demonstrate the ideas discussed and how those ideas could be implemented.

This is the sample code for the `Facade` interface:

```
package reuse;

/* Represents a facade interface to this package */

public interface Facade {

  /* Creates and returns a value object specific to this package
   * @return ValueObject specific to this package
   */
  public ValueObject getValueObject();

  //other facade methods

}
```

The implementation is simple at this stage:

```
package reuse;

/* Represents a facade implementation */

public class FacadeImpl implements Facade {

  /* Creates and returns a value object specific to this package
   * @return ValueObject specific to this package
   */
  public ValueObject getValueObject() {
    return new ValueObjectImpl();
  }

  //other facade methods

}
```

For the `ValueObject` interface, we have used a dynamic property set strategy with weakly typed property values. This is more flexible and reusable than the typical value-object idea based on bean `getX()` and `setX()` methods, but it is weakly typed and thus requires extra validation effort.

Here is the source for the `ValueObject` interface:

```
package reuse;

import java.io.Serializable;
import java.util.Iterator;
```

```
/* A set of dynamic properties expressed as { name, value } pairs.
 * Typically, client code is expected to use the Facade interface
 * to retrieve the correct ValueObject implementation.
 */
public interface ValueObject extends Serializable {

    /* Returns the names of the properties stored in the name space.
     * @return java.util.Iterator
     */
    public Iterator getPropertyNames();

    /* Sets a property to a given value. Validation may be performed for
     * any given value, depending on the implementation being used.
     * @param name  Name of the property to set.
     * @param value New value for the property.
     * @throws ValidationException if the value is incorrect.
     * @throws com.woe.cmi.exception.ValidationException
     */
    public void setProperty(String name, Object value);

    /* Returns the value of a property.
     * @param name Name of the property to retrieve.
     * @return java.lang.Object representing the value, or null if no
     * property has been set with this name.
     */
    public Object getProperty(String name);
}
```

To add a new property, or to extend the existing property set, we will not need to change this interface. We may only need to modify its implementation and possibly add some more validation rules.

The `ValueObjectImpl` class has package visibility only and, therefore, can be easily extended or replaced. This implementation utilizes a `Hashmap` to hold the property set:

```
package reuse;

import java.util.Map;
import java.util.Iterator;
import java.util.HashMap;

/* Provides a ValueObject implementation. */

class ValueObjectImpl implements ValueObject {
    private Map nameMap = new HashMap (10);

    /* Returns the names of the properties stored in this value object
     * @return java.util.Iterator
     */
    public Iterator getPropertyNames() {
        return nameMap.keySet().iterator();
    }

    /* Sets a property to a given value.
```

```
   * @param name   Name of the property to set.
   * @param value New value for the property.
   */
public void setProperty(java.lang.String name, java.lang.Object value) {
  nameMap.put(name, value);
}


 /* Returns the value of a property.
  * @param name Name of the property to retrieve.
  * @return java.lang.Object representing the value, or null if no
  * property has been set with this name.
  */
public Object getProperty(java.lang.String name) {
  return nameMap.get(name);
}

/* returns a string representation of myself */
public String toString() {
  StringBuffer buf = new StringBuffer( this.getClass().getName() + "::\n"
  );
  for (Iterator it = getPropertyNames(); it.hasNext(); ) {
    String name = it.next().toString();
    Object value = getProperty(name);
    buf.append(name + "=" + value);
    if( it.hasNext() ) {
      buf.append( ", " );
    }
  }
  return buf.toString();
}

}
```

The following class diagram shows the interfaces and classes that we have developed so far and their relationships:

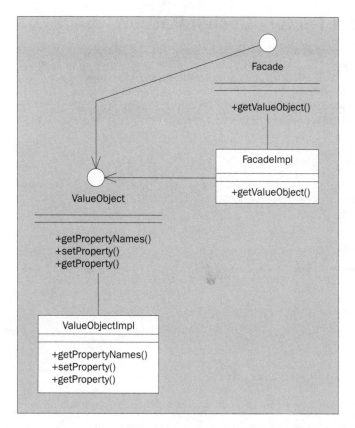

You may already be thinking that having a Façade is not quite enough. We will also need a pattern to create the various value object implementations. Introducing a factory will enforce the possibility of extending the existing set of value object implementations. It also defines a clear and simple framework, which caters for future change.

We may have a number of value object implementations for various future projects. To manage creating the family of value objects, it is suitable use a Factory pattern.

There are two Factory patterns that we could use to create the `ValueObject` classes:

❏ **Factory Method** – defines an interface to create objects but defers instantiation to subclasses

❏ **Abstract Factory** – defines an interface for creating families of related objects

The Factory Method pattern can be used to join two hierarchies of dependent families of objects by using a method called a factory method to do the creation. The Abstract Factory pattern is more focused on the creation of a family of related or dependent objects by introducing a factory interface as shown in the next section. The Factory Method pattern uses a creator, which is not necessarily a factory interface and it can include other functions as well. The Abstract Factory always has a factory interface dedicated for the purpose of creating objects alone. For this reason, we have identified this pattern as the most suitable choice to achieve our objective.

The Abstract Factory Design Pattern

The Abstract Factory pattern allows the creation of families of related or dependent objects without declaring their concrete classes. It helps to control the classes created in an application by allowing clients to use the classes through their abstract interfaces. Therefore the client code does not have any concrete class knowledge. Extending the class family created is also easier to manage, because the client code has no knowledge of the actual concrete class it is using. The following diagram shows the structure of the Abstract Factory design pattern:

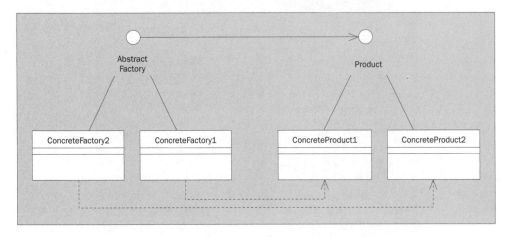

Participants in the Abstract Factory pattern are as follows:

❑ **Abstract Factory** – provides interface abstraction for creating a product

❑ **Product** – provides an interface for a product abstraction

❑ **Concrete Factory** – an abstract factory implementation for creation of a concrete product

❑ **Concrete Product** – the product concrete implementation

Implementing Abstract Factory in the J2EE Context

We have identified two strategies to implement the Abstract Factory pattern in Java. The first strategy is the standard strategy based on naming the product in the factory class definition.

There are two products that we are interested in building for the sake of this example. These are the `ValueObjectA` and `ValueObjectB` and the code for these classes is available with the code download for this book.

Here is the `ValueObjectFactory` interface:

```
package reuse;

/* Value object factory interface */
interface ValueObjectFactory {

  /* Creates a product called ValueObjectA
   * @return the product created
   */
  public ValueObject createValueObjectA();

  /* Creates a product called ValueObjectB
   * @return the product created
   */
  public ValueObject createValueObjectB();

}
```

The implementation of this class is as follows:

```
/* Value object factory implementation */

class ValueObjectFactoryImpl implements ValueObjectFactory {

  /* Creates a product called ValueObjectA
   * @return the product created
   */
  public ValueObject createValueObjectA() {
    return new ValueObjectA();
  }

  /* Creates a product called ValueObjectB
   * @return the product created
   */
  public ValueObject createValueObjectB() {
    return new ValueObjectB();
  }

}
```

This is the modified class diagram, which includes the new factory classes that we have developed:

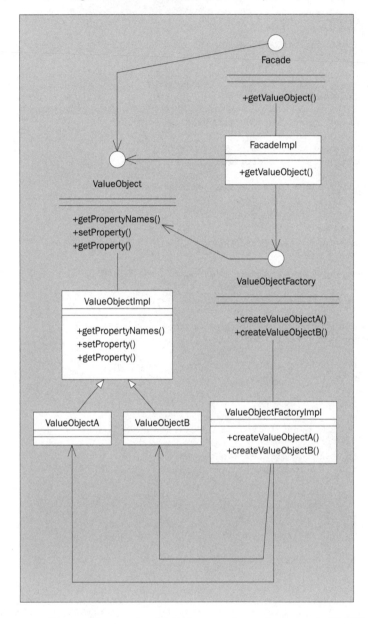

The second strategy is less weakly typed and based on naming a parameter to identify the product and thus allow its creation.

This strategy is more flexible because adding new products does not imply any changes to the code. To do this, we have to change the ValueObjectFactory interface as well as its implementation:

```
package reuse;

/* Value object factory interface */

interface ValueObjectFactory {

  /* Creates a product called based on the name specified
   * @param name of product to create
   * @return the product created
   */
  public ValueObject createValueObject( String name )
                          throws CreateException;


}
```

This is the implementation for the interface shown above:

```
package reuse;

import java.util.*;
import java.lang.reflect.*;

/* Value object factory implemenation */

class ValueObjectFactoryImpl implements ValueObjectFactory {

  private Properties properties = new Properties();
  private final static String VALUE_OBJECT_MAPPING_PROPERTIES =
                          "valueObjectMapping.properties";

  // Creates instance of me
  ValueObjectFactoryImpl() {
    try {
      properties.load( getClass().getResourceAsStream(
      VALUE_OBJECT_MAPPING_PROPERTIES ));
    } catch( java.io.IOException e ) {
      // handle exception here
    }
  }

  /* Creates a product called based on the name specified
   * @param name of product to create
   * @return the product created
   */
  public ValueObject createValueObject( String name )
      throws CreateException {

    try {
      return ( ValueObject )ObjectCreator.createObject(
      properties.getProperty( name ) );
    } catch( Exception e ) {
      throw new CreateException( "Error occured while creating " +
```

```
                                        name, e);
   }
}

static class ObjectCreator {
 // Private constructor. This class cannot be instantiated
    private ObjectCreator() {}

    /* Instantiate an Object from a given class name
     * @param className full qualified name of the class
     * @return the instantaited Object
     * @exception java.lang.Exception if instantiation failed
     */
    public static Object createObject(String className)
        throws Exception {
      return createObject( Class.forName(className));
    }

    /* Instantiate an Object instance
     * @param classObject Class object representing the object type
     * to be instantiated
     * @return the instantaied Object
     * @exception java.lang.Exception if instantiation failed
     */
    public static Object createObject(Class classObject)
        throws Exception {
      Object object = null;
      return  classObject.newInstance();
    }

    /* Instantiate an Object instance, requires a constructor with
     * parameters
     * @param className full qualified name of the class
     * @param params an array including the required parameters to
     * instantiate the object
     * @return the instantaited Object
     * @exception java.lang.Exception if instantiation failed
     */
    public static Object createObject(String className, Object[]
        params) throws Exception {
      return createObject( Class.forName(className), params);
    }

    /* Instantiate an Object instance, requires a constructor with
     * parameters
     * @param classObject, Class object representing the object type
     * to be instantiated
     * @param params an array including the required parameters to
     * instantiate the object
     * @return the instantaied Object
     * @exception java.lang.Exception if instantiation failed
     */
    public static Object createObject(Class classObject, Object[]
        params) throws Exception {
```

```
           Constructor[] constructors = classObject.getConstructors();
           Object object = null;
           for(int counter = 0; counter<constructors.length; counter++) {
             try {
               object = constructors[counter].newInstance(params);
             } catch(Exception e) {
               if(e instanceof InvocationTargetException)
                   ((InvocationTargetException)e).getTargetException().
                       printStackTrace();
                 // Do nothing, try the next constructor
               }
           }
           if(object == null)
             throw new InstantiationException();
           return object;
         }
     }
   }
```

This class reads a set of mappings for property names and class names for value objects from a property file, and instantiates these classes dynamically. This approach is less safe then the approach we described earlier, but is a lot more flexible.

The following is the content of the property file:

```
ValueObjectA=reuse.ValueObjectA
ValueObjectB=reuse.ValueObjectB
```

Finally, we need to amend the Facade interface and its implementation to allow creating the different types of value object products:

```
package reuse;

/** Represets a facade interface to this package
*/

public interface Facade {

  /** Creates and returns a value object specific to this package
* @return ValueObject specific to this package
*/
  public ValueObject getValueObject( String name ) throws CreateException;

  //other facade methods

}
```

To recap, the factory interface and classes used in this package are not visible to other packages. The only public classes in this package, so far, are the Facade interface, its implementation, the ValueObject interface, and the exception classes used in the package. This will make extensibility and maintainability a lot easier because of the reduction of coupling between client and implementation classes.

Here is the modified class diagram, which shows the second strategy of Abstract Factory, which we have developed:

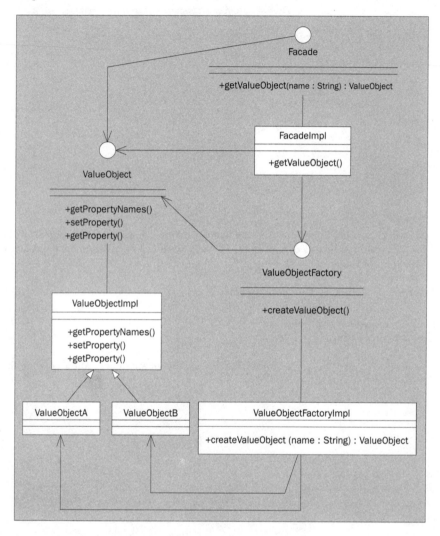

As mentioned earlier, the value object classes that we have developed so far, are flexible and weakly typed. This will necessitate the use of a validation function to validate the content of the value objects. A good way to add validation behavior to a class while maintaining flexibility is to use the Decorator pattern.

For introducing validation, we have two alternatives to choose from:

- ❑ **Using sub-classing**
  Adding responsibilities by sub-classing

- ❑ **Using Decorator**
  Adding responsibilities without sub-classing

In Decorator, new behavior or responsibility can be added transparently without affecting other objects. This is particularly useful if the added behavior needs to be withdrawn or when sub-classing is not practical. Since Java has single inheritance, you may not want to use inheritance for adding different behavior.

The Decorator Design Pattern

The Decorator pattern adds behavior dynamically to another class without sub-classing. It provides a more flexible way to extend a class without sub-classing. This pattern makes a good alternative to sub-classing. The following diagram shows the structure of the Decorator design pattern:

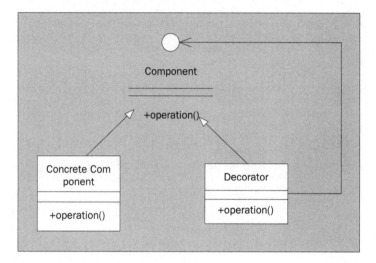

Participants of this pattern are as follows:

- ❑ **Component** – defines an interface for a component, which can be decorated
- ❑ **Concrete Component** – requires some extra behavior or responsibilities to be added
- ❑ **Decorator** – adds behavior dynamically to the concrete component without sub-classing it

Implementing Decorator in the J2EE Context

To do this, we have slightly modified the `ValueObject` interface to throw a `ValidateException` on the `setProperty()` method. We could have left `ValueObject` unchanged and made `ValidateException` extend the runtime exception but it is always a better practice to declare the exception. If this were to introduce many code changes then it is potentially better to make the `ValidateException` a runtime exception.

This is the changed interface:

```
package reuse;

import java.io.Serializable;
```

```
import java.util.Iterator;

/* A set of dynamic properties expressed as { name, value } pairs.
 * Typically, client code is expected to use the Facade interface
 * to retrieve the correct ValueObject implementation.
 */
public interface ValueObject extends Serializable {

    /* Returns the names of the properties stored in the name space.
     * @return java.util.Iterator
     */
    public Iterator getPropertyNames();

    /* Sets a property to a given value. Validation may be performed for
     * any given value, depending on the implementation being used.
     * @param name  Name of the property to set.
     * @param value New value for the property.
     * @throws ValidationException if the value is incorrect.
     * @throws com.woe.cmi.exception.ValidationException
     */
    public void setProperty(String name, Object value)
        throws ValidateException;

    /* Returns the value of a property.
     * @param name Name of the property to retrieve.
     * @return java.lang.Object representing the value, or null if no
       property has
     * been set with this name.
     */
    public Object getProperty(String name);
}
```

The value object decorator class decorates by delegation and not inheritance. This is a more flexible strategy because this decorator class can be used to decorate more than one implementation of the `ValueObject` interface. This is the source for the `DecoratedValueObjectImpl` class:

```
package reuse;

import java.util.Map;
import java.util.Iterator;
import java.util.HashMap;

/* Provides a decorated ValueObject implementation with validation. */
class DecoratedValueObjectImpl implements ValueObject {

    private ValueObject valueObject = null;

    /* Creates instance of me */
    DecoratedValueObjectImpl( ValueObject valueObject ) {
      this.valueObject = valueObject;
    }

    /* Returns the names of the properties stored in this value object
     * @return java.util.Iterator
```

```
    */
    public Iterator getPropertyNames() {
      return valueObject.getPropertyNames();
    }

    /* Sets a property to a given value.
     * @param name  Name of the property to set.
     * @param value New value for the property.
     */
    public void setProperty(java.lang.String name, java.lang.Object value)
        throws ValidateException {
      if( name == null || value == null ) {
        throw new ValidateException("Name or value being set is null");
      } else if ( name != null && name.equals( "" ) ) {
        throw new ValidateException("Name being set is empty value" );
      } else {
        valueObject.setProperty(name, value);
      }
    }

    /* Returns the value of a property.
     * @param name Name of the property to retrieve.
     * @return java.lang.Object representing the value, or null if no
     * property has been set with this name.
     */
    public Object getProperty( java.lang.String name ) {
      return valueObject.getProperty( name );
    }

    /* Returns a string representation of myself */
    public String toString() {
      return valueObject.toString();
    }

}
```

To put the Decorator pattern into effect, we need to change one method in the
ValueObjectFactoryImpl, which is the createValueObject() method that currently looks
like this:

```
public ValueObject createValueObject(String name) throws CreateException {
  try {
    return ( ValueObject )ObjectCreator.createObject(
              properties.getProperty( name ) );
  } catch( Exception e ) {
    throw new CreateException(
                "Error occurred while creating " + name, e );
  }
}
```

After modifying it, the createValueObject() method looks like this:

```
public ValueObject createValueObject(String name) throws CreateException {
  try {
```

```
            return new DecoratedValueObjectImpl(
                    ( ValueObject )ObjectCreator.createObject(
                             properties.getProperty( name ) ) );
    } catch( Exception e ) {
    throw new CreateException(
                "Error occurred while creating " + name, e );
    }
}
```

Note that because all of the value object family of classes and the Value Object Factory implementation classes are not visible to other packages, adding these minor modifications is perfectly safe even if done after the product has matured.

The following diagram shows the DecoratedValueObjectImpl in context with the rest of the Value Object class family:

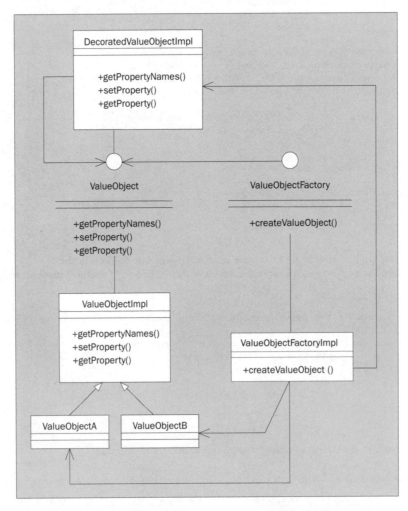

Finally, to make these sets of classes complete, we shall include the source for the `ValidateException` class. This is used by the `ValueObject` interface for validating properties when they are set:

```
package reuse;

import java.io.PrintStream;
import java.io.PrintWriter;

/* Indicates that a validation exceptional condition has occurred */

public class ValidateException extends BaseException {

  /*Creates an instance of me */
  public ValidateException() {
    super();
  }

  /*Creates an instance of me */
  public ValidateException(String msg) {
    super(msg);
  }

  /*Creates an instance of me */
  public ValidateException(String msg, Throwable cause) {
    super(msg, cause);
  }

  /*Creates an instance of me */
  public ValidateException(Throwable cause) {
    super(cause);
  }

}
```

This class extends another exception class called `BaseException`. Please note that this exception introduces the notion of a nested exception. The added feature makes the exception class generic and more reusable in various situations. Our `Facade` interface provides more than just value object creation to be used in other J2EE packages.

The component that we shall develop and design next is the query class family and its related classes. The query classes provide an easy way to construct proprietary queries for a data source through using a Data Access Object. Developers using these query objects need an easy and reliable way to build them. This suggests the need to develop a query builder. The Builder design pattern is ideally suited for this purpose.

The Builder Design Pattern

Unlike the Abstract Factory pattern, which focuses on creating a family of related products, the Builder pattern focuses on constructing a complex object step by step.

This pattern gives finer control over the construction process, defining the steps needed to build the product, and then provides the final product in one go. The following diagram shows the structure of the Builder design pattern:

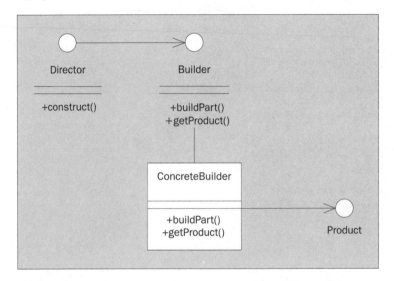

Participants in the Builder design pattern are:

❏ **Builder** – defines an interface for building a product in a set of steps

❏ **Concrete Builder** – defines the steps in which the product is going to be built

❏ **Director** – delegates to the builder to build the products parts

❏ **Product** – complex component composed of a number of parts

The Builder makes the construction process more modular. Also, the product building process can be repeated with variations on the same structure allowing reuse of the building parts.

In addition, different products that share similar components can also be built. This is a powerful tool for future extensibility as shown in the next section.

Implementing Builder in the J2EE Context

Sometimes, in a J2EE application, it is required to use a proprietary data source other than a database. For example, the data source may have a specific query language. Typically, a session or an entity bean will use a Data Access Object to obtain access to the external data source. The Data Access Object will also use a query builder to build and post queries to the external data source.

This is the interface for a query, which is the product of our builder:

```
package reuse;

/* Specifies the interface of a query */
```

```
public interface Query {

  /* Represents the string value of the query
   * @return a String representing me
   */
  public String stringValue();

  /* Returns a String representation of me
   * @return a String representing me
   */
  public String toString();

}
```

The `QueryBuilder` also has an interface defined as follows:

```
package reuse;

/* Interface for building queries uses Builder Pattern */

public interface QueryBuilder {

  /* Builds the header of the query */
  public void buildQueryHeader();

  /* Builds the query token */
  public void buildQueryToken();

  /* Builds the query body */
  public void buildQueryBody();

  /* Returns the built query */
  public Query getQuery();

}
```

We have a package class, which implements the `QueryBuilder` interface. This is the implementation class:

```
package reuse;

import java.util.Iterator;

class QueryBuilderImpl implements QueryBuilder {

  private String queryHeader = "";
  private String queryToken = "";
  private String queryBody = "";
  private ValueObject bodyParams;

  /* Creates instance of me */
  public QueryBuilderImpl( ValueObject bodyParams ) {
```

```
    this.bodyParams = bodyParams;
  }

  /* Builds the header of the query */
  public void buildQueryHeader() {
    queryHeader = "External Data Source Query";
  }

  /* Builds the query token */
  public void buildQueryToken() {
    queryToken = "CR";
  }

  /* Builds the query body */
  public void buildQueryBody() {
    StringBuffer buf = new StringBuffer();
    Iterator propertyNames = bodyParams.getPropertyNames();
    while( propertyNames.hasNext() ) {
      String propertyName = ( String )propertyNames.next();
      buf.append( propertyName + "="
                    + bodyParams.getProperty( propertyName ) );
      if( propertyNames.hasNext() ) {
        buf.append(",");
      }
    }
    queryBody = buf.toString();
  }

  private String getQueryHeader() {
    return queryHeader;
  }

  private String getQueryToken() {
    return queryToken;
  }

  private String getQueryBody() {
    return queryBody;
  }

  /* Returns the built query */
  public Query getQuery() {
    return new QueryImpl( getQueryHeader(),
                          getQueryToken(),
                          getQueryBody() );
  }

}
```

This is the `QueryImpl` class, which implements the `Query` interface:

```
package reuse;

/* Defines a simple implementation of a query */
```

```
class QueryImpl implements Query {

  private String queryHeader = "";
  private String queryToken = "";
  private String queryBody = "";

  QueryImpl( String queryHeader,
             String queryToken,
             String queryBody ) {
    this.queryHeader = queryHeader;
    this.queryToken = queryToken;
    this.queryBody = queryBody;
  }

  public String toString() {
    return stringValue();
  }

  public String stringValue() {
    StringBuffer buf = new StringBuffer();
    buf.append( getQueryHeader() + "|" );
    buf.append( getQueryToken() + "|" );
    buf.append( getQueryBody() + "||" );
    return buf.toString();
  }

  protected String getQueryHeader() {
    return queryHeader;
  }

  protected String getQueryToken() {
    return queryToken;
  }

  protected String getQueryBody() {
    return queryBody;
  }

}
```

Finally, the Facade class that we developed earlier will have a second method to create a query for a client based on a populated ValueObject:

```
package reuse;

/* Represents a facade interface to this package */

public interface Facade {

  /* Creates and returns a value object specific to this package
   * @return ValueObject specific to this package
   */
  public ValueObject getValueObject( String name ) throws CreateException;
```

```
  /* Builds and returns a query for specified value object
   * @param valueObject query parameters
   * @return Query the built query
   */
  public Query getQuery( ValueObject valueObject );

  //other facade methods

}
```

The `FacadeImpl` class acts as a director to construct the query product using the `Builder` interface as shown in the following Java code:

```
package reuse;

/* Represents a facade implementation */

public class FacadeImpl implements Facade {
  ValueObjectFactory factory = new
  ValueObjectFactoryImpl();

  /* Creates and returns a value object specific to this package
   * @return ValueObject specific to this package
   */
  public ValueObject getValueObject( String name ) throws CreateException {
    return factory.createValueObject( name );
  }

  /* Builds and returns a query for specified value object
   * @param valueObject query parameters
   * @return Query the built query
   */
  public Query getQuery( ValueObject valueObject ) {
    QueryBuilder builder = new QueryBuilderImpl( valueObject );
    builder.buildQueryHeader();
    builder.buildQueryToken();
    builder.buildQueryBody();
    return builder.getQuery();
  }

  //other facade methods

}
```

This is the modified class diagram, which shows the query interface and the builder classes for the **query** family of classes:

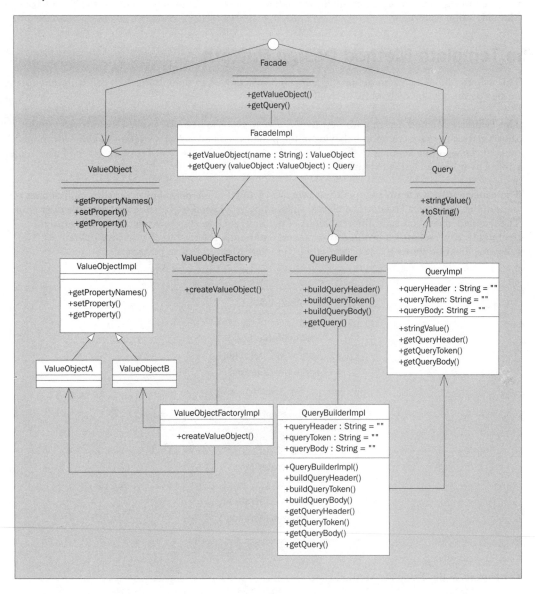

As the façade only exposes the Query interface, it will be very straightforward to vary the implementation of the query without affecting any client code.

The Builder will allow the future developer to easily define new kinds of queries based on the same structure as the current query, with a high proportion of reuse. It will be easy to introduce a new or modified implementation by creating a new builder implementation and a new query implementation.

There is a requirement to define a clear extension framework, while sharing common behavior among the query class family. Due to the possibility of future projects using these queries, the query class family will need to expand. The appropriate design pattern that will help to achieve this is the Template Method design pattern.

The Template Method Design Pattern

This pattern allows a class to define the algorithm structure of an operation while deferring some steps in the operation to be defined by derived classes.

The Template Method design pattern provides a very powerful tool for reusability and extensibility. It allows classes to share common behavior in the parent class and define variation of behavior in the derived classes while keeping to the same structure of method calls. The Template Method also allows control over how a class is extended.

The pattern utilizes a template operation, which is defined in the parent abstract class, and defines the steps of the algorithm. The derived classes should not be allowed to override the template operation. The template operation calls different kinds of methods such as concrete operations and abstract operations. Abstract operations in this context are normally referred to as primitive operations. The following diagram shows the structure of the Template Method design pattern:

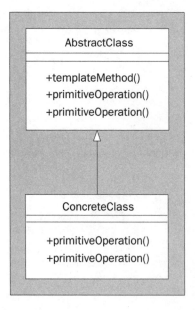

Participants in the Template Method class are:

❑ **Abstract Class** – defines a template method, which implements the steps of an algorithm by calling primitive operations, which are implemented by derived classes

❑ **Concrete Class** – implements primitive operations, which the Abstract Class defines and extends

Implementing Template Method in the J2EE Context

In the J2EE context, as with any Java application, the Template Method design pattern provides a powerful technique to manage extensibility and evolution of a set of related classes.

To demonstrate, we have decided to extend the `QueryImpl` class developed in the previous sections to provide a variation of implementation for the query.

A query was built using the Builder design pattern. It can be sub-classed to support different types of queries. The `QueryImpl` class is now abstract, and defines a template operation called `stringValue()`. This operation is final and cannot be overridden by derived classes. There are six protected concrete and abstract operations called by this operation. The Template Method and the other operations called by it are highlighted in the code below:

```
package reuse;

/* Represents a query implementation */

abstract class QueryImpl implements Query {

  private String queryHeader = "";
  private String queryToken = "";
  private String queryBody = "";

  /* Creates instance of me */
  QueryImpl( String queryHeader,
             String queryToken,
             String queryBody ) {
    this.queryHeader = queryHeader;
    this.queryToken = queryToken;
    this.queryBody = queryBody;
  }

  public String toString() {
    return stringValue();
  }

  public final String stringValue() {
    StringBuffer buf = new StringBuffer();
    buf.append( getQueryHeader() );
    buf.append( getExtraHeaderInfo() + "|" );
    buf.append( getQueryToken() + "," );
    buf.append( getExtraTokens() + "|" );
    buf.append( getQueryBody() + "," );
    buf.append( getExtraBody() + "||" );
    return buf.toString();
  }

  /* A Template method uses a primitive operation */
  protected String getQueryHeader() {
    return queryHeader;
  }
```

```
/* A Template method uses a primitive operation */
protected String getQueryToken() {
  return queryToken;
}

/* A Template method uses a primitive operation */
protected String getQueryBody() {
  return queryBody;
}

/* A primitive operation defined by derived class */
abstract protected String getExtraHeaderInfo();

/* A primitive operation defined by derived class */
abstract protected String getExtraTokens();

/* A primitive operation defined by derived class */
abstract protected String getExtraBody();

}
```

The two classes called QueryA and QueryB extend the QueryImpl class and define the primitive operations highlighted above.

This is the QueryA class:

```
package reuse;

/* A special query of type A */
final class QueryA extends QueryImpl {

  /* Creates instance of me */
  QueryA( String queryHeader,
          String queryToken,
          String queryBody ) {
    super( queryHeader, queryToken, queryBody );
  }

  /* A primitive operation called by super class */
  protected String getExtraHeaderInfo() {
    return "";
  }

  /* A primitive operation called by super class */
  protected String getExtraTokens() {
    return "A";
  }

  /* A primitive operation called by super class */
  protected String getExtraBody() {
    return "className=" + this.getClass().getName();
  }

}
```

This is the QueryB class:

```
package reuse;

/* A special query of type B */

final class QueryB extends QueryImpl {

  /* Creates instance of me */
  QueryB( String queryHeader,
          String queryToken,
          String queryBody ) {
    super( queryHeader, queryToken, queryBody );
  }

  /* A primitive operation called by super class */
  protected String getExtraHeaderInfo() {
    return "";
  }

  /* A primitive operation called by super class */
  protected String getExtraTokens() {
    return "B";
  }

  /* A primitive operation called by super class */
  protected String getExtraBody() {
    return "className=" + this.getClass().getName();
  }

}
```

And finally, this is the class diagram, which shows the Template Method design pattern in action:

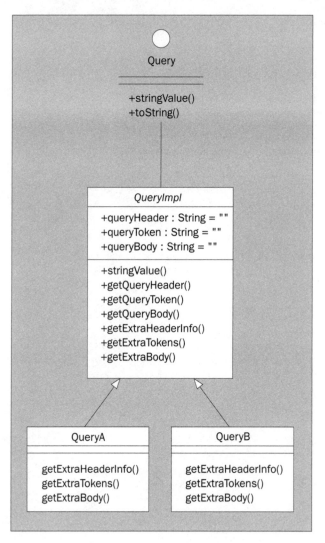

Assembling the Patterns into a Framework

So far, we have described and adopted the following patterns for our generic study:

❑ **The Façade pattern**
Provides a higher-level interface to abstract out the internal complexities of a subsystem to make the subsystem easier to use and to reduce coupling

❑ **The Abstract Factory pattern**
Allows the creation of families of related objects without specifying their concrete classes

❑ **The Decorator pattern**
Adds responsibilities to a class without sub-classing it

❑ **The Builder pattern**
Allows the creation of a complex object in a step-by-step manner and provides the final product in one go

❑ **The Template Method pattern**
Allows a class to define the algorithm structure of an operation, deferring some steps in the operation to be defined by derived classes

And finally, we are going to show all the patterns adopted and discussed earlier assembled into one framework:

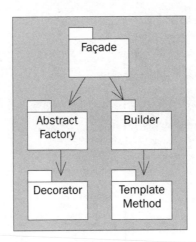

The following diagram shows the actual class relationships and how the patterns map to classes and interfaces:

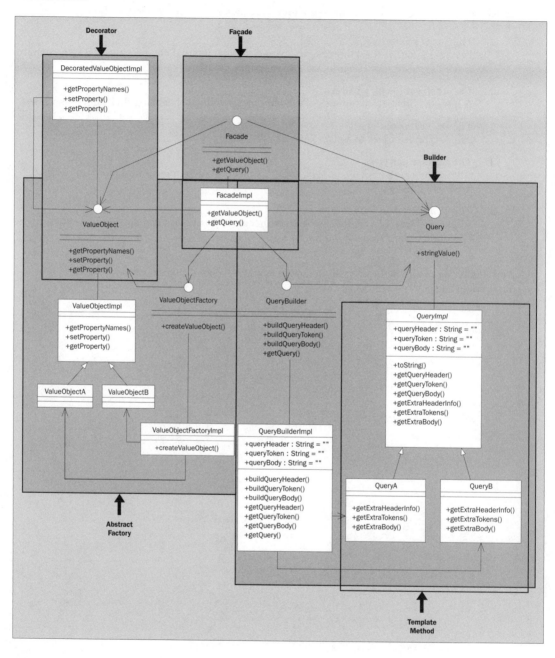

Summary

Many software design patterns can be applied to attain better software reusability, maintainability, and extensibility. This is a list of the patterns we have discussed that help to provide more future extensibility:

- ❑ The Decorator design pattern
- ❑ The Template Method design pattern
- ❑ The Abstract Factory design pattern
- ❑ The Façade design pattern
- ❑ The Builder design pattern

The scope to attain better software reusability, maintainability, and extendibility by applying software patterns is immense. The components that we have developed and designed demonstrate only a few of the many possible patterns available.

The important lessons we have learned are:

- ❑ To make an effective reusable design, the design should have as many interfaces as possible defined in it. It should also provide an `Ximpl` class, which implements the relevant interfaces.

- ❑ Avoid using primitives as parameters or as return values. Instead, use objects, which allow the use of the methods like the `toString()`, `equals()`, and so on. This helps in maintaining cleaner Java code and encourages encapsulation, whereby each object implements its own `toString()` and `equals()` methods for example.

- ❑ The more abstract the component, the more reusable and extendable it is.

- ❑ Adopt design patterns that encourage extendibility (for example Façade, Abstract Factory, Builder, Decorator, and Template Method).

- ❑ Adopt design patterns that encourage better encapsulation and decoupling, for example Façade and Abstract Factory.

- ❑ Try to keep classes small by using delegation, for instance using the Decorator design pattern. Size is not important; small but perfectly formed classes are easier to maintain, extend, and reuse.

- ❑ When designing with inheritance, always make sure that there is a real object-oriented relationship, such as generalization or specialization. In a lot of cases using delegation or aggregation can prove to be a better choice. In many applications, inheritance is overused, which can make an application tightly coupled, and difficult to maintain and reuse.

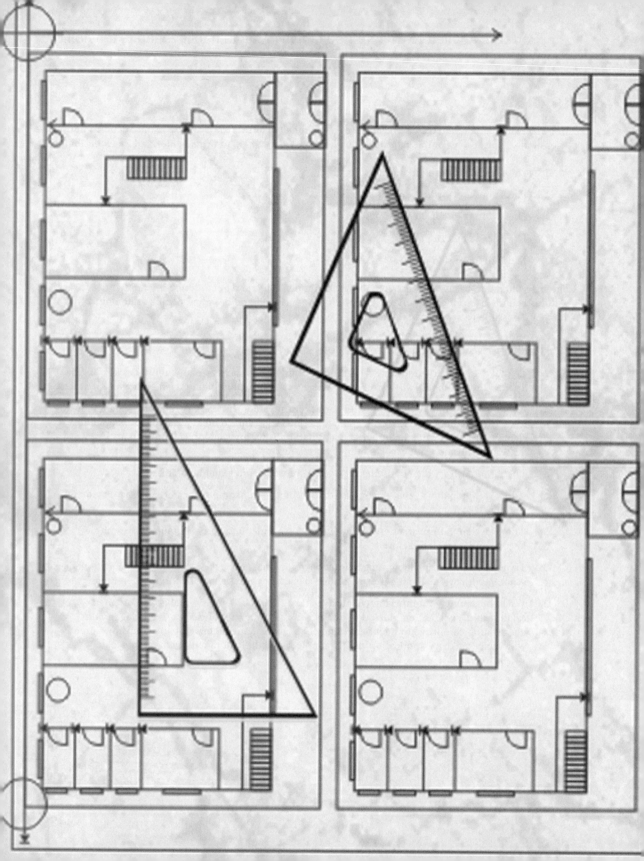

Index

X

Notes

Notes

Notes

ASP Today

The daily knowledge site for professional ASP programmers

ASPToday brings the essence of the Wrox Programmer to Programmer philosophy to you through the web. Every working day, www.asptoday.com delivers a new, original article by ASP programmers for ASP programmers.

Want to know about Classic ASP, ASP.NET, Performance, Data Access, Site Design, SQL Server, and more? Then visit us. You can make sure that you don't miss a thing by subscribing to our free daily e-mail updates featuring ASPToday highlights and tips.

By bringing you daily articles written by real programmers, ASPToday is an indispensable resource for quickly finding out exactly what you need. ASPToday is THE daily knowledge site for professional ASP programmers.

In addition to our free weekly and monthly articles, ASPToday also includes a premier subscription service. You can now join the growing number of ASPToday subscribers who benefit from access to:

- Daily in-depth articles
- Code-heavy demonstrations of real applications
- Access to the ASPToday Living Book, our collection of past articles
- ASP reference material
- Fully searchable index and advanced search engine
- Tips and tricks for professionals

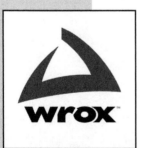

Visit ASPToday at: www.asptoday.com

Got more Wrox books than you can carry around?

Wroxbase is the new online service from Wrox Press. Dedicated to providing online access to books published by Wrox Press, helping you and your team find solutions and guidance for all your programming needs.

The key features of this service will be:

- Different libraries based on technologies that you use everyday (ASP 3.0, XML, SQL 2000, etc.). The initial set of libraries will be focused on Microsoft-related technologies.
- You can subscribe to as few or as many libraries as you require, and access all books within those libraries as and when you need to.
- You can add notes (either just for yourself or for anyone to view) and your own bookmarks that will all be stored within your account online, and so will be accessible from any computer.
- You can download the code of any book in your library directly from Wroxbase

Visit the site at: www.wroxbase.com

wrox

Programmer to Programmer™

Registration Code: | 52884I667NC5N301 |

Wrox writes books for you. Any suggestions, or ideas about how you want
information given in your ideal book will be studied by our team.
Your comments are always valued at Wrox.

Free phone in USA 800-USE-WROX
Fax (312) 893 8001

UK Tel.: (0121) 687 4100   Fax: (0121) 687 4101

Professional J2EE Design Patterns – Registration Card

Name _____

Address _____

_____

_____

City _____ State/Region_____

Country _____ Postcode/Zip_____

E-Mail _____

Occupation _____

How did you hear about this book?

☐ Book review (name) _____

☐ Advertisement (name) _____

☐ Recommendation _____

☐ Catalog _____

☐ Other _____

Where did you buy this book?

☐ Bookstore (name) _____ City_____

☐ Computer store (name) _____

☐ Mail order _____

☐ Other _____

What influenced you in the purchase of this book?

☐ Cover Design   ☐ Contents   ☐ Other (please specify):

_____

How did you rate the overall content of this book?

☐ Excellent   ☐ Good   ☐ Average   ☐ Poor

What did you find most useful about this book? _____

_____

What did you find least useful about this book? _____

_____

Please add any additional comments. _____

_____

What other subjects will you buy a computer book on soon?

_____

What is the best computer book you have used this year?

_____

Note: This information will only be used to keep you updated
about new Wrox Press titles and will not be used for
any other purpose or passed to any other third party.

wrox

Programmer to Programmer™

Note: If you post the bounce back card below in the UK, please send it to:

Wrox Press Limited, Arden House, 1102 Warwick Road,
Acocks Green, Birmingham B27 6HB. UK.

Computer Book Publishers

CAMBRIDGE SCHOOL

Shakespeare

The Taming of the Shrew

Edited by Michael Fynes-Clinton and Perry Mills

Series Editor: Rex Gibson
Director, Shakespeare and Schools Project

CAMBRIDGE UNIVERSITY PRESS

Published by the Press Syndicate of the University of Cambridge
The Pitt Building, Trumpington Street, Cambridge CB2 1RP
40 West 20th Street, New York, NY 10011–4211, USA
10 Stamford Road, Oakleigh, Victoria 3166, Australia

First published 1992

Printed in Great Britain at the University Press, Cambridge

A catalogue record for this book is available from the British Library.

Library of Congress cataloguing in publication data applied for

ISBN 0 521 42505 0 paperback

Designed by Richard Morris, Stonesfield Design
Picture research by Callie Kendall
Illustration by Jones and Sewell Associates

Thanks are due to the following for permission to reproduce photographs:

Jacket: Alastair Muir; detail of the Bradford Table Carpet by courtesy of the board of trustees of
the Victoria & Albert Museum; p. 8, from Scarron's *Comical Romance of a Company of Stage
Players* (1676); p. 20, The Shakespeare Centre Library: Joe Cocks Studio Collection; pp. 32,
80, 88, 118, 146, © Donald Cooper/Photostage; pp. 60, 70, Reg Wilson; p. 78, Laurence
Burns; p. 94; The Shakespeare Centre Library; p. 112, copyright © BBC/photo: David Green;
p. 122, Birmingham City Museum and Art Gallery; p. 177, © Angus McBean; p. 179, King
Features Syndicate

Thanks are due to the following for permission to reproduce extracts from copyright material:

p. 178: extract from an article by Michael Billington in *The Guardian*, reproduced by permission
of the author; extract from *The Female Eunuch* (1970) by Germaine Greer, published by
HarperCollins Publishers Ltd; extract from 'Sexism and the battle of the sexes in *The Taming of
the Shrew*' by Linda Bamber from *Comic Women, Tragic Men: a Study of Gender and Genre in
Shakespeare* (1984), Stanford University Press, reproduced by permission of the publisher; p.
179: extract from '*The Taming* Untamed: or the return of the Shrew' (1966) by R. B. Heilman,
in *Modern Language Quarterly* 27 (1966), pp. 147–61; extracts from interviews with Jonathan
Miller and Michael Bogdanov in *The Shakespeare Myth* (1988) ed. Graham Holderness,
Manchester University Press, reproduced by permission of the publisher.

MFC to Annette
PEM to Mary

Contents

Cambridge School Shakespeare

This edition of *The Taming of the Shrew* is part of the *Cambridge School Shakespeare* series. Like every other play in the series, it has been specially prepared to help all students in schools and colleges.

This *The Taming of the Shrew* aims to be different from other editions of the play. It invites you to bring the play to life in your classroom, hall or drama studio through enjoyable activities that will increase your understanding. Actors have created their different interpretations of the play over the centuries. Similarly, you are encouraged to make up your own mind about *The Taming of the Shrew*, rather than having someone else's interpretation handed down to you.

Cambridge School Shakespeare does not offer you a cut-down or simplified version of the play. This is Shakespeare's language, filled with imaginative possibilities. You will find on every left-hand page: a summary of the action, an explanation of unfamiliar words, a choice of activities on Shakespeare's language, characters and stories.

Between each act and in the pages at the end of the play, you will find notes, illustrations and activities. These will help to increase your understanding of the whole play.

There are a large number of activities to give you the widest choice to suit your own particular needs. Please don't think you have to do every one. Choose the activities that will help you most.

This edition will be of value to you whether you are studying for an examination, reading for pleasure, or thinking of putting on the play to entertain others. You can work on the activities on your own or in groups. Many of the activities suggest a particular group size, but don't be afraid to make up larger or smaller groups to suit your own purposes.

Although you are invited to treat *The Taming of the Shrew* as a play, you don't need special dramatic or theatrical skills to do the activities. By choosing your activities, and by exploring and experimenting, you can make your own interpretations of Shakespeare's language, characters and stories. Whatever you do, remember that Shakespeare wrote his plays to be acted, watched and enjoyed.

Rex Gibson

This edition of *The Taming of the Shrew* uses the text of the play established by Ann Thompson in *The New Cambridge Shakespeare*.

List of characters

The Induction
(set in Warwickshire)

CHRISTOPHER SLY   a tinker
HOSTESS   of an alehouse
A LORD
BARTHOLOMEW   the Lord's page (pretends to be Sly's wife)
Huntsmen and Servingmen attending the Lord
A Troupe of Actors visiting the Lord

who present

The Taming of the Shrew
(set in Padua)

The Minola Family

KATHERINA the Shrew
BIANCA her younger sister
BAPTISTA MINOLA her father

The Suitors

PETRUCHIO
LUCENTIO (pretends to be Cambio)
HORTENSIO (pretends to be Litio)
GREMIO a rich old man

The Servants

GRUMIO   Petruchio's personal servant
TRANIO   Lucentio's personal servant
                       (pretends to be Lucentio)
BIONDELLO   Lucentio's second servant

CURTIS, NATHANIEL, PHILIP, } Petruchio's servants
JOSEPH, NICHOLAS, PETER

Servants attending on Baptista and Lucentio

Other Characters

VINCENTIO Lucentio's father   A MERCHANT (pretends to be Vincentio)
A WIDOW in love with Hortensio   A TAILOR
                                  A HABERDASHER

I

Christopher Sly quarrels with the Hostess who is throwing him out of her tavern. He falls into a drunken sleep. A nobleman returns from the hunt and talks about the day's sport.

1 Sit up and pay attention! (in groups of five)

The Induction opens in the middle of an aggressive argument. Different productions have tried elaborate ways of grabbing the audience's attention (see page 186).

From lines 1–11, gather information about the location and atmosphere. Three of you act as director, designer and stage manager and discuss the most appropriate setting. Consider adding music, other characters or some short introduction.

Rehearse and present lines 1–11 to the rest of the class.

2 Christopher Sly (in groups of three)

Sly does not say much, but his few lines suggest a great deal about his character. Each person chooses one phrase from lines 1–11 and works out a short mime to show something about Sly, using only their phrase as a caption. After the mimes have been shown, talk about Sly's appearance, costume and accent. Do you all agree about what he is like?

3 The Lord (in pairs)

The Lord uses a different style of language from Sly. He has been hunting and tells how one of his hounds is foaming at the mouth from exhaustion ('embossed'), how another detected a scent when all the other hounds seemed to have lost it ('made it good'), and puts a price on the hound's head. Make up a 'modern' version of lines 12–17, for example, substituting cars for hounds.

---

feeze fix
Richard Conqueror Sly's error for William
paucas pallabris few words
Sessa! Be quiet! (or push off!)

denier French coin of low value
thirdborough officer
brach bitch
in the coldest fault where we nearly lost the scent

The Taming of the Shrew

INDUCTION 1
Outside an Alehouse in Warwickshire

Enter CHRISTOPHER SLY *and the* HOSTESS

SLY I'll feeze you, in faith.

HOSTESS A pair of stocks, you rogue!

SLY Y'are a baggage, the Slys are no rogues. Look in the Chronicles;
    we came in with Richard Conqueror. Therefore *paucas pallabris,*
    let the world slide. Sessa!   5

HOSTESS You will not pay for the glasses you have burst?

SLY No, not a denier. Go by, Saint Jeronimy, go to thy cold bed and
    warm thee.

                    [He lies down.]

HOSTESS I know my remedy; I must go fetch the thirdborough.*[Exit]*

SLY Third, or fourth, or fifth borough, I'll answer him by law. I'll not   10
    budge an inch, boy. Let him come, and kindly.

                    He falls asleep.

Wind horns. Enter a LORD *from hunting, with his train* [*of*
            HUNTSMEN *and* SERVINGMEN].

LORD Huntsman, I charge thee, tender well my hounds.
    Breathe Merriman – the poor cur is embossed –
    And couple Clowder with the deep-mouthed brach.
    Saw'st thou not, boy, how Silver made it good   15
    At the hedge corner, in the coldest fault?
    I would not lose the dog for twenty pound.

The Lord challenges the Huntsman's judgement of his hounds. Seeing Sly asleep, he decides to play a trick on the drunkard. When Sly wakes, everyone will pretend he is really a nobleman.

---

1 The foul beast (in groups of three)

While one person reads lines 30–1 aloud, the others form a statue which features both Sly and the Lord in the positions you imagine them to hold at that point. The postures should bring out as much of their characters as possible. Talk together about what you feel about both characters.

2 The jest (in pairs)

The Lord decides to play a trick on Sly which he describes as a 'jest'. Read lines 32–50, alternately a line at a time. Then discuss these questions:

- Do these details sound as if they have been prepared beforehand, or made up on the spur of the moment? Give reasons for your choice.
- Why does the Lord want to play a trick on Sly?
- Why does the Lord want to make Sly 'forget himself'?
- If it's a 'jest', how funny is it?
- Is it fair?

---

fleet fast
sup feed
practise play a trick
wanton erotic, sexy

balm bathe, anoint
distillèd concentrated, perfumed
dulcet melodious

1 HUNTSMAN Why, Belman is as good as he, my lord;
　　　　　He cried upon it at the merest loss,
　　　　　And twice today picked out the dullest scent.　　　　20
　　　　　Trust me, I take him for the better dog.
LORD Thou art a fool. If Echo were as fleet
　　　　　I would esteem him worth a dozen such.
　　　　　But sup them well, and look unto them all:
　　　　　Tomorrow I intend to hunt again.　　　　25
1 HUNTSMAN I will, my lord.
LORD What's here? One dead, or drunk? See, doth he breathe?
2 HUNTSMAN He breathes, my lord. Were he not warmed with ale,
　　　　　This were a bed but cold to sleep so soundly.
LORD O monstrous beast, how like a swine he lies!　　　　30
　　　　　Grim death, how foul and loathsome is thine image!
　　　　　Sirs, I will practise on this drunken man.
　　　　　What think you, if he were conveyed to bed,
　　　　　Wrapped in sweet clothes, rings put upon his fingers,
　　　　　A most delicious banquet by his bed,　　　　35
　　　　　And brave attendants near him when he wakes –
　　　　　Would not the beggar then forget himself?
1 HUNTSMAN Believe me, lord, I think he cannot choose.
2 HUNTSMAN It would seem strange unto him when he waked –
LORD Even as a flatt'ring dream or worthless fancy.　　　　40
　　　　　Then take him up, and manage well the jest.
　　　　　Carry him gently to my fairest chamber
　　　　　And hang it round with all my wanton pictures;
　　　　　Balm his foul head in warm distillèd waters
　　　　　And burn sweet wood to make the lodging sweet;　　　　45
　　　　　Procure me music ready when he wakes
　　　　　To make a dulcet and a heavenly sound;
　　　　　And if he chance to speak, be ready straight
　　　　　And with a low submissive reverence
　　　　　Say, 'What is it your honour will command?'　　　　50

*The Lord gives detailed instructions for the execution of his plan, and Sly
is carried to the Lord's house. Trumpets sound, heralding the arrival of
a company of actors.*

---

1 Luxury (in groups of five)

One person reads aloud lines 42–64. Enjoy the language, which is full
of sensuous details. The others 'echo' words which they associate
with certain topics: one takes wealth; one anything suggesting a
master/servant relationship; the third echoes any words to do with
sex; the fourth concentrates on verbs. The most appropriate way to do
this is to whisper the words back to the reader as soon as you hear
them. Repeat the exercise changing roles, then talk together about
what you notice.

2 'Husbanded with modesty' (in groups of four)

The Lord is sure the trick will be very entertaining as long as no one
takes things too far (line 64). Of course, it is the Lord himself who
decides where to draw the line. Discuss what you think about the
rules of this particular game.

---

ewer jug
diaper towel
kindly naturally, with conviction

passing extremely
to his office perform his duty
An't if it

Let one attend him with a silver basin
Full of rose-water and bestrewed with flowers;
Another bear the ewer, the third a diaper,
And say, 'Will't please your lordship cool your hands?'
Some one be ready with a costly suit   55
And ask him what apparel he will wear;
Another tell him of his hounds and horse,
And that his lady mourns at his disease.
Persuade him that he hath been lunatic,
And when he says he is, say that he dreams,   60
For he is nothing but a mighty lord.
This do, and do it kindly, gentle sirs.
It will be pastime passing excellent,
If it be husbanded with modesty.

1 HUNTSMAN My lord, I warrant you we will play our part   65
As he shall think by our true diligence
He is no less than what we say he is.

LORD Take him up gently and to bed with him,
And each one to his office when he wakes.

[Sly is carried off]

Sound trumpets.

Sirrah, go see what trumpet 'tis that sounds.   70

[Exit Servingman]

Belike some noble gentleman that means,
Travelling some journey, to repose him here.

Enter Servingman.

How now? Who is it?

SERVINGMAN   An't please your honour, players
That offer service to your lordship.

LORD Bid them come near.

7

The Lord welcomes the players and willingly agrees that they should stay at his house. He asks them to perform before a 'lord' (Sly), but warns them that the 'Lord' is given to strange behaviour.

1 The players' entry (in large groups)

Act out the arrival of the actors in all their glory. Use the illustration of a typical band of strolling players for inspiration. Think about the effect the arrival might have on the audience. If you have time, find a copy of *Hamlet* and compare how Hamlet welcomes another troupe of travelling players (Act 2, Scene 2).

2 What does Christopher Sly like? (in groups of five)

One person takes on the role of Sly, the rest of the group question him about his favourite pastimes and forms of entertainment.

---

in happy time just at the right time
The rather for more especially because
doubtful . . . modesties uncertain whether you can control yourselves

over-eyeing observing
merry passion fit of merriment
veriest antic oddest of people
buttery pantry/kitchen
want lack

Enter PLAYERS.

                Now, fellows, you are welcome.   75

PLAYERS We thank your honour.

LORD Do you intend to stay with me tonight?

1 PLAYER So please your lordship to accept our duty.

LORD With all my heart. This fellow I remember
      Since once he played a farmer's eldest son –   80
      'Twas where you wooed the gentlewoman so well –
      I have forgot your name, but sure that part
      Was aptly fitted and naturally performed.

2 PLAYER I think 'twas Soto that your honour means.

LORD 'Tis very true; thou didst it excellent.   85
      Well, you are come to me in happy time,
      The rather for I have some sport in hand
      Wherein your cunning can assist me much.
      There is a lord will hear you play tonight –
      But I am doubtful of your modesties,   90
      Lest over-eyeing of his odd behaviour
      (For yet his honour never heard a play)
      You break into some merry passion
      And so offend him; for I tell you, sirs,
      If you should smile, he grows impatient.   95

1 PLAYER Fear not, my lord, we can contain ourselves
      Were he the veriest antic in the world.

LORD Go, sirrah, take them to the buttery
      And give them friendly welcome every one.
      Let them want nothing that my house affords.   100
                  Exit one with the Players

*The Lord has a new idea. He will provide Sly with a 'wife' in the shape of a
young page dressed as a woman. The Lord himself will act as the
calming influence to dampen excessive hilarity.*

1 One view of women (in groups of three)

The Lord gives elaborate instructions for his page to follow when
dressed up as Sly's 'wife'.

- One person reads through lines 101–24. The others note down the
  key words which suggest how the Lord sees women. Talk about
  what you discover.
- Work together to present a tableau ('frozen moment') which
  reflects this view of women.
- One person reads lines 114–24 aloud while the others mime
  appropriate actions for Sly and his 'wife'. Remember, the audience
  knows they are both male, Sly does not.

2 Laughing with the Lord (in small groups)

A volunteer slowly reads lines 127–34 as the Lord. The rest of the
group become his servants, who are keen to win his favour. Whenever
you have the chance, laugh at the idea of Sly and his 'wife' to show
your approval of the Lord's wit.

At the end, the Lord and two of the servants are cross-questioned
by the others about how the exercise made them feel about master/
servant relationships.

---

esteemèd him thought himself
commanded forced
such a shift such a purpose
in despite against nature
usurp assume, feign

Haply perhaps
abate control
over-merry spleen excessive
  impulse to laughter (the spleen was
  thought to be the seat of the
  emotions)

Sirrah, go you to Barthol'mew my page
And see him dressed in all suits like a lady.
That done, conduct him to the drunkard's chamber,
And call him 'madam', do him obeisance.
Tell him from me – as he will win my love –   105
He bear himself with honourable action
Such as he hath observed in noble ladies
Unto their lords, by them accomplishèd.
Such duty to the drunkard let him do
With soft low tongue and lowly courtesy,   110
And say, 'What is't your honour will command
Wherein your lady and your humble wife
May show her duty and make known her love?'
And then with kind embracements, tempting kisses,
And with declining head into his bosom,   115
Bid him shed tears, as being overjoyed
To see her noble lord restored to health,
Who for this seven years hath esteemèd him
No better than a poor and loathsome beggar.
And if the boy have not a woman's gift   120
To rain a shower of commanded tears,
An onion will do well for such a shift,
Which in a napkin being close conveyed
Shall in despite enforce a watery eye.
See this dispatched with all the haste thou canst;   125
Anon I'll give thee more instructions.
                                    Exit a Servingman

I know the boy will well usurp the grace,
Voice, gait and action of a gentlewoman.
I long to hear him call the drunkard 'husband',
And how my men will stay themselves from laughter   130
When they do homage to this simple peasant.
I'll in to counsel them. Haply my presence
May well abate the over-merry spleen
Which otherwise would grow into extremes.
                                    [*Exeunt*]

Sly wakes up and the Lord's servants carry out their master's instructions. Sly is scornful, but they attempt to persuade the tinker that he is indeed a nobleman who is suffering from a delusion.

1 Change the scene (in pairs)

The previous scene ended with the Lord's soliloquy. This scene returns us to Sly and the start of the Lord's plan, which needs servants and lots of stage properties ('props') to convince Sly that he really is the noble owner of a great house. Work as props assistants on a production and make a list of all the things that might be useful to create the right illusion. They can be props for the actors to use, or larger items with which to dress the set.

2 Who am I? (in small groups)

Because everyone treats him as a nobleman, poor Sly becomes terribly confused in this scene. Read the question Sly asks in lines 15–18, and then think up others he might ask as he desperately tries to hang on to his identity. Use your imagination, but also draw on any material you have come across so far in the play.

When you have a list, one of the group reads out the questions, while the others reply with line 22 or line 23, or with 'All that's a dream, you're really a fine lord!'.

3 Private thoughts (in groups of five)

Read through lines 1–30, each person taking a part as the Lord, Sly and the servingmen. Next, each confesses their private thoughts concerning what is taking place. In particular, what do the servingmen think about what is going on?

---

small ale weakest and cheapest ale/beer
sack sherry or dry white wine (a more refined drink)
conserves candied fruits
overleather leather uppers

cardmaker worker in the wool trade
bear-herd keeper of a performing bear
on the score in debt
bestraught distracted, mad
ancient former
beck summons, nod

INDUCTION 2
The Lord's country house

Enter aloft SLY *with* ATTENDANTS – *some with apparel, basin and*
ewer, and other appurtenances – *and* LORD

SLY For God's sake, a pot of small ale!

1 SERVINGMAN Will't please your lordship drink a cup of sack?

2 SERVINGMAN Will't please your honour taste of these conserves?

3 SERVINGMAN What raiment will your honour wear today?

SLY I am Christophero Sly – call not me 'honour' nor 'lordship'. I ne'er 5
    drank sack in my life, and if you give me any conserves, give me
    conserves of beef. Ne'er ask me what raiment I'll wear, for I have
    no more doublets than backs, no more stockings than legs, nor no
    more shoes than feet – nay, sometime more feet than shoes, or such
    shoes as my toes look through the overleather. 10

LORD Heaven cease this idle humour in your honour!
    O that a mighty man of such descent,
    Of such possessions and so high esteem,
    Should be infusèd with so foul a spirit!

SLY What, would you make me mad? Am not I Christopher Sly, old 15
    Sly's son of Burton-heath, by birth a pedlar, by education a
    cardmaker, by transmutation a bear-herd, and now by present
    profession a tinker? Ask Marian Hacket, the fat ale-wife of Wincot,
    if she know me not. If she say I am not fourteen pence on the score
    for sheer ale, score me up for the lying'st knave in Christendom. 20
    What, I am not bestraught! Here's –

3 SERVINGMAN O, this it is that makes your lady mourn.

2 SERVINGMAN O, this is it that makes your servants droop.

LORD Hence comes it that your kindred shuns your house
    As beaten hence by your strange lunacy. 25
    O noble lord, bethink thee of thy birth.
    Call home thy ancient thoughts from banishment,
    And banish hence these abject lowly dreams.
    Look how thy servants do attend on thee,
    Each in his office ready at thy beck. 30

Sly is offered delightful pastimes to choose from: music and relaxation;
walking and riding; hawking and hunting; viewing erotic paintings. As the
enticing pictures are described, the Lord cunningly introduces the topic of
Sly's beautiful 'wife'.

---

1 The range of pleasures (a whole class activity)

Two volunteers read aloud lines 31–42, one asking the questions, the
other reading the answers in as enticing a way as possible, really
laying out the goodies in front of Sly. To help tempt him even more,
the rest of the group acts out the forms of entertainment with equal
relish. The movements should be excessive, 'over-the-top' and fun!

2 Wanton pictures (in groups of three)

The Lord said he would seduce Sly with 'wanton pictures', and they
are described here in lines 45–56.

- One person reads the lines aloud with as much passion as possible.
  Whenever a word associated with sex is mentioned, another
  member of the group sighs. The third growls on every verb.
- Talk together about the lines, and especially how a feeling of
  sensuality or sexiness is created.
- How does Sly respond to all these classical references?

3 Use the library

Choose one picture from the Lord's collection, and research the
characters in more detail. Find out if any such picture actually exists.
Sketch the picture (whether it exists or not), or work with others to
create a tableau.

Apollo Greek god of music
Semiramis queen famous for her
  voluptuousness
bestrow scatter (with rushes or
  flowers)
trapped decorated

welkin sky
course hunt the hare
breathèd healthy
Adonis, Cytherea, Io,
  Daphne mythical figures of love

Wilt thou have music? Hark, Apollo plays,   *Music*
And twenty cagèd nightingales do sing.
Or wilt thou sleep? We'll have thee to a couch
Softer and sweeter than the lustful bed
On purpose trimmed up for Semiramis.   35
Say thou wilt walk, we will bestrow the ground.
Or wilt thou ride? Thy horses shall be trapped,
Their harness studded all with gold and pearl.
Dost thou love hawking? Thou hast hawks will soar
Above the morning lark. Or wilt thou hunt?   40
Thy hounds shall make the welkin answer them
And fetch shrill echoes from the hollow earth.

1 SERVINGMAN Say thou wilt course, thy greyhounds are as swift
As breathèd stags, ay, fleeter than the roe.

2 SERVINGMAN Dost thou love pictures? We will fetch thee straight   45
Adonis painted by a running brook,
And Cytherea all in sedges hid,
Which seem to move and wanton with her breath
Even as the waving sedges play wi'th'wind.

LORD We'll show thee Io as she was a maid,   50
And how she was beguilèd and surprised,
As lively painted as the deed was done.

3 SERVINGMAN Or Daphne roaming through a thorny wood,
Scratching her legs that one shall swear she bleeds,
And at that sight shall sad Apollo weep,   55
So workmanly the blood and tears are drawn.

LORD Thou art a lord, and nothing but a lord.
Thou hast a lady far more beautiful
Than any woman in this waning age.

1 SERVINGMAN And till the tears that she hath shed for thee   60
Like envious floods o'er-run her lovely face,
She was the fairest creature in the world –
And yet she is inferior to none.

Wondering whether it is all a dream, Sly quickly decides that he is a lord after all. The servants tell him he has slept for fifteen years, saying strange things in his sleep.

1 Sly: better and verse (in groups of eight to ten)

Christopher Sly begins to speak in verse. Try this sequence of activities to explore what is happening in lines 64–71.

First: Read the lines aloud in unison. Think about why Sly is speaking in verse for the first time. Each member of the group chooses a different phrase from the speech and repeats it over and over until it is memorised. What tone of voice suits your line best? Does Sly try to speak like a lord at any point?

Second: Speak the phrases aloud, one at a time, in a random order. Try not to speak over another person's words. Talk together about whether the sense of what he's saying comes through just as well in this random order.

Third: Collect groups of similar kinds of phrases (questions, statements, words to do with the senses, and so on). Talk together about the groups, the selections, any patterns, and which phrases (if any) were missed out altogether.

Fourth: Identify the stages Sly goes through as he becomes convinced he is a lord. Discuss what you think caused Sly to come to his decision.

Finally: What is the effect of Sly's line 'And once again a pot o'th'smallest ale' (line 71)?

2 Sly's dream

Write a dream story involving all the people named in lines 85–90.

---

wit sanity
fay faith
idle meaningless, mad

present her at the leet bring her to trial
sealed quarts official measures of drink
amends recovery

SLY Am I a lord, and have I such a lady?
　　　　Or do I dream? Or have I dreamed till now? 65
　　　　I do not sleep: I see, I hear, I speak,
　　　　I smell sweet savours and I feel soft things.
　　　　Upon my life, I am a lord indeed,
　　　　And not a tinker, nor Christopher Sly.
　　　　Well, bring our lady hither to our sight, 70
　　　　And once again a pot o'th'smallest ale.

[Exit a Servingman]

2 SERVINGMAN Will't please your mightiness to wash your hands?
　　　　O, how we joy to see your wit restored!
　　　　O, that once more you knew but what you are!
　　　　These fifteen years you have been in a dream, 75
　　　　Or when you waked, so waked as if you slept.
SLY These fifteen years! By my fay, a goodly nap.
　　　　But did I never speak of all that time?
1 SERVINGMAN O yes, my lord, but very idle words,
　　　　For though you lay here in this goodly chamber, 80
　　　　Yet would you say ye were beaten out of door,
　　　　And rail upon the hostess of the house,
　　　　And say you would present her at the leet
　　　　Because she brought stone jugs and no sealed quarts.
　　　　Sometimes you would call out for Cicely Hacket. 85
SLY Ay, the woman's maid of the house.
3 SERVINGMAN Why, sir, you know no house, nor no such maid,
　　　　Nor no such men as you have reckoned up,
　　　　As Stephen Sly and old John Naps of Greece,
　　　　And Peter Turph and Henry Pimpernell, 90
　　　　And twenty more such names and men as these,
　　　　Which never were, nor no man ever saw.
SLY Now Lord be thankèd for my good amends!
ALL Amen.

Sly is introduced to his 'wife' (Bartholomew). After some confusion over what to call 'her', he attempts to take 'her' to bed. Bartholomew's quick-thinking saves both his honour and the whole charade.

1 Bartholomew the 'wife' (in groups of three)

Design the costume and make-up necessary for Bartholomew, the page, in this scene. On the Elizabethan stage, female roles were taken by young boys. As you work, talk together about:

a whether Bartholomew's 'female' appearance should be as convincing as that of the Hostess in Induction 1.

b the effect you wish the costume to have on Sly and the audience.

2 Madam's point of view

As Sly gets carried away with the idea of a 'wife' he didn't know he had, 'she' has to think quickly in order to avoid discovery. Look carefully at lines 114–20 and write down what is *really* going on in Bartholomew's mind as he says each line.

3 Stand or fall? (in pairs)

In lines 121–3, Sly makes a sexual joke which turns on the double meaning of the words 'stand' and 'fall'. Work out the double meaning, and suggest stage business with which the actor could accompany the lines.

---

goodman husband
abandoned banished

In peril at the risk of
tarry wait

Enter BARTHOLOMEW, *a page, dressed as a lady, with*
ATTENDANTS, *one of whom gives Sly a pot of ale.*

SLY I thank thee, thou shalt not lose by it.   95
BARTHOLOMEW How fares my noble lord?
SLY Marry, I fare well, for here is cheer enough. [*He drinks.*] Where
    is my wife?
BARTHOLOMEW Here, noble lord, what is thy will with her?
SLY Are you my wife, and will not call me 'husband'?   100
    My men should call me 'lord'; I am your goodman.
BARTHOLOMEW My husband and my lord, my lord and husband,
    I am your wife in all obedience.
SLY I know it well – What must I call her?
LORD 'Madam.'   105
SLY 'Al'ce madam' or 'Joan madam'?
LORD 'Madam' and nothing else. So lords call ladies.
SLY Madam wife, they say that I have dreamed
    And slept above some fifteen year or more.
BARTHOLOMEW Ay, and the time seems thirty unto me,   110
    Being all this time abandoned from your bed.
SLY 'Tis much. Servants, leave me and her alone.
                          [*Exeunt Servingmen*]
    Madam, undress you and come now to bed.
BARTHOLOMEW Thrice noble lord, let me entreat of you
    To pardon me yet for a night or two,   115
    Or, if not so, until the sun be set.
    For your physicians have expressly charged,
    In peril to incur your former malady,
    That I should yet absent me from your bed.
    I hope this reason stands for my excuse.   120
SLY Ay, it stands so that I may hardly tarry so long, but I would be
    loath to fall into my dreams again. I will therefore tarry in despite
    of the flesh and the blood.

Sly and his 'wife' settle to watch the play. Lucentio introduces himself as a well-born young man who has come to Padua with his servant to continue his education.

1 Popular entertainments (in groups of three)

Sly's 'comonty' is his error for the word 'comedy', but a 'gambold' was a frolic and a 'tumbling trick' a performance of acrobatics. Suggest contemporary equivalents for such entertainments, and compare your ideas with other groups. (See pages 54 and 186–7 for more activities on the Induction.)

2 What kind of place is Padua? (in pairs)

What image do you form of 'fair Padua' from the opening lines?

What impression of Padua do you think the designer of this production wished to create? (Royal Shakespeare Company, 1987.)

meet appropriate	**well approved in all** proved by
nurse nourisher	experience to be good in every way
bars prevents, wards off	**breathe** pause
history story, narrative	**haply** perhaps
nursery of arts home of culture	**ingenuous** appropriate to a
and learning	gentleman

Enter a MESSENGER.

MESSENGER Your honour's players, hearing your amendment,
   Are come to play a pleasant comedy;   125
   For so your doctors hold it very meet,
   Seeing too much sadness hath congealed your blood
   And melancholy is the nurse of frenzy –
   Therefore they thought it good you hear a play
   And frame your mind to mirth and merriment,   130
   Which bars a thousand harms and lengthens life.
SLY Marry, I will. Let them play it. Is not a comonty a Christmas
  gambold or a tumbling trick?
BARTHOLOMEW No, my good lord, it is more pleasing stuff.
SLY What, household stuff?   135
BARTHOLOMEW It is a kind of history.
SLY Well, we'll see't.

             [*Exit Messenger*]

   Come, madam wife, sit by my side,
   And let the world slip. We shall ne'er be younger.
       [*They sit down.*]
   [*A flourish of trumpets to announce the play.*]

ACT I   SCENE I
A street in Padua

Enter LUCENTIO and his man TRANIO

LUCENTIO Tranio, since for the great desire I had
   To see fair Padua, nursery of arts,
   I am arrived for fruitful Lombardy,
   The pleasant garden of great Italy,
   And by my father's love and leave am armed   5
   With his good will and thy good company –
   My trusty servant well approved in all –
   Here let us breathe and haply institute
   A course of learning and ingenuous studies.

Lucentio talks about his father and about his desire to study hard. Tranio suggests that they should not be over-serious, or forget that they should also enjoy themselves.

1 What's on Lucentio's mind? (in pairs)

Lucentio packs a great deal into his first speech (lines 1–24). Read the lines through alternately, and then select a key word from each line. Discuss what this list suggests about Lucentio's interests, attitudes and state of mind.

2 Start the play (in groups of three or four)

Imagine you are directing this opening scene. You need to focus the audience's interest on the new story after the highly theatrical Induction. Talk together about how you might do this. Some directors make lines 1–45 funny. Find at least three points where you would attempt to make the audience laugh aloud.

3 Aristotle *v.* Ovid (in pairs)

In lines 25–40, Tranio brings in classical authors to convince Lucentio of the validity of his argument that serious study should be balanced with fun and entertainment. Aristotle was a Greek philosopher, who emphasised in his *Ethics* the idea that happiness can only be achieved through virtuous living. For Tranio, Aristotle represents academic discipline and logic. Ovid, a Roman poet, popular among the Elizabethans for his love poetry, stands for imagination, storytelling, fun.

Suggest similar pairs of 'opposite' people today. Improvise an argument (perhaps between a teenager and a parent) on 'scholarship' versus 'imagination'.

---

deck embellish
plash puddle
Mi perdonato pardon me (Italian)
affected inclined
stoics, stocks people who don't
  care about pleasure

Balk logic bandy words
metaphysics philosophy
stomach appetite
tane taken
affect like
Gramercies many thanks

Pisa renownèd for grave citizens   10
Gave me my being and my father first,
A merchant of great traffic through the world,
Vincentio, come of the Bentivolii.
Vincentio's son, brought up in Florence,
It shall become to serve all hopes conceived   15
To deck his fortune with his virtuous deeds.
And therefore, Tranio, for the time I study,
Virtue and that part of philosophy
Will I apply that treats of happiness
By virtue specially to be achieved.   20
Tell me thy mind, for I have Pisa left
And am to Padua come as he that leaves
A shallow plash to plunge him in the deep
And with satiety seeks to quench his thirst.

TRANIO *Mi perdonato*, gentle master mine,   25
I am in all affected as yourself,
Glad that you thus continue your resolve
To suck the sweets of sweet philosophy.
Only, good master, while we do admire
This virtue and this moral discipline,   30
Let's be no stoics nor no stocks, I pray,
Or so devote to Aristotle's checks
As Ovid be an outcast quite abjured.
Balk logic with acquaintance that you have
And practise rhetoric in your common talk;   35
Music and poesy use to quicken you;
The mathematics and the metaphysics –
Fall to them as you find your stomach serves you.
No profit grows where is no pleasure tane:
In brief, sir, study what you most affect.   40

LUCENTIO Gramercies, Tranio, well dost thou advise.
If, Biondello, thou wert come ashore,
We could at once put us in readiness
And take a lodging fit to entertain
Such friends as time in Padua shall beget.   45

The Taming of the Shrew

Lucentio and Tranio listen as Baptista declares he will not allow his daughter Bianca to marry before Katherina, her elder sister. Katherina quarrels with Hortensio, one of Bianca's suitors. Lucentio appears to be very attracted to Bianca.

1 What were they talking about? (in groups of five)

When Baptista and the others enter, they are obviously in the middle of a conversation. Improvise their dialogue to cover the few moments before they enter. Think especially about what Hortensio and Gremio might have said that led Baptista to protest: 'importune me no farther'.

2 First impressions (in pairs)

Katherina certainly makes her presence felt immediately in this scene. One partner reads aloud Katherina's lines, whilst the other makes moves and gestures which best convey her powerful personality. Then swap roles and repeat. Any differences?

3 'A penny for your thoughts'

Bianca says nothing on the opposite page, and yet she is very important, especially as far as Lucentio is concerned. What's she thinking about and doing whilst the others are talking?

4 Gremio – a pantaloon

A pantaloon was a conventional figure in Italian comedies. He was usually a ridiculous old man whose role was to be an obstacle to young lovers marrying.

---

importune try to persuade
cart her treat her like a convicted prostitute, by taking her in a cart to prison
stale prostitute

mates fellows
Iwis certainly
froward wilful, headstrong, disobedient
Mum! Hush!

Enter BAPTISTA *with his two daughters* KATHERINA *and* BIANCA;
GREMIO, *a pantaloon, and* HORTENSIO, *suitor to Bianca.*

But stay awhile, what company is this?
TRANIO Master, some show to welcome us to town.
Lucentio and Tranio stand by.
BAPTISTA Gentlemen, importune me no farther
 For how I firmly am resolved you know –
 That is, not to bestow my youngest daughter   50
 Before I have a husband for the elder.
 If either of you both love Katherina,
 Because I know you well and love you well,
 Leave shall you have to court her at your pleasure.
GREMIO To cart her rather! She's too rough for me.   55
 There, there, Hortensio, will you any wife?
KATHERINA [*To Baptista*] I pray you, sir, is it your will
 To make a stale of me amongst these mates?
HORTENSIO 'Mates', maid? How mean you that? No mates for you
 Unless you were of gentler, milder mould.   60
KATHERINA I'faith, sir, you shall never need to fear.
 Iwis it is not halfway to her heart –
 But if it were, doubt not her care should be
 To comb your noddle with a three-legged stool
 And paint your face and use you like a fool.   65
HORTENSIO From all such devils, good Lord deliver us!
GREMIO And me too, good Lord!
TRANIO [*Aside to Lucentio*]
 Husht, master, here's some good pastime toward;
 That wench is stark mad, or wonderful froward.
LUCENTIO [*Aside to Tranio*] But in the other's silence do I see   70
 Maid's mild behaviour and sobriety.
 Peace, Tranio.
TRANIO [*Aside to Lucentio*]
 Well said, master. Mum! And gaze your fill.

The two sisters quarrel briefly. Baptista sends Bianca into the house and then suggests that the two suitors find teachers for her. Katherina leaves, asserting her freedom to go whenever she wishes.

1 Eavesdropping (in groups of seven)

Lucentio and Tranio are watching what is going on. Read through lines 74–91, take roles, and work out where to position everyone.

2 The good father (in pairs)

Baptista says he will be 'liberal/To mine own children in good bringing up'. What impressions have you formed so far of Baptista as a father? Try to find two things in the script opposite which support Baptista's remark, and two which contradict it.

3 Two sisters (in pairs)

In lines 78–83, Katherina and Bianca have what seems to be a rather bad-tempered exchange. Read the lines to each other several times, thinking carefully about the different ways in which you can say them. Swap roles.

Next try Katherina's exit lines (lines 102–4). Take it in turns to say these lines and leave, concentrating on creating a different impression with the audience each time. You can have particular fun with Katherina's 'Ha!' just before she departs. Afterwards, talk together about the two sisters – what they are like, and their attitudes towards each other.

---

peat spoilt child
put finger in the eye cry
Minerva goddess of wisdom
strange unkind
mew her up lock her up

prefer recommend
cunning clever
commune discuss
appointed hours told when to stay or go

BAPTISTA Gentlemen, that I may soon make good
　　　　　What I have said – Bianca, get you in.　　　　　　75
　　　　　And let it not displease thee, good Bianca,
　　　　　For I will love thee ne'er the less, my girl.
KATHERINA A pretty peat! It is best put finger in the eye, and she knew
　　why.
BIANCA Sister, content you in my discontent.　　　　　　80
　　　　　Sir, to your pleasure humbly I subscribe.
　　　　　My books and instruments shall be my company,
　　　　　On them to look and practise by myself.
LUCENTIO [*Aside*] Hark, Tranio, thou mayst hear Minerva speak!
HORTENSIO Signor Baptista, will you be so strange?　　　　85
　　　　　Sorry am I that our good will effects
　　　　　Bianca's grief.
GREMIO　　　　　　　　Why will you mew her up,
　　　　　Signor Baptista, for this fiend of hell,
　　　　　And make her bear the penance of her tongue?
BAPTISTA Gentlemen, content ye. I am resolved.　　　　　90
　　　　　Go in, Bianca.
　　　　　　　　　　　　　　　　　　[*Exit Bianca*]

　　　　　And, for I know she taketh most delight
　　　　　In music, instruments and poetry,
　　　　　Schoolmasters will I keep within my house
　　　　　Fit to instruct her youth. If you, Hortensio,　　　95
　　　　　Or Signor Gremio you, know any such,
　　　　　Prefer them hither; for to cunning men
　　　　　I will be very kind, and liberal
　　　　　To mine own children in good bringing up.
　　　　　And so farewell. Katherina, you may stay,　　　100
　　　　　For I have more to commune with Bianca.　　　*Exit*
KATHERINA Why, and I trust I may go too, may I not?
　　　　　What, shall I be appointed hours as though, belike,
　　　　　I knew not what to take and what to leave? Ha!　　*Exit*

Gremio and Hortensio discuss their common problem: they have no chance of marrying Bianca until Katherina is married. They agree to work together to find a husband for her.

1 Proverbs (in pairs)

Gremio and Hortensio use many proverbs, such as 'our cake's dough on both sides', meaning that they have both failed. Collect as many proverbs as you can find in lines 105–36. Think of a modern equivalent for each.

2 Gremio and Hortensio (in groups of three)

Each person lists their impressions of the two suitors – age, looks, ways of speaking, wealth, dress, opinions and attitudes, and so on. Flick back through this scene to gather your information. Pool your ideas and see how similar your interpretations are.

3 Inner voices (in groups of four)

The competing suitors have joined forces, but what are they really thinking to themselves? Two of you read lines 111–27, a sentence at a time. The other pair 'shadow' them by immediately suggesting at the end of each sentence what Gremio and Hortensio are each secretly thinking.

---

the devil's dam the devil's mother, a shrew
blow our nails wait patiently
fast it fairly out survive
wish recommend
brooked parle allowed us to negotiate

as lief as willingly
bar in law legal hindrance (meaning Baptista's decision about Katherina's marriage)
dole destiny

GREMIO You may go to the devil's dam! Your gifts are so good here's 105
none will hold you. There! Love is not so great, Hortensio, but we
may blow our nails together and fast it fairly out. Our cake's dough
on both sides. Farewell. Yet, for the love I bear my sweet Bianca,
if I can by any means light on a fit man to teach her that wherein
she delights, I will wish him to her father. 110
HORTENSIO So will I, Signor Gremio. But a word, I pray. Though the
nature of our quarrel yet never brooked parle, know now, upon
advice, it toucheth us both – that we may yet again have access to
our fair mistress and be happy rivals in Bianca's love – to labour
and effect one thing specially. 115
GREMIO What's that, I pray?
HORTENSIO Marry, sir, to get a husband for her sister.
GREMIO A husband? A devil!
HORTENSIO I say a husband.
GREMIO I say a devil. Think'st thou, Hortensio, though her father be 120
very rich, any man is so very a fool to be married to hell?
HORTENSIO Tush, Gremio. Though it pass your patience and mine to
endure her loud alarums – why, man, there be good fellows in the
world, and a man could light on them, would take her with all faults,
and money enough. 125
GREMIO I cannot tell. But I had as lief take her dowry with this
condition: to be whipped at the high cross every morning.
HORTENSIO Faith, as you say, there's small choice in rotten apples. But
come, since this bar in law makes us friends, it shall be so far forth
friendly maintained till by helping Baptista's eldest daughter to a 130
husband we set his youngest free for a husband – and then have
to't afresh. Sweet Bianca! Happy man be his dole! He that runs
fastest gets the ring. How say you, Signor Gremio?
GREMIO I am agreed, and would I had given him the best horse in Padua
to begin his wooing that would thoroughly woo her, wed her, and 135
bed her, and rid the house of her. Come on.
Exeunt Gremio and Hortensio

*Lucentio tells of his great love for Bianca and asks Tranio to help him.
Tranio tries to bring his master down to earth, reminding him of
the problem of Katherina.*

1 Love at first sight (in small groups)

What has Lucentio been doing to prompt lines 137–8? His sudden
love for Bianca is expressed in a way which you might find rather
extreme. One of the group reads lines 139–49, emphasising the
words and phrases which seem important. The others perform brief
mimes to illustrate what he's saying.

2 'Great Jove' (in pairs)

Lucentio likes displaying his knowledge of the Classics. In lines
159–61 he uses a classical reference to describe Bianca's 'sweet
beauty'. He likens her to Agenor's daughter, Europa, who was famed
for her looks. Jove (the supreme Roman god) fell in love with her. He
disguised himself as a bull and carried her away to Crete. Earlier, in
line 145, Lucentio compared Tranio to Anna, sister and adviser to
Dido, Queen of Carthage.

Replace Lucentio's classical references with appropriate pairs of
twentieth-century 'heroes/heroines'.

3 Master and servant (in pairs)

Tranio is Lucentio's servant yet seems to enjoy a relaxed relationship
with him. Lucentio asks him for 'counsel' or advice. Talk about how
they get on together, and how Tranio responds to Lucentio's request
for advice. (An interesting question to consider is their relative ages.)

---

love-in-idleness the pansy, a
 supposed aphrodisiac
rated driven away by scolding
*Redime te captum quam queas
 minimo* ransom yourself, now you
 have been captured, for as low a
 price as you can

Gramercies thanks
longly for a long time
pith main part
strand shore
curst and shrewd bad-tempered
 and perverse

TRANIO I pray sir, tell me, is it possible
    That love should of a sudden take such hold?
LUCENTIO O Tranio, till I found it to be true
    I never thought it possible or likely.   140
    But see! while idly I stood looking on,
    I found the effect of love-in-idleness,
    And now in plainness do confess to thee
    That art to me as secret and as dear
    As Anna to the Queen of Carthage was –   145
    Tranio, I burn! I pine, I perish, Tranio,
    If I achieve not this young modest girl.
    Counsel me, Tranio, for I know thou canst;
    Assist me, Tranio, for I know thou wilt.
TRANIO Master, it is no time to chide you now;   150
    Affection is not rated from the heart.
    If love have touched you, naught remains but so:
    Redime te captum quam queas minimo.
LUCENTIO Gramercies, lad. Go forward. This contents;
    The rest will comfort, for thy counsel's sound.   155
TRANIO Master, you looked so longly on the maid,
    Perhaps you marked not what's the pith of all.
LUCENTIO O yes, I saw sweet beauty in her face,
    Such as the daughter of Agenor had,
    That made great Jove to humble him to her hand   160
    When with his knees he kissed the Cretan strand.
TRANIO Saw you no more? Marked you not how her sister
    Began to scold and raise up such a storm
    That mortal ears might hardly endure the din?
LUCENTIO Tranio, I saw her coral lips to move,   165
    And with her breath she did perfume the air.
    Sacred and sweet was all I saw in her.
TRANIO Nay, then, 'tis time to stir him from his trance.
    I pray, awake, sir. If you love the maid
    Bend thoughts and wits to achieve her. Thus it stands: 170
    Her elder sister is so curst and shrewd
    That, till the father rid his hands of her,
    Master, your love must live a maid at home,
    And therefore has he closely mewed her up,
    Because she will not be annoyed with suitors.   175

*Lucentio and Tranio arrive at the same solution to enable Lucentio to win
Bianca: Lucentio will become Bianca's schoolteacher! They exchange
clothes, and Tranio adopts Lucentio's identity.*

1 Changing clothes (in groups of four)

As they swap clothes on stage,
there is great opportunity for
farcical stage business. How
much of their clothing do they
take off? Work out how full the
exchange should be. Two of the
group read lines 193–208 whilst
the others exchange clothes,
making it as funny as they can.
Can you fit the lines to
undressing and dressing? (Take
care!)

Who's who? (Royal Shakespeare
Company, 1982.)

2 Swapping roles (in pairs)

'I am content to be Lucentio', says Tranio – as well he might. The
servant is now the master! Talk together about what would be the first
three things you would do if you were made Head or Principal of your
school or college for a week.

hand part
inventions ideas
jump agree
Keep house entertain
ply his book carry on with his
  studies
Basta! Enough!

I have it full I've got it all worked
  out
port lifestyle
Uncase undress
sith since
serviceable eager to serve

LUCENTIO Ah, Tranio, what a cruel father's he!
　　　　　But art thou not advised he took some care
　　　　　To get her cunning schoolmasters to instruct her?
TRANIO Ay, marry, am I, sir – and now 'tis plotted!
LUCENTIO I have it, Tranio!
TRANIO 　　　　　　　　　Master, for my hand, 　　　　　　180
　　　　　Both our inventions meet and jump in one.
LUCENTIO Tell me thine first.
TRANIO 　　　　　　　　You will be schoolmaster
　　　　　And undertake the teaching of the maid –
　　　　　That's your device.
LUCENTIO 　　　　　　　　It is. May it be done?
TRANIO Not possible. For who shall bear your part 　　　　185
　　　　　And be in Padua here Vincentio's son,
　　　　　Keep house, and ply his book, welcome his friends,
　　　　　Visit his countrymen and banquet them?
LUCENTIO *Basta!* Content thee, for I have it full.
　　　　　We have not yet been seen in any house, 　　　　190
　　　　　Nor can we be distinguished by our faces
　　　　　For man or master. Then it follows thus:
　　　　　Thou shalt be master, Tranio, in my stead;
　　　　　Keep house and port and servants as I should.
　　　　　I will some other be – some Florentine, 　　　　195
　　　　　Some Neapolitan or meaner man of Pisa.
　　　　　'Tis hatched and shall be so. Tranio, at once
　　　　　Uncase thee; take my coloured hat and cloak.
　　　　　　　　　　[*They exchange clothes.*]
　　　　　When Biondello comes, he waits on thee,
　　　　　But I will charm him first to keep his tongue. 　　200
TRANIO So had you need.
　　　　　In brief, sir, sith it your pleasure is,
　　　　　And I am tied to be obedient –
　　　　　For so your father charged me at our parting:
　　　　　'Be serviceable to my son', quoth he, 　　　　205
　　　　　Although I think 'twas in another sense –
　　　　　I am content to be Lucentio,
　　　　　Because so well I love Lucentio.

Biondello, another servant, is confused when he sees that his master and Tranio have exchanged clothes. Lucentio invents a story that it is a disguise to prevent his arrest for murder. Biondello is sworn to secrecy.

1 Another servant (in pairs)

Lucentio doesn't seem to trust Biondello as much as he trusts Tranio. Discuss what reasons he may have for not telling Biondello the truth. What clues can you find in the script opposite as to the relative status of the two servants?

2 Private or public? (in pairs)

Read aloud lines 216–28 together in three different ways:

a) in whispers, as if they conceal a vital secret
b) loudly, as if they are military orders
c) with humour, as if they are a practical joke.

Discuss the differences and decide which version works the best.

3 More pretending (in groups of four or five)

It is not clear why Lucentio invents such a dramatic story to explain why he is wearing Tranio's clothes, but he doesn't seem to have any trouble thinking of one. In three tableaux ('frozen moments') bring Lucentio's story to life (lines 218–22).

---

thralled enslaved
frame your manners alter your behaviour
count'nance manner
descried observed

as becomes appropriately
Ne'er a whit not in the least
use your manners behave
execute carry out
make one become one

LUCENTIO Tranio, be so, because Lucentio loves,
And let me be a slave t'achieve that maid   210
Whose sudden sight hath thralled my wounded eye.

Enter BIONDELLO.

Here comes the rogue. Sirrah, where have you been?
BIONDELLO Where have I been? Nay, how now, where are you?
Master, has my fellow Tranio stolen your clothes or you stolen his,
or both? Pray, what's the news?   215
LUCENTIO Sirrah, come hither. 'Tis no time to jest,
And therefore frame your manners to the time.
Your fellow Tranio here, to save my life,
Puts my apparel and my count'nance on,
And I for my escape have put on his;   220
For in a quarrel since I came ashore
I killed a man, and fear I was descried.
Wait you on him, I charge you, as becomes,
While I make way from hence to save my life.
You understand me?
BIONDELLO   Ay, sir. Ne'er a whit.   225
LUCENTIO And not a jot of 'Tranio' in your mouth:
Tranio is changed into Lucentio.
BIONDELLO The better for him! Would I were so too.
TRANIO So could I, faith, boy, to have the next wish after –
That Lucentio indeed had Baptista's youngest daughter.   230
But, sirrah, not for my sake but your master's, I advise
You use your manners discreetly in all kind of companies.
When I am alone, why then I am Tranio,
But in all places else your master Lucentio.
LUCENTIO Tranio, let's go.   235
One thing more rests that thyself execute:
To make one among these wooers. If thou ask me why,
Sufficeth my reasons are both good and weighty.
                                                          Exeunt

Christopher Sly comments ambiguously on the play. In Scene 2, Petruchio, newly arrived from Verona, quarrels with his servant Grumio outside Hortensio's door. He strikes Grumio.

1 Different masters and servants (in pairs)

Here's another master and servant. We've already met Lucentio and Tranio in Scene 1. How alike are the master/servant relationships?
Try this:

First read lines 1–19 from Scene 2.
Then read lines 1–45 from Scene 1.
Then read lines 1–19 from Scene 2 in the manner of the Lucentio/Tranio scene.

Talk together about the similarities and differences.

2 Knock, knock – a pun (in groups of four)

Elizabethans thoroughly enjoyed puns. Petruchio and Grumio play on different meanings of 'knock'. One pair reads lines 1–19 and lines 27–40. At each mention of 'knocking', one of the other two mimes what Petruchio means, and the other what Grumio means.

---

nod sleep
mind watch
trow believe, reckon

rebused Grumio's mistake; he
means abused
pate head
sol-fa sing a scale

The Presenters above speaks.

LORD My lord, you nod; you do not mind the play.

SLY Yes, by Saint Anne, do I. A good matter surely. Comes there any   240
more of it?

BARTHOLOMEW My lord, 'tis but begun.

SLY 'Tis a very excellent piece of work, madam lady. Would 'twere done!
They sit and mark.

ACT 1   SCENE 2
Outside Hortensio's house

Enter PETRUCHIO and his man GRUMIO

PETRUCHIO Verona, for a while I take my leave
To see my friends in Padua, but of all
My best belovèd and approvèd friend,
Hortensio: and I trow this is his house.
Here, sirrah Grumio, knock, I say.   5

GRUMIO Knock, sir? Whom should I knock? Is there any man has
rebused your worship?

PETRUCHIO Villain, I say, knock me here soundly.

GRUMIO Knock you here, sir? Why, sir, what am I, sir, that I should
knock you here, sir?   10

PETRUCHIO Villain, I say, knock me at this gate,
And rap me well, or I'll knock your knave's pate!

GRUMIO My master is grown quarrelsome. I should knock you first,
And then I know after who comes by the worst.

PETRUCHIO Will it not be?   15
Faith, sirrah, and you'll not knock, I'll ring it.
I'll try how you can *sol-fa*, and sing it.
He wrings him by the ears.

GRUMIO Help, mistress, help! My master is mad.

PETRUCHIO Now knock when I bid you, sirrah villain.

37

Hortensio welcomes Petruchio. Grumio continues to complain about Petruchio's 'knocking'. Hortensio urges peace between master and servant. Petruchio explains that his father is dead and that he is now broadening his mind with travel and looking for a wife.

1 When in Italy . . . (in pairs)

Petruchio and Hortensio greet each other in Italian (lines 23–5 mean 'With all my heart well met' and 'Welcome to our house, much honoured Signor Petruchio'). The meaning may be reasonably straightforward, but how would you advise actors to speak this Italian dialogue? Read the lines through twice, changing the style of delivery as much as possible. Try some appropriate gestures too. Afterwards, discuss why you think they use Italian here.

2 Peacemaking (in groups of three)

This is a two-minute activity. Notice how Hortensio tries to restore peace in line 44: 'Your ancient, trusty, pleasant servant Grumio'. Quickly flick through everything Petruchio has said about his servant from line 5. Say aloud in turn every term Petruchio uses to describe Grumio. What a difference from Hortensio's description!

3 Introductions (in pairs)

There are a number of occasions in the play when characters introduce themselves in the same way as in lines 47–55. One person reads the lines aloud, while the other mimes the ideas expressed. What image of himself is Petruchio presenting here?

---

compound settle
ledges alleges
two and thirty, a pip out a bit mad (the expression comes from a card game)

pledge surety: guarantee in a legal case
in a few briefly
maze uncertain action (or muddled world)

Enter HORTENSIO.

HORTENSIO How now, what's the matter? My old friend Grumio and   20
my good friend Petruchio! How do you all at Verona?

PETRUCHIO Signor Hortensio, come you to part the fray?
Con tutto il cuore ben trovato, may I say.

HORTENSIO *Alla nostra casa ben venuto*
Molto honorato signor mio Petruchio.   25
Rise, Grumio, rise. We will compound this quarrel.

GRUMIO Nay, 'tis no matter, sir, what he ledges in Latin. If this be not
a lawful cause for me to leave his service – look you, sir: he bid me
knock him and rap him soundly, sir. Well, was it fit for a servant
to use his master so, being perhaps, for aught I see, two and thirty,   30
a pip out?
Whom would to God I had well knocked at first,
Then had not Grumio come by the worst.

PETRUCHIO A senseless villain! Good Hortensio,
I bade the rascal knock upon your gate   35
And could not get him for my heart to do it.

GRUMIO Knock at the gate? O heavens! Spake you not these words
plain: 'Sirrah, knock me here, rap me here, knock me well, and
knock me soundly'? And come you now with 'knocking at the
gate'?   40

PETRUCHIO Sirrah, be gone, or talk not, I advise you.

HORTENSIO Petruchio, patience. I am Grumio's pledge.
Why this' a heavy chance 'twixt him and you –
Your ancient, trusty, pleasant servant Grumio.
And tell me now, sweet friend, what happy gale   45
Blows you to Padua here from old Verona?

PETRUCHIO Such wind as scatters young men through the world
To seek their fortunes farther than at home
Where small experience grows. But, in a few,
Signor Hortensio, thus it stands with me: 50
Antonio my father is deceased
And I have thrust myself into this maze,
Happily to wive and thrive as best I may.
Crowns in my purse I have, and goods at home,
And so am come abroad to see the world.   55

Hortensio promises Petruchio a rich wife, and Petruchio declares he will marry anyone who has money. Hortensio describes Katherina's good and bad points. Petruchio is eager to meet her at once.

---

1 Money or sex? (in groups of six)

Two volunteers read aloud, slowly, lines 45–73. Everyone else listens carefully. Whenever you hear a word connected with money, 'echo' it in a whisper. Repeat the activity with a different pair of readers, but this time echo every word connected with sex or love.

Afterwards, talk together about what the 'echoing' tells you about Petruchio.

2 Hortensio's motives (in groups of three)

What is Hortensio up to in lines 56–61? Find at least three different ways of speaking his lines, and compare your suggestions. Can you agree on the most effective way of saying them?

3 Petruchio's language (in pairs)

Talk together about the ways in which Petruchio's language changes as he speaks to Grumio or Hortensio. How do you account for the differences?

4 The audience's response (in pairs)

As a director, would you want to make the audience laugh at lines 74–88, even though they mock women? Try reading the passage aloud, but always substitute 'him' for 'her', 'he' for 'she', 'husband' for 'wife', and so on. Afterwards talk together about what differences emerged from changing the gender of the person mocked.

---

come roundly speak directly
Florentius a knight who married an ugly old woman to save his life
Sibyl aged prophetess in classical mythology

Xanthippe notoriously bad-tempered wife of the Greek philosopher
edge intensity
aglet-baby small carved figure
board her seduce her

HORTENSIO Petruchio, shall I then come roundly to thee
          And wish thee to a shrewd ill-favoured wife?
          Thou'dst thank me but a little for my counsel –
          And yet I'll promise thee she shall be rich,
          And very rich. But th'art too much my friend,   60
          And I'll not wish thee to her.
PETRUCHIO Signor Hortensio, 'twixt such friends as we
          Few words suffice, and therefore, if thou know
          One rich enough to be Petruchio's wife –
          As wealth is burden of my wooing dance –   65
          Be she as foul as was Florentius' love,
          As old as Sibyl, and as curst and shrewd
          As Socrates' Xanthippe or a worse,
          She moves me not, or not removes at least
          Affection's edge in me, were she as rough   70
          As are the swelling Adriatic seas.
          I come to wive it wealthily in Padua;
          If wealthily, then happily in Padua.
GRUMIO Nay, look you sir, he tells you flatly what his mind is. Why,
          give him gold enough and marry him to a puppet or an aglet-baby   75
          or an old trot with ne'er a tooth in her head, though she have as
          many diseases as two and fifty horses. Why, nothing comes amiss,
          so money comes withal.
HORTENSIO Petruchio, since we are stepped thus far in,
          I will continue that I broached in jest.   80
          I can, Petruchio, help thee to a wife
          With wealth enough, and young, and beauteous,
          Brought up as best becomes a gentlewoman.
          Her only fault – and that is faults enough –
          Is that she is intolerable curst,   85
          And shrewd and froward so beyond all measure
          That, were my state far worser than it is,
          I would not wed her for a mine of gold!
PETRUCHIO Hortensio, peace. Thou know'st not gold's effect.
          Tell me her father's name and 'tis enough,   90
          For I will board her though she chide as loud
          As thunder when the clouds in autumn crack.

Petruchio is instantly attracted by Hortensio's description of Katherina.
Hortensio admits his own interest in Bianca. He asks Petruchio to introduce
him to Baptista, disguised as a music teacher.

1 Who's who? (in groups of five)

Stand or sit in a circle. One person slowly reads Hortensio's lines
111–22. The others point to a particular person in the group every
time a certain character is referred to (by name, or as he, she, I, and
so on). It sounds complicated, but try it! You'll find it's easy to pick
up. Try the exercise again with a different reader. Afterwards, discuss
what this activity reveals about Hortensio and the plot at this point.

2 What's their view of love? (in pairs)

Hortensio appears to be quite candid with Petruchio about his love
for Bianca. Write a single sentence which sums up what Hortensio
thinks about love, and another for Petruchio.

3 Stereotyping (in groups of three)

'Katherine the curst' say Hortensio and Grumio; and so Katherina is
pigeon-holed by the men. Think up similar labels for other characters
we have met so far in the play:

Bianca the . . .
Petruchio the . . .
Baptista the . . .
Tranio the . . .
Sly the . . .

and so on.

---

give you over leave you
humour mood
rail in his rope-tricks scold in an
  outrageous way
stand challenge
throw a figure hurl words (a figure
  of speech)

disfigure . . . cat stun her into
  silence
other more other lovers
tane given
seen qualified
make love woo, speak about love

HORTENSIO Her father is Baptista Minola,
      An affable and courteous gentleman.
      Her name is Katherina Minola,   95
      Renowned in Padua for her scolding tongue.
PETRUCHIO I know her father, though I know not her,
      And he knew my deceasèd father well.
      I will not sleep, Hortensio, till I see her,
      And therefore let me be thus bold with you   100
      To give you over at this first encounter –
      Unless you will accompany me thither?
GRUMIO I pray you, sir, let him go while the humour lasts. A' my word,
      and she knew him as well as I do, she would think scolding would
      do little good upon him. She may perhaps call him half a score   105
      knaves or so – why, that's nothing. And he begin once, he'll rail
      in his rope-tricks. I'll tell you what, sir, and she stand him but a
      little, he will throw a figure in her face and so disfigure her with
      it that she shall have no more eyes to see withal than a cat. You
      know him not, sir.   110
HORTENSIO Tarry, Petruchio, I must go with thee,
      For in Baptista's keep my treasure is.
      He hath the jewel of my life in hold,
      His youngest daughter, beautiful Bianca,
      And her withholds from me and other more –   115
      Suitors to her and rivals in my love –
      Supposing it a thing impossible,
      For those defects I have before rehearsed,
      That ever Katherina will be wooed.
      Therefore this order hath Baptista tane,   120
      That none shall have access unto Bianca
      Till Katherine the curst have got a husband.
GRUMIO 'Katherine the curst'!
      A title for a maid of all titles the worst.
HORTENSIO Now shall my friend Petruchio do me grace   125
      And offer me disguised in sober robes
      To old Baptista as a schoolmaster
      Well seen in music, to instruct Bianca,
      That so I may by this device at least
      Have leave and leisure to make love to her   130
      And unsuspected court her by herself.

43

Petruchio, Hortensio and Grumio eavesdrop on Gremio. He is giving instructions to Lucentio disguised as Cambio, on how to behave when teaching Bianca.

1 'O this learning, what a thing it is!' (in pairs)

Gremio seems delighted to have found Cambio (Lucentio). We, of course, know that he is not a real schoolteacher, but Lucentio does not seem to have any problems pretending to be one so far. Improvise the conversation when Gremio interviewed him. Remember that Lucentio is very anxious to secure the job, and Gremio is equally keen to gain the services of someone who will please Baptista . . .

2 Lucentio's disguise

In some productions, the actor playing Lucentio is given very little in the way of disguise. Other productions make use of elaborate make-up and costume. Make a list of the things you would give the actor to alter his appearance. Sketch your view of Cambio the schoolteacher.

3 They stand aside (in groups of five)

For most of this scene, there are two groups on the stage:

Hortensio, Petruchio and Grumio
Lucentio and Gremio.

How would you stage this? Work out two tableaux (frozen pictures), one for each group of characters, which show something about the relationships between those in the group. Bear in mind that Grumio is a servant. Would his social status make a difference to his position in the group?

---

proper stripling handsome youth
note list of books
see that at any hand see to that in any case
largess extra sum

as yourself were still in place as if you were there yourself
woodcock idiot
Trow you do you know
fit for her turn just right for her

Enter GREMIO, *and* LUCENTIO *disguised* [*as Cambio, a schoolmaster*].

GRUMIO Here's no knavery! See, to beguile the old folks, how the young
    folks lay their heads together. Master, master, look about you! Who
    goes there, ha?

HORTENSIO Peace, Grumio. It is the rival of my love.   135
    Petruchio, stand by a while.

GRUMIO A proper stripling, and an amorous!

                          [*They stand aside.*]

GREMIO O, very well, I have perused the note.
    Hark you, sir, I'll have them very fairly bound –
    All books of love, see that at any hand –   140
    And see you read no other lectures to her:
    You understand me. Over and beside
    Signor Baptista's liberality
    I'll mend it with a largess. Take your paper too
    And let me have them very well perfumed,   145
    For she is sweeter than perfume itself
    To whom they go to. What will you read to her?

LUCENTIO Whate'er I read to her I'll plead for you
    As for my patron, stand you so assured
    As firmly as yourself were still in place –   150
    Yea and perhaps with more successful words
    Than you, unless you were a scholar, sir.

GREMIO O this learning, what a thing it is!

GRUMIO [*Aside*] O this woodcock, what an ass it is!

PETRUCHIO [*Aside*] Peace, sirrah.   155

HORTENSIO [*Aside*] Grumio, mum.

                      [*Coming forward.*]
                      God save you, Signor Gremio.

GREMIO And you are well met, Signor Hortensio.
    Trow you whither I am going? To Baptista Minola.
    I promised to inquire carefully
    About a schoolmaster for the fair Bianca,   160
    And by good fortune I have lighted well
    On this young man, for learning and behaviour
    Fit for her turn, well read in poetry
    And other books – good ones, I warrant ye.

Hortensio tells Gremio that he has found somebody prepared to marry Katherina. Gremio is amazed, but Petruchio assures him that he knows about Katherina's faults and is still determined to wed her.

1 Petruchio (in small groups)

Petruchio is introduced to other characters as the man prepared to take on Katherina. Discuss how you would say Petruchio's lines on the opposite page. What impression does he want to create? Think carefully about the short line 'Will I live?'. It can be said in many different ways.

2 Another lie? (in pairs)

Hortensio is 'economical with the truth'. He does not own up to Gremio that Petruchio is an old friend. Talk together about possible reasons why you think he doesn't do so.

3 Fatherless (in pairs)

Improvise a short scene in which Petruchio visits his sick father on his deathbed. What is uppermost in the son's mind during the last moments of the father's life?

4 Repetitions

Much of page 47 repeats information that has already been given. Make a list of everything you've read or heard before. Then look back through the play and identify who first said what and to whom.

another another teacher
bags wealth
vent utter
indifferent good equally good
What countryman? Where do you come from?

if you have a stomach, to't a God's name! if you really want to, go for it!
chafèd annoyed

HORTENSIO 'Tis well. And I have met a gentleman   165
        Hath promised me to help me to another,
        A fine musician to instruct our mistress.
        So shall I no whit be behind in duty
        To fair Bianca, so beloved of me.
GREMIO Beloved of me, and that my deeds shall prove.   170
GRUMIO [*Aside*] And that his bags shall prove.
HORTENSIO Gremio, 'tis now no time to vent our love.
        Listen to me, and if you speak me fair,
        I'll tell you news indifferent good for either.
        Here is a gentleman whom by chance I met,   175
                [*Presents Petruchio.*]
        Upon agreement from us to his liking,
        Will undertake to woo curst Katherine,
        Yea, and to marry her, if her dowry please.
GREMIO So said, so done, is well.
        Hortensio, have you told him all her faults?   180
PETRUCHIO I know she is an irksome, brawling scold.
        If that be all, masters, I hear no harm.
GREMIO No? Say'st me so, friend? What countryman?
PETRUCHIO Born in Verona, old Antonio's son.
        My father dead, my fortune lives for me,   185
        And I do hope good days and long to see.
GREMIO O sir, such a life with such a wife were strange.
        But if you have a stomach, to't a God's name!
        You shall have me assisting you in all.
        But will you woo this wildcat?
PETRUCHIO   Will I live?   190
GRUMIO Will he woo her? Ay, or I'll hang her.
PETRUCHIO Why came I hither but to that intent?
        Think you a little din can daunt mine ears?
        Have I not in my time heard lions roar?
        Have I not heard the sea, puffed up with winds,   195
        Rage like an angry boar chafèd with sweat?

Petruchio continues to recount his past exploits and bravery. Gremio is impressed. Hortensio and Gremio are suspicious of Tranio's interest in the Minola family.

1 Petruchio's past (in small groups)

Stand in a circle:

- Read Petruchio's lines 192–204.
- Read them through again stressing the verbs.
- Read them again emphasising all the words concerned with sound.
- One speaks the words from the last two exercises as a kind of running commentary, while the rest mime the story they suggest.
- Talk together – is Petruchio just boasting, or could it all be true?

2 The lovers (in small groups)

Lines 212–30 are complicated but fascinating:

- Hortensio and Gremio are jealous of any interest shown in Bianca by Tranio.
- This is the first time Tranio plays the part of Lucentio.
- Lucentio is on the sidelines, egging Tranio on.

a Comic pairs

Concentrate on a pair of characters (for instance, Hortensio and Gremio). Create a comic tableau to show how the pair see themselves. Then turn it round, and show how the other characters might see them.

b Direct the scene

Discuss how you would direct this section to ensure that the audience finds it amusing.

---

ordnance cannon
'larums calls to arms on the
  battlefield

bugs fantasy, goblins
charge expenses
readiest quickest

Have I not heard great ordnance in the field,
And heaven's artillery thunder in the skies?
Have I not in a pitchèd battle heard
Loud 'larums, neighing steeds and trumpets' clang?   200
And do you tell me of a woman's tongue,
That gives not half so great a blow to hear
As will a chestnut in a farmer's fire?
Tush, tush, fear boys with bugs!

GRUMIO   For he fears none.
GREMIO Hortensio, hark.   205
          This gentleman is happily arrived,
          My mind presumes, for his own good and yours.
HORTENSIO I promised we would be contributors
          And bear his charge of wooing, whatsoe'er.
GREMIO And so we will – provided that he win her.   210
GRUMIO I would I were as sure of a good dinner.

          Enter TRANIO [*disguised as Lucentio*] *and* BIONDELLO.

TRANIO Gentlemen, God save you. If I may be bold,
          Tell me, I beseech you, which is the readiest way
          To the house of Signor Baptista Minola?
BIONDELLO He that has the two fair daughters – is't he you mean? 215
TRANIO Even he, Biondello.
GREMIO Hark you, sir, you mean not her to –
TRANIO Perhaps him and her, sir. What have you to do?
PETRUCHIO Not her that chides, sir, at any hand, I pray.
TRANIO I love no chiders, sir. Biondello, let's away.   220
LUCENTIO [*Aside*] Well begun, Tranio.
HORTENSIO   Sir, a word ere you go.
          Are you a suitor to the maid you talk of, yea or no?
TRANIO And if I be, sir, is it any offence?
GREMIO No, if without more words you will get you hence.
TRANIO Why, sir, I pray, are not the streets as free   225
          For me as for you?
GREMIO   But so is not she.
TRANIO For what reason, I beseech you?
GREMIO For this reason, if you'll know –
          That she's the choice love of Signor Gremio.
HORTENSIO That she's the chosen of Signor Hortensio.   230

Tranio announces his intention to become a suitor to Bianca. Petruchio tells Tranio of his own interest in Katherina and of Baptista's decree.

---

1 Tranio the performer (in pairs)

One person reads Tranio's lines on the opposite page. The other person echoes those parts where Tranio is playing the gentleman. Take it in turns to say the lines with suitable gestures.

2 To what end are all these words? (in small groups)

Gremio complains that Tranio will 'out-talk us all'. Petruchio complains about all the talking. Tranio says Katherina has a 'scolding tongue'. There seems to be a general concern with talking here.

Try reading the opposite page through in a number of different ways:

a very seriously
b with exaggerated accents
c like a fast-moving farce.

Which do you think fits the words best?

Softly gently
Fair Leda's daughter Helen of Troy
Paris a Trojan prince who stole Helen from her husband
prove a jade get tired (like a broken-down horse)

let her go by leave her alone
Alcides Hercules (who took on twelve difficult tasks)
in sooth for certain

TRANIO Softly, my masters! If you be gentlemen,
     Do me this right – hear me with patience.
     Baptista is a noble gentleman
     To whom my father is not all unknown,
     And were his daughter fairer than she is,   235
     She may more suitors have, and me for one.
     Fair Leda's daughter had a thousand wooers;
     Then well one more may fair Bianca have.
     And so she shall: Lucentio shall make one,
     Though Paris came in hope to speed alone.   240
GREMIO What, this gentleman will out-talk us all!
LUCENTIO Sir, give him head. I know he'll prove a jade.
PETRUCHIO Hortensio, to what end are all these words?
HORTENSIO Sir, let me be so bold as ask you,
     Did you yet ever see Baptista's daughter?   245
TRANIO No, sir, but hear I do that he hath two,
     The one as famous for a scolding tongue
     As is the other for beauteous modesty.
PETRUCHIO Sir, sir, the first's for me; let her go by.
GREMIO Yea, leave that labour to great Hercules,   250
     And let it be more than Alcides' twelve.
PETRUCHIO Sir, understand you this of me in sooth:
     The youngest daughter, whom you hearken for,
     Her father keeps from all access of suitors
     And will not promise her to any man   255
     Until the elder sister first be wed.
     The younger then is free, and not before.

Tranio expresses his gratitude to Petruchio for his determination to wed Katherina. He agrees to reward Petruchio if he wins Katherina. Everyone goes off to eat and drink together.

1 Eat and drink as friends (in groups of five or six)

All the characters leave the stage and intend to relax together. Improvise a short scene to show what happens at this gathering. Do you think they will all remain friends, or will there be disagreements? It's worth noting that the deceitfulness and hypocrisy of lawyers was legendary, so perhaps this gives a clue to what happens!

2 Impatient servants (in pairs)

Grumio and Biondello are linked because they share line 273. They seem very anxious to go. Do you think they're hungry? Or greedy? Improvise a few lines of dialogue as they leave the stage.

3 Who's who? (in groups of four)

Act 1 introduces a number of characters, several are in love, some adopt disguises, and some have particular relationships with others. Draw a diagram to show as clearly as possible who's who, who's pretending to be someone else, and the chief relationships among the characters. The list of characters on page 1 will help you.

---

stead help
whose hap shall be whoever shall
 be so lucky
ingrate ungrateful
gratify reward
rest generally beholding are
 indebted

quaff carouses drink toasts
motion idea
I shall be your *ben venuto* I'll pay
 for you

TRANIO If it be so, sir, that you are the man
          Must stead us all, and me amongst the rest,
          And if you break the ice and do this feat –   260
          Achieve the elder, set the younger free
          For our access – whose hap shall be to have her
          Will not so graceless be to be ingrate.
HORTENSIO Sir, you say well, and well you do conceive;
          And since you do profess to be a suitor,   265
          You must, as we do, gratify this gentleman
          To whom we all rest generally beholding.
TRANIO Sir, I shall not be slack; in sign whereof,
          Please ye we may contrive this afternoon
          And quaff carouses to our mistress' health,   270
          And do as adversaries do in law,
          Strive mightily, but eat and drink as friends.
GRUMIO
BIONDELLO } O excellent motion! Fellows, let's be gone.
HORTENSIO The motion's good indeed, and be it so.
          Petruchio, I shall be your *ben venuto*.   275

                                    Exeunt

53

Looking back at Act 1
Activities for groups or individuals

1 Working on the senses

The Lord and his servingmen disorientate Sly when he wakes by working on his senses (Induction 2 lines 1–71). As director, work out the effects you could use in this scene. Consider music and lighting, but allow your imagination full rein. What sounds? What sights? What smells? Write a detailed list of effects for 'Sly's dream'.

2 Sly's point of view

Petruchio and Katherina are being prepared like two mighty opponents. It is inevitable that they will meet – remember the title of the play! What will Christopher Sly think about it all? Allow him to describe the two characters, and give his personal prediction of what will happen when they meet. Try to capture Sly's tone and language.

3 Sisters

Find evidence to support your idea of how the actresses playing the roles should dress, what make-up they should use, and so on.

Design the sisters' clothes: for a modern day production and for some other historical period. (Do some research to make sure you get the details right.) Use simple sketches to show how you would differentiate between Bianca and Katherina. Is one taller than the other?

4 A fatherly act?

Baptista will not allow anyone to marry Bianca until he has got Katherina off his hands.

- What does that tell you about Baptista and about Padua?
- How will this arrangement affect the relationship between the two sisters?
- Is he being more unkind to Bianca or to Katherina?
- Do fathers have that power today?

5 Seeking experience

Lucentio uses a striking image to convey his desire for experience as
he arrives in Padua (1.1.22–4):

> And am to Padua come as he that leaves
> A shallow plash to plunge him in the deep
> And with satiety seeks to quench his thirst.

Petruchio expresses himself with typical force (1.2.52–3):

> And I have thrust myself into this maze,
> Happily to wive and thrive as best I may.

Compare and contrast the two men in as many ways as you can.

6 Friendships

What makes Petruchio and Hortensio close friends? Talk together
about what they have in common and in what ways they are different.

7 Grumio the commentator

Grumio makes a number of critical comments about people throughout the act. Do you take his opinions seriously at all? What might he
have to say about other characters? Improvise a few comments about
Baptista or Hortensio.

8 Cast the play

You are a director about to film the play. Who would you select to
play the characters you've met so far? Choose anyone you like: film or
television actors, singers or other public figures. Say why you think
each is suitable. Or cast from the teachers or students in your school
or college.

9 Describing women – not men

Think about the words used to describe women in Act 1: 'shrewd',
'froward', 'curst', 'ill-favoured', and so on. There are many other
examples. Find them, and organise a discussion on why *women* are
described like this, and not *men*.

Katherina has tied Bianca's hands, and is cross-questioning her about which suitor she loves the most. Bianca tries to pacify her sister, but Katherina strikes her. Baptista rescues Bianca and reprimands Katherina.

1 Stage directions – explicit and implicit (in pairs)

a Take parts and read through lines 1–22.

b Now go through the passage again identifying the obvious stage directions in the language. Quickly run through the lines performing only those gestures and moves.

c Next, suggest appropriate gestures and moves for every line. Run through the passage without words, only the moves.

d Finally, act out lines 1–22 using both language and movements.

2 Envy?

Bianca suggests (line 18) that Katherina envies her. Is that really how Katherina feels towards her sister? What word would you suggest to replace 'envy' to reflect Katherina's feelings more accurately?

3 Baptista (in groups of five or six)

Read Baptista's lines 23–8 round the group. Each person reads a word or phrase (up to a punctuation mark) before handing on to the next person. Talk together about what the lines suggest about Baptista's attitudes towards his daughters. Then read the lines again with great energy to bring out those attitudes.

---

gauds finery, adornments
raiment clothes
dissemble cheat, lie
fancy love
Minion spoilt brat

affect love
but you shall have him if there is no other way for you to have him
fair well-dressed
hilding good-for-nothing

ACT 2   SCENE 1
Baptista's house

Enter KATHERINA *and* BIANCA [with her hands tied]

BIANCA Good sister, wrong me not, nor wrong yourself
To make a bondmaid and a slave of me.
That I disdain. But for these other gauds –
Unbind my hands, I'll pull them off myself,
Yea, all my raiment, to my petticoat,   5
Or what you will command me will I do,
So well I know my duty to my elders.
KATHERINA Of all thy suitors here I charge thee tell
Whom thou lov'st best. See thou dissemble not.
BIANCA Believe me, sister, of all the men alive   10
I never yet beheld that special face
Which I could fancy more than any other.
KATHERINA Minion, thou liest! Is't not Hortensio?
BIANCA If you affect him, sister, here I swear
I'll plead for you myself but you shall have him.   15
KATHERINA O then, belike, you fancy riches more:
You will have Gremio to keep you fair.
BIANCA Is it for him you do envy me so?
Nay then, you jest, and now I well perceive
You have but jested with me all this while.   20
I prithee, sister Kate, untie my hands.
                [Katherina] strikes her.
KATHERINA If that be jest, then all the rest was so.

                Enter BAPTISTA.

BAPTISTA Why, how now, dame! Whence grows this insolence?
Bianca, stand aside. Poor girl, she weeps.
                [He unties her hands.]
Go, ply thy needle; meddle not with her.   25
For shame, thou hilding of a devilish spirit!
Why dost thou wrong her that did ne'er wrong thee?
When did she cross thee with a bitter word?

57

Baptista sends Bianca into the house. Katherina leaves, talking of favouritism and revenge. Petruchio tells Baptista about his interest in Katherina, and presents Hortensio (disguised as Litio) as Bianca's tutor.

1 Katherina's anger (in groups of three)

'Her silence flouts me', says Katherina when asked what Bianca has done to annoy her. Is this really the reason for Katherina's violent behaviour towards her sister? Talk together about what you think *really* motivates Katherina's anger and aggression.

2 Old maid (in small groups)

Katherina uses two expressions which Shakespeare's audience would have understood as referring to her future status as an 'old maid' (the older unmarried sister):

- 'dance barefoot on her wedding day'
- 'lead apes in hell' (apparently because old maids had no children to lead into heaven).

Imagine that Katherina is living today. Would she be so concerned about being the older unmarried sister?

3 An innocent question? (in groups of six to eight)

Shortly after Katherina's strong language, Petruchio uses the words 'fair and virtuous' to describe her. Stage lines 31–42 in a manner which brings out:

Either: the truthfulness of the description
    or: the difference between the report and the reality.

4 Bianca's view (in pairs)

Take parts. Have Bianca comment on every word in lines 47–9, which describes Katherina.

---

flouts mocks
suffer me let me have my own way
mean poor, lower class
orderly in a proper way

entrance to my entertainment
  entrance fee for my reception
Cunning skilful

KATHERINA Her silence flouts me, and I'll be revenged.

Flies after Bianca.

BAPTISTA What, in my sight? Bianca, get thee in.   30

Exit [Bianca]

KATHERINA What, will you not suffer me? Nay, now I see
    She is your treasure, she must have a husband.
    I must dance barefoot on her wedding day
    And, for your love to her, lead apes in hell.
    Talk not to me! I will go sit and weep   35
    Till I can find occasion of revenge.   *[Exit]*

BAPTISTA Was ever gentleman thus grieved as I?
    But who comes here?

Enter GREMIO, LUCENTIO *in the habit of a mean man [disguised as Cambio],* PETRUCHIO *with [*HORTENSIO *disguised as Litio,]* TRANIO *[disguised as Lucentio,] with his boy [*BIONDELLO*] bearing a lute and books.*

GREMIO Good morrow, neighbour Baptista.

BAPTISTA Good morrow, neighbour Gremio. God save you, gentlemen.   40

PETRUCHIO And you, good sir. Pray have you not a daughter
    Called Katherina, fair and virtuous?

BAPTISTA I have a daughter, sir, called Katherina.

GREMIO You are too blunt; go to it orderly.

PETRUCHIO You wrong me, Signor Gremio. Give me leave.   45
    [To Baptista] I am a gentleman of Verona, sir,
    That hearing of her beauty and her wit,
    Her affability and bashful modesty,
    Her wondrous qualities and mild behaviour,
    Am bold to show myself a forward guest   50
    Within your house, to make mine eye the witness
    Of that report which I so oft have heard.
    And for an entrance to my entertainment,
    I do present you with a man of mine,
        [Presents Hortensio.]
    Cunning in music and the mathematics,   55
    To instruct her fully in those sciences,
    Whereof I know she is not ignorant.
    Accept of him, or else you do me wrong.
    His name is Litio, born in Mantua.

Baptista welcomes Petruchio, and accepts Gremio's gift of Cambio (Lucentio) as a teacher for Bianca. Tranio declares that he too wants to be considered as a suitor for Bianca.

1 Plain-speaking (in groups of three)

'I speak but as I find', says Baptista (line 65). Plain speaking is *usually* considered a virtue, but even plain speakers do not always express their real thoughts. Consider each character in turn and judge whether they 'speak as they find' all the time, or whether they sometimes conceal what they really think.

2 Language and character (in groups of three)

Read through what Petruchio, Gremio and Baptista say in lines 60–83. Then choose two phrases from each character's lines. Say the words in turn in different tones, and emphasising different words. Try to fit the way in which you say them to your view of their personality. Finally, talk together about how this exercise has developed the way you perceive these three characters.

Teachers' appearances. Lucentio is introduced in disguise. Suggest an appropriate disguise for Hortensio. Litio is supposed to be a music teacher, so let your imagination run freely.

---

not for your turn not for you
Saving no offence to
Backare! Stand back! (Latin catch-phrase)

marvellous very
I would fain be doing I am eager for action
grateful welcome

BAPTISTA Y'are welcome, sir, and he for your good sake,   60
        But for my daughter Katherine, this I know:
        She is not for your turn, the more my grief.
PETRUCHIO I see you do not mean to part with her,
        Or else you like not of my company.
BAPTISTA Mistake me not; I speak but as I find.   65
        Whence are you, sir? What may I call your name?
PETRUCHIO Petruchio is my name, Antonio's son,
        A man well known throughout all Italy.
BAPTISTA I know him well. You are welcome for his sake.
GREMIO Saving your tale, Petruchio, I pray   70
        Let us that are poor petitioners speak too.
        Backare! You are marvellous forward.
PETRUCHIO O pardon me, Signor Gremio, I would fain be doing.
GREMIO I doubt it not, sir, but you will curse your wooing.
        [To Baptista] Neighbour, this is a gift very grateful, I am sure of   75
        it. To express the like kindness, myself, that have been more kindly
        beholding to you than any, freely give unto you this young scholar
        [Presents Lucentio.] that hath been long studying at Rheims, as
        cunning in Greek, Latin and other languages as the other in music
        and mathematics. His name is Cambio. Pray accept his service.   80
BAPTISTA A thousand thanks, Signor Gremio. Welcome, good Cambio.
        [To Tranio] But, gentle sir, methinks you walk like a stranger. May
        I be so bold to know the cause of your coming?
TRANIO Pardon me, sir, the boldness is mine own
        That, being a stranger in this city here,   85
        Do make myself a suitor to your daughter,
        Unto Bianca, fair and virtuous.
        Nor is your firm resolve unknown to me
        In the preferment of the eldest sister.
        This liberty is all that I request   90
        That, upon knowledge of my parentage,
        I may have welcome 'mongst the rest that woo,
        And free access and favour as the rest,
        And toward the education of your daughters
        I here bestow a simple instrument   95
        And this small packet of Greek and Latin books.
        [Biondello steps forward with the lute and books.]
        If you accept them, then their worth is great.

Baptista welcomes Tranio (Lucentio) and the 'teachers' leave to meet their pupils. Petruchio and Baptista discuss the financial details of Katherina's marriage. Baptista warns that he must first win her love.

1 'Teachers' (in pairs)

Although the audience knows that both teachers are frauds, each teacher believes the other to be genuine. Improvise their conversation as they leave the stage. Remember that neither of them is a teacher, and they are both in love with Bianca.

2 The dowry (in groups of four)

Look carefully at lines 117–23 where the financial arrangements concerning Katherina's marriage are described.

- Draw up the contract setting out the dowry promises.
- 20,000 crowns would have been an extraordinarily high figure. What does this suggest about Katherina and Baptista?
- Act out the lines concentrating on the manner in which Baptista makes the large offer and Petruchio receives the news.

3 'The special thing' (in groups of three)

Talk together about why Baptista lays such emphasis on love in lines 124–5.

4 How men see women (in small groups)

Consider each male character in turn (Baptista, Lucentio, Gremio, Petruchio, Grumio, Tranio, Hortensio). Write a sentence for each stating the opinion each has of women. Is there a dominant male view of women?

Prepare a tableau (a 'frozen moment') to show one male character's view of women. When you show it, can the other groups guess your character?

---

presently immediately
passing extremely
possession immediately, at the
  time of the wedding

specialties contracts
covenants financial arrangements

BAPTISTA Lucentio is your name. Of whence, I pray?
TRANIO Of Pisa, sir, son to Vincentio.
BAPTISTA A mighty man of Pisa. By report   100
    I know him well. You are very welcome, sir.
    [*To Hortensio*] Take you the lute, [*To Lucentio*] and you the
      set of books;
    You shall go see your pupils presently.
    Holla, within!

                Enter a SERVANT.

          Sirrah, lead these gentlemen
    To my daughters, and tell them both   105
    These are their tutors. Bid them use them well.
                [*Exeunt Servant, Hortensio, Lucentio*]
    We will go walk a little in the orchard
    And then to dinner. You are passing welcome,
    And so I pray you all to think yourselves.
PETRUCHIO Signor Baptista, my business asketh haste,   110
    And every day I cannot come to woo.
    You knew my father well, and in him me,
    Left solely heir to all his lands and goods,
    Which I have bettered rather than decreased.
    Then tell me, if I get your daughter's love,   115
    What dowry shall I have with her to wife?
BAPTISTA After my death, the one half of my lands,
    And in possession twenty thousand crowns.
PETRUCHIO And for that dowry I'll assure her of
    Her widowhood, be it that she survive me,   120
    In all my lands and leases whatsoever.
    Let specialties be therefore drawn between us,
    That covenants may be kept on either hand.
BAPTISTA Ay, when the special thing is well obtained,
    That is, her love, for that is all in all.   125

Petruchio confirms his determination to woo Katherina. Hortensio returns injured, and describes Katherina's violent response to her music lesson, but Petruchio appears undaunted.

1 How Petruchio presents himself (a whole class activity)

One volunteer reads slowly, but emphatically, everything Petruchio says in lines 126–33. The rest of the class act out what they understand to be the meaning of what Petruchio says. Throw yourself into this activity, making your gestures as bold as you can.

Afterwards, talk about Petruchio's choice of language.

2 'Twangling Jack' (in pairs)

Work out a series of tableaux to tell Hortensio's story in lines 145–55.

3 Petruchio's response

On hearing that Katherina has smashed the lute over Hortensio's head, Petruchio appears undaunted. Speak lines 156–8 in a manner which confirms this attitude.

Then experiment with speaking the lines in other ways which suggest different attitudes.

4 Stage direction

'*Enter Hortensio with his head broke*' often provokes great laughter in the theatre. Work out how you would stage Hortensio's entrance for the greatest comic effect.

---

peremptory final, admitting to no refusal
to the proof unpiercable armour
break her to the lute teach her to play
frets ridges to help fingering on the lute, or irritations
fume be furious
pate head
pillory a wooden frame used to punish an offender by imprisoning their head and hands
studied planned
lusty spirited

PETRUCHIO Why, that is nothing, for I tell you, father,
    I am as peremptory as she proud-minded,
    And where two raging fires meet together
    They do consume the thing that feeds their fury.
    Though little fire grows great with little wind,   130
    Yet extreme gusts will blow out fire and all.
    So I to her, and so she yields to me,
    For I am rough and woo not like a babe.
BAPTISTA Well mayst thou woo, and happy be thy speed!
    But be thou armed for some unhappy words.   135
PETRUCHIO Ay, to the proof, as mountains are for winds,
    That shakes not though they blow perpetually.

          Enter Hortensio with his head broke.

BAPTISTA How now, my friend! Why dost thou look so pale?
HORTENSIO For fear, I promise you, if I look pale.
BAPTISTA What, will my daughter prove a good musician?   140
HORTENSIO I think she'll sooner prove a soldier!
    Iron may hold with her, but never lutes.
BAPTISTA Why then, thou canst not break her to the lute?
HORTENSIO Why no, for she hath broke the lute to me.
    I did but tell her she mistook her frets   145
    And bowed her hand to teach her fingering,
    When, with a most impatient devilish spirit,
    'Frets, call you these?' quoth she, 'I'll fume with them!'
    And with that word she struck me on the head,
    And through the instrument my pate made way,   150
    And there I stood amazèd for a while,
    As on a pillory, looking through the lute,
    While she did call me rascal fiddler
    And twangling Jack, with twenty such vile terms,
    As had she studied to misuse me so.   155
PETRUCHIO Now, by the world, it is a lusty wench!
    I love her ten times more than e'er I did.
    O how I long to have some chat with her.

Baptista comforts Hortensio. Left alone, Petruchio describes how he plans to woo Katherina. When she arrives, he 'flatters' her and speaks of her reputation for mildness.

1 Petruchio's plans (in groups of three)

In lines 165–76, Petruchio makes clear his strategy for 'wooing' Katherina.

- One person reads, the others, as Katherina and Petruchio, mime what is being described.
- Talk together about whether you think Petruchio's approach will succeed.
- Later in the scene you can compare his intention with what actually takes place.

2 Why does Katherina obey? (in groups of three)

Baptista has said he will *send* Katherina to Petruchio (line 163). Katherina is scarcely the sort of person who enjoys being told what to do, but come she does. One person takes the role of Katherina, the others question her about her reasons for obeying her father.

3 What's in a name? (in pairs)

In lines 178–86, Petruchio provokes Katherina by playing on 'Kate', the familiar version of her name ('cates' were Elizabethan sweets or 'dainties'). Our names are very personal to us, which is why nicknames or corruptions of our names can prove so distressing.

In turn read the lines aloud, emphasising the different 'Kates'. Then think of some other 'Kates' he might have used, and run through the lines again, substituting your own ideas.

Proceed in practice continue your lessons
attend wait for
rail complain
clear calm
piercing moving

pack go away
bonny fair
consolation comfort
sounded proclaimed
moved led

BAPTISTA [*To Hortensio*]
    Well, go with me, and be not so discomfited.
    Proceed in practice with my younger daughter;   160
    She's apt to learn and thankful for good turns.
    Signor Petruchio, will you go with us,
    Or shall I send my daughter Kate to you?
PETRUCHIO I pray you do. I'll attend her here –
                              [*Exeunt all but Petruchio*]
    And woo her with some spirit when she comes!   165
    Say that she rail, why then I'll tell her plain
    She sings as sweetly as a nightingale.
    Say that she frown, I'll say she looks as clear
    As morning roses newly washed with dew.
    Say she be mute and will not speak a word,   170
    Then I'll commend her volubility
    And say she uttereth piercing eloquence.
    If she do bid me pack, I'll give her thanks
    As though she bid me stay by her a week.
    If she deny to wed, I'll crave the day   175
    When I shall ask the banns, and when be married.

                Enter Katherina.

    But here she comes, and now, Petruchio, speak.
    Good morrow, Kate, for that's your name, I hear.
KATHERINA Well have you heard, but something hard of hearing –
    They call me Katherine that do talk of me.   180
PETRUCHIO You lie, in faith, for you are called plain Kate,
    And bonny Kate, and sometimes Kate the curst.
    But Kate, the prettiest Kate in Christendom,
    Kate of Kate-Hall, my super-dainty Kate –
    For dainties are all Kates – and therefore, Kate,   185
    Take this of me, Kate of my consolation:
    Hearing thy mildness praised in every town,
    Thy virtues spoke of and thy beauty sounded –
    Yet not so deeply as to thee belongs –
    Myself am moved to woo thee for my wife.   190

Katherina and Petruchio argue wittily, trying to outdo each other. She is eventually driven to strike him. He promises to return the blow if she hits him again.

1 Sharing the verse (in pairs)

Lines 178–269 are in verse. Notice how certain lines of verse are 'shared', that is, part of the line is spoken by Katherina, part by Petruchio (lines 193–4, 202, 210, 213). Speak these lines, and decide where they sound better with pauses inserted between the dialogue, and where with the cues picked up quickly.

2 Puns

The opposite page is full of puns. Here are some:

movable furniture or changeable person
bear carry or have children
jade worn out horse or sexless man
burden make pregnant or accuse
light slim or promiscuous

Find other puns. In each case, work out why both meanings of the word could apply to Petruchio or Katherina.

3 Give and take (in groups of three)

How does Katherina strike Petruchio? How does he respond? Act out the short passage lines 213–14 with one person as director, assessing and commenting on the performances.

swain country bumpkin or lover
as heavy as my weight should be like a coin that has not been clipped or cut; I'm not 'lightweight', my reputation is intact

tane taken
turtle turtle dove (symbol of love) and peace
try make trial of, test

KATHERINA 'Moved' – in good time! Let him that moved you hither
    Remove you hence. I knew you at the first
    You were a movable.

PETRUCHIO   Why, what's a movable?

KATHERINA A joint stool.

PETRUCHIO   Thou hast hit it. Come sit on me.

KATHERINA Asses are made to bear, and so are you.   195

PETRUCHIO Women are made to bear, and so are you.

KATHERINA No such jade as you, if me you mean.

PETRUCHIO Alas, good Kate, I will not burden thee,
    For, knowing thee to be but young and light –

KATHERINA Too light for such a swain as you to catch,   200
    And yet as heavy as my weight should be.

PETRUCHIO 'Should be'! Should – buzz!

KATHERINA   Well tane, and like a |buzzard.

PETRUCHIO O slow-winged turtle, shall a buzzard take thee?

KATHERINA Ay, for a turtle, as he takes a buzzard.

PETRUCHIO Come, come, you wasp! I'faith you are too angry.   205

KATHERINA If I be waspish, best beware my sting.

PETRUCHIO My remedy is then to pluck it out.

KATHERINA Ay, if the fool could find it where it lies.

PETRUCHIO Who knows not where a wasp does wear his sting?
    In his tail.

KATHERINA   In his tongue.

PETRUCHIO   Whose tongue?   210

KATHERINA Yours, if you talk of tales, and so farewell.
             [*She turns to go.*]

PETRUCHIO What, with my tongue in your tail? Nay, come again.
    Good Kate, I am a gentleman –

KATHERINA   That I'll try.
            She strikes him.

PETRUCHIO I swear I'll cuff you if you strike again.
             [*He holds her.*]

KATHERINA So may you lose your arms.   215
    If you strike me, you are no gentleman,
    And if no gentleman, why then no arms.

PETRUCHIO A herald, Kate? O put me in thy books.

The battle between Katherina and Petruchio continues. He describes her using terms which are the exact opposite of her reputation.

1 C C C K K K (in groups of three)

Lines 219–24 contain much alliteration (words which begin with the same letter or sound):

crest heraldic device or tuft of feathers on a bird's head
coxcomb fool's cap
craven cowardly cock
crab sour crab apple (somebody with a cross face)

Talk together about the effects the actors could create with these words to add force to the quarrel.

2 Reputations
(in groups of three)

Petruchio compares, at some length, Katherina's supposed reputation with his own view of her (lines 232–46). One person reads the lines aloud. The others mime each defect or quality (one takes the bad side, the other the good).

Which line opposite do you imagine best fits this picture? (Royal Shakespeare Company, 1973.)

chafe irritate	**whom thou keep'st command**
coy disdainful (or shy and retiring)	order your own servants about (not
askance with scorn	me)
halt limp	**Dian** goddess of hunting
	sportful amorous

KATHERINA What is your crest – a coxcomb?

PETRUCHIO A combless cock, so Kate will be my hen.   220

KATHERINA No cock of mine; you crow too like a craven.

PETRUCHIO Nay, come, Kate, come; you must not look so sour.

KATHERINA It is my fashion when I see a crab.

PETRUCHIO Why, here's no crab, and therefore look not sour.

KATHERINA There is, there is.   225

PETRUCHIO Then show it me.

KATHERINA   Had I a glass I would.

PETRUCHIO What, you mean my face?

KATHERINA   Well aimed of such a young
     one.

PETRUCHIO Now, by Saint George, I am too young for you.

KATHERINA Yet you are withered.

PETRUCHIO   'Tis with cares.

KATHERINA   I care not.

PETRUCHIO Nay, hear you, Kate – in sooth you scape not so.   230

KATHERINA I chafe you if I tarry. Let me go.

PETRUCHIO Nay, not a whit. I find you passing gentle.
     'Twas told me you were rough and coy and sullen,
     And now I find report a very liar,
     For thou art pleasant, gamesome, passing courteous,   235
     But slow in speech, yet sweet as springtime flowers.
     Thou canst not frown, thou canst not look askance,
     Nor bite the lip as angry wenches will,
     Nor hast thou pleasure to be cross in talk,
     But thou with mildness entertain'st thy wooers,   240
     With gentle conference, soft and affable.
               [He lets her go.]
     Why does the world report that Kate doth limp?
     O sland'rous world! Kate like the hazel twig
     Is straight and slender, and as brown in hue
     As hazel-nuts and sweeter than the kernels.   245
     O let me see thee walk. Thou dost not halt.

KATHERINA Go, fool, and whom thou keep'st command.

PETRUCHIO Did ever Dian so become a grove
     As Kate this chamber with her princely gait?
     O be thou Dian, and let her be Kate,   250
     And then let Kate be chaste and Dian sportful!

Petruchio tells Katherina he intends to marry her and tame her. Baptista returns, anxious to know what has happened. Katherina accuses her father of lack of care for her in wanting her to marry Petruchio.

1 'I will marry you' (in pairs)

Petruchio's lines 255–67 seem to be a mixture of several different feelings. One person reads the speech, whilst the other makes an aggressive gesture every time the language seems harsh or angry and determined. Change over and, during the second reading, softly echo the quieter, loving words.

2 The argument (in pairs)

Take parts and read through lines 178–269 again. Then try some or all of these activities:

a Divide the quarrel into shorter sections, and give each section a subtitle. Present the subtitles to the class. How much agreement is there about the sections?

b Only read out words connected with animals or sex. Then talk together about what these words reveal about the exchange.

c Imagine you are witnessing the whole argument, not as a theatre audience, but as a jury. Whose side are you on at any particular moment? Read through the lines slowly, commenting on how your sympathies shift.

3 'How but well?' (in groups of three)

Do you think Petruchio is telling the truth at line 271? Does he think he is telling the truth? Argue, giving evidence for your point of view.

study learn by heart
extempore without preparation
mother-wit natural intelligence
Witless else her son for her son has no wit of his own
keep you warm but not much (only enough to keep)

for your turn just right for you
Conformable submissive
speed progress
in your dumps unhappy
face the matter out get his own way by sheer impudence

KATHERINA Where did you study all this goodly speech?
PETRUCHIO It is extempore, from my mother-wit.
KATHERINA A witty mother! Witless else her son.
PETRUCHIO Am I not wise?
KATHERINA   Yes, keep you warm.   255
PETRUCHIO Marry, so I mean, sweet Katherine, in thy bed.
    And therefore, setting all this chat aside,
    Thus in plain terms: your father hath consented
    That you shall be my wife, your dowry 'greed on,
    And will you, nill you, I will marry you.   260
    Now Kate, I am a husband for your turn,
    For, by this light whereby I see thy beauty –
    Thy beauty that doth make me like thee well –
    Thou must be married to no man but me,
    For I am he am born to tame you, Kate,   265
    And bring you from a wild Kate to a Kate
    Conformable as other household Kates.

Enter Baptista, Gremio and Tranio.

    Here comes your father. Never make denial –
    I must and will have Katherine to my wife.
BAPTISTA
    Now, Signor Petruchio, how speed you with my daughter?   270
PETRUCHIO How but well, sir? How but well?
    It were impossible I should speed amiss.
BAPTISTA Why, how now, daughter Katherine, in your dumps?
KATHERINA Call you me 'daughter'? Now I promise you
    You have showed a tender fatherly regard   275
    To wish me wed to one half lunatic,
    A mad-cap ruffian and a swearing Jack
    That thinks with oaths to face the matter out.

*Petruchio claims that Katherina loves him. However 'curst' she appears in
public, she is very different in private. Baptista agrees to the match,
and Petruchio leaves to prepare for the wedding.*

1 How much does Katherina hear? (in groups of five)

In any stage production, it makes a difference how much Katherina is
allowed to hear from lines 291 until her exit. Try these two stagings to
explore the difference:

a Read the passage through with Petruchio keeping as much as he
can from Katherina.

b Read it again with Petruchio making sure that Katherina does hear.

Compare the two versions, considering in particular the way
Katherina feels and reacts.

2 'Kiss me, Kate' (in pairs)

This is the first time in the play that Petruchio asks Katherina to kiss
him. Shakespeare gives us no clue as to whether they do kiss or not
before they leave the stage, so the choice is yours. What do you think?

3 Silent exit (in groups of five)

Supply Katherina with a characteristic parting comment before she
exits. Then read through lines 306–13 and finish with your new line.
Finally, talk together about why Shakespeare chose to keep Katherina
silent.

4 Famous ladies

Grissel (line 284) was a famous example of wifely obedience in
Chaucer's *The Clerk's Tale*. Lucrece (line 285) was a legendary
Roman lady famed for her chastity. Shakespeare wrote his long poem
The Rape of Lucrece describing her rape by Tarquin.

---

for policy for her own reasons
froward wilful
hot passionate, hot-tempered
speeding success

goodnight our part we can say
  goodbye to our hopes
vied redoubled
meacock mild
apace rapidly

PETRUCHIO Father, 'tis thus: yourself and all the world
          That talked of her have talked amiss of her.   280
          If she be curst, it is for policy,
          For she's not froward, but modest as the dove;
          She is not hot, but temperate as the morn;
          For patience she will prove a second Grissel,
          And Roman Lucrece for her chastity.   285
          And, to conclude, we have 'greed so well together
          That upon Sunday is the wedding day.
KATHERINA I'll see thee hanged on Sunday first!
GREMIO Hark, Petruchio, she says she'll see thee hanged first.
TRANIO Is this your speeding? Nay then, goodnight our part.   290
PETRUCHIO Be patient, gentlemen. I choose her for myself.
          If she and I be pleased, what's that to you?
          'Tis bargained 'twixt us twain, being alone,
          That she shall still be curst in company.
          I tell you, 'tis incredible to believe   295
          How much she loves me – O the kindest Kate!
          She hung about my neck, and kiss on kiss
          She vied so fast, protesting oath on oath,
          That in a twink she won me to her love.
          O you are novices! 'Tis a world to see   300
          How tame, when men and women are alone,
          A meacock wretch can make the curstest shrew.
          Give me thy hand, Kate. I will unto Venice,
          To buy apparel 'gainst the wedding day.
          Provide the feast, father, and bid the guests.   305
          I will be sure my Katherine shall be fine.
BAPTISTA I know not what to say, but give me your hands.
          God send you joy, Petruchio! 'tis a match.
GREMIO
TRANIO } Amen say we. We will be witnesses.
PETRUCHIO Father, and wife, and gentlemen, adieu.   310
          I will to Venice – Sunday comes apace.
          We will have rings, and things, and fine array,
          And kiss me, Kate, 'We will be married a' Sunday.'
                 Exeunt Petruchio and Katherina [separately]

Gremio and Tranio argue about the strength of their love for Bianca. Baptista tells them that the person who brings the greatest wealth into the marriage will win. Gremio lists his assets.

1 The love merchant

Lines 315–33 are full of references to money and merchandise. Make a list of them, and think about what they suggest to you about Baptista's attitude to his family. Does it match what you know of his character so far?

2 Youth and age (in groups of six)

GREMIO 'Tis age that nourisheth.
TRANIO But youth in ladies' eyes that flourisheth.

Devise a series of four to six silent tableaux which convey your understanding of the meaning of these lines.

3 The rich lover (in small groups)

Gremio's list of his wealth is detailed. He takes real delight in his possessions. It is rather like the Lord's description of great wealth in Induction 1 lines 42–58. Today Gremio might well have used a superior dating agency, and made a video to sell himself to his prospective partner.

Plan Gremio's video using his speech opposite (and any other information you have gathered from the play). Act it out. If you have the facilities, video it.

4 Bianca and love (in groups of three)

At no point in arranging Bianca's marriage does Baptista mention the importance of love. Yet he did so in connection with Katherina's marriage (lines 124–5). Interview Baptista (one of you in role) in order to learn his motives for this difference.

---

clapped up fixed up in a hurry.
desperate mart a very risky deal
commodity piece of merchandise
 (Kate)
fretting wearing out
Skipper playboy
compound settle

lave wash
arras counterpoints tapestry
 counterpanes
milch-kine milking cows
answerable to this portion in
 proportion for an estate on this
 scale

GREMIO Was ever match clapped up so suddenly?
BAPTISTA Faith, gentlemen, now I play a merchant's part,   315
        And venture madly on a desperate mart.
TRANIO 'Twas a commodity lay fretting by you.
        'Twill bring you gain, or perish on the seas.
BAPTISTA The gain I seek is quiet in the match.
GREMIO No doubt but he hath got a quiet catch!   320
        But now, Baptista, to your younger daughter:
        Now is the day we long have lookèd for;
        I am your neighbour and was suitor first.
TRANIO And I am one that love Bianca more
        Than words can witness, or your thoughts can guess.   325
GREMIO Youngling, thou canst not love so dear as I.
TRANIO Greybeard, thy love doth freeze.
GREMIO   But thine doth fry.
        Skipper, stand back! 'Tis age that nourisheth.
TRANIO But youth in ladies' eyes that flourisheth.
BAPTISTA Content you, gentlemen; I will compound this strife.   330
        'Tis deeds must win the prize, and he of both
        That can assure my daughter greatest dower
        Shall have my Bianca's love.
        Say, Signor Gremio, what can you assure her?
GREMIO First, as you know, my house within the city   335
        Is richly furnishèd with plate and gold,
        Basins and ewers to lave her dainty hands;
        My hangings all of Tyrian tapestry;
        In ivory coffers I have stuffed my crowns,
        In cypress chests my arras counterpoints,   340
        Costly apparel, tents and canopies,
        Fine linen, Turkey cushions bossed with pearl,
        Valance of Venice gold in needlework,
        Pewter and brass, and all things that belongs
        To house or housekeeping. Then at my farm   345
        I have a hundred milch-kine to the pail,
        Six score fat oxen standing in my stalls,
        And all things answerable to this portion.
        Myself am struck in years I must confess,
        And if I die tomorrow this is hers,   350
        If whilst I live she will be only mine.

Tranio and Gremio make their rival bids for Bianca. Baptista finds
Tranio's offer the more attractive, and awards him Bianca, subject to
confirmation of the dowry. Wedding dates are arranged.

1 Insult by implication (in groups of four)

'That "only" came well in' (line 352) is insulting to Gremio. It
suggests that, if Bianca is stupid enough to marry him, it will not be
long before she will be unfaithful. Is this a fair comment on either
Gremio or Bianca? Talk together about Tranio's insult in the light of
what you know of the characters.

2 The woman's point of view (in groups of four)

We don't know what Bianca thinks about the way she is being traded
by the men. Take parts as Baptista, Tranio, Gremio and Bianca, and
read lines 330–87 aloud, with Bianca providing a running commentary on their 'business deal'.

Tranio and Baptista. In this 1978 Royal Shakespeare Company production,
Baptista's calculator exploded as he eagerly tapped in the figures. Talk
together about what kind of society it is that, even in a comedy, is seen to
measure everything by wealth.

---

ducats Venetian gold coins
jointure settlement to provide for
  her widowhood
pinched put pressure on
argosy largest merchant ship

Marsellis' road Marseilles' safe
  anchorage
galliasses cargo vessels
tight sound
out-vied out-bidden
cavil frivolous minor point

TRANIO That 'only' came well in. Sir, list to me:
    I am my father's heir and only son.
    If I may have your daughter to my wife,
    I'll leave her houses three or four as good   355
    Within rich Pisa walls as any one
    Old Signor Gremio has in Padua,
    Besides two thousand ducats by the year
    Of fruitful land, all which shall be her jointure.
    What, have I pinched you, Signor Gremio?   360
GREMIO Two thousand ducats by the year of land?
    [*Aside*] My land amounts not to so much in all! –
    That she shall have, besides an argosy
    That now is lying in Marsellis' road. –
    What, have I choked you with an argosy?   365
TRANIO Gremio, 'tis known my father hath no less
    Than three great argosies, besides two galliasses
    And twelve tight galleys. These I will assure her,
    And twice as much whate'er thou off'rest next.
GREMIO Nay, I have offered all. I have no more,   370
    And she can have no more than all I have.
    If you like me, she shall have me and mine.
TRANIO Why, then the maid is mine from all the world
    By your firm promise. Gremio is out-vied.
BAPTISTA I must confess your offer is the best,   375
    And, let your father make her the assurance,
    She is your own; else, you must pardon me.
    If you should die before him, where's her dower?
TRANIO That's but a cavil. He is old, I young.
GREMIO And may not young men die as well as old?   380
BAPTISTA Well, gentlemen, I am thus resolved.
    On Sunday next you know
    My daughter Katherine is to be married.
    Now, on the Sunday following shall Bianca
    Be bride to you, if you make this assurance.   385
    If not, to Signor Gremio.
    And so I take my leave, and thank you both.

Gremio comments on the foolishness of Tranio's father in giving away all his money to his son. Tranio realises that as 'Lucentio' he must find a 'Vincentio', his 'father'.

1 Money and marriage

Money is clearly an important consideration for Baptista in the marriage of his daughters.

Talk together about how far you think money is still important today in finding a partner.

2 Age versus youth (in pairs)

After Baptista leaves, Gremio allows his anger to come to the surface, and he hurls several insults at Tranio. Face one another and use these insults and Tranio's reply (line 393) to begin an insult-match. Develop more insults of your own, but still in role as Gremio and Tranio.

3 Tranio thinks aloud
   (in groups of three)

Tranio's soliloquy (lines 393–400) completes a very busy and fast-moving act of the play. Talk together about the different ways in which he might say the lines – and why. Try out different tones of voice: breathless excitement, crafty and cunning, as the loyal servant, to the audience, to himself . . . Agree on the most effective style.

Does this picture match your image of the disguised Tranio?

Set foot under thy table live on your charity
toy joke
faced it bluffed my way through

card of ten a low value card
A child shall get a sire a child will produce a father

GREMIO Adieu, good neighbour.

Exit Baptista

Now I fear thee not.
Sirrah, young gamester, your father were a fool
To give thee all and in his waning age   390
Set foot under thy table. Tut, a toy!
An old Italian fox is not so kind, my boy.   *Exit*

TRANIO A vengeance on your crafty withered hide!
Yet I have faced it with a card of ten.
'Tis in my head to do my master good: 395
I see no reason but supposed Lucentio
Must get a father called supposed Vincentio.
And that's a wonder – fathers commonly
Do get their children, but in this case of wooing
A child shall get a sire, if I fail not of my cunning.   *Exit*   400

Looking back at Act 2
Activities for groups or individuals

1 Sly's comments

What is Sly's reaction to what he has witnessed so far? Choose four key moments and improvise appropriate comments from Sly.

2 What's going on?

Imagine *The Taming of the Shrew* is to be performed on the radio. The audience cannot see the complicated disguises in Act 2. Write a series of short, helpful speeches to be spoken by a narrator at appropriate moments in order to help the radio audience.

3 Fight in the dark (whole class activity)

How does your audience respond to physical violence?

A pair takes on the roles of a guard and a prisoner. The rest of the class position chairs around the edge of a square and sit facing inwards. The guard and the prisoner are blindfolded, and the guard is armed with a rolled newspaper. 'Treasure' (a bunch of keys or some other object which makes a noise when moved) is secretly placed somewhere in the square, and the game can begin. The object is for the prisoner to capture the 'treasure' without being detected by the guard. Obviously, they have to listen very carefully for each other as they search the square, so the rest of the group must remain silent. If the guard finds the prisoner, punishment can be administered with the newspaper – unless the prisoner manages to hide again! Play this game with several different pairs and then talk together about how the 'audience' responded. Then discuss how the exercise offers insights into possible audience responses to the way in which Petruchio treats Katherina in Act 2 Scene 1.

4 Research the Classics

There are many references to the Classics (Greek and Latin literature) in the play. Find as many as you can in Act 2, such as Dian and Lucrece. Research into these classical characters in the library. Report your findings back to the rest of the class.

5 Shakespeare's language

These are three difficult exercises, but they reveal a lot about Shakespeare's craftsmanship. They'll also help you with your own writing.

a Sentences in single syllables

Go through the whole act but read aloud only these one-line sentences which have only single syllable words in them. The first is line 22:

'If that be jest, then all the rest was so.'

The last monosyllabic line in the act is line 394:

'Yet I have faced it with a card of ten.'

When you have made your own list, talk together about how Shakespeare uses these monosyllabic sentences to create feeling and atmosphere. How do they give insight into character?

b Rhymes

Now repeat the activity, but this time read aloud only those pairs of lines which rhyme. How does the sound help you to understand the meaning and emotions?

c Know, known, knowledge

Words connected with 'knowing' abound in the play. Flick through the act again, reading out those sentences which contain such words. Talk together about why you think so many of these words occur.

6 Boxing ring, pantomime, circus . . . ?

The Taming of the Shrew has been performed in a variety of ways. It has been set in a circus and in a boxing ring. Parts of it have been played as a pantomime. Make a list of those episodes which you think would fit such particular settings and styles. Then try to match characters from the play with figures from those settings and styles. For example, who would be

the ringmaster?	the boxers?	the two robbers?
the clown?	the referee?	the cheeky servant?
the lion tamer?	the principal boy?	the old widow (in drag!)?

Can you suggest other unusual settings and styles which would work? Give some reasons for your suggestions, arguing what they might reveal about the play.

The two suitors, disguised as teachers, compete for Bianca's attention. She reminds them that she is not a schoolchild, and chooses Cambio (Lucentio) for her first lesson rather than Litio (Hortensio).

1 Work *v.* play (in groups of six)

Lucentio tells us what he thinks is the value of music (lines 11–12): relaxation after hard work. Put together a radio advertisement which aims to sell recorded music on this basis. The advert must not last more than forty-five seconds.

2 'As I please myself' (in pairs)

Take it in turns to read Bianca's lines 16–23.

Firstly, read in a relaxed way as if you were trying to calm the quarrel. After your reading, your partner should respond as one of the suitors. How does the suitor feel now?

Next, swap roles, and this time read the speech as angrily and selfishly as you can. As you do so, your partner points to you every time you refer to yourself.

3 The Latin lesson

At lines 28–9, Lucentio begins his lesson with some lines in Latin from Ovid:

'Here ran the river Simois, here is the Segeian land,
Here stood old Priam's lofty palace.'

a Speak the Latin in different ways (slowly, swiftly, full of significance, as if you don't understand a word, and so on). Accompany each reading with appropriate stage business.

b Talk together about what you think is the most appropriate way to speak lines in a foreign language. Try out your ideas on other lines in the play (Induction 1.4; 1.1.25; 1.1.153; 1.1.189; 1.2.23–5; 3.1.28–9; 4.3.130; 4.4.89–90).

---

pedant fussy academic
prerogative priority
lecture lesson
Preposterous putting things in the wrong order

serve in serve up, contribute
braves insults
breeching in breeches, young
Conster translate

84

ACT 3   SCENE 1
Baptista's house

Enter LUCENTIO [*as Cambio*], HORTENSIO [*as Litio*] *and* BIANCA

LUCENTIO Fiddler, forbear! You grow too forward, sir.
    Have you so soon forgot the entertainment
    Her sister Katherine welcomed you withal?
HORTENSIO But, wrangling pedant, this is
    The patroness of heavenly harmony.   5
    Then give me leave to have prerogative,
    And when in music we have spent an hour,
    Your lecture shall have leisure for as much.
LUCENTIO Preposterous ass, that never read so far
    To know the cause why music was ordained!   10
    Was it not to refresh the mind of man
    After his studies or his usual pain?
    Then give me leave to read philosophy
    And, while I pause, serve in your harmony.
HORTENSIO Sirrah! I will not bear these braves of thine!   15
BIANCA Why, gentlemen, you do me double wrong
    To strive for that which resteth in my choice.
    I am no breeching scholar in the schools:
    I'll not be tied to hours nor 'pointed times
    But learn my lessons as I please myself.   20
    And, to cut off all strife, here sit we down.
    Take you your instrument; play you the whiles;
    His lecture will be done ere you have tuned.
HORTENSIO You'll leave his lecture when I am in tune?
LUCENTIO That will be never. Tune your instrument.   25
BIANCA Where left we last?
LUCENTIO Here, madam. [*He reads.*]
    Hic ibat Simois, hic est Sigeia tellus,
    Hic steterat Priami regia celsa senis.
BIANCA Conster them.   30

Lucentio reveals his true identity to Bianca, who, though cautious, offers him hope. After two unsuccessful attempts, Hortensio wins the right to begin his music lesson.

1 Secrets (in pairs)

Lucentio reveals his love for Bianca in a carefully guarded manner, hidden amongst Latin phrases. Try your hand at something similar. Use another language, or a code, or even mime, to convey a secret to a partner. Ensure that anyone overhearing will not get the drift of what you are really talking about.

2 Bianca's role (in groups of four)

Bianca's reply (lines 39–42) is worth close attention. At first, work in pairs.

Pair 1 One person reads the lines phrase by phrase; the other states Lucentio's emotional reaction at each point.

Pair 2 Read the passage as before, but the other person considers Bianca's emotional response at each phrase.

Compare these simple 'emotional graphs', and discuss how confident Lucentio can afford to feel.

3 Where is Hortensio? (in pairs)

Talk about where on the stage Hortensio might position himself during lines 25–55. Remember that he needs to deliver an aside to the audience, and is obviously interested in what the other two are doing and saying.

Identify anything in the script opposite that Lucentio and Bianca intend Hortensio to hear. In particular, does he overhear lines 48–52?

---

port appearance, status
Spit . . . hole try again!
Pedascule little pedant (a scornful phrase)

Aeacides Ajax Greek warrior at the siege of Troy
pleasant teasing

LUCENTIO *Hic ibat* – as I told you before; *Simois* – I am Lucentio; *hic est* – son unto Vincentio of Pisa; *Sigeia tellus* – disguised thus to get your love. *Hic steterat* – and that Lucentio that comes a-wooing; *Priami* – is my man Tranio; *regia* – bearing my port; *celsa senis* – that we might beguile the old pantaloon.   35

HORTENSIO Madam, my instrument's in tune.

BIANCA Let's hear. [*He plays.*] O fie! The treble jars.

LUCENTIO Spit in the hole, man, and tune again.

BIANCA Now let me see if I can conster it. *Hic ibat Simois* – I know you not; *hic est Sigeia tellus* – I trust you not; *Hic steterat*   40
Priami – take heed he hear us not; *regia* – presume not; *celsa senis* – despair not.

HORTENSIO Madam, 'tis now in tune.

                  [*He plays again.*]

LUCENTIO   All but the bass.

HORTENSIO The bass is right; 'tis the base knave that jars.

    [*Aside*] How fiery and forward our pedant is!   45
    Now, for my life, the knave doth court my love.
    Pedascule, I'll watch you better yet.

BIANCA In time I may believe, yet I mistrust.

LUCENTIO Mistrust it not, for sure Aeacides
    Was Ajax, called so from his grandfather.   50

BIANCA I must believe my master, else, I promise you,
    I should be arguing still upon that doubt.
    But let it rest. Now, Litio, to you.
    Good master, take it not unkindly, pray,
    That I have been thus pleasant with you both.   55

HORTENSIO [*To Lucentio*]
    You may go walk, and give me leave awhile.
    My lessons make no music in three parts.

LUCENTIO Are you so formal, sir? Well, I must wait –
    [*Aside*] And watch withal, for, but I be deceived,
    Our fine musician groweth amorous.   60

Hortensio attempts to woo Bianca during a 'lesson', but she rejects him. Bianca is summoned to prepare for Katherina's wedding, so Lucentio also leaves. Hortensio is suspicious of both of them.

1 No musician (in groups of four)

Teachers are usually experts in their own subjects, but imagine that Hortensio were not a skilled musician. Talk together about how this could add to the fun in this scene.

Bianca at her schooldesk (Royal Shakespeare Company, 1982). Talk together about the sort of pupil she appears to be.

2 Hortensio's suspicions (in pairs)

In lines 84–9, Hortensio voices his suspicions, and describes how he would respond if he thought Bianca had eyes for anyone but him. Read the lines aloud to one another in different ways, for example: aggressively, humorously, conspiratorially. Talk together about his attitude to rivals. Then write out and complete this sentence in fewer than twenty extra words: Hortensio is a . . . because . . .'.

---

gamut the musical scale	**seize . . . list** anyone who wants you can have you
effectual effective	
nice fussy	**quit with** rid of
stale false lover	

HORTENSIO Madam, before you touch the instrument
   To learn the order of my fingering,
   I must begin with rudiments of art,
   To teach you gamut in a briefer sort,
   More pleasant, pithy and effectual   65
   Than hath been taught by any of my trade;
   And there it is in writing, fairly drawn.
BIANCA Why, I am past my gamut long ago.
HORTENSIO Yet read the gamut of Hortensio.
BIANCA [*Reads*]
   '*Gamut* I am, the ground of all accord: 70
   A re, to plead Hortensio's passion;
   B mi, Bianca, take him for thy lord;
   C fa ut, that loves with all affection;
   D sol re, one clef, two notes have I;
   E la mi, show pity or I die.'   75
   Call you this 'gamut'? Tut, I like it not!
   Old fashions please me best. I am not so nice
   To change true rules for odd inventions.

       Enter a SERVANT.
SERVANT Mistress, your father prays you leave your books,
   And help to dress your sister's chamber up.   80
   You know tomorrow is the wedding-day.
BIANCA Farewell, sweet masters both, I must be gone.
         [*Exeunt Bianca and Servant*]
LUCENTIO Faith, mistress, then I have no cause to stay. [*Exit*]
HORTENSIO But I have cause to pry into this pedant:
   Methinks he looks as though he were in love.   85
   Yet if thy thoughts, Bianca, be so humble
   To cast thy wand'ring eyes on every stale,
   Seize thee that list! If once I find thee ranging
   Hortensio will be quit with thee by changing.   *Exit*

The wedding day has arrived, the family and guests are ready, but Petruchio is missing. Katherina complains bitterly about her treatment and, although Tranio tries to cheer her up, she leaves in tears.

1 Left in the lurch (in pairs)

'What says Lucentio to this shame of ours?', asks Baptista. What would you say in a similar situation? Improvise as many explanations as you can to give to the father of a bride who has been left waiting at the church.

2 Responses to Katherina (in groups of four)

Read lines 8–20 round the group, one sentence per person. Then each of you select a character from those on stage, and tell the others how much sympathy your character feels for Katherina.

3 Description of Petruchio (in groups of six)

Look carefully at Tranio's portrait of Petruchio (lines 22–5). Contrast it with the way in which Katherina has just described him. Find lines from earlier in the play which confirm these views. Suggest a few aspects of his personality not mentioned by Tranio or Katherina, and find lines to support these too.

Present your findings as a short dramatic poem entitled 'Petruchio – the man'.

'pointed appointed
want lack
rudesby lout
spleen changeable temper
to . . . for to get a reputation as

merry humorous
means but well has only good
intentions
fortune . . . word mishap stops
him from keeping his promise to be
here

ACT 3   SCENE 2
Outside Baptista's house

Enter BAPTISTA, GREMIO, TRANIO disguised as Lucentio, KATHERINA,
BIANCA, LUCENTIO disguised as Cambio, other GUESTS and
ATTENDANTS

BAPTISTA [*To Tranio*] Signor Lucentio, this is the 'pointed day
  That Katherine and Petruchio should be married,
  And yet we hear not of our son-in-law.
  What will be said? What mockery will it be
  To want the bridegroom when the priest attends   5
  To speak the ceremonial rites of marriage!
  What says Lucentio to this shame of ours?
KATHERINA No shame but mine. I must, forsooth, be forced
  To give my hand, opposed against my heart,
  Unto a mad-brain rudesby, full of spleen,   10
  Who wooed in haste and means to wed at leisure.
  I told you, I, he was a frantic fool,
  Hiding his bitter jests in blunt behaviour.
  And to be noted for a merry man,
  He'll woo a thousand, 'point the day of marriage,   15
  Make feast, invite friends, and proclaim the banns,
  Yet never means to wed where he hath wooed.
  Now must the world point at poor Katherine
  And say, 'Lo, there is mad Petruchio's wife
  If it would please him come and marry her!'   20
TRANIO Patience, good Katherine, and Baptista too.
  Upon my life, Petruchio means but well,
  Whatever fortune stays him from his word.
  Though he be blunt, I know him passing wise;
  Though he be merry, yet withal he's honest.   25
KATHERINA Would Katherine had never seen him though!
     Exit weeping [followed by Bianca and others]

As Baptista sympathises with Katherina, Biondello brings news of the bridegroom's approach. He describes Petruchio's fantastic appearance. Grumio is dressed in a similarly strange manner.

1 Biondello's language (whole class activity)

Biondello gives a very detailed picture of Petruchio, his horse and Grumio. Everything is described with great invention and relish.

a Read lines 41–62 round the class, one phrase from each person (speak only up to the next piece of punctuation and then allow the next person to carry on). Fluency will come with a couple of run-throughs.

b Read through the lines again. If your phrase makes complete sense to you, 'stage whisper' it. If any part of it puzzles you, shout it out. At the end of this exercise, talk about how much of the passage is hard to follow.

c The description of Petruchio's horse presents a particular problem for the actor. Should he attempt to make the meaning as clear as possible to the audience, or should he perform it in some other way (for example, at express speed)? Or should it simply be cut? Split into pairs and each 'perform' lines 45–56 ('his horse . . . packthread') for your partner. Use vocal and facial expressions, gestures, mimes – anything which will help you to convey the meaning. Next, choose a different style (for example, slowly, quickly, amused, shocked) and 'perform' it again.

   To help you, all these are horses' ailments: 'hipped', 'glanders', 'mose in the chine', 'lampass', 'fashions', 'windgalls', 'spavins', 'yellows', 'fives', 'staggers', 'bots', 'shoulder-shotten', 'near-legged'.

d Write a modern equivalent about a bridegroom arriving at the church in a clapped-out car.

---

tane taken
chapeless without a scabbard
half-cheeked wrongly adjusted
headstall, girth, crupper parts of the saddle

caparisoned fitted out
kersey woollen
list strip of cloth
for instead of

BAPTISTA Go, girl. I cannot blame thee now to weep,
    For such an injury would vex a very saint,
    Much more a shrew of thy impatient humour.

Enter BIONDELLO.

BIONDELLO Master, master, news! And such old news as you never 30
    heard of!
BAPTISTA Is it new and old too? How may that be?
BIONDELLO Why, is it not news to hear of Petruchio's coming?
BAPTISTA Is he come?
BIONDELLO Why no, sir. 35
BAPTISTA What then?
BIONDELLO He is coming.
BAPTISTA When will he be here?
BIONDELLO When he stands where I am and sees you there.
TRANIO But say, what to thine old news? 40
BIONDELLO Why, Petruchio is coming in a new hat and an old jerkin;
    a pair of old breeches thrice turned; a pair of boots that have been
    candle-cases, one buckled, another laced; an old rusty sword tane
    out of the town armoury, with a broken hilt and chapeless; with
    two broken points; his horse hipped – with an old mothy saddle 45
    and stirrups of no kindred – besides, possessed with the glanders
    and like to mose in the chine; troubled with the lampass, infected
    with the fashions, full of windgalls, sped with spavins, rayed with
    the yellows, past cure of the fives, stark spoiled with the staggers,
    begnawn with the bots, swayed in the back and shoulder-shotten, 50
    near-legged before, and with a half-cheeked bit and a headstall of
    sheep's leather, which, being restrained to keep him from stumbling,
    hath been often burst and now repaired with knots; one girth six
    times pieced, and a woman's crupper of velour, which hath two
    letters for her name fairly set down in studs, and here and there 55
    pieced with packthread.
BAPTISTA Who comes with him?
BIONDELLO O sir, his lackey, for all the world caparisoned like the
    horse, with a linen stock on one leg and a kersey boot-hose on the
    other, gartered with a red and blue list; an old hat and the humour 60
    of forty fancies pricked in't for a feather; a monster, a very monster
    in apparel, and not like a Christian footboy or a gentleman's lackey.

Biondello distracts Baptista with more word-play until Petruchio makes his entrance. Petruchio appears puzzled by the amazement that greets him.

1 Baptista's joy (in pairs)

Does Baptista mean what he says in line 65? Compare it with his exchange with Petruchio (lines 78–9).

2 The appearance of Petruchio and Grumio (in groups of eight)

a Rehearse this entry in order to make it as striking as possible.

b Cut the action after line 77 from Petruchio. Then, each member of the group comes forward in role, introduces themselves, and sums up their feelings in one sentence only.

pricks urges
mean-apparelled poorly dressed
all one the same thing
Were it better even if I were better
 dressed
monument portent

prodigy omen
unprovided unprepared
habit outfit
estate position, status
occasion of import important
 matter

TRANIO 'Tis some odd humour pricks him to this fashion,
 　　　　Yet oftentimes he goes but mean-apparelled.
BAPTISTA I am glad he's come, howsoe'er he comes.　　　65
BIONDELLO Why, sir, he comes not.
BAPTISTA Didst thou not say he comes?
BIONDELLO Who? That Petruchio came?
BAPTISTA Ay, that Petruchio came.
BIONDELLO No, sir, I say his horse comes with him on his back.　　70
BAPTISTA Why, that's all one.
BIONDELLO 　Nay, by Saint Jamy,
 　　　　I hold you a penny,
 　　　　A horse and a man
 　　　　Is more than one,　　　　　75
 　　　　And yet not many.

Enter PETRUCHIO *and* GRUMIO.

PETRUCHIO Come, where be these gallants? Who's at home?
BAPTISTA You are welcome, sir.
PETRUCHIO 　　　　　　　　And yet I come not well.
BAPTISTA And yet you halt not.
TRANIO 　　　　　　　　Not so well apparelled
 　　　　As I wish you were.　　　　　80
PETRUCHIO Were it better, I should rush in thus.
 　　　　But where is Kate? Where is my lovely bride?
 　　　　How does my father? Gentles, methinks you frown,
 　　　　And wherefore gaze this goodly company
 　　　　As if they saw some wondrous monument,　　85
 　　　　Some comet or unusual prodigy?
BAPTISTA Why, sir, you know this is your wedding-day.
 　　　　First were we sad, fearing you would not come,
 　　　　Now sadder that you come so unprovided.
 　　　　Fie, doff this habit, shame to your estate,　　90
 　　　　An eye-sore to our solemn festival.
TRANIO And tell us what occasion of import
 　　　　Hath all so long detained you from your wife
 　　　　And sent you hither so unlike yourself.

Petruchio brushes questions aside and insists on going to the church to be married dressed as he is. The rest of the family and guests follow. Tranio and Lucentio remain, discussing their plans to win Bianca.

1 Why has Katherina gone? (in pairs)

Petruchio seems surprised that Katherina is not there to greet him (line 100). A meeting between the two at this point might well cause sparks to fly. One of you take on the role of Katherina, and the other, as an interviewer, asks you your reasons for leaving.

Afterwards, the interviewer becomes Petruchio. Improvise a meeting between the bride and bridegroom outside the church.

2 What is Grumio doing?

Grumio doesn't speak from the time he arrives with Petruchio to his departure after line 113. Yet he must be fully involved in the action. Make a list of as many suggestions as you can to help the actor playing the part.

3 'He hath some meaning in his mad attire' (in pairs)

Once again Tranio is the one who tries to explain what Petruchio is up to, although he doesn't get very far. Talk together about what 'meaning' there might be in Petruchio's behaviour at this point. Try to produce an explanation that might be offered, however implausible.

Sufficeth it is enough
digress change my plans
wears is passing
Good sooth yes indeed
wear wear out (a sexual joke)

lovely loving
event outcome
concerneth us it is important for us
skills matters

PETRUCHIO Tedious it were to tell, and harsh to hear.   95
    Sufficeth I am come to keep my word
    Though in some part enforcèd to digress,
    Which at more leisure I will so excuse
    As you shall well be satisfied with all.
    But where is Kate? I stay too long from her.   100
    The morning wears, 'tis time we were at church.
TRANIO See not your bride in these unreverent robes;
    Go to my chamber, put on clothes of mine.
PETRUCHIO Not I, believe me; thus I'll visit her.
BAPTISTA But thus, I trust, you will not marry her.   105
PETRUCHIO Good sooth, even thus. Therefore ha' done with words;
    To me she's married, not unto my clothes.
    Could I repair what she will wear in me
    As I can change these poor accoutrements,
    'Twere well for Kate and better for myself.   110
    But what a fool am I to chat with you
    When I should bid good morrow to my bride
    And seal the title with a lovely kiss!

Exit [with Grumio]

TRANIO He hath some meaning in his mad attire.
    We will persuade him, be it possible,   115
    To put on better ere he go to church.
BAPTISTA I'll after him and see the event of this.

Exit [with Gremio, Biondello and Attendants]

TRANIO *[To Lucentio]* But, sir, to love concerneth us to add
    Her father's liking, which to bring to pass,
    As I before imparted to your worship,   120
    I am to get a man – whate'er he be
    It skills not much, we'll fit him to our turn –
    And he shall be Vincentio of Pisa
    And make assurance here in Padua
    Of greater sums than I have promisèd.   125
    So shall you quietly enjoy your hope
    And marry sweet Bianca with consent.

Lucentio and Tranio review their plot to win Bianca. Gremio returns and tells them about Petruchio's strange behaviour at the church – he has struck the priest.

1 Twenty lines (in groups of eight)

When Gremio departs with the rest of the party at line 117, Lucentio and Tranio have only twenty lines to fill before Gremio returns with news of what happened at the church. Their conversation is a report on the progress (or lack of it) made with their plot to enable Lucentio to marry Bianca. For some reason Shakespeare chose not to stage the wedding itself, but to insert these twenty lines marking time with the sub-plot.

Franco Zeffirelli, the Italian director, *did* show Katherina and Petruchio's wedding in his 1966 film of the play starring Elizabeth Taylor and Richard Burton. The scene is very lively and entertaining, and yet Shakespeare seems to have ignored this option. Why?

Divide into two groups, the Shakespeares and the Zeffirellis, and debate the merits of the two approaches. See the video of the film if you can.

2 'The narrow-prying father' (in pairs)

Look back through the play so far and decide whether line 136 is an accurate description of Baptista.

3 Opposites? (in groups of three)

Read lines 145–7 aloud, one line each. Work out a series of three tableaux, one to illustrate each line. Present your tableaux to the rest of the class.

---

steal our marriage elope
watch our vantage wait for an
  opportunity
quaint cunning
groom lout

dam mother
fool harmless innocent
gogs-wouns God's wounds (an
  oath)
list pleases to

LUCENTIO Were it not that my fellow schoolmaster
      Doth watch Bianca's steps so narrowly,
      'Twere good, methinks, to steal our marriage,   130
      Which once performed, let all the world say no,
      I'll keep mine own despite of all the world.
TRANIO That by degrees we mean to look into
      And watch our vantage in this business.
      We'll overreach the greybeard Gremio,   135
      The narrow-prying father Minola,
      The quaint musician, amorous Litio,
      All for my master's sake, Lucentio.

Enter Gremio.

      Signor Gremio! Came you from the church?
GREMIO As willingly as e'er I came from school.   140
TRANIO And is the bride and bridegroom coming home?
GREMIO A bridegroom, say you? 'Tis a groom indeed –
      A grumbling groom, and that the girl shall find.
TRANIO Curster than she? Why, 'tis impossible.
GREMIO Why, he's a devil, a devil, a very fiend!   145
TRANIO Why, she's a devil, a devil, the devil's dam!
GREMIO Tut, she's a lamb, a dove, a fool, to him.
      I'll tell you, Sir Lucentio: when the priest
      Should ask if Katherine should be his wife,
      'Ay, by gogs-wouns!' quoth he, and swore so loud   150
      That, all-amazed, the priest let fall the book,
      And as he stooped again to take it up,
      This mad-brained bridegroom took him such a cuff
      That down fell priest and book, and book and priest!
      'Now take them up', quoth he, 'if any list.'   155
TRANIO What said the wench when he rose again?

Gremio describes how, at the wedding, Petruchio raged, threw wine over the sexton, and kissed Katherina very enthusiastically. When the wedding party returns, Petruchio announces that he must leave immediately.

1 The wedding (in large groups)

Gremio's description of the wedding is very detailed (lines 148–72). Try the following versions of the wedding scene:

a Each person chooses what they consider to be the funniest piece of outrageous behaviour by Petruchio. Explain your choice to the rest of the group.

b Stage the scene as described by Gremio, emphasising the humour. You may be able to find some appropriate music to accompany your actions.

c Improvise a contemporary version of the wedding, but this time make it the bride who misbehaves. This is to be a 'society wedding', so spend some time preparing the right atmosphere in the 'church'. Would a woman employ the same disruptive style and techniques as Petruchio?

d Discuss the two versions. Focus on the different effects of the bride's, rather than the bridegroom's, misbehaviour.

2 Petruchio's motives (a whole class activity)

Clear a space in the classroom (or use the hall or drama studio). Everyone walks around the room reading aloud Petruchio's lines 174–8 and lines 180–7. At each punctuation mark, stop abruptly, turn at least 90° and then continue reading and moving.

Repeat the exercise several times. Don't be afraid to put plenty of energy and enthusiasm into your reading. At the end, talk together about what you notice about how the language matches Petruchio's moods and decisions.

---

for why because	**sops** pieces of cake soaked in wine
cozen cheat	**hungerly** as if ill-fed
aboard on board ship	**rout** crowd (of guests)
carousing drinking healths	**cheer** food and drink
muscadel sweet white wine	**Make . . . wonder** don't be surprised

GREMIO Trembled and shook, for why he stamped and swore
As if the vicar meant to cozen him.
But after many ceremonies done
He calls for wine. 'A health', quoth he, as if   160
He had been aboard, carousing to his mates
After a storm; quaffed off the muscadel
And threw the sops all in the sexton's face,
Having no other reason
But that his beard grew thin and hungerly   165
And seemed to ask him sops as he was drinking.
This done, he took the bride about the neck
And kissed her lips with such a clamorous smack
That at the parting all the church did echo.
And I, seeing this, came thence for very shame,   170
And after me, I know, the rout is coming.
Such a mad marriage never was before!
Music plays.
Hark, hark! I hear the minstrels play.

*Enter Petruchio, Katherina, Bianca, Hortensio [as Litio], Baptista,
[Grumio and others].*

PETRUCHIO Gentlemen and friends, I thank you for your pains.
I know you think to dine with me today   175
And have prepared great store of wedding cheer,
But so it is, my haste doth call me hence,
And therefore here I mean to take my leave.
BAPTISTA Is't possible you will away tonight?
PETRUCHIO I must away today, before night come.   180
Make it no wonder; if you knew my business,
You would entreat me rather go than stay.
And, honest company, I thank you all
That have beheld me give away myself
To this most patient, sweet and virtuous wife.   185
Dine with my father, drink a health to me,
For I must hence, and farewell to you all.

Petruchio ignores all pleas to stay – even Katherina's. When she refuses to go with him, he orders the guests to go to the wedding breakfast, but insists that she accompanies him.

1 'If you love me . . .' (in pairs)

Read out lines 190–4 several times in different tones of voice. Compare different pairs' efforts, trying to find:

- the most amusing reading
- the most unpleasant reading.

2 'I please myself' (in groups of four)

Between lines 190–210 Katherina fights back – and loses. She says she has 'a spirit to resist', and she tries a number of different tactics during the scene. Read the whole of the opposite page, with one member of the group playing all the parts other than Petruchio and Katherina. The fourth person stops the reading every few lines to comment on Katherina's state of mind at that point.

3 What would Father say? (in pairs)

Katherina refuses to listen to Baptista, sweeping him aside in line 206. Make up four lines that he could have said, if he had had the chance.

4 Katherina v. Petruchio (in groups of four)

One person reads aloud lines 211–16, while the others mime as Petruchio instructs them. On the last line, Petruchio must make some gesture, emphasising his clear statement of intent. At this point, the others tell Petruchio, one by one, exactly what they think of him.

---

the oats . . . horses they've fed (or is Grumio just being silly?)
green fresh (a proverbial phrase for hastening the departure of an unwelcome guest)
jolly arrogant

roundly boldly
What . . . do? What has it got to do with you?
stay my leisure wait until I am ready
work seethe, rage
domineer feast luxuriously

TRANIO Let us entreat you stay till after dinner.
PETRUCHIO It may not be.
GREMIO   Let me entreat you.
PETRUCHIO It cannot be.
KATHERINA   Let me entreat you.   190
PETRUCHIO I am content.
KATHERINA   Are you content to stay?
PETRUCHIO I am content you shall entreat me stay –
     But yet not stay, entreat me how you can.
KATHERINA Now, if you love me, stay.
PETRUCHIO   Grumio, my horse!
GRUMIO Ay, sir, they be ready – the oats have eaten the horses.   195
KATHERINA Nay then,
     Do what thou canst, I will not go today!
     No, nor tomorrow – not till I please myself.
     The door is open, sir, there lies your way;
     You may be jogging whiles your boots are green.   200
     For me, I'll not be gone till I please myself.
     'Tis like you'll prove a jolly surly groom
     That take it on you at the first so roundly.
PETRUCHIO O Kate, content thee; prithee be not angry.
KATHERINA I will be angry. What hast thou to do?   205
     – Father, be quiet. He shall stay my leisure.
GREMIO Ay, marry, sir, now it begins to work.
KATHERINA Gentlemen, forward to the bridal dinner.
     I see a woman may be made a fool
     If she had not a spirit to resist.   210
PETRUCHIO They shall go forward, Kate, at thy command.
     Obey the bride, you that attend on her.
     Go to the feast, revel and domineer,
     Carouse full measure to her maidenhead,
     Be mad and merry – or go hang yourselves.   215
     But for my bonny Kate, she must with me.

Insisting that Katherina is his property, Petruchio 'defends' his wife against attack from the wedding party and rushes off with her. The guests are left confused and amused, and decide to go to the feast.

1 Women's lib? (a whole class activity)

'I will be master of what is mine own,
She is my goods, my chattels; she is my house,
My household-stuff, my field, my barn,
My horse, my ox, my ass, my anything,
And here she stands.'

'These are the most unpleasant words Shakespeare ever wrote', said one student. Do you agree? To explore your reactions to Petruchio's lines, try one or more of the following:

a Male students kneel. Female students chant the lines at them, substituting 'he' for 'she'.

b In pairs. One student reads, pausing at each punctuation mark. The other says at each pause: 'O no I'm not, because . . .' (give reasons).

c A volunteer, as Petruchio, stands in a circle of students and reads, trying to convince all the others who heckle his reading.

d Experiment with different styles of speaking the lines, for example: as a formal lecture, as a ranting politician, as a comedian. Can you find a style to fit the language?

e Substitute modern items (television set, car, and so on) for Petruchio's nouns.

f Organise a class debate on the theme: 'Petruchio is simply a male chauvinist pig'.

g Is there any danger of these lines being taken too seriously? Are they, after all, just a joke?

---

look not big don't defy me
chattels movable possessions
buckler shield
Went they not if they hadn't gone
Kated afflicted with 'the Kate' (as if a disease)

wants . . . supply are not here to fill
there . . . junkets there is no lack of delicacies

Nay, look not big, nor stamp, nor stare, nor fret;
I will be master of what is mine own.
She is my goods, my chattels; she is my house,
My household-stuff, my field, my barn,   220
My horse, my ox, my ass, my anything,
And here she stands. Touch her whoever dare,
I'll bring mine action on the proudest he
That stops my way in Padua. Grumio,
Draw forth thy weapon – We are beset with thieves!   225
Rescue thy mistress, if thou be a man.
– Fear not, sweet wench, they shall not touch thee, Kate;
I'll buckler thee against a million!

> *Exeunt Petruchio, Katherina [and Grumio]*

BAPTISTA Nay, let them go – a couple of quiet ones!
GREMIO Went they not quickly, I should die with laughing.   230
TRANIO Of all mad matches never was the like.
LUCENTIO Mistress, what's your opinion of your sister?
BIANCA That being mad herself, she's madly mated.
GREMIO I warrant him, Petruchio is Kated.
BAPTISTA

Neighbours and friends, though bride and bridegroom wants   235
For to supply the places at the table,
You know there wants no junkets at the feast.
[*To Tranio*] Lucentio, you shall supply the bridegroom's
      place,
And let Bianca take her sister's room.
TRANIO Shall sweet Bianca practise how to bride it?   240
BAPTISTA She shall, Lucentio. Come, gentlemen, let's go.

> *Exeunt*

Looking back at Act 3
Activities for groups or individuals

1 'What will the neighbours say?'

Baptista, perhaps surprisingly, shows sympathy for Katherina's plight (3.2.27–9). He is also very worried by the threat of public humiliation as he waits for the missing Petruchio before the wedding (3.2.4–5). Prepare a short scene in which a handful of neighbours gossip abut 'that Minola wedding'.

2 Characters' 'wants'

- List each character who appears in this act. Write a single sentence for each which begins 'What I want is . . .'.
- How much agreement is there in the class about each character's motive?
- Add another layer of complexity – A says about B: 'What *I* think *they* want is . . .'.

3 An agony aunt replies to a plea

Imagine you are an 'agony aunt' for a magazine. One character (Petruchio, Baptista, Bianca or Katherina) contacts you with their problem. Write their letter to you and your advice.

4 Pardon?

Turn to Biondello's lively description of Petruchio, his horse and Grumio (3.2.41–62). Choose your favourite phrase and try to decide why it appeals to you.

Talk together about how you can enjoy a speech – and even find it funny – when you don't fully understand every word. Find appropriate examples from this speech and from others.

5 'To me she's married, not unto my clothes'

Petruchio's words might well strike a chord with many people who feel that too often others judge them on their appearance. Talk together about this idea, and make a list of the kinds of occasion when this issue might arise. Improvise one such scene.

6 Shakespeare and schools

In Act 3, Scene 2 Gremio says 'As willingly as e'er I came from school' (line 140). Schools and schoolteachers often seem to receive a bad press from Shakespeare. For example:

> And then the whining schoolboy, with his satchel
> And shining morning face, creeping like snail
> Unwillingly to school.
> > (*As You Like It* 2.7.145–7)

> Love goes toward love, as schoolboys from their books,
> But love from love, toward school with heavy looks.
> > (*Romeo and Juliet* 2.2.157–8)

In *Antony and Cleopatra* Antony's schoolmaster is presented as a 'feeble' messenger. In *Love's Labours Lost* we meet the pompous Holofernes; and the 'exceedingly fantastical' Sir Hugh in *The Merry Wives of Windsor*.

Use the information in these references to write a short essay entitled: 'The problem with teachers – by William Shakespeare'.

7 Telling lies – is it always wrong?

A large number of lies are told in this play. Most of the characters lie at some point, some do so often.

> Bianca lies to Hortensio during her music lesson.
> Lucentio pretends to be Cambio, Hortensio pretends to be Litio.
> Tranio pretends to be Lucentio.
> Biondello lies when he tells Baptista about Petruchio's approach.
> Petruchio pretends that the wedding party threatens Katherina.

Talk together about whether you think any of the characters have good reasons for lying. When is it acceptable to lie?

8 'What a picture!' (in large groups)

Some time has passed and everyone, apart from Petruchio, Katherina and Grumio, has reached the wedding breakfast. Devise between six and ten 'still photographs' for the Minola family album. Make sure that future generations will be able to gain a fair idea of what the guests were thinking from these pictures. Accompany each one with a witty or pithy caption (perhaps a brief quotation from the play).

*Grumio arrives at Petruchio's house, cold and tired. He orders Curtis
to light a fire, threatening to complain to their new mistress. Curtis
asks for news.*

1 After the interval (in pairs)

Many productions place the interval between Acts 3 and 4, so that
Grumio's arrival opens the second half. How would you stage lines
1–8 to seize the audience's attention? Take it in turns to read the
lines. Devise actions and gestures, with one of you acting as director.

2 Chez Petruchio (in groups of three or four)

The scene has changed to Petruchio's house. Houses often suggest a
great deal about a person's character. Talk together about the sort of
house Petruchio might live in, its furnishings, pictures, decoration.
Then make a quick sketch as a starting point for a set design for a
theatre production.

3 Another servant (in pairs)

What is Curtis like? Read lines 1–30 aloud twice, swapping roles.
Talk together about what evidence there is in the passage for Curtis's
age, manner, relationship with Grumio and even sex (the part has
often been played by a woman). Decide on two clearly distinct
versions of the character, and read the lines through again developing
each in turn.

---

jades worn-out horses
rayed spattered with mud
a little . . . hot a small person with
 a short temper
taller bolder
run running start

thy horn . . . least my penis is as
 big as yours
hot office job of making fire
have thy duty earn your reward
as wilt thou as you could wish
cony-catching trickery

ACT 4   SCENE 1
Petruchio's country house

Enter GRUMIO

GRUMIO Fie, fie on all tired jades, on all mad masters, and all foul ways!
Was ever man so beaten? Was ever man so rayed? Was ever man
so weary? I am sent before to make a fire, and they are coming after
to warm them. Now were not I a little pot and soon hot, my very
lips might freeze to my teeth, my tongue to the roof of my mouth,   5
my heart in my belly, ere I should come by a fire to thaw me. But
I with blowing the fire shall warm myself, for, considering the
weather, a taller man than I will take cold. Holla, ho! Curtis!

Enter CURTIS.

CURTIS Who is that calls so coldly?

GRUMIO A piece of ice. If thou doubt it, thou mayst slide from my   10
shoulder to my heel with no greater a run but my head and my
neck. A fire, good Curtis.

CURTIS Is my master and his wife coming, Grumio?

GRUMIO O ay, Curtis, ay, and therefore fire, fire! Cast on no water.

CURTIS Is she so hot a shrew as she's reported?   15

GRUMIO She was, good Curtis, before this frost. But thou know'st
winter tames man, woman and beast; for it hath tamed my old
master, and my new mistress, and myself, fellow Curtis.

CURTIS Away, you three-inch fool, I am no beast!

GRUMIO Am I but three inches? Why, thy horn is a foot, and so long   20
am I at the least. But wilt thou make a fire, or shall I complain on
thee to our mistress, whose hand – she being now at hand – thou
shalt soon feel, to thy cold comfort, for being slow in thy hot office.

CURTIS I prithee, good Grumio, tell me, how goes the world?

GRUMIO A cold world, Curtis, in every office but thine, and therefore,   25
fire. Do thy duty, and have thy duty, for my master and mistress
are almost frozen to death.

CURTIS There's fire ready, and therefore, good Grumio, the news.

GRUMIO Why, 'Jack boy, ho boy!' and as much news as wilt thou.

CURTIS Come, you are so full of cony-catching.   30

Grumio checks on the state of the house and servants. Curtis is anxious to hear the news, and Grumio eventually tells the story of the disastrous journey from the wedding.

1 Telling the tale (in pairs)

Once again, Curtis asks Grumio for news (line 37). Grumio takes a long time to tell the story, and he certainly makes the most of it. Read lines 37–62. Then go through Grumio's lines reading out only the key words. There are a number of words over which he takes particular delight. Finally, talk together about how successful Grumio is as a story-teller, and about how funny he could be made to seem on stage.

2 Film it (in groups of four)

Grumio describes what happens during the journey in lines 53–62. You are making a film of the play, and have decided to develop a major scene out of these ten lines. With one of you acting as director, see how much fun you can get from Grumio's lines. You can add any amount of comic business, as long as the scene follows the outline given.

3 Petruchio (in groups of three)

'He is more shrew than she', comments Curtis. From what you've learned so far in the play, do you think this is a fair comment? Talk about what could be said for or against Curtis's view.

---

rushes strewed the floor prepared (with fresh reeds)
fustian coarse cloth, garments
officer servant
Jacks and Jills male and female servants, drinking cups

feel experience
sensible easily understood
Imprimis to begin
crossed interrupted
bemoiled covered with mud
crupper saddle-strap

GRUMIO Why, therefore fire, for I have caught extreme cold. Where's the cook? Is supper ready, the house trimmed, rushes strewed, cobwebs swept, the servingmen in their new fustian, their white stockings, and every officer his wedding garment on? Be the Jacks fair within, the Jills fair without, the carpets laid, and everything in order? 35

CURTIS All ready, and therefore, I pray thee, news.

GRUMIO First know my horse is tired, my master and mistress fallen out.

CURTIS How? 40

GRUMIO Out of their saddles into the dirt, and thereby hangs a tale.

CURTIS Let's ha't, good Grumio.

GRUMIO Lend thine ear.

CURTIS Here.

GRUMIO There. 45

[He boxes Curtis's ear.]

CURTIS This 'tis to feel a tale, not to hear a tale.

GRUMIO And therefore 'tis called a sensible tale; and this cuff was but to knock at your ear and beseech listening. Now I begin. *Imprimis* we came down a foul hill, my master riding behind my mistress.

CURTIS Both of one horse? 50

GRUMIO What's that to thee?

CURTIS Why, a horse.

GRUMIO Tell thou the tale. But hadst thou not crossed me, thou shouldst have heard how her horse fell, and she under her horse; thou shouldst have heard in how miry a place, how she was 55 bemoiled, how he left her with the horse upon her, how he beat me because her horse stumbled, how she waded through the dirt to pluck him off me, how he swore, how she prayed that never prayed before, how I cried, how the horses ran away, how her bridle was burst, how I lost my crupper – with many things of worthy 60 memory which now shall die in oblivion, and thou return unexperienced to thy grave.

CURTIS By this reckoning he is more shrew than she.

Grumio calls for the other servants to appear. He is anxious that their appearance and manners satisfy Petruchio. When Petruchio does arrive, he shouts at them angrily, accusing them of negligence.

'Four or five servingmen'. These 'spruce companions', Italian servants with very English names, have little to say, but certainly have much to do. Actors playing these parts would want to give each servant a distinctive identity to suggest a unique life history. Work in groups of five or six. Each person becomes one servant and introduces his or her character to the others in a few sentences.

1 Katherina's appearance (in pairs)

Kate's wedding outfit is likely to have been ruined during the course of the journey. Suggest possible changes which the wardrobe and make-up departments could make to her appearance.

blue the usual colour for servants
indifferent unobtrusive
left legs thought to be a more submissive way of kneeling
countenance pay your respects to

credit honour
spruce lively
Cock's God's
hold my stirrup help me dismount
logger-headed stupid

GRUMIO Ay, and that thou and the proudest of you all shall find when
  he comes home. But what talk I of this? Call forth Nathaniel,   65
  Joseph, Nicholas, Philip, Walter, Sugarsop and the rest. Let their
  heads be slickly combed, their blue coats brushed, and their garters
  of an indifferent knit. Let them curtsy with their left legs, and not
  presume to touch a hair of my master's horse-tail till they kiss their
  hands. Are they all ready?   70
CURTIS They are.
GRUMIO Call them forth.
CURTIS Do you hear, ho? You must meet my master to countenance
  my mistress.
GRUMIO Why, she hath a face of her own.   75
CURTIS Who knows not that?
GRUMIO Thou, it seems, that calls for company to countenance her.
CURTIS I call them forth to credit her.
GRUMIO Why, she comes to borrow nothing of them.

Enter four or five SERVINGMEN.

NATHANIEL Welcome home, Grumio.   80
PHILIP How now, Grumio.
JOSEPH What, Grumio.
NICHOLAS Fellow Grumio.
NATHANIEL How now, old lad.
GRUMIO Welcome you; how now you; what you; fellow you; and thus   85
  much for greeting. Now, my spruce companions, is all ready, and
  all things neat?
NATHANIEL All things is ready. How near is our master?
GRUMIO E'en at hand, alighted by this. And therefore be not – Cock's
  passion, silence! I hear my master.   90

Enter PETRUCHIO *and* KATHERINA.

PETRUCHIO Where be these knaves? What, no man at door
  To hold my stirrup, nor to take my horse?
  Where is Nathaniel, Gregory, Philip?
ALL SERVINGMEN Here! Here sir, here sir!
PETRUCHIO 'Here sir, here sir, here sir, here sir'!   95
  You logger-headed and unpolished grooms!
  What, no attendance? No regard? No duty?
  Where is the foolish knave I sent before?

113

Petruchio accuses Grumio of failing to organise the servants. Grumio apologises for their poor state and appearance. Petruchio demands food, strikes the servants and accuses everyone of incompetence.

1 Petruchio's performance (whole class)

Stand in a circle and read aloud lines 100–26 together. Now go round the circle, each person taking a phrase, sharing the words out as they are divided up by the punctuation. Remember which phrase was yours, and move round the room repeating it until you can remember it without having to look at the page. To help you remember, greet other students with your phrase.

After two minutes, the whole group stands still and speaks the lines in order.

Next form yourself into five groups according to your phrase:

a the orders to servants
b the orders to Kate
c the insults
d the questions
e the snatches of song.

Of course, you are likely to belong to several different groups. Every time you form a new group, loudly call out your phrase.

Finally, talk together about what you have learned about Petruchio's state of mind at this point.

2 Silent Kate (in small groups)

Katherina has said nothing since her entry, in spite of the fact that she is spoken to frequently by her husband. Talk together about possible reasons for this. What is she thinking?

---

whoreson bastard, illegitimate child
malthorse drudge slow, heavy horse
all unpinked lacking proper decoration

link blacking
sheathing being fitted with a scabbard
orders grey in a grey robe
mend make a better job of

GRUMIO Here sir, as foolish as I was before.

PETRUCHIO You peasant swain! You whoreson malthorse drudge!   100
        Did I not bid thee meet me in the park
        And bring along these rascal knaves with thee?

GRUMIO Nathaniel's coat, sir, was not fully made,
        And Gabriel's pumps were all unpinked i'th'heel.
        There was no link to colour Peter's hat   105
        And Walter's dagger was not come from sheathing.
        There were none fine but Adam, Rafe and Gregory;
        The rest were ragged, old and beggarly.
        Yet, as they are, here are they come to meet you.

PETRUCHIO Go, rascals, go, and fetch my supper in.   110

                                        Exeunt Servingmen

        [*Sings*] Where is the life that late I led?
                Where are those –
        Sit down, Kate, and welcome. Food, food, food, food!

                Enter Servants with supper.

        Why, when, I say? Nay, good sweet Kate, be merry.
        Off with my boots, you rogues, you villains! When?   115
        [*Sings*] It was the friar of orders grey
                As he forth walkèd on his way –
        Out, you rogue! You pluck my foot awry.
        Take that!
                        [*He strikes the Servant.*]
                And mend the plucking off the other.
        Be merry, Kate. Some water here! What ho!   120

                Enter one with water.

        Where's my spaniel Troilus? Sirrah, get you hence
        And bid my cousin Ferdinand come hither –
                                        [*Exit a Servant*]
        One, Kate, that you must kiss and be acquainted with.
        Where are my slippers? Shall I have some water?
        Come, Kate, and wash, and welcome heartily.   125
        You whoreson villain! Will you let it fall?
                        [*He strikes the Servant.*]

Katherina unsuccessfully tries to calm Petruchio. He invites her to eat, but finds fault with the food and throws it at the servants. He tells her they will fast instead and takes her off to the bridal chamber.

1 Kate's speeches (in pairs)

One person reads Kate's lines (lines 127 and 139–40) in an aggressive and 'shrewish' manner. The other reads them in a completely different tone. Discuss which styles of speaking are available to Kate here. How would you advise her to speak them?

2 Insults (in pairs)

Find all the insulting words and phrases used on the opposite page. Go back to the beginning of the act and add others to your list. Choose your favourite and practise hurling the insults at each other. Talk together about whether you think Petruchio intends them seriously of not.

3 'He kills her in her own humour' (in small groups)

First discuss what you think this line means. Then develop a tableau which you feel expresses its meaning for you.

Think up a different caption which would also suit your tableau. Share your ideas with the rest of the class.

---

unwilling not deliberate
stomach appetite
give thanks say grace before the meal
trenchers wooden plates
heedless joltheads careless fools
I'll . . . straight I'll be after you

disquiet upset
if you . . . contented if only you were in a better humour
choler anger
mended put right
for company together

KATHERINA Patience, I pray you. 'Twas a fault unwilling.
PETRUCHIO A whoreson, beetle-headed, flap-eared knave!
        Come, Kate, sit down, I know you have a stomach.
        Will you give thanks, sweet Kate, or else shall I?   130
        What's this? Mutton?
FIRST SERVINGMAN   Ay.
PETRUCHIO   Who brought it?
PETER   I.
PETRUCHIO 'Tis burnt, and so is all the meat.
        What dogs are these! Where is the rascal cook?
        How durst you villains bring it from the dresser
        And serve it thus to me that love it not?   135
        There, take it to you, trenchers, cups and all!
        [*He throws the food and dishes at them.*]
        You heedless joltheads and unmannered slaves!
        What, do you grumble? I'll be with you straight.
                         [*Exeunt Servants*]
KATHERINA I pray you, husband, be not so disquiet.
        The meat was well, if you were so contented.   140
PETRUCHIO I tell thee, Kate, 'twas burnt and dried away,
        And I expressly am forbid to touch it,
        For it engenders choler, planteth anger;
        And better 'twere that both of us did fast,
        Since, of ourselves, ourselves are choleric,   145
        Than feed it with such over-roasted flesh.
        Be patient. Tomorrow't shall be mended,
        And for this night we'll fast for company.
        Come, I will bring thee to thy bridal chamber.
                            Exeunt

Enter Servants severally.

NATHANIEL Peter, didst ever see the like?   150
PETER He kills her in her own humour.

Grumio and Curtis talk about Katherina's confused state of mind.
Petruchio tells the audience about his plan to tame Katherina by depriving
her of food and sleep.

1 'Pour soul' (in pairs)

Do you think that Curtis's sympathy for Katherina is justified? Talk together about your own feelings for Katherina at this point.

2 Challenge: taming Kate (in small groups)

In the last two lines, Petruchio challenges anyone in the audience to come up with a better idea to tame a shrew. Reply to him with ideas of your own.

3 Challenge: taming Petruchio (in small groups)

Does Petruchio need a taste of his own medicine? How should *he* be tamed? Write your own prescription.

In the 1982 Royal Shakespeare Company production, a live falcon was brought on stage at this point in the play. Argue together about how it could highlight Petruchio's speech – or how it might prove distracting.

continency self-control	**haggard** wild hawk
rates scolds	**watch her** keep her awake
politicly with a calculated plan	**bate and beat** flap and flutter their
sharp hungry	wings
passing extremely	**intend** pretend
stoop obeys me, flies to the lure	**charity** public spirited
full-gorged fully fed	

Enter Curtis.

GRUMIO Where is he?
CURTIS In her chamber,
    Making a sermon of continency to her,
    And rails and swears and rates, that she, poor soul,   155
    Knows not which way to stand, to look, to speak,
    And sits as one new-risen from a dream.
    Away, away, for he is coming hither.

                                       [Exeunt]

Enter Petruchio.

PETRUCHIO Thus have I politicly begun my reign,
    And 'tis my hope to end successfully.   160
    My falcon now is sharp and passing empty,
    And till she stoop she must not be full-gorged,
    For then she never looks upon her lure.
    Another way I have to man my haggard,
    To make her come and know her keeper's call,   165
    That is, to watch her, as we watch these kites
    That bate and beat and will not be obedient.
    She ate no meat today, nor none shall eat;
    Last night she slept not, nor tonight she shall not.
    As with the meat, some undeservèd fault   170
    I'll find about the making of the bed,
    And here I'll fling the pillow, there the bolster,
    This way the coverlet, another way the sheets.
    Ay, and amid this hurly I intend
    That all is done in reverend care of her.   175
    And, in conclusion, she shall watch all night,
    And if she chance to nod I'll rail and brawl
    And with the clamour keep her still awake.
    This is a way to kill a wife with kindness,
    And thus I'll curb her mad and headstrong humour.   180
    He that knows better how to tame a shrew,
    Now let him speak – 'tis charity to show.   *Exit*

Tranio and Hortensio are watching Bianca and Lucentio. Hortensio throws off his disguise in disgust. Tranio suggests that this is the moment that they should both give up Bianca.

---

1 Stage direction: *They court* (in pairs)

Suggest what Lucentio and Bianca might be doing which so outrages Hortensio at this point.

2 Disguises (in groups of four)

Three people on stage are disguised, but only one (Hortensio) reveals his true identity (lines 16–21). Improvise a brief scene in which all three characters reveal their true identity. Make sure each revelation is made in a way which suits the character.

The fourth member of the group should respond to each in the role of Bianca.

3 Irony (in pairs)

'I tell thee, Litio, this is wonderful.'
Tranio's words in line 15 can mean different things to different people.
Talk about what is understood:

a by Hortensio
b by Tranio himself
c by you as a member of the audience.

---

she bears . . . hand she is
  deceiving me beautifully
satisfy convince
resolve answer
profess practise
Quick proceeders apt students

marry by St Mary
wonderful amazing
cullion low-class person
lightness fickleness
Forswear give up, renounce

ACT 4   SCENE 2
Outside Baptista's house

Enter TRANIO [*disguised as Lucentio*] *and* HORTENSIO [*disguised as Litio*]

TRANIO Is't possible, friend Litio, that mistress Bianca
    Doth fancy any other but Lucentio?
    I tell you, sir, she bears me fair in hand.
HORTENSIO Sir, to satisfy you in what I have said,
    Stand by, and mark the manner of his teaching.   5
                [They stand aside.]

Enter BIANCA [*and* LUCENTIO *disguised as Cambio*].

LUCENTIO Now, mistress, profit you in what you read?
BIANCA What, master, read you? First resolve me that.
LUCENTIO I read that I profess, *The Art to Love.*
BIANCA And may you prove, sir, master of your art.
LUCENTIO While you, sweet dear, prove mistress of my heart.   10
                [They court.]
HORTENSIO Quick proceeders, marry! Now tell me, I pray,
    You that durst swear that your mistress Bianca
    Loved none in the world so well as Lucentio.
TRANIO O despiteful love, unconstant womankind!
    I tell thee, Litio, this is wonderful.   15
HORTENSIO Mistake no more – I am not Litio,
    Nor a musician as I seem to be,
    But one that scorn to live in this disguise
    For such a one as leaves a gentleman
    And makes a god of such a cullion.   20
    Know, sir, that I am called Hortensio.
TRANIO Signor Hortensio, I have often heard
    Of your entire affection to Bianca,
    And since mine eyes are witness of her lightness,
    I will with you, if you be so contented,   25
    Forswear Bianca and her love for ever.

Hortensio vows to reject Bianca in favour of a wealthy widow, whom he says he intends to marry in three days' time. Tranio, Lucentio and Bianca are delighted.

1 Unworthy of Hortensio (in pairs)

One person reads Hortensio's lines aloud while the other echoes the key words. Talk together about what it reveals about Hortensio's attitude to Bianca.

2 The taming-school

Tranio says that Hortensio has gone to 'the taming-school'. Bianca asks whether such a place exists, but Tranio's answer is short on detail. See if you can help him out from your experience of the previous scene and this nineteenth-century painting by Sir John Gilbert.

fondly foolishly	**in resolution** determined
unfeignèd sincere	**'longeth** belongs
beastly like an animal	**tane you napping** caught you
haggard wild hawk	unawares
Kindness constant affection	**tricks eleven . . . long** tricks of
	exactly the right kind

HORTENSIO See how they kiss and court! Signor Lucentio,
   Here is my hand, and here I firmly vow
   Never to woo her more, but do forswear her
   As one unworthy all the former favours   30
   That I have fondly flattered her withal.
TRANIO And here I take the like unfeignèd oath
   Never to marry with her though she would entreat.
   Fie on her! See how beastly she doth court him.
HORTENSIO Would all the world but he had quite forsworn! 35
   For me, that I may surely keep mine oath,
   I will be married to a wealthy widow
   Ere three days pass, which hath as long loved me
   As I have loved this proud disdainful haggard.
   And so farewell, Signor Lucentio.   40
   Kindness in women, not their beauteous looks,
   Shall win my love; and so I take my leave,
   In resolution as I swore before.   [Exit]
    [Tranio joins Lucentio and Bianca.]
TRANIO Mistress Bianca, bless you with such grace
   As 'longeth to a lover's blessèd case!
   Nay, I have tane you napping, gentle love, 45
   And have forsworn you with Hortensio.
BIANCA Tranio, you jest – but have you both forsworn me?
TRANIO Mistress, we have.
LUCENTIO   Then we are rid of Litio.
TRANIO I'faith, he'll have a lusty widow now   50
   That shall be wooed and wedded in a day.
BIANCA God give him joy!
TRANIO Ay, and he'll tame her.
BIANCA   He says so, Tranio?
TRANIO Faith, he is gone unto the taming-school.
BIANCA The taming-school? What, is there such a place? 55
TRANIO Ay, mistress, and Petruchio is the master,
   That teacheth tricks eleven and twenty long
   To tame a shrew and charm her chattering tongue.

Biondello has found someone who will serve as Lucentio's father. Tranio scares the Merchant into the role by inventing a tale that anyone from Mantua found in Padua will be executed because of a political quarrel.

This map of Italy shows all the places mentioned in the play. Make a copy, and enter on it where the characters have come from, where they are going, and other information from the play. Make your map tell as much of the story of the play as possible.

ancient angel old man, the answer
  to my prayer
serve the turn will do for our
  purposes
marcantant merchant
trust believe

let me alone rely on me
farre farther
goes hard is a serious matter
stayed detained
'Tis marvel it's strange

Enter BIONDELLO.

BIONDELLO O master, master, I have watched so long
    That I am dog-weary, but at last I spied   60
    An ancient angel coming down the hill
    Will serve the turn.
TRANIO   What is he, Biondello?
BIONDELLO Master, a marcantant, or a pedant,
    I know not what, but formal in apparel,
    In gait and countenance surely like a father.   65
LUCENTIO And what of him, Tranio?
TRANIO If he be credulous and trust my tale,
    I'll make him glad to seem Vincentio
    And give assurance to Baptista Minola
    As if he were the right Vincentio.   70
    Take in your love, and then let me alone.
           [*Exeunt Lucentio and Bianca*]

Enter a MERCHANT.

MERCHANT God save you, sir.
TRANIO   And you, sir. You are welcome.
    Travel you farre on or are you at the farthest?
MERCHANT Sir, at the farthest for a week or two,
    But then up farther, and as far as Rome,   75
    And so to Tripoli, if God lend me life.
TRANIO What countryman, I pray?
MERCHANT   Of Mantua.
TRANIO Of Mantua, sir? Marry, God forbid!
    And come to Padua careless of your life?
MERCHANT My life, sir? How, I pray? For that goes hard.   80
TRANIO 'Tis death for anyone in Mantua
    To come to Padua. Know you not the cause?
    Your ships are stayed at Venice, and the Duke,
    For private quarrel 'twixt your Duke and him,
    Hath published and proclaimed it openly.   85
    'Tis marvel – but that you are but newly come,
    You might have heard it else proclaimed about.
MERCHANT Alas, sir, it is worse for me than so.
    For I have bills for money by exchange
    From Florence, and must here deliver them.   90

Tranio claims that the wealthy Vincentio is his father. The Merchant believes him and agrees to impersonate Vincentio to avoid arrest. Tranio mentions that his father is coming to Padua to complete the marriage arrangements.

1 Biondello's catch-phrase (in pairs)

'As much as an apple doth an oyster' is a striking phrase which forcefully expresses Biondello's opinion of Tranio's lie. Suggest modern versions of what he might have said.

2 Tranio's con trick (in pairs)

Tranio is totally in charge of the situation as he develops his plot. Imagine that the Merchant is not conned so easily. Improvise his questions and Tranio's replies.

3 Further disguises (in small groups)

Now someone else is to put on a disguise – the Merchant 'becomes' Vincentio. The play may be becoming a bit confusing! Make sure that everyone knows what's going on: work out which characters are in disguise, who they are pretending to be, and why. Present your findings as a diagram, ensuring that you haven't left anybody out!

Finally, identify which characters know the most about what is going on, and which are the most in the dark.

4 'Clothe you as becomes you'

Clothing is very important in this play, especially clothes which turn a character into someone else. Make some notes or draw a simple sketch to show the Merchant 'before' and 'after' he disguises himself as Vincentio. Use the library to research details about costumes of the time.

---

all one just the same
credit status
undertake assume
take upon you play your role

repute you think of you
make the . . . good carry out the
  plan
looked for expected
pass assurance make a settlement

TRANIO Well, sir, to do you courtesy,
          This will I do, and this I will advise you –
          First tell me, have you ever been at Pisa?
MERCHANT Ay, sir, in Pisa have I often been,
          Pisa renownèd for grave citizens.   95
TRANIO Among them know you one Vincentio?
MERCHANT I know him not, but I have heard of him,
          A merchant of incomparable wealth.
TRANIO He is my father, sir, and sooth to say,
          In count'nance somewhat doth resemble you.   100
BIONDELLO [*Aside*] As much as an apple doth an oyster, and all one!
TRANIO To save your life in this extremity,
          This favour will I do you for his sake –
          And think it not the worst of all your fortunes
          That you are like to Sir Vincentio –   105
          His name and credit shall you undertake,
          And in my house you shall be friendly lodged.
          Look that you take upon you as you should –
          You understand me, sir? So shall you stay
          Till you have done your business in the city.   110
          If this be court'sy, sir, accept of it.
MERCHANT O sir, I do, and will repute you ever
          The patron of my life and liberty.
TRANIO Then go with me to make the matter good.
          This, by the way, I let you understand: 115
          My father is here looked for every day
          To pass assurance of a dower in marriage
          'Twixt me and one Baptista's daughter here.
          In all these circumstances I'll instruct you.
          Go with me to clothe you as becomes you.   120
                                              Exeunt

Katherina, starving and exhausted, pleads with Grumio to fetch her some food. Grumio teases her, offering tempting delicacies and then finding reasons to deny her.

---

1 Katherina's state (in pairs)

One person reads Katherina's speech (lines 2–16) aloud. The other makes suitable gestures or acts out simple mimes every time her physical state is mentioned.

2 Poor little rich girl (in pairs)

Katherina comes from a wealthy home, and, as she says 'never knew how to entreat,/Nor never needed that I should entreat'. Now she does need to beg. Read lines 15–30, and then talk together about how skilled she is at begging from Grumio. Suggest other ways in which she could have tried to win his support.

3 Master and servant (in groups of three)

First, talk together about Grumio's tactics and how closely they parallel Petruchio's earlier in the scene. Imagine what Petruchio might have thought if he had been listening to lines 17–30. Improvise a soliloquy in which Petruchio comments on what he has just seen and heard.

4 Violent Kate (in groups of three)

The stage direction 'beats him' suggests Katherina becomes very angry, but how violent is she? Rehearse this little episode with the third member of the group acting as director/referee. Experiment with different degrees of theatrical violence, and talk together about the effect you would wish different styles to have upon the audience. Remember the golden rule of all stage violence: no one gets hurt!

The more my wrong the more
  wrong done to me
famish starve
upon entreaty when they ask
present alms immediate help

meat food
spites irritates
neat calf or ox
passing extremely
choleric anger-provoking

ACT 4   SCENE 3
Petruchio's house

Enter KATHERINA *and* GRUMIO

GRUMIO No, no, forsooth, I dare not for my life!
KATHERINA The more my wrong, the more his spite appears.
 What, did he marry me to famish me?
 Beggars that come unto my father's door
 Upon entreaty have a present alms;   5
 If not, elsewhere they meet with charity.
 But I, who never knew how to entreat,
 Nor never needed that I should entreat,
 Am starved for meat, giddy for lack of sleep,
 With oaths kept waking, and with brawling fed.   10
 And that which spites me more than all these wants,
 He does it under name of perfect love,
 As who should say, if I should sleep or eat
 'Twere deadly sickness or else present death.
 I prithee go and get me some repast –   15
 I care not what, so it be wholesome food.
GRUMIO What say you to a neat's foot?
KATHERINA 'Tis passing good. I prithee let me have it.
GRUMIO I fear it is too choleric a meat.
 How say you to a fat tripe finely broiled?   20
KATHERINA I like it well. Good Grumio, fetch it me.
GRUMIO I cannot tell, I fear 'tis choleric.
 What say you to a piece of beef and mustard?
KATHERINA A dish that I do love to feed upon.
GRUMIO Ay, but the mustard is too hot a little.   25
KATHERINA Why then, the beef, and let the mustard rest.
GRUMIO Nay then, I will not. You shall have the mustard,
 Or else you get no beef of Grumio.
KATHERINA Then both, or one, or anything thou wilt.
GRUMIO Why then, the mustard without the beef.   30
KATHERINA Go, get thee gone, thou false deluding slave
     Beats him.
 That feed'st me with the very name of meat.

Petruchio and Hortensio arrive with food for Katherina. They sit down to dine, but Hortensio has strict orders to eat all the food. Petruchio talks about fine clothes, and a tailor is announced.

1 Thanks (in pairs)

Discover as many different ways as possible for Kate to deliver line 47: 'I thank you, sir'. Compare the two versions you find most effective with those of another pair.

2 Hortensio's attitude (in groups of four)

In the previous scene, Tranio said that Hortensio was eager to enrol at Petruchio's 'taming-school'. But what kind of pupil is he? Look carefully at his behaviour in lines 36–51 for evidence of his attitude towards Katherina. Talk together about what you think of Hortensio.

3 Eating and talking (in groups of three)

After Petruchio has told Hortensio to eat all the food, he talks to Katherina at some length, describing a long list of fashion accessories. What is happening at the table during this speech? One person reads lines 51–8, while the other two mime a scene between Hortensio and Katherina.

4 Silent Kate (in pairs)

Once again, Katherina is silent during a long stretch of Petruchio's outrageous behaviour. One person reads Petruchio's lines 50–60 in as provocative a way as possible, pausing at the end of each line. The other, as Katherina, provides appropriate interjections in each pause.

---

amort depressed
what cheer? how are you?
all my . . . proof all my labour has
  been in vain
apace quickly
bravely spendidly dressed

farthingales hooped skirts
brav'ry finery
knav'ry nonsense
stays awaits
ruffling ornate

Sorrow on thee and all the pack of you
That triumph thus upon my misery!
Go, get thee gone, I say.   35

Enter PETRUCHIO *and* HORTENSIO *with meat.*

PETRUCHIO How fares my Kate? What, sweeting, all amort?
HORTENSIO Mistress, what cheer?
KATHERINA   Faith, as cold as can be.
PETRUCHIO Pluck up thy spirits; look cheerfully upon me.
    Here, love, thou seest how diligent I am
    To dress thy meat myself, and bring it thee.   40
    I am sure, sweet Kate, this kindness merits thanks.
    What, not a word? Nay then, thou lov'st it not,
    And all my pains is sorted to no proof.
    Here, take away this dish.
KATHERINA   I pray you, let it stand.
PETRUCHIO The poorest service is repaid with thanks,   45
    And so shall mine before you touch the meat.
KATHERINA I thank you, sir.
HORTENSIO Signor Petruchio, fie, you are to blame.
    Come, Mistress Kate, I'll bear you company.
PETRUCHIO [*Aside*] Eat it up all, Hortensio, if thou lov'st me –   50
    [*To Katherina*] Much good do it unto thy gentle heart.
    Kate, eat apace. And now, my honey love,
    Will we return unto thy father's house
    And revel it as bravely as the best,
    With silken coats and caps, and golden rings,   55
    With ruffs and cuffs and farthingales and things,
    With scarves and fans and double change of brav'ry,
    With amber bracelets, beads and all this knav'ry.
    What, hast thou dined? The tailor stays thy leisure,
    To deck thy body with his ruffling treasure.   60

Enter TAILOR.

Come, tailor, let us see these ornaments.
Lay forth the gown.

A haberdasher brings in a hat, but Petruchio dismisses it in spite of Katherina's protests that she likes it. The gown brought on by the tailor is also rejected by Petruchio.

1 Threat? (in groups of four)

Divide into two pairs. One pair presents lines 71–2 in a way which might raise a laugh. The other plays them with heavy, serious emphasis and significance. Decide which is the more effective, or think of another way to play them.

2 How can you make men listen? (in pairs)

In her long-awaited response (lines 73–80) Katherina states her right to be angry, and to express her anger in words. It is an inspired speech. She speaks not only for herself, but for all women in every century, in a passionate plea for the female voice to be heard. But will men listen?

- Work out a presentation of the speech as a radio broadcast. The words are all the audience has to go on, no pictures, no faces. Your task is to present the speech in a way to make men really hear what is being said.
- Collect images from newspapers and magazines to illustrate Katherina's impassioned plea.

3 But Petruchio is deaf (in groups of four)

In lines 81–3, Petruchio once again denies, ignores or twists what Katherina is saying. He has already used this technique, designed to cause maximum frustration, at their first meeting. Is this typical male behaviour? Talk together about whether Petruchio's technique is successful here, and whether you think it is commonly used by men towards women.

---

bespeak order
porringer small basin
cockle cockle shell
knack knick-knack, trifle
toy something of no value
trick joke

doth fit the time is the fashion
custard-coffin pastry case for custard
masking stuff extravagant clothes for the stage
demi-cannon large gun
censer incense burner

Enter HABERDASHER.

What news with you, sir?
HABERDASHER Here is the cap your worship did bespeak.
PETRUCHIO Why, this was moulded on a porringer –
          A velvet dish! Fie, fie, 'tis lewd and filthy.   65
          Why, 'tis a cockle or a walnut-shell,
          A knack, a toy, a trick, a baby's cap.
          Away with it! Come, let me have a bigger.
KATHERINA I'll have no bigger. This doth fit the time,
          And gentlewomen wear such caps as these.   70
PETRUCHIO When you are gentle you shall have one too,
          And not till then.
HORTENSIO [*Aside*]   That will not be in haste.
KATHERINA Why, sir, I trust I may have leave to speak,
          And speak I will. I am no child, no babe.
          Your betters have endured me say my mind,   75
          And if you cannot, best you stop your ears.
          My tongue will tell the anger of my heart,
          Or else my heart concealing it will break,
          And, rather than it shall, I will be free
          Even to the uttermost, as I please, in words.   80
PETRUCHIO Why, thou say'st true – it is a paltry cap.
          A custard-coffin, a bauble, a silken pie!
          I love thee well in that thou lik'st it not.
KATHERINA Love me or love me not, I like the cap,
          And it I will have, or I will have none.   85
PETRUCHIO Thy gown? Why, ay. Come, tailor, let us see't.
                                             [*Exit Haberdasher*]
          O mercy God! What masking stuff is here?
          What's this – a sleeve? 'Tis like a demi-cannon.
          What, up and down carved like an apple-tart?
          Here's snip and nip and cut and slish and slash,   90
          Like to a censer in a barber's shop.
          Why, what a devil's name, tailor, call'st thou this?
HORTENSIO [*Aside*] I see she's like to have neither cap nor gown.
TAILOR You bid me make it orderly and well,
          According to the fashion and the time.   95

Petruchio and Katherina disagree about the gown, and Petruchio turns on the tailor with a string of insults. Grumio quarrels with the tailor over the order for the gown.

---

1 Puppet on a string (in groups of three)

Read lines 103–5 aloud several times in as many different ways as you can. Then talk together about the effect of these three lines when they are spoken in rapid succession. How would the audience react to the three characters at this point?

2 More insults (in pairs)

Insult each other with lines 106–10 by speaking alternate phrases to each other. Then make up similar lists of 'job-related insults' in the same style.

3 Silent Kate (in pairs)

Once more Katherina says very little. Work together on advice a director could give to the actress about her behaviour throughout the dialogue in the script opposite.

---

mar it . . . time ruin it by following the fashion
kennel gutter
quaint ingeniously designed
nail a measure for cloth (5.7 cm/ 2.25in)
braved defied

quantity scrap
bemete measure, but also beat
as thou . . . liv'st that you'll think twice before telling such lies
stuff material
faced/braved trimmed/provided with finery

PETRUCHIO Marry, and did. But if you be remembered,
    I did not bid you mar it to the time.
    Go, hop me over every kennel home,
    For you shall hop without my custom, sir.
    I'll none of it. Hence, make your best of it.   100
KATHERINA I never saw a better-fashioned gown,
    More quaint, more pleasing, nor more commendable.
    Belike you mean to make a puppet of me.
PETRUCHIO Why, true, he means to make a puppet of thee.
TAILOR She says your worship means to make a puppet of her.   105
PETRUCHIO O monstrous arrogance! Thou liest, thou thread, thou
    thimble,
    Thou yard, three-quarters, half-yard, quarter, nail!
    Thou flea, thou nit, thou winter-cricket thou!
    Braved in mine own house with a skein of thread?
    Away, thou rag, thou quantity, thou remnant!   110
    Or I shall so bemete thee with thy yard
    As thou shalt think on prating whilst thou liv'st.
    I tell thee, I, that thou hast marred her gown.
TAILOR Your worship is deceived. The gown is made
    Just as my master had direction.   115
    Grumio gave order how it should be done.
GRUMIO I gave him no order; I gave him the stuff.
TAILOR But how did you desire it should be made?
GRUMIO Marry, sir, with needle and thread.
TAILOR But did you not request to have it cut?   120
GRUMIO Thou hast faced many things.
TAILOR I have.
GRUMIO Face not me. Thou hast braved many men; brave not me. I
    will neither be faced nor braved. I say unto thee, I bid thy master
    cut out the gown, but I did not bid him cut it to pieces. *Ergo*, thou   125
    liest.
TAILOR Why, here is the note of the fashion to testify.
PETRUCHIO Read it.
GRUMIO The note lies in's throat if he say I said so.

Grumio and the Tailor continue to argue about the details of the order. The gown is rejected by Petruchio. He secretly asks Hortensio to pay the Tailor later.

1 Design the dress

Read through the script opposite up to line 149, noting all the details given about the design of the dress. Find other details given earlier in the scene. Design the dress, bearing in mind material, colour and particular features.

2 'What's your conceit in that?' (in groups of six)

Much of what Grumio says is again deliberate misunderstanding, usually to make a dirty joke. Four of you read through the opposite page. The remaining two interrupt each time they think there is a dirty joke or a sexual reference intended. You could take on the role of someone disgusted at the 'smut', and protest vigorously. Or you could be somebody really keen to find as many rude innuendoes as possible. Afterwards, talk together about how funny you could make this episode on stage.

3 'Take no unkindness . . .' (in pairs)

Hortensio seems to be part of Petruchio's plan here, apologising to the Tailor (lines 160–2). How happy do you think the Tailor would be, and just what does Hortensio tell him? Improvise the dialogue between them, with the Tailor still smarting at his treatment, and Hortensio faced with the problem of deciding how much to explain.

Imprimis first
loose-bodied loose-fitting
(Grumio takes it to mean suitable for a loose woman)
bottom spool
compassed cut in a circle
trunk full

curiously carefully, elaborately
prove upon thee prove by fighting you
unto thy . . . use for your master to do what he can
conceit implication

TAILOR [*Reads*] '*Imprimis*, a loose-bodied gown –'   130
GRUMIO Master, if ever I said 'loose-bodied gown', sew me in the skirts
    of it and beat me to death with a bottom of brown thread. I said
    'a gown'.
PETRUCHIO Proceed.
TAILOR 'With a small compassed cape.'   135
GRUMIO I confess the cape.
TAILOR 'With a trunk sleeve.'
GRUMIO I confess two sleeves.
TAILOR 'The sleeves curiously cut.'
PETRUCHIO Ay, there's the villainy.   140
GRUMIO Error i'th'bill, sir, error i'th'bill! I commanded the sleeves
    should be cut out and sewed up again – and that I'll prove upon
    thee, though thy little finger be armed in a thimble.
TAILOR This is true that I say, and I had thee in place where thou
    should'st know it.   145
GRUMIO I am for thee straight. Take thou the bill, give me thy mete-yard
    and spare not me.
HORTENSIO God-a-mercy, Grumio, then he shall have no odds.
PETRUCHIO Well, sir, in brief, the gown is not for me.
GRUMIO You are i'th'right sir, 'tis for my mistress.   150
PETRUCHIO Go, take it up unto thy master's use.
GRUMIO Villain, not for thy life! Take up my mistress' gown for thy
    master's use?
PETRUCHIO Why, sir, what's your conceit in that?
GRUMIO O sir, the conceit is deeper than you think for.   155
    Take up my mistress' gown to his master's use?
    O fie, fie, fie!
PETRUCHIO [*Aside*] Hortensio, say thou wilt see the tailor paid.
    [*To Tailor*] Go, take it hence; be gone and say no more.
HORTENSIO [*Aside*] Tailor, I'll pay thee for thy gown tomorrow,   160
    Take no unkindness of his hasty words.
    Away I say, commend me to thy master.
                         Exit Tailor

Petruchio lectures Katherina on the unimportance of clothes. He tells her they are about to leave for Baptista's, making a deliberate mistake about the time of day. Katherina corrects him and the trip is cancelled.

1 What's the lesson? (in groups of three)

Read lines 163–74 aloud. Each person reads two lines, then hands on to the next. Repeat the exercise several times to become familiar with the verse style. Then talk together about Petruchio's moral lesson. Do you think he really means it, or is he being ironic?

Work together on a short reply from Katherina using the same moralising style of couplets (two line units).

2 Hortensio's comment (in pairs)

What advice would you give to the actor playing Hortensio about how to say line 190? You will need to consider carefully how Hortensio feels about what has gone on in this scene.

One point to consider – could Hortensio have said the line to one of the characters, rather than to the audience?

3 Shrews

Read this scientific description of the shrew:

'Shrews are very active, solitary, surface-dwellers. They are very voracious and suffer from lack of food within a few hours . . . Shrews are preyed upon extensively by birds, but much less so by mammalian carnivores . . . Dispersion is maintained by aggressive behaviour at all times, except during the brief period of oestrus and copulation. The fighting is stereotyped and involves great use of the voice, resulting in "squeaking matches".'

(Corbet, *The Terrestrial Mammals of Western Europe*)

Do you think Katherina is anything like this description? Think about the whole of this scene and earlier scenes.

---

mean habiliments poor clothes
peereth peeps through
habit outfit
painted colourful
furniture dress
lay it on blame

frolic be happy
dinner-time about midday
supper-time about 7.00 p.m.
Look what whatever
crossing opposing

PETRUCHIO Well, come, my Kate, we will unto your father's
    Even in these honest mean habiliments.
    Our purses shall be proud, our garments poor,   165
    For 'tis the mind that makes the body rich,
    And as the sun breaks through the darkest clouds,
    So honour peereth in the meanest habit.
    What, is the jay more precious than the lark
    Because his feathers are more beautiful?   170
    Or is the adder better than the eel
    Because his painted skin contents the eye?
    O no, good Kate; neither art thou the worse
    For this poor furniture and mean array.
    If thou account'st it shame, lay it on me,   175
    And therefore frolic! We will hence forthwith
    To feast and sport us at thy father's house.
    [*To Grumio*] Go call my men, and let us straight to him,
    And bring our horses unto Long-lane end,
    There will we mount, and thither walk on foot.   180
    Let's see, I think 'tis now some seven o'clock,
    And well we may come there by dinner-time.
KATHERINA I dare assure you, sir, 'tis almost two,
    And 'twill be supper-time ere you come there.
PETRUCHIO It shall be seven ere I go to horse.   185
    Look what I speak, or do, or think to do,
    You are still crossing it. Sirs, let't alone.
    I will not go today, and, ere I do,
    It shall be what o'clock I say it is.
HORTENSIO [*Aside*] Why so this gallant will command the sun.   190
                 [*Exeunt*]

Tranio completes the preparations to turn the Merchant into Vincentio. Biondello confirms that he will play his part in the deception. Tranio introduces his 'father' to Baptista.

1 Nostalgia (in small groups)

Obviously well trained, the Merchant is running through his lines as Vincentio. Baptista and the supposed Vincentio were 'twenty years ago in Genoa/Where we were lodgers at the Pegasus'. Invent some of the experiences they might have had together as young men in Genoa. Might they have been similar to those of the young people in the play?

To help you, find a copy of *The Second Part of King Henry IV* and look at Act 3, Scene 2, where old men reminisce about the wild times they had in their youth.

2 'Set your countenance' (in pairs)

Tranio warns the Merchant to put on the right expression as Baptista approaches. Imagine the Merchant has a panic attack just at this moment. Improvise a brief scene in which Tranio calms him down and gives him advice.

---

hold your own keep up your disguise
schooled instructed
looked for expected
tall capable

hold thee . . . drink take that to buy yourself a drink
patrimony inheritance

ACT 4   SCENE 4
Outside Baptista's house

Enter TRANIO [disguised as Lucentio] *and the* MERCHANT, *booted and
bare headed, dressed like Vincentio*

TRANIO Sir, this is the house. Please it you that I call?
MERCHANT Ay, what else? And, but I be deceived,
   Signor Baptista may remember me
   Near twenty years ago in Genoa
   Where we were lodgers at the Pegasus.   5
TRANIO 'Tis well. And hold your own, in any case,
   With such austerity as 'longeth to a father.
MERCHANT I warrant you.

      Enter BIONDELLO.

     But, sir, here comes your boy;
   'Twere good he were schooled.
TRANIO Fear you not him. Sirrah Biondello,   10
   Now do your duty throughly, I advise you:
   Imagine 'twere the right Vincentio.
BIONDELLO Tut, fear not me.
TRANIO But hast thou done thy errand to Baptista?
BIONDELLO I told him that your father was at Venice,   15
   And that you looked for him this day in Padua.
TRANIO Th'art a tall fellow; hold thee that to drink.
      [*He gives him money.*]

  Enter BAPTISTA *and* LUCENTIO [*disguised as Cambio*].

   Here comes Baptista. Set your countenance, sir.
   Signor Baptista, you are happily met.
   Sir, this is the gentleman I told you of.   20
   I pray you stand good father to me now:
   Give me Bianca for my patrimony.

The Merchant plays his part convincingly and agrees to the marriage.
Baptista therefore gives it his blessing. It is decided that detailed
arrangements should be made at Tranio's lodgings.

1 'Plainness and shortness' (in groups of six)

Taking a phrase at a time, read lines 23–37 round the group. Discuss the Merchant's style of speaking – how accurate is Baptista's comment in line 39? Think about such details as sincerity, tone, manner, and gesture.

After your discussion, prepare some notes for the actor playing the Merchant on how to deliver his lines.

2 'Pitchers have ears' (in groups of six)

Read line 52 round the group, each person trying to give it a different emphasis. Then create a tableau which illustrates it and reflects Baptista's state of mind.

3 The Merchant

Of the several new characters in this act, it's the Merchant who has the greatest impact on the plot. Look at what he says, and also at what other people say about him.

a Discuss the different ways in which the part of the Merchant could be played.
b Can you think of an actor from television, stage or film who could play him today?

Soft just a moment
weighty cause serious question
to stay ... not in order not to keep him waiting
to like to be satisfied
curious over-particular
affied formally betrothed

assurance tane legal arrangements made
as shall ... stand to satisfy both sides
Pitchers jugs
heark'ning lying in wait
happily perhaps

MERCHANT Soft, son.
    Sir, by your leave, having come to Padua
    To gather in some debts, my son Lucentio   25
    Made me acquainted with a weighty cause
    Of love between your daughter and himself.
    And – for the good report I hear of you,
    And for the love he beareth to your daughter,
    And she to him – to stay him not too long,   30
    I am content, in a good father's care,
    To have him matched. And if you please to like
    No worse than I, upon some agreement
    Me shall you find ready and willing
    With one consent to have her so bestowed,   35
    For curious I cannot be with you,
    Signor Baptista, of whom I hear so well.
BAPTISTA Sir, pardon me in what I have to say.
    Your plainness and your shortness please me well.
    Right true it is your son Lucentio here   40
    Doth love my daughter, and she loveth him –
    Or both dissemble deeply their affections –
    And therefore, if you say no more than this,
    That like a father you will deal with him,
    And pass my daughter a sufficient dower,   45
    The match is made and all is done:
    Your son shall have my daughter with consent.
TRANIO I thank you, sir. Where, then, do you know best
    We be affied and such assurance tane
    As shall with either part's agreement stand?   50
BAPTISTA Not in my house, Lucentio, for you know
    Pitchers have ears, and I have many servants.
    Besides, old Gremio is heark'ning still,
    And happily we might be interrupted.
TRANIO Then at my lodging, and it like you.   55
    There doth my father lie, and there this night
    We'll pass the business privately and well.

*Baptista arranges for Cambio (Lucentio) to tell Bianca what has happened.
Tranio leads Baptista off to his lodgings. Biondello explains to Lucentio
that Baptista was deceived, and Bianca almost won.*

1 Servants 1: 'Shall I lead the way?' (in small groups)

Resourceful servants feature in a number of Shakespeare's plays.
Discuss to what extent Tranio has 'led the way' throughout the play
up to this point.

2 Servants 2: 'To expound the meaning' (in pairs)

Biondello is another clever servant. In the script opposite, he tries to
explain what is happening to a rather slow-witted Lucentio. Take
parts and read through lines 73–103.

- Talk about what purpose these lines serve.
- What would be lost if the whole passage were cut, as it sometimes
  is in performance?
- Try to find examples (not necessarily from Shakespeare) where a
  servant is cleverer than his or her master.

3 Food (in small groups)

Food plays a very important part in the play. In the passage opposite,
Tranio seems very worried that the food will be insufficient ('a thin
and slender pittance').

Do some research in the library about what people ate in the
sixteenth century. Plan a menu for this meal, assuming that Tranio is
worrying unnecessarily, and that there is plenty to eat.

---

scrivener notary (to draw up
 agreements)
presently at once
thin . . . pittance meagre meal
hie you hurry off

straight immediately
mess dish
cheer entertainment
moralise interpret
safe out of the way

Send for your daughter by your servant here.
[*He indicates Lucentio and winks at him.*]
My boy shall fetch the scrivener presently.
The worst is this, that at so slender warning   60
You are like to have a thin and slender pittance.
BAPTISTA It likes me well. Cambio, hie you home,
And bid Bianca make her ready straight,
And, if you will, tell what hath happenèd:
Lucentio's father is arrived in Padua,   65
And how she's like to be Lucentio's wife.

                                  [*Exit Lucentio*]

BIONDELLO I pray the gods she may, with all my heart!
TRANIO Dally not with the gods, but get thee gone.

                               Exit Biondello

– Signor Baptista, shall I lead the way?
Welcome. One mess is like to be your cheer.   70
Come sir, we will better it in Pisa.
BAPTISTA I follow you.

                                    Exeunt

Enter Lucentio [disguised as Cambio] and Biondello.

BIONDELLO Cambio!
LUCENTIO What say'st thou, Biondello?
BIONDELLO You saw my master wink and laugh upon you?   75
LUCENTIO Biondello, what of that?
BIONDELLO Faith, nothing – but 'has left me here behind to expound
the meaning or moral of his signs and tokens.
LUCENTIO I pray thee, moralise them.
BIONDELLO Then thus: Baptista is safe, talking with the deceiving   80
father of a deceitful son.
LUCENTIO And what of him?
BIONDELLO His daughter is to be brought by you to the supper.
LUCENTIO And then?
BIONDELLO The old priest at Saint Luke's church is at your command   85
at all hours.

Biondello urges Lucentio to organise his secret wedding quickly. On the way to Baptista's, Petruchio insists that it is night not day. When Katherina contradicts him, he orders everyone home.

1 Lucentio's soliloquy (in groups of three)

Each person reads lines 100–3 in a different way: confident, confused, romantic . . . Which do you think provides the most effective conclusion to the scene?

2 What's the story?

There's surely a fascinating story behind Biondello's 'I knew a wench married in an afternoon as she went to the garden for parsley to stuff a rabbit'. Tell it.

Royal Shakespeare Company, 1982, Act 4 Scene 5. What comic business could you invent, using the bicycle, for lines 1–11?

Take you assurance make sure
cum privilegio ad imprimendum
solum with exclusive rights to
father children
against you come in preparation
for your coming

appendix Bianca
roundly boldly
list please
Or e'er before
crossed contradicted

LUCENTIO And what of all this?

BIONDELLO I cannot tell, except they are busied about a counterfeit
assurance. Take you assurance of her *cum privilegio ad imprimendum
solum*. To the church! Take the priest, clerk and some sufficient   90
honest witnesses.

    If this be not that you look for, I have no more to say,
    But bid Bianca farewell for ever and a day.

LUCENTIO Hear'st thou, Biondello?

BIONDELLO I cannot tarry. I knew a wench married in an afternoon   95
as she went to the garden for parsley to stuff a rabbit. And so may
you, sir; and so adieu, sir. My master hath appointed me to go to
Saint Luke's to bid the priest be ready to come against you come
with your appendix.   *Exit*

LUCENTIO I may and will, if she be so contented.   100
    She will be pleased – then wherefore should I doubt?
    Hap what hap may, I'll roundly go about her.
    It shall go hard if Cambio go without her.   *Exit*

ACT 4   SCENE 5
On the road to Padua

Enter PETRUCHIO, KATHERINA, HORTENSIO [*and* SERVANTS]

PETRUCHIO Come on, a God's name! Once more toward our
    father's.
    Good Lord, how bright and goodly shines the moon!

KATHERINA The moon? The sun! It is not moonlight now.

PETRUCHIO I say it is the moon that shines so bright.

KATHERINA I know it is the sun that shines so bright.   5

PETRUCHIO Now, by my mother's son – and that's myself –
    It shall be moon or star or what I list
    Or e'er I journey to your father's house.
    [*To Servants*] Go on and fetch our horses back again.
    Evermore crossed and crossed, nothing but crossed!   10

HORTENSIO Say as he says, or we shall never go.

Katherina accepts what Petruchio says – she will see the world as he instructs. Petruchio tests her by asking her to greet Vincentio as if he were a young girl.

1 Change the emphasis (in groups of six to eight)

A number of lines on the opposite page can be spoken in different ways to evoke different audience responses:

'And be it moon or sun or what you please' (line 13)
'I know it is the moon' (line 17)
'And the moon changes even as your mind' (line 20)
'And so it shall be so for Katherine' (line 22)
'Petruchio, go thy ways. The field is won' (line 23)
'My mistaking eyes . . . green' (lines 45–7).

Work your way through the above lines (and any others you collect) as follows:

- Speak each in turn round the group, but each person changes the emphasis.
- One person acts as 'ringmaster' and stops the proceedings occasionally to ask the person speaking to explain and justify their interpretations.
- What was it supposed to show about that character at that moment?

2 Confessions (in pairs)

One person plays Katherina and the other interviews her. What you want to know is why she responded as she did each time she spoke in the script opposite.

3 Cruel or funny (in small groups)

Read lines 26–47. Members of the group who are not reading listen carefully, judging whether the lines are funny or cruel, or whether something else is going on. Make up similarly ridiculous or offensive ways of greeting somebody.

---

go thy ways well done
against the bias against nature
where away where are you going

fresher more youthful
green youthful

KATHERINA Forward, I pray, since we have come so far.
    And be it moon or sun or what you please;
    And if you please to call it a rush-candle,
    Henceforth I vow it shall be so for me.   15
PETRUCHIO I say it is the moon.
KATHERINA   I know it is the moon.
PETRUCHIO Nay then you lie, it is the blessèd sun.
KATHERINA Then God be blessed, it is the blessèd sun.
    But sun it is not, when you say it is not,
    And the moon changes even as your mind.   20
    What you will have it named, even that it is,
    And so it shall be so for Katherine.
HORTENSIO [*Aside*] Petruchio, go thy ways. The field is won.
PETRUCHIO Well, forward, forward! Thus the bowl should run
    And not unluckily against the bias.   25

      Enter VINCENTIO.

    But soft, company is coming here.
    [*To Vincentio*] Good morrow, gentle mistress, where away?
    Tell me, sweet Kate, and tell me truly too,
    Hast thou beheld a fresher gentlewoman?
    Such war of white and red within her cheeks!   30
    What stars do spangle heaven with such beauty
    As those two eyes become that heavenly face?
    Fair lovely maid, once more good day to thee.
    Sweet Kate, embrace her for her beauty's sake.
HORTENSIO [*Aside*] A will make the man mad, to make the woman of   35
  him.
KATHERINA Young budding virgin, fair and fresh and sweet,
    Whither away, or where is thy abode?
    Happy the parents of so fair a child!
    Happier the man whom favourable stars   40
    Allots thee for his lovely bedfellow.
PETRUCHIO Why, how now, Kate! I hope thou art not mad.
    This is a man – old, wrinkled, faded, withered –
    And not a maiden, as thou say'st he is.
KATHERINA Pardon, old father, my mistaking eyes   45
    That have been so bedazzled with the sun
    That everything I look on seemeth green.

Vincentio introduces himself as Lucentio's father. Petruchio tells him that his son is married to Katherina's sister. Hortensio vows to tame his widow as Petruchio has tamed Katherina.

1 Petruchio's sixth sense (in pairs)

Is Petruchio clairvoyant, or has Shakespeare slipped up? In lines 59–63, Petruchio reveals that Lucentio has married Bianca, although he can hardly know this yet. A similar problem arises when Hortensio confirms the marriage (line 74), and seems to have forgotten that he and 'Lucentio' forswore Bianca's love in Act 4, Scene 2. Do you think these inconsistencies matter? Discuss whether you think an audience would notice these things during a performance.

2 A good wife (in groups of three)

Petruchio describes Bianca in glowing terms to Vincentio (lines 64–7), but does he tell the whole truth? Talk together about a less flattering picture of Bianca, which might be equally true (or more so!).

3 Hortensio (in small groups)

Yet another scene which ends with a brief monologue. As Hortensio, try speaking it in different styles: to the audience, to yourself, determinedly, joyfully . . .

4 Beginnings and endings

Look back at the first and last sentence of each scene in this act.

a Talk together about the impression made on you by each opening sentence.
b Now do the same for the last sentence of each scene.
c Finally, alter the first and last lines so that your response will be different.

---

encounter manner of greeting
so qualified having such qualities
beseem become, be fitting to ·
pleasant humorous

break a jest play a trick
jealous suspicious
froward difficult
untoward stubborn

Now I perceive thou art a reverend father.
Pardon, I pray thee, for my mad mistaking.
PETRUCHIO Do, good old grandsire, and withal make known   50
Which way thou travellest – if along with us
We shall be joyful of thy company.
VINCENTIO Fair sir, and you, my merry mistress,
That with your strange encounter much amazed me,
My name is called Vincentio, my dwelling Pisa,   55
And bound I am to Padua, there to visit
A son of mine which long I have not seen.
PETRUCHIO What is his name?
VINCENTIO   Lucentio, gentle sir.
PETRUCHIO Happily met – the happier for thy son.
And now by law as well as reverend age   60
I may entitle thee my loving father.
The sister to my wife, this gentlewoman,
Thy son by this hath married. Wonder not,
Nor be not grieved. She is of good esteem,
Her dowry wealthy, and of worthy birth;   65
Beside, so qualified as may beseem
The spouse of any noble gentleman.
Let me embrace with old Vincentio,
And wander we to see thy honest son,
Who will of thy arrival be full joyous.   70
VINCENTIO But is this true, or is it else your pleasure,
Like pleasant travellers, to break a jest
Upon the company you overtake?
HORTENSIO I do assure thee, father, so it is.
PETRUCHIO Come, go along and see the truth hereof,   75
For our first merriment hath made thee jealous.
                              Exeunt [all but Hortensio]
HORTENSIO Well, Petruchio, this has put me in heart!
Have to my widow, and if she be froward,
Then hast thou taught Hortensio to be untoward.   *Exit*

Looking back at Act 4
Activities for groups or individuals

1 What happens?

A great deal happens in this act. Tell the story in newspaper headlines. Use as few as possible, but don't leave anything out.

2 Design

Find out how many locations are used in this act. Imagine that you have been asked to produce some sketches for the stage design for a production. You have been warned that there is very little money.

a Given your small budget, how would you locate each scene using the minimum of design? You must ensure that one scene flows into another.

b Now think about how your designs might need to be changed if the production is staged 'in the round', with the audience sitting all around the stage.

3 Language

Make a list of four examples from this act of each of these types of language:

- technical language (about tailoring, for example)
- sarcastic humour
- sayings or proverbs
- very serious statements or threats.

Talk together about which characters use each particular type of language most often.

4 Masters and servants (in small groups)

Many servants appear in Act 4. What are their stories? Each person chooses a particular servant. Include those who say very little (or nothing at all), as well as Grumio, Curtis and Biondello. Tell their stories around a circle. Keep to the plot in broad terms, but think about how events looked from their point of view. What about their hidden off-stage life?

5 Who talks to us? (in pairs)

Some of the characters talk directly to the audience and some don't. These activities will help you to think about why Shakespeare gave some characters asides and soliloquies.

a Make a list of the characters in this act who are given asides or soliloquies. Talk together about what these moments add to the play. How might the audience be affected?

b Discuss whether there are moments when you think a character should have been given the chance to speak directly to the audience, but wasn't. Perhaps they could have made something clearer or presented their own point of view. Choose four occasions, and improvise a brief aside to the audience in modern English. Make sure you place the comments or reactions exactly in context.

6 'Why so this gallant will command the sun'

Write two newspaper articles about Petruchio. One should be full of admiration for his strengths. The other article is by somebody who detests him. Decide in which particular newspaper the articles appear.

7 Brainwashing

Most people feel that brainwashing is evil.

Make notes on the techniques Petruchio uses in Act 4, and write the first page of a manual entitled: 'Brainwashing techniques and how to resist them'.

8 Funny or serious?

Two episodes in Act 4 can be made either funny or cruel in productions: Scene 3, lines 1–35, and lines 61–162.

a In small groups, read through these two passages.
b Identify the lines which support a 'cruel' interpretation.
c Identify the lines which support a 'funny' reading.
d Read through the lines again, emphasising one or the other interpretation.

Lucentio and Bianca leave to be married. Petruchio shows Vincentio to his son's lodgings. The Merchant, still pretending to be Vincentio, is not very welcoming.

1 'Backstage' (in groups of three)

Remind yourself of what's happening behind the scenes. Where are all the characters who aren't on stage at this moment, and what are they doing?

2 On stage

Study this artist's reconstruction of an Elizabethan theatre. Talk together about how you would stage lines 1–15 in this space.

I'll see . . . back I'll see you safely married	**is toward** can be expected
	withal with
bears lies	**frivolous circumstances** idle chatter

ACT 5   SCENE 1
Outside Lucentio's lodgings

Enter first GREMIO, *then* BIONDELLO, LUCENTIO [*as himself*] *and*
BIANCA

BIONDELLO Softly and swiftly, sir, for the priest is ready.
LUCENTIO I fly, Biondello. But they may chance to need thee at home;
    therefore leave us.

Exit Lucentio [with Bianca]

BIONDELLO Nay, faith, I'll see the church a'your back, and then come
    back to my master's as soon as I can.   *Exit* 5
GREMIO I marvel Cambio comes not all this while.

Enter PETRUCHIO, KATHERINA, VINCENTIO, GRUMIO, *with*
ATTENDANTS.

PETRUCHIO Sir, here's the door, this is Lucentio's house.
        My father's bears more toward the market-place;
        Thither must I, and here I leave you, sir.
VINCENTIO You shall not choose but drink before you go.   10
        I think I shall command your welcome here,
        And by all likelihood some cheer is toward.
He knocks.
GREMIO They're busy within. You were best knock louder.
MERCHANT looks out of the window.
MERCHANT What's he that knocks as he would beat down the gate?
VINCENTIO Is Signor Lucentio within, sir?   15
MERCHANT He's within, sir, but not to be spoken withal.
VINCENTIO What if a man bring him a hundred pound or two to make
    merry withal?
MERCHANT Keep your hundred pounds to yourself. He shall need none
    so long as I live.   20
PETRUCHIO Nay, I told you your son was well beloved in Padua. Do
    you hear, sir? To leave frivolous circumstances, I pray you tell
    Signor Lucentio that his father is come from Pisa and is here at
    the door to speak with him.

The Merchant and Vincentio both claim to be Lucentio's father.
Vincentio recognises Biondello, who denies knowing him. Vincentio
beats him angrily.

---

1 'Come hither, crack-hemp' (in pairs)

Rehearse lines 33–46 between Vincentio and Biondello, making the
scene as lively as possible. Talk about how successfully Biondello
scores points off Vincentio.

2 Who is telling the truth? (in small groups)

Two of the group take on the roles of Vincentio and the Merchant.
The rest ask questions as if you were members of a crowd trying to
decide who is telling the truth. Remember that it is quite possible for
the 'real' Vincentio to lose if he is not quick witted enough.

3 Observers

There have been a number of stage audiences in this play. Suggest
different positions from which Petruchio and Katherina can watch
what is going on. Use the sketch on page 154 to help you. Show your
suggestions to another student, and justify your choices.

---

flat bare-faced
a means to cozen he means to
 cheat
countenance name
shipping voyage (marriage)

undone ruined
crack-hemp villain
choose please myself/choose my
 own master

MERCHANT Thou liest. His father is come from Mantua and here   25
looking out at the window.

VINCENTIO Art thou his father?

MERCHANT Ay, sir, so his mother says, if I may believe her.

PETRUCHIO [*To Vincentio*] Why, how now, gentleman! Why, this is flat
knavery, to take upon you another man's name.   30

MERCHANT Lay hands on the villain. I believe a means to cozen
somebody in this city under my countenance.

Enter Biondello.

BIONDELLO [*Aside*] I have seen them in the church together – God send
'em good shipping! But who is here? Mine old master, Vincentio!
Now we are undone and brought to nothing!   35

VINCENTIO Come hither, crack-hemp.

BIONDELLO I hope I may choose, sir.

VINCENTIO Come hither, you rogue! What, have you forgot me?

BIONDELLO Forgot you? No, sir. I could not forget you, for I never
saw you before in all my life.   40

VINCENTIO What, you notorious villain! Didst thou never see thy
master's father, Vincentio?

BIONDELLO What, my old worshipful old master? Yes, marry, sir, see
where he looks out of the window.

VINCENTIO Is't so indeed?   45

He beats Biondello.

BIONDELLO Help! Help! Help! Here's a madman will murder me!

[*Exit*]

MERCHANT Help, son! Help, Signor Baptista! [*Exit from the window*]

PETRUCHIO Prithee, Kate, let's stand aside and see the end of this
controversy.

[*They stand aside.*]

Vincentio is astonished to see Tranio pretending to be Lucentio. He fears for his son's life. Despite Gremio's suspicions, Vincentio is on the point of arrest.

1 Tranio caught red-handed (in pairs)

Read aloud only what Tranio and Vincentio say opposite. Then compare how Tranio deals with the shock of Vincentio's arrival with how Biondello managed earlier. Talk together about these differences in terms of the characters of Tranio and Biondello.

2 What are you wearing? (in small groups)

Vincentio appears to be very angry that Tranio is wearing grand clothes. Tranio rather impertinently comments on Vincentio's 'sober' (respectable) habit which disguises a madman. Imagine a modern dress production of the play. Suggest what Tranio, Vincentio, the Merchant and Baptista might be wearing. Remember that two of them are not who they seem. How successful are their disguises?

3 Suspicious Gremio (in groups of three)

What is it that makes Gremio suspicious? One of you take his part, and the other two ask him why he suspects a trick and yet is afraid to swear to it on oath.

offer dare
fine richly dressed
copatain dome-shaped
husband manager
what 'cerns . . . you what business
  is it of yours?

maintain afford
forthcoming available for trial
cony-catched tricked
dotard old fool
haled dragged about

Enter Merchant [below] with SERVANTS, BAPTISTA *and* TRANIO
[*disguised as Lucentio*].

TRANIO Sir, what are you that offer to beat my servant?   50
VINCENTIO What am I, sir? Nay, what are you, sir? O immortal gods!
    O fine villain! A silken doublet, a velvet hose, a scarlet cloak, and
    a copatain hat! O I am undone, I am undone! While I play the good
    husband at home my son and my servant spend all at the university.
TRANIO How now, what's the matter?   55
BAPTISTA What, is the man lunatic?
TRANIO Sir, you seem a sober ancient gentleman by your habit, but your
    words show you a madman. Why, sir, what 'cerns it you if I wear
    pearl and gold? I thank my good father, I am able to maintain it.
VINCENTIO Thy father? O villain! He is a sail-maker in Bergamo.   60
BAPTISTA You mistake, sir; you mistake, sir. Pray, what do you think
    is his name?
VINCENTIO His name? As if I knew not his name! I have brought him
    up ever since he was three years old, and his name is Tranio.
MERCHANT Away, away, mad ass! His name is Lucentio and he is mine   65
    only son, and heir to the lands of me, Signor Vincentio.
VINCENTIO Lucentio? O, he hath murdered his master! Lay hold on
    him, I charge you in the Duke's name. O my son, my son! Tell
    me, thou villain, where is my son Lucentio?
TRANIO Call forth an officer.   70

[*Enter an* OFFICER.]

    Carry this mad knave to the jail. Father Baptista, I charge you see
    that he be forthcoming.
VINCENTIO Carry me to the jail?
GREMIO Stay, officer. He shall not go to prison.
BAPTISTA Talk not, Signor Gremio. I say he shall go to prison.   75
GREMIO Take heed, Signor Baptista, lest you be cony-catched in this
    business. I dare swear this is the right Vincentio.
MERCHANT Swear, if thou dar'st.
GREMIO Nay, I dare not swear it.
TRANIO Then thou wert best say that I am not Lucentio.   80
GREMIO Yes, I know thee to be Signor Lucentio.
BAPTISTA Away with the dotard, to the jail with him!
VINCENTIO Thus strangers may be haled and abused. O monstrous
    villain!

Lucentio begs Vincentio to forgive him. He explains to Baptista that he is Bianca's husband. Baptista and Vincentio are not entirely satisfied.

---

1 Discovery! (in large groups)

Lines 85–8 make an intensely dramatic and funny episode. Suddenly all is revealed! With one person as director and the others as characters, stage what happens. Make the action as entertaining for the audience as you possibly can, also making sure that they understand exactly what's going on.

2 'Counterfeit supposes' (in small groups)

Baptista's eyes have been bleared with 'counterfeit supposes'. The 'supposes' are the deceptions, intrigues and misunderstandings that are the basis of the Bianca sub-plot. They all come to an end at this point in the play. Imagine that Lucentio lists each of the deceptions that have been played. He presents them like a Master of Ceremonies, calling out titles to a series of tableaux:

'First, I disguised myself as Cambio, a musician!'
'Second, Tranio disguised himself as me!'
'Third, . . .'

Complete the list and present Lucentio's list of 'counterfeit supposes'.

3 'Love wrought these miracles' (in pairs)

Or so Lucentio says. One person reads lines 98–102 aloud several times. Talk together about the type of language Lucentio uses here. Then, the other person reads the lines again, but this time exaggerating language and gesture. Remember that Lucentio and Bianca are both on their knees.

---

spoiled ruined
bleared thine eyne deceived your eyes
packing plotting

faced and braved outfaced and defied
wrought made
My cake is dough I have failed

Enter Biondello, Lucentio and Bianca.

BIONDELLO O, we are spoiled, and yonder he is! Deny him, forswear   85
him, or else we are all undone.
Exeunt Biondello, Tranio and Merchant, as fast as may be
LUCENTIO Pardon, sweet father.
Lucentio and Bianca kneel.
VINCENTIO   Lives my sweet son?
BIANCA Pardon, dear father.
BAPTISTA   How hast thou offended?
Where is Lucentio?
LUCENTIO   Here's Lucentio,
Right son to the right Vincentio,   90
That have by marriage made thy daughter mine
While counterfeit supposes bleared thine eyne.
GREMIO Here's packing, with a witness, to deceive us all!
VINCENTIO Where is that damnèd villain, Tranio,
That faced and braved me in this matter so?   95
BAPTISTA Why, tell me, is not this my Cambio?
BIANCA Cambio is changed into Lucentio.
LUCENTIO Love wrought these miracles. Bianca's love
Made me exchange my state with Tranio
While he did bear my countenance in the town,   100
And happily I have arrived at the last
Unto the wishèd haven of my bliss.
What Tranio did, myself enforced him to;
Then pardon him, sweet father, for my sake.
VINCENTIO I'll slit the villain's nose that would have sent me to the   105
jail!
BAPTISTA But do you hear, sir? Have you married my daughter without
asking my good will?
VINCENTIO Fear not, Baptista, we will content you. Go to. But I will
in to be revenged for this villainy.   *Exit*   110
BAPTISTA And I, to sound the depth of this knavery.   *Exit*
LUCENTIO Look not pale, Bianca, thy father will not frown.
Exeunt [Lucentio and Bianca]
GREMIO My cake is dough, but I'll in among the rest,
Out of hope of all but my share of the feast.   *[Exit]*

Katherina reluctantly kisses Petruchio. He feels very pleased with the way things have turned out. Lucentio welcomes everyone to the banquet held to celebrate the three weddings.

1 'Kiss me, Kate' (in pairs)

As Katherina kisses Petruchio, two passers-by comment on what they see and hear. Improve their conversation.

2 The banquet (in large groups)

Using chairs and tables, set up the scene for the feast. Who sits where? Decide where the audience is, and make sure that they can see and hear the important guests. If you don't have space to set the scene, draw a plan of the stage set for the banquet scene.

3 'If music be the food of love' (in groups of three)

The scene opens with a musical image, suggesting that harmony has returned. Imagine a production set in the present day. What music would you use to accompany Lucentio's speech?

---

scapes escapes
overblown gone by
close our stomachs up finish the
  meal (signifies the end of quarrels)

affords provides
kind affectionate, natural

KATHERINA Husband, let's follow, to see the end of this ado.   115
PETRUCHIO First kiss me, Kate, and we will.
KATHERINA What, in the midst of the street?
PETRUCHIO What, art thou ashamed of me?
KATHERINA No sir, God forbid – but ashamed to kiss.
PETRUCHIO Why then, let's home again.   120
      [*To Grumio*] Come, sirrah, let's away.
KATHERINA Nay, I will give thee a kiss.
               [*She kisses him.*]
      Now pray thee, love, stay.
PETRUCHIO Is not this well? Come, my sweet Kate,
      Better once than never, for never too late.   125
                           Exeunt

ACT 5   SCENE 2
Lucentio's lodgings

Enter BAPTISTA, VINCENTIO, GREMIO, *the* MERCHANT, LUCENTIO *and*
BIANCA, HORTENSIO *and the* WIDOW, PETRUCHIO *and* KATHERINA,
TRANIO, BIONDELLO *and* GRUMIO *with* SERVINGMEN *bringing
in a banquet*

LUCENTIO At last, though long, our jarring notes agree,
      And time it is when raging war is done
      To smile at scapes and perils overblown.
      My fair Bianca, bid my father welcome,
      While I with selfsame kindness welcome thine.   5
      Brother Petruchio, sister Katherina,
      And thou Hortensio, with thy loving widow,
      Feast with the best, and welcome to my house.
      My banquet is to close our stomachs up
      After our great good cheer. Pray you, sit down,   10
      For now we sit to chat as well as eat.
PETRUCHIO Nothing but sit and sit, and eat and eat!
BAPTISTA Padua affords this kindness, son Petruchio.
PETRUCHIO Padua affords nothing but what is kind.

The guests exchange witty repartee, especially the Widow and Katherina, encouraged by the men. Bianca leads the women from the room.

---

1 Proverb (in groups of six)

'He that is giddy thinks the world turns round', says the Widow at line 26. Her remark seems to rankle with Kate, who demands to know her meaning. Discuss what the phrase means in this context. Create a tableau or a short mime to express it. Compare your version with those of other groups.

2 Swapping witticisms (in small groups)

At first, the guests seem to indulge in good-natured banter, but do you think the tone changes at a particular point?

There are a number of sexual puns in the script opposite. Here are a few:

conceive become pregnant (or understand)
tale sexual organ (or story)
bush pubic hair (or place)

See if you can find others. Talk together about how appropriate this language is to the characters who use it.

3 'To her!' (in groups of four)

In lines 16–37, the two men champion their wives in a battle of wits. Take parts and read them through twice. As you read them the second time, the two group members who are Kate and the Widow set up an arm-wrestling contest. As the battle of words is fought, respond physically so that you can show success or failure. Is there a clear winner?

Roundly boldly
mean meaning spiteful meaning
I am . . . you my behaviour is moderate compared with yours
like an officer someone who does their duty

Ha' here's
bitter shrewd
bird target (as in sport of killing sitting birds)

HORTENSIO For both our sakes I would that word were true.   15
PETRUCHIO Now, for my life, Hortensio fears his widow!
WIDOW Then never trust me if I be afeard.
PETRUCHIO You are very sensible, and yet you miss my sense:
      I mean Hortensio is afeard of you.
WIDOW He that is giddy thinks the world turns round.   20
PETRUCHIO Roundly replied.
KATHERINA   Mistress, how mean you that?
WIDOW Thus I conceive by him.
PETRUCHIO Conceives by me! How likes Hortensio that?
HORTENSIO My widow says, thus she conceives her tale.
PETRUCHIO Very well mended. Kiss him for that, good widow.   25
KATHERINA 'He that is giddy thinks the world turns round.'
      I pray you tell me what you meant by that.
WIDOW Your husband, being troubled with a shrew,
      Measures my husband's sorrow by his woe –
      And now you know my meaning.   30
KATHERINA A very mean meaning.
WIDOW   Right, I mean you.
KATHERINA And I am mean indeed, respecting you.
PETRUCHIO To her, Kate!
HORTENSIO To her, widow!
PETRUCHIO A hundred marks my Kate does put her down.   35
HORTENSIO That's my office.
PETRUCHIO Spoke like an officer. Ha' to thee, lad.
               He drinks to Hortensio.
BAPTISTA How likes Gremio these quick-witted folks?
GREMIO Believe me, sir, they butt together well.
BIANCA Head and butt! An hasty-witted body   40
      Would say your head and butt were head and horn.
VINCENTIO Ay, mistress bride, hath that awakened you?
BIANCA Ay, but not frighted me; therefore I'll sleep again.
PETRUCHIO Nay, that you shall not. Since you have begun,
      Have at you for a bitter jest or two.   45
BIANCA Am I your bird? I mean to shift my bush,
      And then pursue me as you draw your bow.
      You are welcome all.
               Exeunt Bianca, [Katherina and Widow]

The men joke about whose wife is least obedient. Petruchio proposes a
wager – each husband will send for his wife to see which one obeys most
promptly. Lucentio begins the contest.

1 The ladies withdraw (in pairs)

Discuss why the ladies leave the banquet table. As a director, what
reason (for example, a piece of 'business') could you provide which
would make sense to a modern audience?

2 Sporting images

The opposite page contains a number of images taken from sports
which were popular in Elizabethan times. Identify as many as you can.

3 Drunk as a lord (in small groups)

Act lines 65–76 as if the wine has been flowing a bit too freely. Then
run it again as if everyone were sober. Which do you think works
better?

4 Confident father (in pairs)

Baptista seems to be pretty sure that Bianca will do as she's told. Do
you think his confidence is well placed? Think back carefully to
earlier scenes which give clues about Bianca's character.

5 Role reversal (in groups of three)

Improvise the situation in lines 66–76 the other way round: the
women are left alone and take bets on the men's responses. What
happens?

---

slipped unleashed
gird gibe, barbed joke
A has a little galled me he's
  annoyed me a bit

good sadness proper seriousness
be your half take half your bet

PETRUCHIO She hath prevented me. Here, Signor Tranio,
This bird you aimed at, though you hit her not –   50
Therefore a health to all that shot and missed.
TRANIO O sir, Lucentio slipped me like his greyhound,
Which runs himself and catches for his master.
PETRUCHIO A good swift simile, but something currish.
TRANIO 'Tis well, sir, that you hunted for yourself –   55
'Tis thought your deer does hold you at a bay.
BAPTISTA O, O, Petruchio! Tranio hits you now.
LUCENTIO I thank thee for that gird, good Tranio.
HORTENSIO Confess! Confess! Hath he not hit you here?
PETRUCHIO A has a little galled me, I confess,   60
And as the jest did glance away from me,
'Tis ten to one it maimed you two outright.
BAPTISTA Now in good sadness, son Petruchio,
I think thou hast the veriest shrew of all.
PETRUCHIO Well, I say no, and therefore, Sir Assurance,   65
Let's each one send unto his wife,
And he whose wife is most obedient
To come at first when he doth send for her
Shall win the wager which we will propose.
HORTENSIO Content. What's the wager?
LUCENTIO   Twenty crowns.   70
PETRUCHIO Twenty crowns?
I'll venture so much of my hawk or hound,
But twenty times so much upon my wife.
LUCENTIO A hundred then.
HORTENSIO   Content.
PETRUCHIO   A match! 'Tis done.
HORTENSIO Who shall begin?
LUCENTIO   That will I.   75
Go Biondello, bid your mistress come to me.
BIONDELLO I go.   *Exit*
BAPTISTA Son, I'll be your half Bianca comes.
LUCENTIO I'll have no halves; I'll bear it all myself.

Biondello returns with the news that neither Bianca nor the Widow will come. Katherina, however, answers the summons. Petruchio sends her back to bring in the other two wives.

1 1–2–3! (in groups of six)

Rehearse lines 80–98. Read the lines through first to gain an initial impression. Talk together about ways of raising the tension: facial expressions, gestures, pauses, music, lighting, sound, movement, 'business'. Then place yourselves as if you were sitting at the banquet and run it through again, adding as many effects as possible.

2 What are they doing? (in groups of five)

The audience sees what is happening amongst the men. Improvise the scene 'backstage' with the three women, Biondello and Grumio making their appearances.

3 'What is your will, sir?' (in pairs)

Katherina's entry should be a very striking theatrical moment.

- Take turns to read line 100 in as many ways as possible.
- Talk together about the effect you would wish it to have on an audience.
- Explore how the characters on stage might respond.

One person reads the line giving it a particular interpretation, while the other responds in role as one of the characters in the scene. Say a quick aside to the audience, telling them what you think about Katherina at this point. You should first give the name of the character you have chosen, then your response.

Keep swapping over. Remember that what a character thinks may well be influenced by the way in which the line is spoken.

The fouler . . . mine the worse my
  luck
my holidame the Virgin Mary
  ('holy dame')
Swinge me them beat them for me

Enter Biondello.

How now, what news?

BIONDELLO   Sir, my mistress sends you word   80
That she is busy, and she cannot come.

PETRUCHIO How? 'She's busy and she cannot come'!
Is that an answer?

GREMIO   Ay, and a kind one too.
Pray God, sir, your wife send you not a worse.

PETRUCHIO I hope better.   85

HORTENSIO Sirrah Biondello, go and entreat my wife
To come to me forthwith.

Exit Biondello

PETRUCHIO   O ho, 'entreat' her!
Nay then, she must needs come.

HORTENSIO   I am afraid, sir,
Do what you can, yours will not be entreated.

Enter Biondello

Now, where's my wife?   90

BIONDELLO She says you have some goodly jest in hand.
She will not come. She bids you come to her.

PETRUCHIO Worse and worse! 'She will not come'! O vile,
Intolerable, not to be endured!
Sirrah Grumio, go to your mistress.   95
Say I command her come to me.

Exit [Grumio]

HORTENSIO I know her answer.

PETRUCHIO   What?

HORTENSIO   She will not.

PETRUCHIO The fouler fortune mine, and there an end.

Enter Katherina.

BAPTISTA Now, by my holidame, here comes Katherina!

KATHERINA What is your will, sir, that you send for me?   100

PETRUCHIO Where is your sister, and Hortensio's wife?

KATHERINA They sit conferring by the parlour fire.

PETRUCHIO Go fetch them hither. If they deny to come,
Swinge me them soundly forth unto their husbands.
Away, I say, and bring them hither straight.   105

[Exit Katherina]

Baptista congratulates Petruchio and adds another dowry. On Katherina's return with Bianca and the Widow, Petruchio instructs her to tell the other women the duty they owe their husbands.

---

1 Petruchio's view of marriage (in groups of three)

What does Petruchio think about Katherina's behaviour? While one person speaks lines 108–10, the others echo the key words. Talk together about what these words suggest about Petruchio's idea of marriage.

2 The wager

Look carefully at lines 116–18. Why do you think Petruchio insists on giving further proof of Katherina's obedience?

3 She obeys (in pairs)

But just how does Katherina obey? A huge range of options are open to the actress, depending on how she sees the actual relationship between Katherina and Petruchio. Experiment, and decide which style you think is the most appropriate.

4 Lucentio and Bianca (in pairs)

Read lines 125–9 aloud, then swap roles and read them again. Improvise a brief discussion between the two about what each of them expects from their marriage.

5 I agree! (in small groups)

Read aloud lines 123–35. Then read them again, but this time the rest of the group acts as a collection of hecklers. They could be feminist supporters of the Widow and Bianca, male chauvinists who feel that women should know their place, or anybody else who might be pleased or angry with what's happening on stage. Make it as lively as you can.

---

bodes foretells
awful commanding respect
what not everything

fair befall thee good fortune to you
froward disobedient
laying betting

LUCENTIO Here is a wonder, if you talk of a wonder.
HORTENSIO And so it is. I wonder what it bodes.
PETRUCHIO Marry, peace it bodes, and love, and quiet life,
  An awful rule and right supremacy
  And, to be short, what not that's sweet and happy.   110
BAPTISTA Now fair befall thee, good Petruchio!
  The wager thou hast won, and I will add
  Unto their losses twenty thousand crowns,
  Another dowry to another daughter,
  For she is changed, as she had never been.   115
PETRUCHIO Nay, I will win my wager better yet,
  And show more sign of her obedience –
  Her new-built virtue and obedience.

    Enter Katherina, Bianca and Widow.

  See where she comes, and brings your froward wives
  As prisoners to her womanly persuasion.   120
  Katherine, that cap of yours becomes you not:
  Off with that bauble – throw it underfoot!
    [*She obeys.*]
WIDOW Lord, let me never have a cause to sigh
  Till I be brought to such a silly pass!
BIANCA Fie, what a foolish duty call you this?   125
LUCENTIO I would your duty were as foolish too.
  The wisdom of your duty, fair Bianca,
  Hath cost me a hundred crowns since supper-time.
BIANCA The more fool you for laying on my duty.
PETRUCHIO Katherine, I charge thee, tell these headstrong women   130
  What duty they do owe their lords and husbands.
WIDOW Come, come, you're mocking. We will have no telling.
PETRUCHIO Come on, I say, and first begin with her.
WIDOW She shall not.
PETRUCHIO I say she shall. And first begin with her.   135

Katherina rebukes Bianca and the Widow for their aggression and for failing to recognise their husbands' superior status. She compares women with a prince's subjects who should serve and obey.

1 Men and women (in groups of seven)

Katherina's long speech about the relationship between men and women presents a challenge to the actress, director and audience. Past productions have shown Katherina as genuinely submissive, believing what she says; as humorously ironic, showing that she will, in fact, be the one in charge; as expressing genuine and equal love of Petruchio. One production showed her as insane, quite literally driven mad by Petruchio's tormenting.

One person reads Katherina's speech. The others choose particular aspects of the speech to concentrate on: men, women, love, weakness, strength and rank. As the speech is read, echo the words which reflect your chosen aspect. Don't worry if more than one of you thinks that the words are yours!

Then talk together about the picture you get of the relationship between the sexes in this scene.

2 Duty (in small groups)

Read lines 155–6 carefully. Use them as the basis for two tableaux. In the first one, show what Katherina is saying. In the second, present an alternative, critical view of her words, by showing a different attitude to the relationship between the sexes.

3 Break it up (in small groups)

One of the group reads Katherina's speech. When you feel she moves on to another subject or changes her tone or approach, stop. The next person takes over, and so on. When you have finished the speech, talk together about the different sections and agree on short, clear titles for each

---

unkind unnatural, harsh
blots disfigures
meads fields
Confounds thy fame destroys
  your reputation
moved made angry

ill-seeming unpleasant, angry
thick clogged with dirt
watch stay awake during
honest honourable
graceless sinful

KATHERINA Fie, fie, unknit that threatening unkind brow,
And dart not scornful glances from those eyes
To wound thy lord, thy king, thy governor.
It blots thy beauty as frosts do bite the meads,
Confounds thy fame as whirlwinds shake fair buds,   140
And in no sense is meet or amiable.
A woman moved is like a fountain troubled,
Muddy, ill-seeming, thick, bereft of beauty,
And while it is so, none so dry or thirsty
Will deign to sip, or touch one drop of it.   145
Thy husband is thy lord, thy life, thy keeper,
Thy head, thy sovereign; one that cares for thee
And for thy maintenance; commits his body
To painful labour both by sea and land,
To watch the night in storms, the day in cold,   150
Whilst thou li'st warm at home, secure and safe,
And craves no other tribute at thy hands
But love, fair looks and true obedience –
Too little payment for so great a debt.
Such duty as the subject owes the prince,   155
Even such a woman oweth to her husband.
And when she is froward, peevish, sullen, sour,
And not obedient to his honest will,
What is she but a foul contending rebel
And graceless traitor to her loving lord?   160
I am ashamed that women are so simple
To offer war where they should kneel for peace,
Or seek for rule, supremacy and sway,
When they are bound to serve, love and obey.
Why are our bodies soft, and weak, and smooth,   165
Unapt to toil and trouble in the world,
But that our soft conditions and our hearts
Should well agree with our external parts?

Katherina concludes her speech by stressing women's weakness. She says she will place her hand beneath Petruchio's foot as a token of submission. He is delighted, and they go off to bed.

1 Funny? (in pairs)

Are there any laughs in Katherina's speech? Experiment with parts of it. Remember that you can raise laughs in many different ways – some characters may laugh, for example, if another person is made to feel uncomfortable.

2 Memories (in groups of four)

One person reads, the others interrupt with mimed snapshots of what Katherina is remembering at this point. Then, for each mime, choose one line from the play which best fits the memory.

3 Faces in the crowd (in large groups)

Almost all the characters are on stage at this point. One person reads the speech through quite slowly, while the other members of the group play the characters who are on stage listening. Don't say anything, just respond with facial expressions at the appropriate moment.

4 Debate it! (a whole class activity)

What do you think of Katherina's speech – 'Thy husband is thy lord . . .'? Is he? You may prefer to put Shakespeare on trial for writing a sexist play!

5 The end (in large groups)

What will be the final image the audience sees in your production of the play, just before the lights are cut? Show it.

---

unable worms feeble creatures
big proud
haply perhaps
That seeming . . . are claiming our weaknesses as our strengths
vail your stomachs suppress your pride

no boot no use
go thy ways well done
toward obedient
sped done for
hit the white hit the target (Bianca's name means white)

Come, come, you froward and unable worms,
My mind hath been as big as one of yours,   170
My heart as great, my reason haply more,
To bandy word for word and frown for frown.
But now I see our lances are but straws,
Our strength as weak, our weakness past compare,
That seeming to be most which we indeed least are.   175
Then vail your stomachs, for it is no boot,
And place your hands below your husband's foot.
In token of which duty, if he please,
My hand is ready, may it do him ease.
PETRUCHIO Why, there's a wench! Come on and kiss me, Kate.   180
LUCENTIO Well, go thy ways, old lad, for thou shall ha't.
VINCENTIO 'Tis a good hearing when children are toward.
LUCENTIO But a harsh hearing when women are froward.
PETRUCHIO Come, Kate, we'll to bed.
We three are married, but you two are sped.   185
[*To Lucentio*] 'Twas I won the wager, though you hit the
      white,
And being a winner, God give you good night.
                    Exeunt Petruchio [and Katherina]
HORTENSIO Now, go thy ways; thou hast tamed a curst shrew.
LUCENTIO 'Tis a wonder, by your leave, she will be tamed so.
                                          [*Exeunt*]

Looking back at Act 5
Activities for groups or individuals

1 'Love wrought these miracles'

Lucentio claims that it was the powerful force of love which led to all the amazing revelations in Act 5, Scene 1. To find out how far you agree with him, consider the following questions:

- Is the play written from a male or female point of view?
- Is it a play about young love?
- What do the lovers find attractive about each other?
- Does anybody end up with their ideal partner?

Collect evidence for your views and present your findings in as vivid a way as you can (for example, a series of drawings, a poem or short one-act play, a closely argued talk).

2 Fathers

In Act 5, Scene 1, all the tangled elements in the Bianca plot are unravelled. The audience knows the truth all along, and enjoys watching how the various characters respond to the relevations. But the two fathers, Vincentio and Baptista, don't seem to be altogether satisfied. Their final words in the scene are:

VINCENTIO But I will in to be revenged for this villainy.
BAPTISTA And I, to sound the depth of this knavery.

Improvise a conversation between them as they go off at the end of the scene.

3 Happily ever after?

'You two are sped', says Petruchio to Hortensio and Lucentio at the end of the play. He means that their marriages are doomed before they start. But is Petruchio's judgement sound?

Gather evidence for and against his view, by listing individual lines said by the Widow and Bianca.

Try saying the lines in different ways. Present them in a way to refute Petruchio's suggestion and reassure the two husbands that everything will turn out happily.

At the end of this experiment, what do *you* think? Will the marriages last?

Royal Shakespeare Company, 1960. Identify as many of the characters as you can. Give each of them a thought to suit the moment – and their expression!

4 Looking back

As time passes, people's memories often play tricks on them. They remember selectively.

- What story would Baptista tell his grandchildren?
- What does Katherina recall in her diary twenty years later?
- In old age, Petruchio writes his autobiography. What does he remember?
- Lucentio meets his old servant Tranio twenty years on. What do they recall about old times?
- Grumio sells his story to a popular newspaper. What does he tell the reporter who interviews him?
- Christopher Sly turns up at Marian Hacket's alehouse in Wincot. What does he say in response to her probing questions?

A sexist play?

Some people think this play should be issued with a government health warning! The portrait it offers of the relationship between men and women arouses strong feelings:

'There is, however, a larger question at stake. It is whether there is any reason to revive a play that seems totally offensive to our age and society. My own feeling is that it should be put back firmly and squarely on the shelf.'

(Michael Billington, 1978)

'Kate has the uncommon good fortune to find Petruchio, who is man enough to know what he wants and how to get it.'

(Germaine Greer, 1970)

'One cannot help thinking a little wistfully that Petruchian discipline had something to say for itself.'

(Sir Arthur Quiller-Couch, 1928)

'Kate is less powerful, less wealthy, less cheerful, less in the playwright's confidence – less everything than Petruchio. When the conflict with women is stressed but unequal, as it is here, we are surely justified in levelling the charge of sexism.'

(Linda Bamber, 1984)

'This *Shrew* was being played as Sly's dream, a male supremacist's fantasy of revenge upon women.'

(Royal Shakespeare Company programme note, 1978)

'I think it's an irresponsible and silly thing to make that play into a feminist tract. It (is) not simply the high jinks of an intolerably selfish man who was simply destroying a woman to satisfy his own vanity, but a sacramental view of the nature of marriage.'

(Jonathan Miller, 1988)

'The play shows a possibility of marriage as a rich, shared sanity.'

(David Daniell, 1986)

'I will be master of what is mine own.
She is my goods, my chattels; she is my house,
My household-stuff, my field, my barn,
My horse, my ox, my ass, my anything.'

(Petruchio, 3.2.218–21)

'Shakespeare underwrote the idea that the state, whether it was the small state of the family or the larger state of the country, required and needed the unquestioned authority of some sort of sovereign.'

(Jonathan Miller, 1981)

'Altogether disgusting to modern sensibility.'   (George Bernard Shaw)

'Such duty as the subject owes the prince,
Even such a woman oweth to her husband.'   (Katherina, 5.2.155–6)

'I believe Shakespeare was a feminist.'   (Michael Bogdanov, 1988)

'The truth is that Kate's great victory is, with Petruchio's help, over herself; she has come to accept herself as having enough merits so that she can be content without having the last word and scaring everybody off.'   (R. B. Heilman, 1966)

1 What do you think?

a In small groups, give yourselves thirty minutes to prepare a radio discussion programme, dealing with some of the issues raised in these comments. Invite suitable 'experts' and celebrities onto the panel.

b Write an assignment on the treatment of women in *The Taming of the Shrew.*

c Read through the comments on these pages, and match up pairs of contrasting views. Select one pair and debate the views expressed in class. Is this a sexist play? Take a vote on it before and after the debate.

Staging the play

The Taming of the Shrew has always been a popular play. It is not only very funny, but it also reflects contemporary discussion of marriage and the role of women. The play has therefore always had strong appeal for audiences: the intrigues and disguises of the Bianca plot; the potential for knockabout farce; its continuing relevance as a play about the relationship between the sexes.

Adaptations

Like other Shakespeare plays, it has inspired many adaptations. While Shakespeare was still alive, John Fletcher wrote *The Woman's Prize or The Tamer Tamed*, in which, as the title suggests, Katherina gets her own back. Some adaptations heightened the violence and brutality in the scenes between Petruchio and Katherina. Other dramatists were more concerned to change the end of the play to avoid any suggestion of Katherina's defeat. In the eighteenth century, David Garrick rewrote the final lines of the play so that Petruchio promised to calm down and looked forward to 'one gentle stream/Of mutual love'. Garrick's version held the stage for a hundred years.

The twentieth century

The liberation of women from traditional roles in marriage and society created new opportunities for challenging interpretations. Modern audiences find some parts of the play distasteful, so directors have sought different solutions. One answer is to concentrate on the play's potential for farce. This type of humour, often with an element of violence, comes from a long tradition of drama going back to Roman plays by Plautus. Punch and Judy shows are a part of this tradition, as are some modern television comedies. The Richard Burton/Elizabeth Taylor film of the play directed by Franco Zeffirelli in 1966 contained much of this kind of lively action. Jonathan Miller's BBC television production was very different. There is plenty of fun and life, but his interpretation is based on the way in which Miller views marriage in Shakespeare's time. It ends with peace and harmony as the characters sing a psalm around the table.

In strong contrast, Michael Bogdanov's 1978 production for the Royal Shakespeare Company emphasised the violence and cruelty of the play. So too did Charles Marowitz in his version *The Shrew*, which opened with Bianca and Katherina fighting, and ended with a hysterical Kate. The action was interwoven with a modern parallel which provided little optimism or light relief. The Royal Shakespeare's Company's 1982 production avoided such a serious emphasis and included all kinds of jokes and comic effects (for example, the four-person bicycle on page 146).

Some directors have tried to avoid both light-hearted romps and unrelievedly bleak interpretations. For them, the play is about two misfits who find true contentment with each other. In such productions, a feminist argument is not central. Meryl Streep, Katherina in a 1978 New York production, said: 'What I'm saying is, I'll do anything for this man . . . Why is selflessness wrong here? Service is the only thing that's important about love'.

Direct your own production

You have become the director for a new production of the play.

- Do you go for laughs and make the play as funny as possible?
- Do you treat it as a 'problem' play, which looks at relationships between the sexes in a serious way?
- How much of a bully should Petruchio be?
- Do you keep the Induction or cut it?
- Will your ending aim at happiness or a feeling of trouble to come?

Argue for your own solutions to these problems.

Publicity

How will you advertise your production? Make a list of five things to emphasise in your publicity campaign. Use those ideas to design a large poster and a small 'flyer' (a leaflet about your show).

Programme

Collect examples of theatre programmes. Use them to produce the programme for your own production. It must reflect the ideas that you have about the play (for example, including newspaper headlines, pictures and stories).

The Induction

The Royal Shakespeare Company's production at Stratford-upon-Avon in 1978 began with a quarrel in the audience. A drunk argued with an usherette, shouting: 'no bloody woman is going to tell me what to do'. The man leapt onto the stage, ripped down the scenery, and then collapsed. The lights dimmed and, to the accompaniment of hunting horns, brightened to reveal the Lord and his Huntsmen in hunting pinks. The drunk was Christopher Sly who, as the play proceeded, became Petruchio. This modern-dress production of the play emphasised the brutality of the story and the society.

There are many puzzles about the Induction, but perhaps the major question is 'Why did Shakespeare bother with it at all?'. Shakespeare used the device of a play within a play in several other plays: the masque in *The Tempest*; the 'tragical comedy' of Pyramus and Thisbe in *A Midsummer Night's Dream*; and, perhaps most famously, the murder of Gonzago in *Hamlet*. In all of these cases, the play within the play is an integral part of the main play. Yet here, the Induction acts as a 'frame' for the main play, *The Taming of the Shrew*. Shakespeare employed various devices for framing his plays (the Chorus in *Henry V*, Rumour in *The Second Part of King Henry IV*). However, *The Taming of the Shrew* is unique in the sophistication and complex allusiveness of the Induction. To explore that complexity, work on some of the following activities:

1 The Induction

a Why do Christopher Sly and the rest disappear after the end of 1.1? Do you miss him?

b Imagine Christopher Sly reappears at the end of the play. Improvise a final scene for him.

Find a copy of the *New Cambridge Shakespeare* edition of the play (edited by Ann Thompson). Compare your version with the final scene of another play of the period called *The Taming of a Shrew*.

c You are in a group about to put on the play. Half want to cut the Induction, half want to keep it. Argue together about what is gained and what is lost.

2 On stage audience

'Come, madam wife, sit by my side', says Sly as he prepares to watch the play. The opening stage direction of Induction 2 includes the phrase 'enter aloft', suggesting that they look down from a gallery above the stage. Copy the stage design on page 154 and sketch the following positions:

- Where do Sly and his 'wife' sit? (Ensure that they can both see and be seen.)
- Where do Lucentio and Tranio play out their scene?

3 The hare, to the hunter

Are the minds of men, become so void of sense,
That they can joy to hurt a harmless thing?
A silly beast, which cannot make defence?
A wretch? A worm that cannot bite, nor sting?
If that be so, I thank my Maker than,
For making me a beast, and not a man.

The Lord and the Huntsmen treat Christopher Sly as though he were a 'monstrous beast' and 'a swine' (Induction 1.30). Use the lines above, written from the hare's point of view, as a model, and write your own poem entitled: 'Christopher Sly, to the Lord'.

4 Links, echoes, parallels

The Induction is a highly theatrical device. It presents as 'theatre', foretells, echoes and offers comments on much that follows in the play itself:

disguise	hunting
masters and servants	cruelty
relationship between men and women	money
love	dreams and reality
clothes and costumes	food and feasts
watching	humour
taming	classical references

- **a** Take each element above and identify an example of it in both the Induction and the main play.
- **b** Identify other ideas, situations or relationships from the Induction which find parallels in the main play.
- **c** What does this activity suggest about the function of the Induction?

The language of
The Taming of the Shrew

---

1 Prose and verse

Some characters speak only in verse (Katherina, Petruchio, Baptista, Bianca), some only in prose (Curtis). A few speak in both verse and prose (Sly, Grumio, Biondello). Talk together about why you think these characters speak as they do.

Look back at these moments:

  Sly Induction 2.64
  Biondello 1.1.225
  Grumio 1.2.32.

At each of these points, the characters shift from prose to verse. Can you suggest reasons why they change? Find other points where similar shifts occur, and discuss the significance of these moments.

2 Quick-fire exchanges

In this favourite form of dialogue, two characters swiftly and wittily compete in a war of words:

  Petruchio and Grumio 1.2.1–19
  Petruchio and Katherina 2.1.178–269
  Grumio and Curtis 4.1.1–79.

a Which present-day pairs of comedians (double-acts) perform similar exchanges? Who could you imagine performing these particular scenes?

b Prepare one of these exchanges, rehearse it, and present it.

3 Puns – something to find out

A pun is a play on words where one word has more than one meaning. *The Taming of the Shrew* is full of such word-play. Grumio and Biondello revel in puns (frequently with sexual associations), and so does Tranio. Even Bianca plays on the various meanings of 'butt', 'horn' and 'bush' in 5.2.40–8.

a Does every character in the play use puns? Discover the first pun each character uses.

b Are puns always funny? Is there such a thing as a serious pun?

4 Imagery

The Taming of the Shrew is rich in imagery (language which calls up pictures in the mind). One particularly vivid string of images is that related to the hunting and taming of animals or birds. These are often used to striking theatrical effect. In one production, a fox's pelt was thrown onto Sly in the Induction. In another, Petruchio carried a fierce live falcon on his wrist (see page 118 and 4.1.159–82).

a Make a list of all the animals or birds mentioned in the play.
b Find three examples each of images of food, education and clothes.
c Identify which characters use which images. What conclusions can you draw?

5 Reporting off-stage events

Certain events happen off-stage, but news of them is related on stage (for example Hortensio's unsuccessful lute lesson with Katherina in 2.1.138–55).

Find other examples of off-stage events told on stage. They are often like the patter of stand-up comedians: energetic, swiftly-moving, full of colourful comparisons. Prepare one example to show to the rest of the class.

6 Creating atmosphere . . .

Shakespeare creates atmosphere through words. Choose a favourite scene or part of a scene. Talk together about its atmosphere (aggressive, fearful, joking). Compile a 'language list' of phrases or lines which create atmosphere. Use your list to present and record a short radio play with your own invented plot and characters.

7 . . . Creating character

You can learn a great deal about characters from their language:

● the proverbs used by Gremio and Hortensio in 1.1
● the exaggeration of Lucentio as the traditional romantic lover
● the bombastic aggression of Petruchio.

Select three characters from the play and compile a list of examples of their 'typical' language.

Talk together about what features make each style distinct.

Money, society and status

'Shakespeare shows women totally abused – like animals – bartered to the highest bidder . . . There is no question of it, his sympathy is with the women, and his purpose, to expose the cruelty of a society that allows these things to happen.'

(Michael Bogdanov)

Padua is an upper middle-class world, in which wealth has a very important place. Baptista is obviously anxious to marry Bianca to a suitably rich partner who comes from the right sort of family. Prospective sons-in-law are likely to come from other wealthy mercantile families.

The play is full of social rituals: banquets, weddings, discussions about dowries, shopping, employing tutors for the children. Such activities reveal much about the priorities of the main characters. Padua is an acquisitive society, concerned with money and possessions, ways of showing off, or gaining status over others. Women are the pawns in this status game. But the play is about much more than money, or the sexism of so many of the characters.

Katherina's story is not only about the way in which she is mistreated, but also about a rebel who rejects the rules and 'respectability' of her father's world, and who fights fiercely to maintain her personal integrity.

a 'Hot seat' a character about their attitude to money and status.

b You are directing a modern-dress production of the play. List five objects you want to bring on stage to suggest the type of society that is Padua.

c Imagine that you are writing a society page for a glossy magazine. You have been asked to cover the lifestyle of some of the important people and families in Padua. Choose who you are going to write about. Then:
  ● write one article in a gushing, uncritical style.
  ● write another article which is an unflattering report on high society in the city, aiming to expose it as cruel, unfeeling and materialistic.

d Is Bogdanov right about the society in the play?

Activities

Asides and soliloquies

Asides are when a character comments to the audience, unheard by the other characters on stage. Grumio gives his opinion of Gremio in an aside (1.2.154). A soliloquy is when a character is alone on stage (or believes himself or herself to be alone), and speaks his or her thoughts to the audience. Petruchio's soliloquy at 2.1.165 tells the audience what to expect during his wooing of Katherina.

Identify other asides and soliloquies in the play. Compare your collection with other groups in the class. What different sorts of function do these asides and soliloquies perform?

Work on Petruchio's soliloquy (4.1.159–82) in pairs. Present it to the class as if you were 'two voices' inside his head. Which of you speak which phrases or words? Do you ever speak together? Talk about what guides your decisions.

The wicker basket

The strolling players who present *The Taming of the Shrew* at the Lord's house carry the minimum of costumes and props with them. Imagine all the items were transported in one large wicker basket. Open it and list the contents. To help you, look back at each scene and every character. How will you convey each place and each character?

Edit *The Padua Gazette*

Your aim is to produce a full edition of the paper in two hours, using as much of Shakespeare's language as possible. The class becomes a newspaper office. Choose a point in the play at which the paper will be produced. Divide into pairs, each pair taking responsibility for one or two sections of the paper:

news	reviews	readers' letters
gossip	agony aunt	book reviews
advertisements	sport	crossword

Add other sections as you wish. Remember that you have a deadline to meet! As in a real newspaper office, there will be intense pressure.

William Shakespeare 1564–1616

1564 Born Stratford-upon-Avon, eldest son of John and Mary Shakespeare.
1582 Married to Anne Hathaway of Shottery, near Stratford.
1583 Daughter, Susanna, born.
1585 Twins, son and daughter, Hamnet and Judith, born.
1592 First mention of Shakespeare in London. Robert Greene, another playwright, described Shakespeare as 'an upstart crow beautified with our feathers . . .'. Greene seems to have been jealous of Shakespeare. He mocked Shakespeare's name, calling him 'the only Shake-scene in the country' (presumably because Shakespeare was writing successful plays).
1595 A shareholder in 'The Lord Chamberlain's Men', an acting company that became extremely popular.
1596 Son Hamnet died, aged eleven.
     Father, John, granted arms (acknowledged as a gentleman).
1597 Bought New Place, the grandest house in Stratford.
1598 Acted in Ben Jonson's *Every Man in His Humour*.
1599 Globe Theatre opens on Bankside. Performances in the open air.
1601 Father, John, dies.
1603 James I granted Shakespeare's company a royal patent: 'The Lord Chamberlain's Men' became 'The King's Men' and played about twelve performances each year at court.
1607 Daughter, Susanna, marries Dr John Hall.
1608 Mother, Mary, dies.
1609 'The King's Men' begin performing indoors at Blackfriars Theatre.
1610 Probably returned from London to live in Stratford.
1616 Daughter, Judith, marries Thomas Quiney.
     Died. Buried in Holy Trinity Church, Stratford-upon-Avon.

The plays and poems
(no one knows exactly when he wrote each play)

1589–1595 *The Two Gentlemen of Verona, The Taming of the Shrew, First, Second and Third Parts of King Henry VI, Titus Andronicus, King Richard III, The Comedy of Errors, Love's Labour's Lost, A Midsummer Night's Dream, Romeo and Juliet, King Richard II* (and the long poems *Venus and Adonis* and *The Rape of Lucrece*).

1596–1599 *King John, The Merchant of Venice, First and Second Parts of King Henry IV, The Merry Wives of Windsor, Much Ado About Nothing, King Henry V, Julius Caesar* (and probably the *Sonnets*).

1600–1605 *As You Like It, Hamlet, Twelfth Night, Troilus and Cressida, Measure for Measure, Othello, All's Well That Ends Well, Timon of Athens, King Lear*.

1606–1611 *Macbeth, Antony and Cleopatra, Pericles, Coriolanus, The Winter's Tale, Cymbeline, The Tempest*.

1613 *King Henry VIII, The Two Noble Kinsmen* (both probably with John Fletcher).

1623 Shakespeare's plays published as a collection (now called the First Folio).